D1807729

MOTTO:
Life doesn't come in a trial pack

FUTURES

How to Survive Life after Thirty

by

SHIRLEY CONRAN

and

ELIZABETH SIDNEY

THE LEISURE CIRCLE

First published in Great Britain in 1979
by Sidgwick and Jackson Limited

Copyright © Shirley Conran and Elizabeth Sidney 1979

Original line drawings by M. Ricketts

For

JEAN MEDAWAR

ISBN 0 283 98490 2

Printed in Great Britain
for The Leisure Circle Limited
York House, Empire Way, Wembley,
Middlesex HA9 0PF

5279.5

Acknowledgements

Many people have worked hard on this book, particularly researchers Mileva Ross and Eileen Totten, together with publisher William Armstrong, and editors Margaret Willes (who knows that Neanderthal man did not battle with dinosaurs but with sabre-toothed tigers), George Seddon (who has battled with many a modern sabre-toothed tiger), Celia Brayfield and Derek .French. Nann du Sautoy, Sonja Stern, Christine Cordell and Mike Ricketts have also shown enthusiasm and encouragement.

Help has been given by Dr Jonathan Gould, Dr James Cyriax, Professor Richard Beard, Dr John Cardwell, Dr Robert Chartham, Dr Robert Rapoport, Dr Margaret Rheinhold, Dr Henry Sandford and Dr Howard Jacobs, as well as Veronica Cotgrove, Nigel and Valerie Bolitho, Graham Mack, Arthur Balaskas, John Reynolds, Fred Thornton, Duncan Hill, Michael Norris, Jeremy MacClancy, Keith Wells, Barbara Henderson, Dee Wells, Katharine Whitehorn, Yvette Monfumat, Wendy Ruis, Nicola Henriques, Mary Stott, Deirdre McSharry, Shirley Lowe, Pat Miller, Pat Hewitt, Erin Pizzey, Heather Jenner, Katherine Allen, Marie Jamieson, Dr Eric Trimmer, Dr Philip Boyd, John Baker, Gilly Kingsley, Mary Allen, Mike Arthur, R. S. Lindenau, Stanley Carslake, Stanley Ward, Bob Dorman, John Snuggs, Peter Bolton and Anne Bottomley.

Organizations that have helped include the Family Planning Association, the National Association of Citizens' Advice Bureaux, the National Council for Civil Liberties, the Women's Research and Resources Group, the Magistrates Association, the Law Society, Rights of Women, Child Poverty Action Group, the Institute for Research into Family and the Environment, Barclays Bank, Coutts & Co., Lloyds Bank, and Williams & Glyn's Bank. Thanks also to Bantam Books Inc., for permission to use quotations from Gail Sheehy's *Passages*.

PUBLISHER'S NOTE

All prices, addresses and telephone numbers are correct at time
of going to press, but such items
often change, so please check anything important with the many
sources given throughout the
book.

Contents

Introduction

This book is about how to survive after thirty. It is for women who want to make their one and only life as interesting and enjoyable as possible. It is a new look at what a woman can be and do in middle life.

Every woman over thirty, whether or not she is happily married, may need to reassess what she's got, what she hasn't got and what she wants from life. The second half of her life lies ahead. She should make sure that she enjoys it *more* than the first half.

There is also a crisis guide for when disaster strikes, because it is no use pretending that life isn't sometimes tough, and you sometimes have to fight for your rights in ways that you never dreamed possible: this book shows you how, and offers you the ammunition. If a chapter doesn't apply to you, then skip it. You may need it later, or perhaps a child, friend or relative might ask you for advice in that area. In most cases 'he' and 'she' are interchangeable.

For the first time in history, the average woman over thirty can now *improve* her life in a spectacular fashion. She's going to have far more life to live (thanks to advances in medicine and nutrition). She's going to look and feel ten years younger (at least) and better than her mother did at the same age. She can have more money, new interests, a new career, and new educational opportunities. She can certainly expect to lead a far more stimulating, exciting and rewarding life than her mother or grandmother would have considered suitable. Their aim was to 'grow old gracefully' and *that* meant sinking into the background with touches of white at the collar and suffering in silence if necessary.

This book shows you how to grow old disgracefully. There's a glorious, golden sunny afternoon and evening ahead of you, provided that you are sensibly selfish. Make sure that what lies ahead is what *you* want and that you know how to get it.

What do you plan to do with the rest of your life?

'I'm 45 and what have I done with my life and where do I go from here?' – *Sunday Times* reader

When is Middle Age? It's when you stop thinking that pensions are a joke. It's when you start wondering what exactly a face lift is (and how much it costs). It's when the problem of how to get the man you want turns into the problem of how to want the man you've got.

It's when you suddenly realize that Motherhood is not a lifetime occupation (or a life sentence) but a period of a life. It is when you stop confidently expecting an improvement in your looks, income, home or work (whichever is the most important to you) and start vaguely worrying about decay, decrepitude, dependency or death (whichever you had previously thought about least).

Most people shrink from the idea of 'Middle Age' as if it were leprosy. You don't think twice when using the phrase to describe someone else, but it is shattering to hear the label applied to yourself. Middle Age is always five years older than you are.

In fact most people feel seventeen in the head for ever and prefer to avoid thinking about Middle Age. They skip it, jumping from the young mother - with - immaculate - holeless-infant daydream to the young - grandmother - with - roses - round - the - cottage - door daydream. What lies between is a dreary grey blur that no one wants to think about.

Those are the *feelings* about Middle Age. The *facts* are that, statistically, you have a life expectation of seventy-five and the Midlife period is twenty-five to fifty (ouch), so thirty is not too young to stocktake, reassess and possibly reroute your life along a more agreeable road.

The Midlife period has traditionally been a time of change, but it is only *one* period of change in a number of different time periods that all add up to one big lifetime. You don't have one life, you have a *series* of lives. Potentially, we are all cats: we can all hope for at least nine lives, if not ten and a half, when counting in Biblical seven-year spans (which some psychologists do).

For women there are three main reasons why it's time to break the mould and create a new Midlife Concept.

First, because we are just emerging from a youth-besotted era. Never before in human history have the young been so influential or have the old so desperately tried to ape them as in the past twenty years.

Secondly, because looking good and fascinating (if that's what you want) is no longer considered a question of age. A few vintage fascinators are Melina Mercouri (1923), Zsa Zsa Gabor (1926), Honor Blackman (1926), HSH Princess Grace of Monaco (1928), Gina Lollobrigida (1929), Jacqueline Onassis (1929), Katie Boyle (1929), Petula Clark (1930), Ann Bancroft (1931), Joan Collins (1931), Elizabeth Taylor (1932), Brigitte Bardot (1933), Sophia Loren (1933), Elsa Martinelli (1933), Mary Quant (1934), Sian Phillips (1935) and Ursula Andress (1936). Only three of them have had plastic surgery (and why not?).

The third, and by far the most important reason, is because, for the first time in history, a woman's life can really unfold when her child-rearing years are over. The women who are now in the Midlife period are the first ones to benefit from the enormous world-wide changes in attitude and opportunity initiated by the Women's Movement. Many myths about women have been shattered: we've now seen female

prime ministers, dictators, self-made tycoons and captains of industry.

It is now known that genuine differences between the sexes (apart from the reproductive essentials) are fewer than were once believed. Physically, the recent athletic records show diminishing differences between the best records of men and women. Both on the track and in the swimming-pool women have been catching up with men. Some doctors think that these performance differences between the sexes may eventually disappear altogether; one doctor has even suggested that in a conventionally scored swimming match there's a strong possibility that Australian females could now beat New Zealand males. This doesn't mean that you can now celebrate your fiftieth birthday by swimming the Channel but it does mean that most women are capable of doing more than they have been encouraged to think that they can.

Midlife is a natural time of change and the most important change should be that of attitude. Shakespeare probably didn't think much about the menopause but he did write, 'There is nothing either good or bad, but thinking makes it so', and every situation depends on how you care to look at it.

The menopause, for example, can mean freedom from menstruation, not the end of physical attraction or sex life. Children that leave home no longer need to be looked after. (Although you will still be tied to them by an invisible umbilical cord of anxiety: you will worry; they won't. Always.)

Some of the Midlife changes are vaguely expected, some come as a nasty shock. There can't be a woman in the country who doesn't know about the menopause, but there are probably few women who expect an identity crisis at the age of forty or who can see it as a happy event when it happens.

An identity crisis can vary from a mild but persistent depression (when just to keep going requires enormous effort) to a full-scale nervous breakdown. And it often needs a lot of guts just to face the fact that (perhaps contrary to outward appearances) something, somewhere, somehow FEELS wrong.

What's bad is just to sink into apathy and Valium; to start looking backwards in order to blame other people (parents, teachers, mates) for what went wrong or didn't happen.

Good signs of creative discontent are feeling restless and dissatisfied, if not downright demanding. Of wanting *more* from life, even if you don't know exactly what; of seeking change.

You cannot always build a new life without flattening the old foundations. Your life is unlikely to improve unless you examine it and decide what's wrong with it and whether you're going to do anything about it.

It is often necessary to reassess (a) what you've got, (b) what you want and (c) what you definitely don't want.

In Midlife you should have a better knowledge of yourself than you did when you were in your early twenties, trying to be trendy and following the crowd. Perhaps you no longer want the things you used to want or do (however desirable these may seem to others). Perhaps you no longer want to see the same people or be the same person that you have been to date. This can be disturbing at first, but then exciting – once you've recognized this feeling instead of repressing it and once you've decided to make a few changes. The healthiest sign of all is when you stop caring what people think about you and start caring about what *you* think about them.

But what about the changes that you *don't* seek, the ones that are forced on you by circumstances? Even in the happiest situation, for better or for worse, jobs can change or disappear, marriages can change or disappear, so can friends and relatives, homes, lifestyles and budgets.

Today women often find themselves leading a life for which they were not properly prepared or equipped. Some of them may (unexpectedly and whether they like it or not) have to get a job after twenty years of home life and with no qualifications.

In this age of specialization, when it sometimes feels as though you have to have five O levels before you can qualify as a park attendant, no one teaches us honestly how to run our own lives, while the morality we were taught doesn't always seem to work (in money, sex or marriage, for instance).

Perhaps because women aren't

prepared for these changes many of them see only the darker side of the clouds and cannot see the silver opportunities that really *do* line them. Such women may feel defeated, bitter, ill-used or useless. Self-pity and blaming other people may set in just at the time when what is really needed is to keep one's head and recreate one's life. Oddly enough, it can be easier to do this in the Midlife phase, when a woman is more experienced, more wary and more in charge of events, than when she was knee-deep in Spock or office deadlines.

What is important is to cultivate one vital attitude. *You* may worry about sagging body changes but what other people (especially the young) are more likely to notice are changing attitudes of mind. So don't get set, cement-like, in your ways or your opinions. Don't become a Lady Blimp; don't go to the opposite extreme and become a pathetic middle-aged trendy. What keeps you alive and vital is an open, enquiring, critical mind plus a small dollop of self-discipline. You've got to keep far more alert after thirty in order to deal with probable changes, possible crises and exciting developments.

And you should be prepared *to make an effort* to get what you want. Things are not going to be handed to you on a plate, as they were in your youth, when indulgent allowances were made for your age and attitudes, when you could squander health and beauty by staying up all night, getting stoned and living on yogurt and Mars bars for months on end. Whatever you want to do now (especially if it is simply less) will probably require a determined effort.

In Midlife some women want to know more. Writer Mary Kenny

moaned for many of us when she complained that although the nuns had taught her the foxtrot, a little elocution, a little piano-playing and a lot about the Thirty Years War, the sciences (maths, chemistry) were thought to be unsuitable minority interests. 'How I wish I'd been taught other things,' she said. 'For example, how electricity works . . . about stocks and shares . . . mortgages and bank rates . . . about the property business, insurance and the law.'

If that's what you want there's no need to feel timid, foolish or hopeless – just go and find out. Turn on the radio, hop into the library and if you feel you didn't get the education you now want, it's not now too hard to catch up. There's a huge range of educational courses that are available, including ones that can be taken by women who are tied to the home. More than 14 per cent of Open University graduates are housewives. The government TOPS get-paid-as-you-learn schemes have encouraged women to become car mechanics, electricians, carpenters and plumbers and to enter other lucrative trades hitherto surrounded by male mystique (for how to do it, see *Superwoman in Action*).

Even if you don't much want to be a plumber, golden opportunities are going to show themselves. It's just that you have to go out and look for them. (Try the personal columns of *The Times* any morning for a few crazy ideas, such as importing second-hand Bokharas or making up a fourth on a jeep trip to Bangkok.)

And if this seems to make Middle Age reminiscent of a cross between 'Opportunity Knocks' and a Commando Course, it is only because that's often what it is.

DEMOLISHING A FEW MYTHS

'If way to the Better there be, it exacts a full look at the worst.' – Thomas Hardy

There's no doubt that not all the Midlife period is good news. But the bad news (and you may not consider all of it bad) is simply what has happened to every woman throughout time.

You're not going to be fertile, you're going to be increasingly liable to get certain diseases, your family is going to alter and your older relatives are going to become more wobbly and dependent. In fact the only two real menaces are disease and dependants and they may not affect you.

Most women consider that losing their looks is their personal tragedy of Middle Age. Of course you're not what you were at eighteen but then you don't want to attract those dreadful fellows that you had at eighteen.

And once a woman stops being totally obsessed by her exterior she often becomes *more* self-confident and *more* attractive. It's self-confidence that's important, and this should flower in the middle years because, by definition, it is knowing who you are and what you want and not wasting time on anything (or anyone) else. Midlife need not be a great disaster but a great, great liberation.

Of course nobody thinks that they have enough self-confidence but that doesn't matter if you have enough sturdy common sense to evaluate what is important (as opposed to urgent) and what is real as opposed to mythical. Myths are dangerous because they drive out reality, and we have been reared on some very dangerous myths, which are bound to encourage discontent and disappointment.

Because these myths have been repeated to us *ad nauseam* and because they are often more attractive and comfortable than reality, the phoney tends to replace the real and we gradually accept the myth as the norm – finally believing that we are entitled to it.

Many of the most influential modern myth-makers are advertisers who want to make you feel that you're being left out of something (but you won't be if you buy their products). They encourage unrealistic expectations and attack your self-confidence in the most intimate way. (For a start, you do *not* need Phyllosan or vaginal deodorants.)

So, if you're feeling wistful, remember that it may be nostalgia for a fantasy that never existed. A lot of what you regret not having done probably never happened in its entirety to anyone. Just to illustrate the point, look at SOME MODERN MYTHOLOGY:

1 *Christmas is a time of family happiness.* Not for everyone, it isn't. It is because days such as Christmas, Easter and Mother's Day are associated with fantasies of how life ought to be, that these periods are the peak times for depression and suicide attempts, according to one expert.
2 *The old-maid myth.* That anyone living alone is unhappy, unfulfilled and on the prowl. But you can feel at your loneliest as part of a couple and more married women break down or attempt suicide than single women.
3 *A broken marriage is a tragedy.* Not if the marriage was a tragedy.

4 *The myth of the job satisfaction of home-making (housework).* Not for any thinking female who has to wash up for a family three times a day, a thousand times a year. Inexorably, the plates keep coming back at you, like onions.

5 The expectation that *motherhood lasts for ever*, and is for ever fulfilling. But when your baby leaves home and your star part is suddenly turned into a minor supporting role (you're still allowed to do his laundry) many women feel disconsolate and redundant.

6 *You and he will grow old together* and he'll be there in your old age, so that you can totter into the sunset together.

7 *Marriage will provide you with support, security and sexual comfort.* Women still cling to this myth, especially if they are very happily married to a good, loving man. But not all marriages fulfil this perfect three-point plan and statistics show that many marriages are ended by early death or divorce.

★ In Britain there is now one divorce for every three marriages and one in five of these couples has been married for over twenty years.

★ More than one in six families with dependent children are headed by a lone woman, who probably didn't expect that.

★ In 1971 over a quarter of a million British women were supporting a husband.

Such statistics show the difference between myth and reality.

No one can tell what Fate is going to clobber you with next, which is why real security doesn't lie in things, money or other people, but in self-reliance, in knowing your own capabilities and being able to cope calmly in a crisis.

When CRUSE (the widows' support association) started, a quarter of the widows were aged between twenty and thirty-nine; well over half were between forty and fifty-nine. They were ill-equipped, at a time of tremendous shock, suddenly to develop independence, deal with funeral arrangements, insurance, finance, wills, lawyers and property, and delve into other tedious labyrinths, that He had always looked after.

Few modern women have been taught how to be self-reliant. Most women want to be taken care of (and have been *told* they will be). Many women, now in their middle years, were brought up to believe that it is unfeminine to be responsible ('Oh, I don't understand about the rates, I leave all that to John'). This is because a woman's welfare has traditionally been the responsibility of a father or husband. Well, that's fine so long as he thinks so as well, and so long as he's *there* – and able to do it.

But in a state of mind that ranges from obstinacy to panic, many women refuse even to consider learning to look after themselves. Their reasoning is as follows: 'If I learn to look after myself then they'll make me do it. And if I *don't* learn to look after myself, then I *won't ever* have to do it, because I won't be able to.'

You don't need the brain of a Bertrand Russell to spot a few flaws in that attitude. It's a dotty dolly mixture of warding-off magic, refusal to face facts and crafty peasant cunning. Such tactics often work very well in the short run, but they quite often don't in the long run.

8 *The myth of femininity*. This is a bit more subtle and difficult to spot.

Women are supposed to behave in a way that is defined as 'feminine', and if we don't, we run the risk of being called 'neurotic', 'hysterical', 'unbalanced', 'disturbed', 'lesbian' or even in some way 'mentally unstable'.

Being assertive, refusing to behave like a doormat, showing guts, gumption, tenacity, asking questions or showing a competitive streak are still regarded by many men as exclusively masculine characteristics. They often feel threatened, more than you can possibly imagine: if his own masculinity is fairly wobbly, such a man can destroy your self-confidence with such subtlety that you don't even *notice* the dagger in your back.

And many a kindly GP, when you limp in as one of the walking wounded (without even *knowing* you're in a sex war), will assume that your anxiety indicates emotional inadequacy rather than the stress of having to suppress your own personality and adjust to a mythical role. You will be handed tranquillizers.

9 *The myth of Middle Age* as being a time when you look back on life, take up a few harmless hobbies and settle for what you've got because it's too late to change. No woman need accept this myth of Middle Age any more than she would step into a constricting pair of whalebone stays.

If you are anything but reasonably happy and contented, Midlife is the time to spring-clean your existence, sweep out the myths, sort out your priorities, reassess your interests and redefine success. From now on your life is determined BY YOU.

GROWING

'When I look up there shall thee be and when you look up there shall I be,' said Gabriel Oak to the beautiful Bathsheba in Hardy's *Far from the Madding Crowd*

That's what we all want and if you have it you are lucky indeed but such a relationship does not always endure: Time and Chance may whip your Oak away.

The absence of Oak can leave you with practical matters to deal with. You may need hurriedly to come to terms with yourself and decide who you are, as a human being, and who you need, as a human being and on what terms.

In a sense, you're doing this all your life but Midlife is a natural time to think again about human relationships. Widowhood and divorce can be an unexpected test of values and attitudes. You may have to reassess your strengths and weaknesses, reorganize your priorities.

We all have many conflicting feelings. In every one of us is all the people that we have been: the demanding baby, the protected child, the fresh young girl, the hopeful bride and the fascinating, experienced adult.

We are also echoes of all the people who have looked after us, the parents, grandparents and teachers. They all taught us how to behave and what to believe, and our behaviour and beliefs basically still accord with what we were taught: what is good and what is bad; what is right and what is wrong; what is proper and what is improper; what is acceptable behaviour and what is unacceptable; what is expected and what isn't.

Whether you like it or not, you are the sum of everyone you have been and everything you have learned and everything that you have done. And you can't eliminate it all and start again. But you *can* become aware of it and take command of your own self.

Midlife is time to take a hard look at what you were taught and decide how much of it still applies in a world that your mentors never knew and couldn't imagine. No doubt they did the best they could, but which of those voices telling you how to behave was right and which was wrong?

Were they right about virginity? Were they right about the rewards of the Puritan ethic? In these days of inflation, were they right about saving? Were they right and realistic about divorce and fidelity and loyalty? (If so, what went wrong?) Were they right to define a man's masculinity by the length of his hair or the dryness of his eye? Were they right to teach that a woman should always be protected? Is she?

Certainly, lots of us feel entitled to protection, as a sort of Divine Right of Women (double Divine for Mothers) but part of you knows damn well that this is neither true nor, indeed, reasonable. There has *never* been a man or a Welfare State that could guarantee permanent protection. There ain't no permanent cradle, purse, sun or safety net. The part of you that acknowledges these Facts of Life is the experienced, sensible adult.

But the part of you that fights such a thought is the protected child in you. 'I did what you taught, I kept to the rules, I deserve to be protected,' you may be howling (conveniently forgetting when you didn't).

It is always difficult to fight your instincts, but then if you had stuck to your instincts you might have had sixteen children and weigh sixteen stone by now. And a lot of what you believe to be instinct may, by now, be just old-fashioned thinking.

You may have been brought up to believe that, apart from being pretty and charming, the ideal woman is gentle, never stubborn, quietly accepts her husband's decisions, but naturally exercises the feminine privilege of changing her mind. In a mysterious, Scarlett O'Hara way she is also sensitive, emotional and excitable.

Let's have another look at that word picture of the ideal, old-fashioned, dream-girl-next-door.

What is the difference between being gentle and being unaggressive?

What is the difference between changing your mind and being indecisive?

What is the difference between quietly accepting your husband's decisions and being passive?

What is the difference between never being stubborn and being persuadable?

The answer is not much. But psychiatrists describe a person in poor mental health as being:

> Unaggressive
> Indecisive
> Passive
> Persuadable
> Excitable
> Emotional
> Sensitive

So, in modern medical terms, you may have been brought up to be slightly sick.

Certainly, such a woman would traditionally have been brought up not to handle her own affairs and certainly, today, a lot of such women are having to do so.

This 'sheltered' unrealistic upbringing also explains any rebelliousness you might feel at having to handle a screwdriver or change a wheel or even, for Heaven's sake, having personally to pump air or petrol into a car.

It also explains some far more important, hurtful feelings that a woman might suffer from in middle life. Such feelings might easily prevent the growth and flowering of her personality at a time when – at last – she has more freedom and the opportunity to blossom in her own right, whether this involves lying in bed until 11 in the morning and reading *Chéri* or studying archaeology.

These feelings are indicated by such questions as:

1 (*a*) Do you love me?
  (*b*) How do I know you really love me?
2 Why aren't the children more grateful/considerate?
3 Why do I get all the work and none of the credit?
4 Why didn't anyone tell me?
5 Why is life so unfair?
6 Why did it have to be me?
7 Why do I have to manage on my own when other women don't?
8 Why aren't I the most important person to anyone any more?

Lots of women are perfectly happy as they are and don't want to grow or flower or blossom or read French novels. That's fine, so long as they have protection and are able to stay in that state. But the women who are asking some of those questions are *not* in that state and they will perhaps continue to feel bitter and aggrieved. These questions will continue to fill the backs of their minds and help them see the world through dun-coloured spectacles until they can reassess and rebalance their lives.

Reassessing and rebalancing your life isn't as difficult as it sounds, provided that you keep your childish I-want, I-hate, I-hurt feelings in their playpen and are prepared to stand up to your authority figures and break the rules that you were taught at school. You must judge everything and find out everything for yourself, according to what *you* have experienced and what *you* feel and to allow for the needs of *you* and the people you care for.

This is how a psychiatrist commented on those eight questions:

1 (*a*) and (*b*) *Do you really love me? How do I know you really love me?* The insecure child is asking the question. The experienced adult knows that love is shown by behaviour, not always by words – which is why so many men reply, when asked, 'Well, I wouldn't be here if I didn't, would I?'

2 *Why aren't the children more grateful/considerate?* An indoctrination response. Why should they be? You chose to invest a lot of your life in them and you may think you're getting a poor return. But they had no part in the bargain and may not even *approve* of all your efforts. As they will endlessly tell you, they never asked to be born. Why should they thank you for doing what *you* wanted to do. It's hardly their *fault* that you lost your freedom, they didn't ask you to slave away for them or make all those sacrifices or whatever you're on about. Children are not grateful until they become parents, then they are fervently grateful for everything.

Until then, they see no merit in washing behind their ears or owning up or giving him up or coming in when they said they would. They see you as leading a dreary life when you might be enjoying eating chocolate ice cream or going to India in a bus. They can't see the invisible umbilical cord that keeps you awake when they're out until 4 in the morning and stops you hitch-hiking to Delhi. They don't treat the place like a hotel; that is how they treat a home. They behave *much* better in hotels.

3 *Why do I get all the work and none of the credit?* Sir George Sitwell, father of Osbert, Edith and Sacheverell, complained there was always more laughter in the next room. And so no doubt there was; he was not a man to promote relaxed cheerfulness in the people around him.

If you feel overburdened and unrecognized, it may be because you keep doing all that work which nobody notices unless it isn't done (housework). Your family have never thanked you for clearing up after them, you have always done it, and it might strike them as *mad* that you should expect their gratitude.

Whether or not it concerns housework, if you keep getting some response from other people which isn't in accordance with what you hope, it's sensible to ask yourself: Why on earth go on doing it? Whatever the answer, it will be in *your* chosen interests. People who think that they have an undue share of the work and not a fair reward are the cause of most disputes in industry. So ignore your indoctrination. Go on strike or shut up, in your own interests.

4 *Why didn't anyone tell me?* asked a small rider at a Pony Club meeting when, after a faultless round on her pony, she was disqualified for leaving the ring at the wrong exit. In fact the signs were up, but she didn't notice them. In life there may be no signs or you may not notice them or they may be downright misleading (after all, many road signs point direct to Heaven).

The main reason why nobody told you may have been because nobody knew. If leading politicians can't run the country properly, if with the aid of our leading scientists, they can't run the Present efficiently, let alone the Future, then how can you blame your parents for not predicting the unpredictable? For not teaching you what *they* didn't know and hadn't been taught?

5 *Why is life so unfair?* Because it just *is*, and you should not have been indoctrinated to believe otherwise. The Headmistress of Sherborne,

accused of being unjust, once snorted, 'Justice, justice! There's no justice in the world and there's certainly not going to be any in my school!' This splendid note of realism is seldom allowed to creep into debates on child upbringing and teaching.

Although *Ecclesiastes* warned us that 'the race is not to the swift, nor the battle to the strong', you were probably taught to play fair and to expect fair play in return. So no wonder you're shattered when you play fair and then the game changes; like Alice's croquet party, you discover that the mallet is a flamingo and the croquet ball a hedgehog, who unrolls himself just as you are about to strike.

It is not fair that diseases should strike at random, that hard work should be undervalued, that some marriages and fortunes prosper when apparently equally deserving ones do not. But life is like that – not fair – and *you* are not going to change it.

6 *Why did it have to be me?* Some people seek disaster, some earn disaster, some have disaster thrust upon them. You may fall into one of these categories – but which? Of course you didn't choose to reduce your life savings to confetti money through world inflation; that was thrust upon you. But suppose you lent your savings to the blue-eyed window cleaner with the infallible business scheme that only needed a bit of capital, and he has not yet reappeared? Was your behaviour innocent, trusting and incautious or greedy and unrealistic? Were you *asking* for trouble?

7 *Why do I have to manage on my own when other women don't?* Experi-enced adults know that other women *do* have to manage on their own, in increasing numbers, whatever is happening in Lower Middle Wallop or wherever you are at the moment. If statistics don't convince you, ask Gingerbread (the pressure group for one-parent families), who will help you to face the facts and stop asking the question. Every woman always has to manage on her own, whatever she may think or appear to be doing.

8 *Why aren't I the most important person to anyone any more?* A protected child is confident that at least one person minds enormously about her. Her ultimate threat is 'One day I'll die and then you'll be sorry.' Rows and arguments there may be but she still doesn't question the loving relationship, or doubt her own total importance to the other person.

In marriage, to some extent, we renew that early state of dependency on Mum, without the biological reasons. You and your mate may be the most important people in the world to each other for a lot of the time. But too overwhelming a single, central relationship may cut you off from the rest of the world and prevent you having other relationships. The least that this can do is to cut you off from a lot of interesting experiences and self-development, and it may prove to be crippling if your marriage ends.

An experienced adult knows that a happy early-childhood relationship and a happy marriage (however short the happy part) are precious assets, but not rights. The most important person to you should be YOU.

How to grow old disgracefully

(Your situation, and how to improve it)

Every woman feels at some point that she could have done better. Very few women are lucky enough to see life as having taken a totally predicted, satisfying course. Everyone feels at some point she could have done better, if only she could have had *a second chance*. Here it is.

Men and women are the only creatures on earth who can reflect on their past experience and learn from it so as to plan changes for the future. As any teenager will tell you, it's difficult to learn from anyone else's experience but every woman can learn a lot from her own. This section should help you to sort out your values (what means more to you than you thought

WE'RE OUT OF GIN!!

and what means less), to spotlight any *special* areas that you need to protect or alter, and to analyse any bad experiences or bad situations to check whether they are a part of your behaviour pattern that you will have to watch like a hawk in future. Don't waste time worrying about mistakes (there will of course be dozens of them) unless they recur (you're always being let down or robbed or raped).

The point of what follows it to help you improve your life, if that's possible. First, you have to sort out what you like and what you *don't* like. You may find, to your surprise, that you don't really like babies, or parties, or foreign travel, or a big house in the country, or something else that's supposed to be universally desirable. You also have to sort out what you've got (your assets), what you can't avoid (your commitments), what you really want (your aims), and what you really want to DUMP.

Industrial management consultants start to solve a problem by locating and defining what's good, what's bad and what's unnecessary in the overall situation. (Not as obvious as you think, especially not to the people on the spot.) The five assessment questionnaires on pages 14, 15 and 16 may tell you more than you expect about who you are, how you've changed, what you want and how to get it.

Don't for Heaven's sake fill in the questionnaires: you know how revealing it is to come across a quiz in a magazine that has been filled in by someone else. Instead, write down the answers in a little notebook and hide it. When answering the questions, constantly try to catch yourself out. Instead of defending yourself (as we all do), quietly try the opposite approach. Ask yourself: Is that my REAL opinion, or what I think I *ought* to think? Do I want to change my attitude? Is that Fact or Hope? (That last can be a nasty one.)

Your Personal Happiness Barometer (*see page* 14) is to help sort out your priorities. You can spend an absorbing half-hour deciding whether flirting counts as sex (yes) or whether the deep freeze is essential equipment or a consumer luxury and whether you award it +2 ('happiness sometimes' because instead of cooking you can shove some frozen dish in the oven, then shove it in front of them) or −1 ('persistent dull ache' because you know you should defrost the thing and refill it).

Double-check your answers in case you gave any pat, indoctrinated response. There should be a certain amount of crossing out, hesitation and recategorizing at this point. Does sex *really* bring you great happiness or do you merely think it ought? Do you *really* rate your mate and children as +3, or do they constantly shuffle around from −2 to +2, or stick at zero? Do you find, to your surprise, that religion, social life and exercise are all rated similarly important (also zero). Do you discover that what you really want *most* in life is fame, animals, adventure and excitement? This doesn't automatically indicate a TOPS course for lady lion tamers. One recently divorced forty-six-year-old, who realized that these were her interests, lost 20 lb at a health farm, then went to Louisiana and started an English riding school (no point in starting one in Britain, where there are dozens).

WHAT DO YOU SINCERELY WANT MOST?

The next step is to consider what you sincerely want MOST. If you're pretending to be interested in things that really don't interest you (for reasons of duty, prestige, snobbery or to please someone) you may have a sure-fire recipe for unhappiness.

Check whether you really WANT to do the things you are doing. To be successful you have to build on real motivations. Consider your answers to the following questions and what they tell you about your *real* wants, however unattainable, unworthy or immoral they may be. They are what really turn you on and should be pursued.

Watch out for conflicting wishes and realize that you will have to choose only one. You can't have

Your Personal Happiness Barometer

	Degree of happiness these aspects give you					
ASPECTS OF YOUR LIFE AT PRESENT	Great happiness	Happiness sometimes	Contentment	Nothing much	Persistent dull ache	Great unhappiness
	+3	+2	+1	0	−1	−2
Marriage or long-term relationship						
Being a parent						
Being a daughter						
Family/home life generally						
Sex life/love life						
Friends						
Social life						
Animals						
Physical health						
Peace of mind, tranquillity						
Looking attractive						
Exercise (sport, dancing, etc.)						
Time off						
Holidays, travel						
Leisure pursuits (a) passive (theatre, opera, ballet) (b) active (playing an instrument, birdwatching, painting)						
Learning						
Consumer luxuries						
Your home						
Where you live						
Financial situation, including debts (peace of purse)						
Job or primary activity						
Recognition, success						
Religion, personal beliefs						
Equality and justice						
Independence						
Freedom						
Self-respect						
Anything else that is important to you (such as noise, silence, isolation, bad weather)						

peace of mind and tranquillity as well as adventure and excitement. You can't be Einstein with one CSE, three children under five and a flourishing overdraft.

GROUP A
Scribble three answers to each of these questions:
1 What gives you most satisfaction?
2 What do you enjoy most?
3 What fascinates you?
4 What irritates you most?
5 What do you find time for NO MATTER WHAT?
6 What do you always try to wriggle out of (sometimes at the last minute)?
7 What would you cancel anything for? An invitation to Buckingham Palace, twenty-four hours with Robert Redford (or someone you actually love), a day afloat with Clare Francis, a first night at Covent Garden, a trip to Hawaii?

GROUP B
Give one answer only:
8 When were you last really happy and why?
9 When were you last really bored and why?
10 When were you last really miserable and why?

GROUP C
11 Do you want any of the following? If so, list up to six in the total list in order of importance to you.

(i)
To be really good at something.
To be genuine.
To have your own distinctive style.
To be original.
To be creative.
To be clever.
To be witty.

(ii)
To prove your usefulness, your worth, your value as a person.
To be really appreciated by your family.
Respect and recognition from other people.
To be considered important in your district.
Power in a small way.
Power in a big way.
Fame.

(iii)
Sex.

(iv)
Children.
A close companion.
A lover.
A husband.
Friends.
To be passionately adored.
More men.

(v)
To do less.
To have more time for yourself.
To lead a less stressful life.
Fewer ties.
Fewer responsibilities (things or people).

To do more.
More money.
More excitement.
Promotion at work.
A new job.
A new life.
Fresh air.

(vi)
More possessions.
More clothes.
A new car.
A new home.
To travel.
To move to town.
To move to the country.
To move to the seaside.
To move abroad.

12 Why do you want these things?
13 What are you prepared to give up
    for them?

There are no 'right' or 'wrong' things
to want in the list in question 11, but
here are some (tentative) comments
about choices from the various num-
bered sections:

  (i) You can't be clever or witty to
        order; for the rest you only need
        be firmly yourself.
 (ii) The first two points show a lack
        of self-confidence which it is
        very important to deal with; the
        rest   indicate   Town-
        Councilloritis.
(iii) A whole different ball game, but
        there's plenty of it around, if
        that's *all* you want. Have a look
        at *Forum* (if only to collapse with
        relief at your simple needs).
 (iv) To want three of the first five
        items is only human; to want the
        rest indicates romantic illusion
        (been reading too much Barbara
        Cartland), if not greed.
  (v) These aims can be achieved but
        you may need self-discipline,
        tenacity, courage, firmness and
        sacrifice (from other people as
        well as yourself).
 (vi) These need money. What are
        you prepared to pay – and how?

GROUP D
14 Do you model your life on anybody you know and, if so, what do
you admire about her (or him)?
15 Who are your three favourite fantasy heroines and why? Here are a
few suggestions:

  (a) Dorothy Parker, Nell
        Gwyn, Lucille Ball, Nancy
        Mitford.
  (b) Greta Garbo, Diane de Poit-
        iers, Mata Hari, the Queen
        of Sheba, Elizabeth Taylor,
        Cora Pearl.

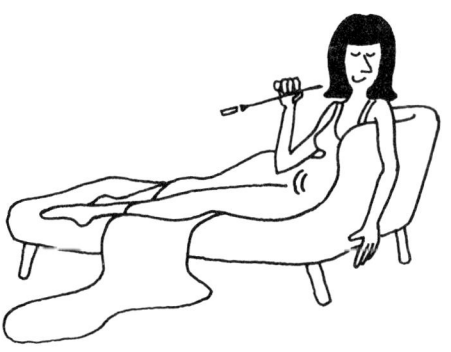

  (c) Queen Victoria, Catherine
        de' Medici, Rose Kennedy.
  (d) Queen Elizabeth I, Helena
        Rubinstein, Catherine the
        Great of Russia, Queen
        Christina of Sweden.
  (e) Jacqueline Onassis, the
        Empress Josephine.
  (f) Mme de Stäel, Mme Curie,
        George Sand, Coco Chanel,
        Sarah Bernhardt, Simone de
        Beauvoir.
  (g) Boadicea, Edith Cavell, Sis-
        ter Theresa, Lady Macbeth.

Now for the good news: we often
admire a bigger dose of what is
already in ourselves, to a certain
extent. So you may already be a bit of
your fantasy heroine. You may

Commitments Chart

PEOPLE	NO	YES (essential)	YES (optional)
1 Your marriage or relationship			
2 Your children			
3 Your parents (or his)			
4 The rest of your family			
5 Your friends			
6 Other relationships (old loves, working relationships, etc.)			
MONEY			
7 Debts			
8 Financial commitments (mortgage, HP, etc.)			
OTHER COMMITMENTS			
9 Work, paid			
10 Work, voluntary			
11 Animals, pets			
12 Social			
13 Others			

already be (reading from top to bottom) a funny lady, a beautiful vamp, a matriarch, a woman of power and determination, an extravagant perfectionist, a creative thinker, or a brave woman of action.

YOUR COMMITMENTS

Women in Midlife nearly always have commitments; sometimes they are a pleasure, sometimes a burden. Sometimes you can discharge them (give away the cat), sometimes your sense of responsibility won't allow this (Dad). The commitments that you are stuck with (Dad) are essential; those that you choose to have are optional. Surprisingly, your essential commitments often change faster than you expect. Check your present commitments; don't bother to work out whether or not they are enriching, just write them down (*see above*).

Do you feel you have too many commitments? Can you shed any and fulfil your obligations in other ways (such as contributing to the hospital fund instead of collecting for it).

Most commitments can be cut, once you have firmly decided that that's vital to your survival (after all, you have a commitment to *yourself* and you can't get a gallon out of a pint pot).

If you can't see any alternatives, ask a friend to look at your lists.

Don't fall into the trap of immediately explaining why all their suggestions won't work. Just listen (especially to the more ludicrous suggestions). Sometimes an idea only needs turning round a bit to work very well.

Next, list the three commitments which most limit your tentative plans for yourself, and the ways in which they limit you, and *for how long*. For instance, a daughter taking A levels may need a lot of support right now but none at all in a few months' time when she's pony trekking in Wales or being a cook on a yacht in the Mediterranean.

Are any of these limiting factors self-inflicted injuries? For instance, do you over-protect your children? (A sixteen-year-old doesn't need a babysitter.) Do you carry more than *your* share of what is a *family* responsibility (Dad)?

Underline any items (and there are almost bound to be some) where you *choose* to be the limiting factor.

Take one of your underlined commitments and think of two ways (however outlandish) in which you could overcome the difficulty and how, and write them down.

The point of going into this in such ponderous detail is to prove to yourself that nothing (however unlikely) is impossible and that *some* day your limiting factor will be gone. And in the meantime, perhaps there is something that you might be doing to prepare for the Great Day, such as taking evening classes in Arabic in order to teach them English, or learning all about a place you intend to visit. The Custodian of the fabulous San Antonio Museum in Texas is Roger, a former London policeman. He spent several years saving up and studying Texan history before he set off for his

Effects of Commitments

DO YOUR COMMITMENTS AFFECT:	*Very much*	*Moder- ately*	*Not much*	*For how many months?*	*For how many years?*	*Indefin- itely*
Where you live						
Your mobility						
What spare time you have						
When you have any spare time						
What money you have						
What money you might have (could earn)						
What resources you have (use of car, etc.)						
Anything else						

Plans to Overcome Commitments

Limitation	Plans to overcome it	The first step to realizing these plans	When they will start to show results (e.g. three months from now)
1		Plan 1, Step 1	
2		Plan 2, Step 1	

heart's desire – to visit the Alamo. When he got there, he knew so much about the place that they offered him this plum job on the spot!

YOUR ASSET CHECK

Perhaps you think that your assets are few and that, compared to your menfolk or the modern miss, you have missed out on fun, confidence, travel, education or a career. But you may have more assets than you realize (and the biggest one may be a negative one – no limiting illness).

HEALTH
1 How is your general health? strength? stamina? Rate 1 for poor to 10 for excellent.
2 Have you a physical disability and, if so, what does it prevent you doing?

APTITUDE, ABILITY AND EXPERIENCE
3 What were your *best subjects* at school?
4 What did you like doing outside school?
5 What have you done since leaving school (including running a home)? Which experience did you enjoy most (anything from being detec-tive at the church bazaar to laying a concrete terrace)?
6 What are your practical skills (such as jam-making, typing, driving, cooking for a sudden multitude . . .)?
7 What are your *skills with people* (coaxing, caring, encouraging . . .)?
8 What are your *creative skills* (making clothes, gardening, arranging flowers, inventing stories . . .)?
9 What are your *intellectual abilities* (inventing, organizing, analyzing . . .)?
10 Have you had any *education* since leaving school? Any extra classes? Any *retraining* (probably not)? Any skills or knowledge that is *self-taught* (do you read historical biographies or geographical travel books?) or *overheard*? Listen to what other people's friends have to say. Dee Wells, the wife of philosopher Sir Alfred Ayer, said that she learned how to argue on television from listening to *his* friends as she carved the leg of lamb. We cannot all be married to one of the stainless steel brains of Britain but the friends of your friends and your family all have something to offer, if you stop talking and start listening. Or you may have learned about plumbing in sheer self-defence, after the third disastrously wrong installation!

CHARACTER STRENGTHS

There are two sides to the coin: your strengths and your weaknesses. Funnily enough, you often don't realize what they are, because you take your good points for granted and simply *cannot* see the bad points. For instance, if you are, by nature, extremely patient, then patience will seem the norm to you. Isn't everybody? And anybody who is impatient will probably deny it impatiently. 'Me? Impatient! Nonsense!! Of course I can't stand hanging around or wasting time and I don't suffer fools gladly and there's no point in saying anything *twice* but that's entirely understandable.'

11 Check your *strengths* (e.g. patience, persistence, tenacity, tolerance, guts and authority) and ask your mother or your oldest woman friend whether they can add any further virtues to your list. On no account ask your mate, who may think the question hilarious.

12 Then check your *weaknesses* (e.g. impatience, intolerance, laziness, bossiness, aggression, a butterfly brain). Again, ask your parent or someone you have known a long, long time and who is fond of you but not too close.

Weaknesses can often be *great* advantages *if you understand and exploit them*. System-Improvers may be lazy and impatient; many good journalists have butterfly brains; major reformers often need to have intolerance, bossiness, aggression (and a thick hide).

13 It's also vital to admit the tarnished side of the coin that every human being possesses. There's a bit of Hitler and Lucrezia Borgia in all of us. It's important to acknowledge (and watch out for) the human weaknesses of the standard model, not only to control one's worst impulses (which doesn't necessarily mean repressing them) but to prevent shame of what is only, alas, natural to human nature (no doubt for some good biological reason) and to understand these impulses in others.

It is not too hard to be good when there is no reason to be bad. It may not be too difficult for a teenager to be optimistic, loving and giving, a brave believer that humanity is basically entirely good and that perfection is just around the corner if only you would stop interfering.

Happy and successful people are generally generous, helpful and tolerant.

Unfortunately it is the sad, battering experiences of life that tend to bring out the worst in one, that summon up anxiety, bitterness, envy, greed, jealousy, destructive cruelty and Old-Man-of-the-Sea dependency. These can be crippling to the personality if not recognized and held in check (it is too much to expect to uproot them).

MATERIAL ASSETS

Scribble everything down: you will find that you have more than you think.

14 Any personal income (earned, unearned, pension).

15 Any savings, investments, expectations (but *never* rely on Aunt Mary).

16 Any material assets (jewellery,

clothes, furs, furniture, books, pictures, silver, collections).

17 Space (in your home).
18 Household equipment (electric mixer, floor polisher).
19 Other equipment (typewriter, piano, stereo).
20 Transport (car, bicycle).
21 *Any other invaluable assets* . . . such as time, a stimulating job or partner, helpful children, supportive relatives or friends.

WHAT YOU WANT AND HOW TO GET IT

You have now analyzed your character, your situation, your limitations and your assets.

Perhaps you are entirely happy with your situation and don't feel an urgent need to develop your personality by learning Arabic, dumping your husband or starting to market the best shortbread this side of Inverness (why *else* would your electric mixer be an asset?).

Some people never stop to enjoy the view because they feverishly hope for a better view, just a bit further on (demonstrate by trying to get a man to pull off the road for a family picnic). Knowing when to stop is almost as great an asset as not being afraid to go on.

If you want to go on, the second step is to Dump the Dream. By now you know which of the things you want are impossible goals and, hopefully, which of your wants might be easier to fulfil than you thought.

Be prepared for a few setbacks. Don't expect your present situation to go on and on, like an Edwardian summer, and don't expect everything to go according to plan, because life isn't like that, and adaptability is still the prime essential of survival. Don't hang on, move on, is the rule that works.

Be prepared to take a few risks. You can't just sit back and expect life to happen to you. You have to help *make* it happen, to be a little adventurous, and sometimes even to take life by the throat and shake it.

As in dieting, the secret is to START NOW, not tomorrow or after the weekend, the wedding or the holiday. So check over your answers and your comments on this section. Then:

1 Write down one long-term aim.
2 Write down what it will involve in time, energy, money, resources, ruthlessness and sacrifices (yours or anyone else's).
3 Write down three steps you can take within the next three months.
4 Write down a tentative Project-Completion Date. Now double the time you have allowed.
5 Write down what you can do TODAY to get started. Write a letter, make a telephone call, visit the library, the travel agency, Job centre, throw out your nightie, buy a rucksack, make a down payment on a bicycle, or whatever.

If you want to do something, but don't know exactly what, then start being more selfish. Start doing what you *feel* like doing, in small ways, especially if it is NOTHING.

NOTHING is good for you. It encourages the front of your mind to shut up, so that you can hear the tiny voice at the back of your mind (this is the voice of the Real You). NOTHING encourages quiet thought about your life and whether you like it and, if not, which bits? This self-examination can help you sort out what you *don't* want, which is one way of finding out what you *do* want, which is how you discover, and encourage the blossoming of, the Real You.

NOTHING is best done in a deckchair or a warm bath or cosily in front of the fire, *but not in bed* (you go to sleep). NOTHING needs concentration and should not be accompanied by music, smoking, drinking, knitting or anyone else.

Try lowering your standards and doing a few enjoyable things with no future to them: perhaps some pursuits that you're not particularly good at but that you enjoy, such as dud double tennis matches (getting it over the net any old how is all that counts) or why not start a Bad Bridge Club (everyone reasons the bidding aloud)?

Forget what you're supposed to do, what you were brought up to do (never sneak, suffer in silence, etc.) and start doing exactly what you feel like. This helps you to sort out what's right *for you* and what's wrong *for you*; this is how you meet, recognize and start to enjoy the Real You.

How to stop killing yourself

All studies of really long-lived healthy people show that they live on very light diets that contain little animal fat, they take a great deal of exercise, have vigorous sex lives, do useful work and are valued by the community.

Before you rush off to the Indies or Kashmir or Southern Russia to join these yogurt-eating, gnarled peasants in their simple geriatric pleasures, there are a lot of gerontological findings that you can make use of right where you are.

Geriatric experts think that many people live to be one hundred – and enjoy it – because they *put their minds to it.* 'Positive thinking is extremely important,' said one specialist, 'because psychotic illnesses can be brought on by negative thinking.' Irritation, greed, hatred, anger, envy and general negative thinking can upset your hormonal balance and make you age faster. Whereas the age-old virtues of love, respect, charitable thinking and consideration seem to encourage serenity, improve your digestion, maintain your level blood pressure and keep your hormones in balance. So loving kindness may do more for you than medicine.

For serenity, increased energy, and concentration try yoga (get the paperback *Wake up to Yoga* by Lynn Marshall, published by Ward Lock), or transcendental meditation (which you can learn in a week at evening classes). Look up in your local telephone directory or ask your library where the nearest class is. Incidentally, yoga can also make you supple and agile.

The Big Three Killers of Women in England and Wales are:

	per cent
Circulatory malfunction (heart attacks and strokes)	51
Cancer	21.1
Respiratory malfunction	14
	86.1

Heart attacks and strokes have accounted for the same percentage of deaths amongst women for the past twenty years. The numbers don't go up and they don't go down. They are associated with obesity, high blood pressure, lack of exercise, smoking and a family history of heart trouble. *You* can do a lot to remove the first four troublemakers.

The death rate for women over forty-five from cancer has risen steadily in the last twenty years. Of these deaths, 20 per cent are breast cancers, 12 per cent are lung and 11 per cent intestinal cancers. So have a regular breast check and try to stop smoking to reduce your chances of contracting these diseases.

The respiratory killers include bronchitis and emphysema, both badly aggravated by smoking.

THE NEW ETIQUETTE

Traditional good manners about smoking, eating and drinking need rethinking. A New Etiquette might not only cut down the voracious cost of the health service, but might easily make you live a *lot* longer. So:

1 Never offer cigarettes to anyone.
2 Try not to smoke in public, in transport, or in an office. It's unfair to non-smokers, especially children, who can suffer from secondary smoking.
3 Never insist that a person smokes, drinks or eats, *whatever* their reason for refusing. In particular, don't insist that *you* won't enjoy *yours* unless they do.
4 Curb your maternal instinct. Don't buy sweets or chocolates as presents or offer them to children (give a no-eat treat instead). Don't overload plates or praise overweight babies.
5 Don't make the family life revolve around meals.
6 Offer friends delicious non-alcoholic drinks (apple juice, home-made lemonade, Ribena milk shake), not just disgusting, synthetic squashes.
7 Don't think it's hospitable to keep topping up the glass of someone who has to drive home.
8 Don't refill wine glasses before they are empty. Then a guest knows how much he or she is drinking.
9 Serve a fresh salad as a first course.
10 Don't serve a meal with a high fat content. (And this means cream.)
11 Anyone who has a business lunch shouldn't have a big evening meal. The less *anyone* eats in the evening, the better for their health and weight.

WHAT CAUSES STRESS?

Although no one explains the behaviour of Romeo and Juliet, Heloise and Abelard or Charles I or Joan of Arc by saying that they were in extreme stress situations, stress is not a modern invention: it has always been with us.

But stress diseases are now major killers. Some doctors believe that over 75 per cent of all illnesses and over 50 per cent of all deaths are from stress-related disorders.

British doctors write over sixty million prescriptions a year for tranquillizers and anti-depressants. Aspirin, cigarettes and drink are often consumed to suppress stress symptoms – but these palliatives do not remove the reasons for stress and they *can* make stress worse by putting off a showdown.

Everyone feels stress. It's not poss-

ible to avoid emotional upsets and anxiety – they are part of life and have always been. However, it is often possible to avoid or diminish the anxieties that cause it.

Some parts of life are more over-burdened and stressful than others, and many of the life changes that are likely to promote stress occur most often in Midlife. The bad stress patches in our society are in late adolescence, early middle age (the attempted suicide rate for women drops off after forty-five) and late old age.

Stress is most likely to occur in periods of change. In late adolescence, many major decisions have to be made for the first time (first big exams, first job, first love affair, end of first love affair). In Midlife, when responsibilities are often heaviest and dramatic, stress-menacing changes may occur in work and family life (promotion, redundancy, children or spouse leaving home). And in late old age there may be illness, bereavement and poverty to cope with alone.

It's easier to cope with stress if you can see light at the end of the tunnel – say, for instance, that you're going to be in debt for about another nine months but then you'll be clear. A permanently leaden situation, such as a resident, tetchy, elderly relative, must be carefully watched in order to minimize the stress effects on you and your family.

Incidentally, stress can also be triggered off by things or events that are traditionally viewed as pleasant, such as having a baby, getting married or winning the pools.

Some studies show that a series of unexpected crises can actually lead to serious illness, while there is an abnormally high death rate amongst widows and widowers in the year after bereavement.

Too much happening too fast has now been scientifically proved to be a major cause of stress. You can take one or two big changes, but however great your natural stability, you can't cope with too many changes at once.

The amount of strain you *can* take varies from person to person and from year to year. You may be able to cope with a lot of stress at twenty-five and very little at forty-five – or *vice versa*. Studies show that the ability to tolerate stress is largely inborn, as is intelligence. However, as it's also a question of training, environment and practice, you can't just sit back happily and say, 'I was *born* unable to cope; someone else will have to do it for me.'

If you do feel that you can't cope, then perhaps you could try to organize your life so that you don't run into any of the big stress situations that can lead to a breakdown (see the following Stress Check). If you are very dependent upon somebody else, you should seriously plan what you would do if he or she were suddenly removed.

THE STRESS LEAGUE TABLE
DIVISION 1
Death of a mate.
Divorce.
Marital separation.
Death of a close family member.
Personal injury or illness.
Remarriage.
Compulsive destructive behaviour of a family member (such as alcoholism or taking drugs).

DIVISION 2
Being sacked from your job.
Marital reconciliation.
Retirement (even if planned).
Pregnancy (even if planned).
Having to look after more children than you can cope with.
Living in stressful surroundings (high-rise flats, a very noisy street, five yards from the railway, next to a building site).
Sex difficulties.
Illness in the family.
A razor-edge business anxiety (your firm will only survive if this deal goes through . . . Can Bloggs and Scrum really sue you for £100,000?).
A very responsible job.
A very harassing job (taxi driver, journalist, doctor, airport traffic controller are the highest job risks).
A severe shock (burglary, eviction, a flood, a car accident).
Relentless, constant overwork.
Doing too many things at once (doing a second job in the evening and at weekends).

DIVISION 3
Gain of a family member (new baby, stepfather, stepmother, stepchildren, Grandad).

Financial change (winning the pools can prove to be as upsetting to your equilibrium as bankruptcy).
Change of work or job.
Guilt concerning a minor undiscovered crime.
Death of a very close friend.
Increased marital arguments.
Enforced separation from a loved one.
Infidelity.
Infidelity (discovery of).

DIVISION 4
A debt of more than a year's income.
Major stress affecting someone close to you (parent, lover, friend, child).
A change in your job (promotion or demotion).
A son or daughter leaving home.
A child marrying.
Trouble with in-laws.
Outstanding personal achievement (fame can be very upsetting).
Beginning or stopping work. (Remember your first day at school?).

DIVISION 5
A change in personal habits (a rigorous diet or stopping smoking).
Trouble with boss.
Change in work hours or conditions.
Moving home.

The scoring of these items is based on the reactions of many people, although yours may be different. Count your score as follows:

> For each Division 1 stress, score 50.
> For each Division 2 stress, score 40.
> For each Division 3 stress, score 30.
> For each Division 4 stress, score 20.

For each Division 5 stress, score 10.

If you score under 50 you're very lucky. If you score over 100 you should carefully consider your stress areas and whether you can do anything to cut them down or alleviate them. If you score over 150, you are overloaded with problems.

HOW TO RECOGNIZE STRESS (PHYSICAL SYMPTOMS)

Small irritations can seem unbearable if they come on top of the situations in the Stress League Table, so can festive occasions such as a holiday or Christmas. These can trigger off a major outburst or even collapse. It really *is* the last straw that breaks the camel's back – 'Can't you turn that bloody thing off when I come home?' 'Why must the bus be extra late this morning, when it's so cold?' Any of these events can trigger off strong emotional reactions such as:

★ Frustration.
★ Irritability.
★ Depression.
★ Anxiety.
★ Rage.

These emotions then produce body changes which you can actually see and feel.

Stress reactions to intense emotion were designed to save us in caveman days when we led simple, dangerous lives. The mental message is: DO SOMETHING; YOU ARE IN DANGER. To Neanderthal man this reaction meant fight or flight, and it still does.

These are the physical reactions: the adrenal glands flood the body with 'fight or flight' hormones, which prepare your body to deal with danger. Very helpful if you are facing a sabre-toothed tiger but not so useful if you are sitting in a traffic jam or facing an irate boss. The effect is that:

1 *Your blood pressure rises.* Your heart bangs faster, you breathe faster and all your muscles – including your stomach muscles – tighten. The whole machine is ready for action. (Pirates, Cossacks and plundering armies used to de-tense by rape and pillage. Less extreme methods are violent, physical exercise, such as squash, scrubbing the floor, cleaning the car, or digging the garden.)
2 *The gastro-intestinal system becomes much more active*, which churns your stomach and leads to *constipation, stomach pains, indigestion* and possibly *ulcers.*
3 *The lymphatic system shrinks.* The blood flow changes so that more blood goes to your brain (to think) and heart (to pump out red energy). Consequently your hands and feet may go cold, your hair stand on end, and your fingertips tingle fifteen seconds *after* you've just missed the other car.

Stress can also *alter your hormone pattern* and suppress the immune responses which protect your body, *lowering your resistance to illness*. That is probably why many people go down with colds or other illnesses during or after a crisis.

Tension and anxiety affect different people in many ways but they are nearly always *exhausting*. Stress saps the energy and *disturbs sleep*. As well as fatigue, it can also lead to *headaches, skin rash, cramp, shoulder or neck pains* (which may lead to a *slipped disc*), *fainting* or *vomiting*. It can also lead to over-smoking, over-drinking and compulsive eating or *loss of appetite*.

If you experience stress for a long period, you may set up a permanent body reaction. Your blood pressure may be permanently raised and your blood vessels changed and this may make you more liable to a stroke. A stroke is a major cause of death amongst women aged over forty-five.

HOW TO RECOGNIZE STRESS
(count how many A, B, C, D or E items affect you)

Sleep	You regularly wake up before 5 in the morning.	A
	You regularly can't get to sleep before 2 in the morning.	C
	You think you haven't gone to sleep all night.	B
Libido	You lose interest in sex (although this can be natural if you have no partner).	B
	You quarrel with your partner about sex.	C
Mood	You feel unusually, unreasonably harassed and irritated by little things.	B
	You are depressed without real cause.	C
	You don't want to see anyone (everyone irritates or bores you) and yet you feel lonely.	A
	Your feelings fluctuate wildly. One hour gaiety, the next hour down in the dumps.	C
	You have constant feelings of pressure.	D
	You have sudden, distressing day-dreams (daymares) which pop into your mind uninvited, generally on the same subject.	B
	You can't concentrate; your mind keeps darting about.	B
	You seem unable to grasp some bits of information . . .	C
	and your memory is unreliable.	C
	You can't make yourself think about certain problems and will think of any little excuse to avoid them.	B
	You can't stop thinking about one or two crucial matters which may not be really important. They go endlessly round and round in your head.	B
Physical	You feel permanently exhausted.	B
	You have unusual persistent indigestion, headaches, pain in neck, shoulder or back, spots.	B
	You start twitching or develop a nervous tic or cough.	C
	Finally, you feel apathetic and past caring for things that you really know are important to you.	A
Habits	You can't be bothered to eat.	E
	You can't stop eating.	E
	You smoke more than usual.	D
	You start smoking.	E
	You drink more than usual, especially in the morning.	C
	You drink alone.	C
	You develop what other people consider an obsession.	B

Count your score as follows:

> For each A symptom, score 50.
> For each B symptom, score 40.
> For each C symptom, score 30.
> For each D symptom, score 20.
> For each E symptom, score 10.

The highest possible score is 810. If you score under 150 you're extremely lucky. If you score over 250 you should carefully consider your situation, and if you score over 500 you may be in serious trouble and should certainly consult your doctor.

SIGNS OF STRESS THAT YOU MAY NOT NOTICE . . . BUT OTHERS DO

You can ask your nearest and dearest to check whether you score a zero on this list (don't snap at him if you don't – that's an added sign of stress). You can also use this list to check on your nearest and dearest:

You suddenly smoke or drink more than before.   E

You take an unusually long time to recover from an illness or accident.   C

You always seem to be denying the obvious (such as that you look tired, have lost or put on weight, seem to be constantly forgetting things).   B

You begin to refuse invitations because they're too much trouble to accept and dress up for.   A

You are less interested in family affairs and in friends (they're too exhausting).   A

You persistently go to bed excessively early.   B

You become indecisive. It takes you an unusually long time to make a decision about elementary things such as shopping lists or planning a simple journey.   C

You have a series of small personal accidents. A burnt finger, a scraped shin, inexplicable small bruises.   B

You are capricious: you change your mind and your feelings; you speak fondly of someone, then shortly afterwards say something bitchy about him or her.   C

You make unusually sweeping judgements, feel unusually weepy if someone mildly contradicts you, you are stubborn, you unreasonably cling to your views. B

You make unreasonable complaints.   D

You expect other people to be impossibly understanding, because they ought to realize how you feel.   B

You complain about other people's faults which now tend to be your own: being abrupt, being rude and unhelpful, shouting, showing lack of consideration for others and being forgetful.   C

One or many facets of your normal behaviour shows a marked change: you used to be meticulously reliable and now you don't even pay the milkman on time; you used to be reasonably untidy and now you yell at the children if they leave anything out of place.   B

You just don't seem to care any more . . . (this could be about your person, your home, your job, your children).   A

Count your score as follows:

> For each A symptom, score 50.
> For each B symptom, score 40.
> For each C symptom, score 30.

For each D symptom, score 20.
For each E symptom, score 10.

The highest possible score is 750. If you score under 100 this can be taken as normal family complaint; 100–200 indicates a stress situation; 200–400 indicates serious stress. *Any* A score is threatening.

UNSTRESS YOURSELF

Coping with stress is relatively easy. The difficult part is to *recognize* that you are in a state of stress, rather than doing something about it.

A series of minor upsets and irritations (or a life of them, as in a newspaper office) may be more disorientating than the big problems of life (such as a large mortgage repayment which you have, after all, thought about carefully and worked out a plan for).

A day or a week or a month of unexpected minor irritations (especially when you are busy) that you regard as unfair, maddening and a waste of your time can be more stressful than a major problem. Ask yourself, is this a *worry* (your son has suddenly abandoned his college course and gone off with a pop group), a *problem* (within six months Mother won't be able to manage on her own if her arthritis gets worse), or a *bunch of irritations* (the cat knocks over the milk, the saucepan burns while you're clearing it up, a door-to-door salesman worms his way in, the phone never stops ringing and then they start drilling the street outside)?

You may then perhaps see that what is causing you stress are the minor exasperations rather than the big league bothers. It is then much easier to deal with them.

HOW TO MINIMIZE STRESS

1 *Learn to differentiate between a problem, a worry and an irritation,* and recognize them for what they are. You can then try to dismiss the irritations and deal with the problems. Try to keep problems in perspective. Ask yourself: Will this matter in five years' time, or even next week? Remember that in three months most people will have forgotten, whatever it is. In two years *you* will have forgotten.
2 *Ask yourself: Is the problem the event or my mood?*
3 If it is your mood, *check whether you are over-reaching or feeling tearful* because you're in a nervy or edgy state (premenstrual tension, the menopause).
4 *Ignore the Joneses.* Be Yourself. Let the Joneses live to your standards.
5 *You cannot do better than your best.* If you are doing that, then no one can expect any more, and if they do you can't give it. So relax and concentrate on only one thing at a time, and finish it properly before moving on to the next thing.
6 *Exercise and learn to breathe correctly* to ease tension. Try yoga or transcendental meditation.

You have only one life. There is only one way to cope with stress: reduce the causes. You may have to settle for less but you'll have longer to enjoy it.

You may have to be a bit tough at times, but remember that it's in the cause of sensible self-defence. You can be useful to yourself and other people only if you are functioning efficiently. Don't be romantic; don't be a martyr; remember that being realistic doesn't mean being unkind. Even if it seems like that to others.

HOW TO RELAX

This is a simple exercise but you need to concentrate and firmly push all other thoughts out of your mind. Ten minutes will refresh you, longer should send you to sleep. Take off your shoes and anything else that is tight. Your waist should be unconstricted.

1 Lie down flat in a warm place (such as bed, sofa or on the carpet), support your neck with a low cushion, cover your body with a rug.
2 Feet should be about 15 cm (6 in) apart. Arms should lie loosely at your side, palms held upward.
3 Take slow regular breaths to a count of six in, six out.
4 On breathing out, tense, then immediately relax, one part of your body. Start with toes, then knees, anus, stomach and ribcage. Then fingers, elbows, back of neck, shoulders, jaw, mouth, eyes, eyebrows, scalp.
5 Check that your body is totally limp, your breathing slow and regular.
6 Imagine yourself slowly sinking through the floor. Switch off all thoughts for ten minutes. Think of nothing but black velvet, then stretch, yawn, open your eyes and slowly get up, or continue step 5 until you go to sleep.

HOW TO GET TO SLEEP

'At three in the morning I used to be sleeping
But lately I wake and reflect that my girlhood has gone and I'll now have to manage without it.
They tell me I'm heading into my prime.
From the previews I do not expect to be crazy about it.'
From *How Did I Get to Be 40* by Judith Viorst

Although sleep isn't yet fully understood, the massive amount of research that has been done in the last ten years looks as though Shakespeare was right. It *does* knit up the ravelled sleeve of care, and the rest it gives the mind is probably more important than the rest it gives the body.

The amount of sleep you need varies from person to person. Extroverts sleep less, introverts sleep more than average. You probably need *more* sleep at times of stress, bereavement, depression, when you're making a lot of mental effort, when you're dieting or when you change jobs. You need *less* sleep when your life is running smoothly.

A recent American study together with work at Cambridge show that *short sleepers* are more likely to be efficient, energetic and ambitious about their lives. They are not worriers, they deal with worries by keeping busy.

Long sleepers (nine hours plus) are more likely to have a great range of employments, they tend to be non-conformists and critical. They often complain of many aches and pains and most have mild or moderate neurotic problems. They may be artistic and creative; they may not be very sure of themselves, their career choices or their lifestyles. Some long sleepers use sleep as an escape from reality and its problems.

Sleeping problems are very common in Midlife when the amount of sleep you need may change. Overwork may make it difficult to get to sleep until the small hours. Anxiety or unhappiness (such as a broken love affair) may wake you up much earlier in the morning and so can depression. In the wee small hours of the morning it's so much easier to remember what you haven't done or what you have done wrong, rather than the things you have done right.

Although prolonged sleep deprivation can be serious, many people worry unnecessarily about a few bad nights (four hours instead of eight). One good early night is generally enough to make you feel fit again. Although you may not *look* your best, a bad night makes little difference to your work performance (unless it's a boring, repetitive task, such as assembly-line work).

Remedies for sleeplessness have ranged from hot-water bottles and camomile tea to an alcoholic nightcap and *Vogue*'s earnest suggestion of a very close friend. Waterbeds were first recommended as sleep inducers in the 1850s, but most people prefer lying on a firm mattress to wobbling about on a hot Li-Lo.

Some people fail to get to sleep because they're thinking about something fascinating and they don't do what they tell the children – avoid too much excitement before bedtime. Try to switch your mind off earlier, *before* going to bed (television is wonderful for this). Try to tire yourself physically, then take a warm (not hot) bath before you go to bed. Once in bed, fill your mind with a pleasant image. Retrace your steps on a favourite long walk or imagine yourself in a garden or a boat on a warm sunny day.

Alternatively, try self-hypnosis:
1 Concentrate on the velvety blackness behind your closed eyelids.
2 Tense, then relax each muscle and breathe slowly (see How to Relax).
3 Imagine a tiny yellow speck in the bottom left-hand corner and glide towards it, as though in a cave. Slowly whisper aloud, 'sleep, sleep, sleep', until you drop off.

If you wake up in the middle of the night and can't get to sleep again, get up, put on a warm dressing-gown and open the window. Take a few deep breaths and then make a cup of *weak* herbal tea or hot water with honey or a few drops of peppermint essence. Sip it slowly. Then go back to bed and pretend it's five minutes before you have to get up. Even if you don't get back to sleep, it will seem less of a misery, more of a treat, to be in bed.

IF YOU CAN'T SLEEP

In the maddening way of experts, sleep doctors say that if you can't sleep it's vital to stop worrying about insomnia. Nothing dreadful will happen if you don't sleep tonight. Some time you will sleep again (perhaps tomorrow night, or next week). Remember that even political torturers have difficulty in deliberately keeping a prisoner awake for more than three or four days. Things might be worse. You won't look your best in the morning (so force yourself to make up well) but as soon as you start doing something interesting, you'll forget that you haven't slept. Don't make a big fuss about it. You will sleep when you are tired enough.

Sometimes you may be unable to get to sleep because you're too cold, or your partner is restless, or the room is stuffy, or you had a huge indigestible late supper or drank strong tea or coffee (which are stimulants) after 6 p.m., or you've been popping some sort of pep pill (even if medically prescribed).

Sometimes a problem stops you sleeping. It is an effort of will to *stop* thinking about problems, but trying to make decisions in the middle of the night is a useless exercise. Molehills turn into mountains in the small hours. If you want proof of this keep a notebook at the bedside, jot down all those amazing thoughts and see how few you actually use. Never, never try to assess a situation or reach a decision in the middle of the night.

Try to avoid taking sleeping-pills except for a couple of nights in order to break a sleeplessness pattern. Some chronic sleeping problems develop *because* you take barbiturates; you can't get to sleep without swallowing the little pill but your body quickly learns to tolerate barbiturates, so the effect is probably more psychological than physical. If you find that your sleeping-pill is not helping you physically you may take a stronger dose. In this way you can build up to massive doses of barbiturates which *still* don't help you sleep properly. And even if you do sleep, barbiturates don't give satisfying sleep and can interfere with your dream pattern, just as tranquillizers and anti-depressants do. And barbiturates give you a bad hangover so that you feel thick in the head and dopey or sick the next day.

If you can't get to sleep, *get up* (don't read in bed) and do some undemanding chore that's not much of a brain strain, such as sorting out your desk or the china cupboard.

American sleep clinics treat chronic insomniacs by breaking the habit of sleeplessness and reassociating bed with sleep. The patient is not allowed to stay in bed if she gets restless. If she doesn't get to sleep within ten minutes of lying down she has to get up and leave the room and she mustn't return to bed for an hour or until she's practically asleep on her feet. There are no sleep clinics in Britain, but this therapy can easily be tried at home.

CAN ANYONE LEARN TO LOVE EXERCISE?

Middle Age is when you take body maintenance seriously, or else your health, strength and mental well-being will suffer. And it's not your size that stamps you as middle-aged, it's your shape and agility.

Women who suddenly realize this tend to rush off and sign up at an expensive gym (where it *sounds* as though the exercise will be painless – a simple matter of signing a cheque) or else buy mysterious contraptions made of very thick elastic which you attach to a door knob and then heave (what happens is that the door knob flies off).

Unfortunately, there's only one

way to keep your muscles in trim – to exercise them. The body deteriorates if you don't use it. You only have to spend a few days in bed to realize how quickly muscles become weak when they are not used. They need to be stretched to work efficiently and do their proper job, which is to strengthen and cushion the joints and prevent the joints from stiffening. *Which?* has produced a chart showing that exercise should give you *endurance*, *suppleness* and *strength*, and different sorts of exercise are needed for each of these three assets. For instance, jogging, strenuous walking, cycling and swimming will build up your *endurance*, keep-fit classes and yoga will keep you *supple* (and yoga will improve your *concentration*), swimming smoothly builds your *strength*.

It is particularly important to adopt some organized programme of regular exercise in the Midlife period when, as children get older, the hard physical work of looking after a family decreases, but *whatever* your age and condition you need exercise, particularly if you work at a desk.

Almost everyone hates the idea of exercise – especially first thing in the morning, but getting up fifteen minutes earlier (except on Sunday) isn't much of a price to pay for agility and suppleness. Or you might have a forty-minute session twice a week. The Keep Fit Association provides addresses of local teachers and classes and leaflets on home exercises. Write to them at 70 Brompton Road, London SW3 1HE.

Or get a list of classes run by the Women's League of Health and Beauty from 45 Rosedene Avenue, London SW16 2LS (☎ 01-769 3577) or 2 Rosebery Gardens, London W13 0HD (☎ 01-997 9524).

Once you're fit you should also think of taking up a sport or outdoor activity at least once a week. Jogging is best (ugh), fifteen minutes three times a week. Swimming is second best.

Your health will greatly benefit and you will feel less tired. You will sleep correctly, you will feel more relaxed, less tense, because you will have externalized the pent-up frustrations and stress of modern life.

OUCH! GASP! PANT! UGH!

WHEN DO YOU NEED TO EXERCISE?

1 When you always wake up stiff.
2 When you start creaking as you turn and twist.
3 When any extra physical effort (such as a dash for the bus) leaves you a panting wreck. *Never* dash for the bus; always wait for the next one.
4 When you can't walk along briskly and talk at the same time.
5 When you can no longer find time for your favourite sport.
6 When a normal day's work leaves you physically exhausted.
7 When you regularly can't get to sleep.
8 When you find that you're increasingly pessimistic or depressed.
9 When you haven't looked at yourself naked in the mirror for a month because you know you won't like what you'll see.

WHEN NOT TO EXERCISE

1 When overtired.
2 When ill.
3 When it's too cold (but don't make it an excuse). (Incidentally, never exercise in winter with the window open, unless you're well wrapped up. That way pneumonia lies.)
4 When your rhythm of exercise slows down (that means you've had enough).
5 When your recommended pulse rate is being exceeded (see end of this section).

HOW TO BEGIN

1 Slowly and with caution. (Especially if starting yoga, never, never strain. You risk tearing a ligament or damaging a muscle, because yoga is not nearly as mild as it seems.)
2 Especially slowly if you're a heavy smoker.
3 Until your heart thumps.

HOW TO KNOW WHETHER YOU'RE FIT ENOUGH TO START EXERCISES

1 Ignore complicated charts relating your weight, height, age to the number of miles you should run in fifteen minutes. (One such chart seriously recommends a running performance level for normal adults just below that of Roger Bannister's four-minute record.)
2 Try this instead (especially good test for over thirty-fives):
(a) Take your normal pulse rate.
(b) Go for a brisk ten-minute walk.
(c) Take your pulse rate again immediately.
If it's over 100 or if, after five minutes, it hasn't returned to 10 per cent above the normal level, plan to build up slowly, rather than start with vigorous exercises.

WHEN YOU START TO EXERCISE

Expect some stiffness at first. If you're really starting to use your muscles again they're bound to ache a bit the following day. Have a warm (not hot) bath and carry on.

HOW TO TAKE YOUR PULSE

Place tips of the *fingers* of left hand on the inside of the right wrist, near the base of the thumb of the right hand until you feel the thing throbbing weakly. Count the beats for six seconds on your watch and multiply by ten, to get the number of beats per minute. Do *not* take your pulse with your thumb – you have a tiny pulse in your thumb which can confuse matters.

RECOMMENDED PULSE RATE

As a rough guide, stop and rest when your pulse beats faster than the recommended maximum rate for your age:

Age	Rate per minute
35	130
40	127
45	124
50	120
55	115

WHERE TO FIND FRESH AIR AND ENJOY IT

If you *are* cautiously considering some sport or outdoor activity perhaps the most important thing to take up is the pen or telephone – NOW!

Choose something that you might enjoy, that you can do regularly (say, once a week) and conveniently, and where you can progressively increase your pace and effort. It's easier to keep up good intentions if you join a friend or a group. Dancing, which many women enjoy, is terrific for improving endurance and suppleness. (*Floodlight* lists forty-five varieties of dancing class. Ask at your local library for details of your local classes.)

The following organizations can tell you where your nearest centre is.

Archery. Secretary, Grand National Archery Society, National Agricultural Centre, Stoneleigh Park, Kenilworth, Warwickshire CV8 2LG (☎ Coventry [0203] 23907).

Badminton. Badminton Association of England, 44–45 Palace Road, Bromley, Kent BR1 3JU (☎ 01-464 0031).

Bowls. English Bowling Association, 2a Eddesleigh, Bournemouth, Dorset BH3 7JR (☎ Bournemouth [0202] 22233).

Canoeing. British Canoe Union, 70 Brompton Road, London SW3 1DT (☎ 01-584 9229).

Cycling. Cyclists Touring Club, Cotterell House, 69 Meadrow, Godalming, Surrey GU7 3HS (☎ Godalming [048 68] 7217).

Fell walking. British Mountaineering Council, Crawford House, Precinct Centre, Booth Street East, Manchester M13 9RZ (☎ 061-273 5835).

Fishing. National Anglers Council, 5 Cowgate, Peterborough PE1 1LR (☎ Peterborough [0733] 54084).

Golf. Golf Development Council, 3 The Quadrant, Richmond, Surrey TW9 1BY (☎ 01-940 0038).

Ice-skating. National Skating Association, Charterhouse, Charterhouse Square, London EC1M 6AT (☎ 01-253 3824).

Orienteering. (A cross between a paper chase, a treasure hunt and a map-reading course. You do it on foot.) British Orienteering Federation, Lea Green, Matlock, Derbyshire DE4 5GJ (☎ Dethick [062 984] 628).

Rambling. Ramblers' Association, 1–4 Crawford Mews, York Street, London W1H 1PT (☎ 01-262 1477).

Riding. British Horse Society, National Equestrian Centre, Stoneleigh Park, Kenilworth, Warwickshire CV8 2LR (☎ Coventry [0203] 27192).

Sailing. (Ted Heath took it up in his fifties.) Royal Yachting Association, 15 Victoria Way, Woking, Surrey GU21 1EQ (☎ Woking [048 62] 5022).

Skiing. Ski Club of Great Britain, 118 Eaton Square, London SW1W 9AF (☎ 01-235 4711).

Swimming. Amateur Swimming Association, Harold Fern House, Derby Square, Loughborough, Leicestershire LE11 0AL (☎ Loughborough [0509] 30431).

Table tennis. English Table Tennis Association, 21 Claremont, Hastings, East Sussex TN34 1HF (☎ Hastings [0424] 433121).

Water skiing. British Water Skiing Federation, 70 Brompton Road, London SW3 1EG (☎ 01-584 9229).

EATING FOR HEALTH

The middle-aged are often told that they will inevitably put on weight because they are taking less exercise and getting more sedentary and therefore need less food. You can suddenly pile it on in a few months without seeming to change your ways at all. And once it's there, you can't seem to shift it.

If you've suddenly put on weight for no apparent reason, tell your doctor, because it just might be due to hormone changes. On the other hand, it could be your feeble excuse.

Your looks, general health and energy are all mainly dependent on your daily diet. General faulty nutrition or constant, ill-balanced dieting can result in lethargy, fatigue, 'nerviness', skin problems, overweight, underweight, dull hair, dandruff and breaking nails.

It is not enough just to eat the foods that don't make you fat. You must eat the right combination of foods to keep you fit and well. Improving your diet will not only make you look and feel good, it can be a protection against future problems associated with ageing, such as heart failures, high blood pressure and bowel cancer, as well as obesity.

In recent years there has been growing medical interest in studying the long-term effects of certain foods in normal diets. Many leading medical authorities are now convinced that there is a link between the rich fatty foods of Western diets and the growing incidence of heart disease and strokes. They have advised cutting down foods with a high cholesterol content. (Cholesterol is a fairly complex organic compound found in body cells which may thicken the artery walls, which can lead to heart attacks and strokes.)

For ten years now, American males have seriously tackled the cholesterol problem and their death rate from heart failure is coming down, whereas British males, who haven't changed their habits, are dying from heart failure at an increasing rate.

In Britain, the death rate from heart attacks in men aged thirty-five to fifty has been going up since the 1950s. During the same period women's deaths under the age of forty-five from heart disease have shown little change, but deaths from this cause after forty-five have increased sharply and steadily.

During the reproductive years it is thought that women are protected against heart trouble by the hormone, oestrogen, that circulates in the body. After the start of menopause (which is often before the menstrual flow stops) the reduction of oestrogen may lead to an increased level of cholesterol in the blood. This can be countered by a low-cholesterol diet.

Other findings suggest that there should be some modification of the traditional sacred twentieth-century Western 'balanced diet' which recommends daily helpings of meat (or fish, eggs, chicken, milk), fats, bread and cereals, fruit and vegetables, and that this diet may be too rich for your health.

Dorothy Hollingsworth, formerly director-general of the British Nutrition Foundation, was one of the nutritionists at the Ministry of Food who worked out the ideal diet during the Second World War ('rations' were so called because they were based on a rationale). As a group, Britons had *never* been as healthy as during those austerity years.

Today, Ms Hollingsworth says that we should eat more vegetables and gap-fillers. Rice, spaghetti and potatoes should be the main centre foods, she says, leaving the concentrated protein in rich meat reduced to a tiny side helping. We will also get more protein from cereals, bread and vegetables, including pulses. What we *won't* get is fattening fat.

She suggests that we change our diet by starting to think Mediterranean. We should imitate the crafty

Italian ways to make a little meat feed a lot of mouths by serving pastas, rice with a meat or tomato sauce, and pizzas. Also good is Spanish paella with vegetables and tiny chunks of chicken and fish.

She also praises Indian curries and Scandinavian salads based on beans, rice or potatoes with a little tuna fish or chopped smoked sausage thrown in.

Obviously this will be a lot cheaper than the roast beef of Olde Englande or the frozen lamb of New Zealand which, increasingly, few of us can afford. But you may wonder how anyone can *avoid* getting fatter on spaghetti and potatoes.

The answer is to eat far, far less of everything. Serve smaller portions. Live longer by being stingier!

TAKING THE ROUGH WITH THE SMOOTH

Recent research indicates that some forms of cancer of the bowel could also be prevented by increasing the roughage in the diet.

Another important change in modern nutritional thinking is the increasing importance of foods that are high in fibre. These are fruit, vegetables and whole-grain cereals. Eating more of these foods increases 'roughage', which increases bowel movement and prevents constipation. Until now Western doctors have said that a bowel movement once a day isn't necessary and that once a week still counts as 'regular'. This uncomfortable philosophy is now becoming redundant and we are getting back to what those Kensington Garden nannies always knew.

It is now thought that one of the main advantages of wholewheat flour over refined white flour, lies not so much in the extra vitamins, protein and iron it contains (we get adequate amounts of these if we eat a good balanced diet) but in its roughage.

One of the quickest, most effective ways to increase roughage in the diet is to take one or two tablespoons of bran each day added to milk, fruit juice or yogurt. Get wheat bran without additive or with wheat-germ added from health-food shops. All-Bran has a high concentration of bran per spoonful, but also has flavouring added.

Modern nutritious advice can be summed up as:

1 Reduce the protein intake.
2 Cut consumption of dairy products (milk, butter, cream, cheese) and animal fats by at least one-third.
3 Avoid alcohol and refined sugar as much as possible (see diet that follows).

THE BACK-TO-NATURE DIET (LOW FAT AND PROTEIN, HIGH ROUGHAGE)

This is not a diet – it's a new eating pattern, based on the way that the rude, healthy peasants of the world have eaten for centuries. Follow it with one eye on the vitamin tables.

You don't just do it for a fortnight, if it suits you. You gradually switch to it for ever. You don't count calories, you just eat as little as possible until you are your favourite size. Chew slowly and enjoy it. Alcohol will sabotage your efforts because it's so high in calories.

LOW FAT AND PROTEIN, HIGH ROUGHAGE DIET

Don't eat   White or brown sugar of any sort (use honey to sweeten)
White flour (use only whole-wheat flour)
Cream
Cakes, biscuits, puddings
Jam
Tinned fruit in syrup
Sweetened fruit juices
Anything fried (except in vegetable oil)
Any 'junk' food, synthetically produced
Any factory-made sauces or pickles
Boxed breakfast cereal

Eat a small amount of the following (but on no account cut them out)
Meat   Lean meat, fish and eggs (liver once a week)
Dairy products   Milk, cheese (cottage cheese is low in fat), butter, unsweetened low-fat yogurt
Fruit and veg   Fresh fruit (unpeeled if possible)
Fresh salad (no mayonnaise, or only a stingy portion now and then)
Fresh vegetables (raw if possible, or cooked so that they are still crunchy, except for potatoes, which should be eaten in their skins if possible)

Eat moderately   Unprocessed honey
Nuts
Dried fruit
Not more than half a pot of yogurt daily

Eat regularly   One or two tablespoons a day of wheat bran

Don't drink   *Any* alcohol of any sort (that's the catch)

Drink   Lots of water (at least five mugs a day). This is necessary to swell the high roughage content of the diet
Tea
Coffee
Cocoa made from unsweetened cocoa powder sweetened with honey

Cook with   Soya or whole-wheat flour (from health-food shops). For your nearest supplier, contact the Soil Association Headquarters, Walnut Tree Manor, Haughley, Stowmarket, Suffolk IP14 3RS (☎ Haughley [044 970] 235)
Unprocessed honey to sweeten
Yogurt
Polyunsaturated oil, such as corn or groundnut oil or margarine (not all margarines are polyunsaturated but some are, e.g. Flora)

Cook   Roast a joint on a grid in the baking tin, so the fat drains off; baste with vegetable oil
Home-made bread, pizza, pancakes
Only spaghetti and rice   that

Vitamin Chart

Vitamin	Benefits	Sources	Too little results in	Too much results in
A	Helps eyesight, protects against sunburn and infections	Liver, butter, cheese, milk, carrots, tomatoes	Sore eyes, itchy skin, hair loss, eventually swelling and pains in arms and leg bones	No appetite, hair loss, pains in arms and leg bones
B	There are many vitamins in the B group. The most important are:			
B1 (thiamine)	Nourishes the brain cells, stimulates the appetite	Cereals, yeast, wheat-germ	Eventual nerve and brain damage, swelling – especially of hands and legs	No problems, excess is excreted
B2 (riboflavin)	Aids growth, improves your hair, makes you more alert	Liver, kidney, milk, green vegetables, mushrooms	Itchy eyes and tongue, cracks at corner of mouth	No problems, excess is excreted
B12 (niacin)	Boosts energy, reduces cholesterol, checks nerve degeneration	Liver, kidney, red meat, eggs, dairy produce	Anaemia	No problems
C	Helps develop cartilage and tissues between cells. Nobel Prize winner Linus Pauling says that 0·1 gram a day keeps influenza away. And it does. Best value is Boots' own brand	Citrus fruits, currants, berries melons, lettuce, green peppers, Brussels sprouts, raw cabbage	Scurvy, bleeding gums, haemorrhages, cuts heal slowly	No problems unless you take enormous amounts over a long period (over 2 grams per day). Then you *might* get kidney stones
D	Strengthens bones, teeth, helps keep muscles supple	Sunlight, animal fats, tuna, sardines, herrings, eggs, butter, margarine	Bone softening (rickets in children)	Hardening of tissues, especially kidneys, loss of appetite
E	Sometimes called the sex vitamin. Stimulates glands, hormone production, reproductive organs. Best value is Boots' own brand	Vegetable fats, especially maize oil, soya beans, peanuts and coconut	May contribute to sterility, hair loss	No problems
K	Helps blood to clot efficiently (not too much, not too little)	Kale, spinach, any dark green vegetables	Haemorrhage	No problems

aren't factory processed to cook fast

Hot soya beans served with traditional Italian pasta sauces (tomato or meat)

Vegetable soups and stews, thickened with whole-wheat or soya flour

Soups based on beans such as soya, split pea, mung beans, black eye beans or lentils

Salads – a salad is not only lettuce and tomato (see *Superwoman* for more ideas)

Salads of haricot and soya beans (boiled for forty minutes, then cooled). Thoroughly toss in a French dressing made from polyunsaturated oil, then add one or two of the following: anchovies, olives, nuts, sliced hard-boiled eggs, slices of tomatoes, onion rings, raw pimento slices.

Get into the habit of always leaving a bowl of beans to soak overnight

VITAMINS

Vitamins are vital for the building and repair processes of the body. Although they are essential, we need only a few milligrams of each per day. A good varied diet should provide you with all the vitamins you need, provided you are in good health.

If you need any extra vitamins (especially after illness or strain) you can take them in pill form. Try Gevral or Boots Multivite. For stress conditions (or a quick boost after flu) you can take B complex vitamins in high concentration with vitamin C in Orovite pills or Parentrovite injections.

Note that excessive amounts of vit-amins A and D can produce nasty side-effects (*see chart, opposite*).

MINERALS

You also need mineral elements to make healthy tissue. You need most of them in very small amounts and, as with vitamins, you should get all you need from a good, varied diet. What is a good varied diet? The Back-to-Nature Diet provides the minerals you need (*see chart, overleaf*).

You can take supplementary minerals in tablet form. Get a multimineral one like Minalca, which contains calcium, potassium, magnesium, sodium, manganese, copper, zinc, cobalt and some vitamin D. Some people swear by kelp tablets, made from seaweed, which contain iodine, sodium and chlorine. You can also get kelp powder to sprinkle on other foods, from health-food stores. Although most excess minerals are excreted, you should never take more than the prescribed dose.

Mineral Chart

Mineral	Needs	Source
Calcium	Active adults need 500 mg daily, to harden bones and teeth. Growing children, pregnant women and nursing mothers need *more* (pregnant women up to 1200 mg daily)	Milk, cheese, yogurt, whole-grain cereals
Iodine	Too little iodine prevents the thyroid gland functioning properly. Thyroid helps metabolism and its failure shows in lethargy, a heavy shape and slow mental and physical reactions	Sea salt and seafoods, vegetables grown where seaweed is used as manure
Iron	Iron is a vital constituent of blood. Adult women need 12 mg daily (more than men). If you don't have enough you become anaemic, especially if you suffer from heavy periods. You may need to take supplementary iron tablets	Red meat, offal, sardines, beans, peas. Berries, such as raspberries. Barley and whole-grain cereals. The acids in citrus fruit and yogurt help you to absorb iron
Magnesium	Adults need 350 mg a day	Whole-grain cereals and green vegetables
Phosphorus	Very important, but phosphorus is a constituent of all animal and plant cells so deficiency is unknown	All foods, but especially animal foods (milk, meat, etc.) Also nuts and whole-grain cereals
Potassium	Potassium and sodium in balance are essential to life. Between them, they help maintain the water balance in your body	All foods, but especially all vegetables
Sodium	You need sodium to help you digest proteins and combat infections. Salt is sodium chloride, but be sparing with its use because it is also present in many foods and is added to bread and butter in the making (you usually have to *ask* if you want unsalted butter)	All meats, milk, eggs, bread, butter (unless you've asked for unsalted)
Sulphur		Animal foods (meat, dairy produce)

You also need traces of several other minerals: *chromium, chlorine, cobalt, copper, manganese, selenium* and *zinc.* When dieticians talk about a trace, they mean a very small amount. It is detected by its *absence* rather than its presence, and the amount you need can be stored in your body for some time so doesn't need daily replenishing. Foods which give you iron will also supply your needs for manganese and copper.
The recommended daily amounts quoted here (except for magnesium) come from *The Manual of Nutrition,* Ministry of Agriculture, Fisheries and Food, HMSO 1977.

Changing

The two most difficult physical problems of a woman's Midlife period may be whether or not she has a late baby and whether she sails through the menopause or has a tough time with it.

THE CONS AND PROS OF HAVING A LATE BABY

Many women want and welcome a late baby. Sometimes they have remarried; sometimes they feel it's their last chance (especially if they've never had one before). Sometimes it's a marriage-cementing idea; sometimes it's a subconscious panic move, to stop themselves feeling redundant in the woman's job – being a mother. Sometimes it's an amazing surprise (as with actor Harry Secombe's wife who said that although she was distressed when she found she was pregnant, the baby made her feel young again, and all the family enjoyed it).

Against this, there's no doubt that bringing up a late baby is physically very, very exhausting and you often lack the patience that you had when you were young and had more stamina. You might feel slightly 'out of things' or even as stranded as the Great White Whale because the other mothers at the health clinic and kindergarten are half your age and have different interests. In fact, you might find them incredibly boring.

Unless you're very rich (and there *isn't* always more spare money as you get older) you're going to be tied to the home (perhaps just when you were planning to spread your wings and do something for yourself at last). So you will have to limit your social activities (especially evenings out with your mate) and you won't have spare time for any absorbing hobbies, new or old. In fact, you won't have any spare time.

The only physical disadvantage to a Midlife mother of giving birth to a late baby is that your body probably won't be as fit and supple as when you were twenty-two, so carefully stick to a correct diet, regular exercise and *never* skip your pre natal check up.

Your chances of conceiving are less than when you were twenty-two but if you are normally fertile they are still high. If you don't conceive within a few months (and you've been practising hard and at the correct times) go to the fertility clinic (they are attached to family planning clinics) where you and your partner can be tested for fertility. Look in the telephone directory (under 'Family Planning Service') for a list of local family planning clinics, or consult your GP, the CAB, the local library or your Area Medical Officer. You don't need an introduction from your GP to go to the clinic, although the clinic doctors may ask you if you have consulted your GP.

Your partner will have to give a sperm sample, which he does by masturbating into a bottle or clear jar. This *can* be done at home, but he has to be ready to dash to the clinic with the bottle, because the contents have to be analysed within the hour.

Male fertility declines after their twenties (but very little and very gradually) and they can easily conceive well into their eighties (look at Charlie Chaplin and Picasso). Subfertility in men can be helped by bathing the testicles in cold water and by giving vitamin B12 injections. Men can also be given testosterone tablets (hormone tablets, the proprietary name is Pro-Viron) which can help to improve the sperm count.

Another problem may be that your mate's sperm cannot survive in your particular cervical mucus. To test this *you* have to go to the clinic twelve to twenty-two hours after intercourse so that the doctor can take a swab from your cervical mucus.

Another cause of infertility in women is that their Fallopian tubes become blocked. This can be tested by a machine that blows carbon dioxide gently through the uterus and tubes. It measures the pressure, and that shows whether or not the gas is passing freely into the abdominal cavity. (It doesn't harm you because if carbon dioxide passes into the abdominal cavity it is absorbed into the blood.) In another test, water-soluble iodine may be introduced into your uterus and Fallopian tubes. You are then X-rayed to determine where the fluid has reached.

Or you can have a laparoscopy. A blue dye is injected through the cervix and an instrument like a thin telescope is inserted through a small incision in the abdominal wall. The instrument photographs the Fallopian tubes and shows where the dye has reached. Laparoscopy is performed under a general anaesthetic and takes two to three days in hospital.

Other possible causes of infertility arise from hormonal insufficiency. If you are short of oestrogen, your womb lining may not be developing properly to receive the fertilized egg or the follicle may not be bursting so that the egg is never released.

To test whether this is the problem, you can have the lining of your womb analyzed. This is usually done by giving you a dilatation and curettage (known as a D & C) under a general anaesthetic. Alternatively, you can have a mini-curettage in which only a tiny piece of your womb lining is removed; a general anaesthetic is not necessary for this.

If you are not ovulating or your womb lining is not developing you can be treated with hormonal drugs, but this has to be done very carefully to avoid multiple pregnancy. The only thing potentially more exhausting than a late baby is late triplets.

A miscarriage is a spontaneous abortion, which you did nothing to help. You are more likely to miscarry as you grow older, especially if you have miscarried in earlier years. You can have a number of *abortions* (i.e. induced miscarriages) but this does not affect your subsequent likelihood of miscarrying.

The only certain child-bearing risk that increases with age seems to be the risk of having a malformed child. It increases noticeably after thirty-five and more steeply after forty. The most precise figures relate to mongolism (Down's syndrome); the average mother's chances of having a mongol child are as follows:

Under thirty: 1 in 2000
Between thirty and thirty-nine: 1 in 1100
Over thirty-nine: 1 in 76
Over forty-five: 1 in 50, and then the risk leaps steeply

Apart from mongolism the risks of all forms of malformation rise after the age of thirty-five. For instance, the risk of spina bifida (failure to close the spinal column) also rises.

If you are in doubt about the risk you run, get *genetic counselling*. A geneticist takes the family history of yourself and your mate and from that he can check the likelihood of your having a defective child. He may also get a chromosome analysis from blood samples taken from you and your husband.

Genetic counselling gives you negative information, rather than positive: it tells you that you are *unlikely* to run a certain risk. Don't expect to be told *before* you conceive it, whether or not you will have a defective child.

After conception, some forms of malformation of the foetus can be assessed just from an analysis of the mother's blood. For example, a blood analysis may indicate that your child has a neural tube defect (spina bifida).

You can be tested in the fifteenth week of your pregnancy for foetal abnormality. You go to hospital and have an amniocentesis test under a local anaesthetic. A small incision is made in your abdomen and uterus. The doctor withdraws some of the amniotic fluid (the water in which the baby floats) which is analyzed and will show if the foetus is suffering from defects due to chromosomal or metabolic abnormality.

If the foetus is abnormal you will find it easy to get an abortion, although you may prefer to have the child.

THE CHANGE

'I think my mother's got it. She's so ratty and she's depressed because she's getting fatter and she's getting double vision. My dad thinks she should go to a psychiatrist because she's so odd but she says she won't go to the doctor because she's not ill.' – Twenty-year-old boy

'When you get to my age, my girl, you'll call it the Blessing not the Curse: the Change is a terrible thing.' – Seventy-year-old grandmother

You may be one of the lucky 15 per cent of British women who sail through the menopause without noticing; you may be one of the 75 per cent who have mild-to-serious trouble; or one of the 10 per cent who really have a tough time and whose whole family can be affected as a result.

In medical terms the menopause means positively your last period and the *climacteric* means the end of the reproductive stage in your life cycle. It is more generally known as 'the change of life' or simply 'the change'.

The crucial things that happen are that:

1 Your ovaries cease to manufacture as much as they previously did of a hormone called oestrogen. (This is not *only* produced by the ovaries, but also by the adrenal glands, which are not affected by the menopause.)
2 You cease to release an egg each month and your monthly menstrual flow stops.

A woman's periods may still be regular but, *without realizing it*, she may have menopausal symptoms because her hormone level is reducing.

You can expect the menopause at any time between forty and fifty-five, although it can start in the early thirties if you're infertile or if early menopause runs in your family. There's evidence that the average age of menopause is rising and is now about fifty-one in Europe.

Women who are reasonably content with their family and personal lives, and who have had children, seem less likely than others to become seriously depressed and disturbed at the menopause.

Your family can make a great difference to the effect it has on you. Your husband and children should be told that this is a temporarily difficult time, and they should know what the menopause is and what to expect (get them to read this chapter). They might even spot that you've got it before *you* do.

Menopausal changes vary from woman to woman and very few of them are outwardly visible. You don't come out in a rash of green spots (so you get no sympathy) but menopausal effects can nevertheless be sudden, violent and really frightening. Many of the symptoms concern your feelings – and these are not always apparent to *you*, although your family may notice that you become more irritable, moody, or hysterical. However, clinical depression may now affect as few as 10 per cent of women, owing to the increasing opportunities available to them. The menopause is no longer a taboo or shaming subject and many symptoms can be easily helped by simple medicine.

And a bonus is that the menopause is a heaven-sent excuse for any bad behaviour on your part, from delayed nymphomania to shop-lifting.

THE MOST COMMON MENOPAUSAL SYMPTOMS

Apart from the notorious hot flush what *are* the symptoms? What happens? And how can you tell when your menopause is starting?

First signs are likely to be a change in menstrual pattern, say from regular to irregular or from scanty to heavy loss of blood at period time. But some women cease to menstruate suddenly: this is often associated with a shock such as a bereavement or moving house.

Often women don't recognize the symptoms and often doctors don't like to suggest menopausal changes for fear the patient will have hysterics on the spot. But any change you recognize is less alarming than one that other people have to point out – and recent discoveries in hormone replacement therapy (HRT) can combat many of the physical problems.

As with pregnant women, extra

oestrogen supplied by HRT can also *improve* hair, skin and general well-being.

CHANGES BEFORE AND DURING THE CLIMACTERIC

The symptoms starred* can be arrested by HRT. Percentages given are based on a 1972 Dutch study of 6000 women and a British study in 1973. For Heaven's sake don't think you're going to get them all. The most common symptoms are:

Fatigue (43 per cent).
*Night sweats (39 per cent) you may wake to find yourself in a really wet bed.
Headaches (38 per cent).
Palpitations sudden heart thumping (24 per cent). These upset many women who think they are developing heart disease.
Sleeplessness (32 per cent). This can continue up to five years afterwards.
*Irritability (29 per cent).
*Dizziness (24 per cent).
*Hot flushes (29 per cent). These can be a combination of several other symptoms. For instance, you may feel fine one minute, then the next minute have a sudden, frightening feeling of being swamped by an instant sauna heat, sweat, shortness of breath, singing in the ears and dizziness. It can be like an invisible wave breaking over you. Try not to move (especially not downstairs). Sit down (if necessary on the floor), say 'I think I'm going to faint' (no further explanation is then necessary) and expect everyone to think you're dead drunk, if it's after 8 p.m.
*Depression which has a physical cause, due to lack of amino-acids in the blood (30 per cent).
Depression due to external causes or attitude to your condition that cannot be relieved by hormone therapy.
Formication, which feels like an army of ants crawling under your skin (22 per cent).
*Skin becomes dry, papery, wrinkled and shrivelled due to less sodium and water in the skin.
*Vaginal dryness.
*Vaginal itching, irritation or infection. This may be more common than doctors think, because not all women like to talk about sexual difficulties. However, changes in vaginal secretion are directly related to oestrogen changes in the body and can certainly be relieved by HRT.
Hypertension or high blood pressure.
*Possible changes in libido. You may find yourself disinterested in sex or abnormally interested in the postman.

Many women find that they become *moody* and *prone to get easily upset* over small matters and generally *'more emotional'. Short temper, edginess* and *fatigue* are very common.

Other emotional problems can include *forgetfulness, inability to make decisions,* and *anxiety.*

CHANGES AFTER MENSTRUATION CEASES

Weight increase
*Change in weight distribution. You may still weigh the same but it seems to have slipped down: breasts are smaller, thighs are bigger. HRT can reduce women to their normal weight and size.
*Vaginal dryness and atrophy (shrivel-

ling). Helped by HRT and also vaginal lubricants.

Pain in bones and joints, which may be due to *osteoporosis*. This is a loss of calcium and phosphate which eventually leads to bone fragility (so that bones, such as the hip, break easily and don't mend). Between the ages of fifty and eighty you may lose 15 per cent of your skeleton. In older women osteoporosis can lead to:

*Dowager's hump
*Lower back pain
*Loss of height.

HRT can prevent the development of osteoporosis and *also* arrest the condition once it has started. It cannot help the pain, but painkillers can be prescribed.

WHY IT HAPPENS

Why should the human female become infertile half-way through her life, when men don't?

One theory is that as females are born with all their eggs (whereas males create fresh ones at every ejaculation) an older mother's eggs may have got stale in storage. (The marked increase in deformities in children born to older women suggests this.)

The second reason may be to ensure that children are not born to mothers who won't live long enough to rear them. In the Roman Empire the average life of a woman was approximately twenty-five years. At the discovery of America (in the 1490s) the average life of a woman was approximately thirty years. During the Victorian age the average life of a woman was approximately forty-five

years. Today the average life of a woman is seventy-seven years.

Many of the unpleasant physical effects of the menopause are due to the jerky unbalanced reduction of female hormones as the whole reproduction system slows down. The lucky 15 per cent who do not seem to age suddenly or suffer are those who slow down smoothly and who have very active adrenal glands to give them a still adequate and steady supply of oestrogen.

WHAT IS HORMONE REPLACEMENT THERAPY AND HOW CAN IT HELP?

Hormone replacement therapy (HRT) can help women to stay as young as possible, for as long as possible. You generally take a daily pill (looks similar to a vitamin pill) which provides the oestrogen that you lack. Many doctors are enthusiastic about this treatment, including Sir John Peel who was, until his recent retirement, gynaecologist to HM the Queen.

The pioneer of HRT was Robert Wilson, a British doctor who was determined to find some way to make the menopause easier for women after seeing how much his mother suffered. He emigrated to America in the 1920s where (as a result) HRT is still very much more readily prescribed than it is in Britain.

However, many British GPs still regard HRT as a new-fangled American fad for women who are chasing the secret of youth or a fantasy of sex and glamour and don't see why this costly, self-indulgent dream should be supplied free by the National Health Service.

Most doctors are male, so they can't *ever* know what the menopause really feels like and many doctors tend to think you should just put up with it – when there is no reason to do so.

It is clear that we have already improved on nature with regard to the birth rate and the death rate. Women who feel uneasy about taking oestrogen ('We weren't meant to interfere with nature') might re-member that it's not more unnatural than wearing clothes, cooking meat, living in a mud hut or taking anti-biotics.

Whatever the reasons, there is no doubt that most British doctors are markedly more sour and ill-informed about HRT than are the Ameri-cans – although as menopause clinics open in big cities, and the results are plainly visible, there is a growing enthusiasm among doctors with experience of HRT.

CAN HRT HELP EVERYONE?

Of the women who have trouble and discomfort at the menopause it is calculated that about 25 per cent are experiencing a serious oestrogen shortage and could benefit enorm-ously from taking this small oes-trogen pill daily. HRT may also help relieve *specific symptoms* for many other women. *But some menopausal troubles are not due to hormone defi-ciency and these are not cured by HRT.*

HRT is generally given in pills of varying strengths. It is also possible to have a tiny hormone pellet inserted into the lower abdomen or buttock muscles. The pellet is replaced every six months. A third method is to take the oestrogen in the form of a pessary or cream which is put into the vagina.

The disadvantage of the implant and pessary methods is that the body is forced to absorb a large dose of oestrogen at once. This can cause – on a massive scale – the sort of side-effects and mood swings of pre/dur-ing/post menstrual tension. NHS doctors are therefore wary of implants, although they are used after a full hysterectomy (*see* 'Women's Operations, *page 52*).

Dr Howard Jacobs says that often doctors prescribe a too-high dosage of oestrogen. A safe and effective pill dose should be between 5 and 15 micrograms a day, prescribed on a twenty-one-day cycle (like the con-traceptive pill). You have a week off when (as with the pill) you get an artificially induced period. Of course, your own doctor may have a very good reason for altering this prescrip-tion. But always ask *why* you are being given a certain size dose, *what* it is, and *keep a note of the answers*.

Whatever dose your doctor advises or however he suggests you take it, you won't run any risk of becoming pregnant. All HRT doses are far below the level required for ovula-tion.

As the correct dosage varies from woman to woman, you can appreciate why you need an expert's opinion. Very rarely will your GP be an expert. Ask him to send you to a specialist gynaecologist or to a menopause clinic. You should have a twice-yearly check.

IS IT SAFE?

If you get your correct dosage and have your checks, then the risk is very low. Many American women have been taking HRT for twenty years and stayed in excellent health.

However, *some* of the earlier HRT studies would not meet modern research standards, and there is no doubt that hormones have powerful effects on the body, some of which cannot be accurately assessed for many years. So HRT may be risky if *it is not carefully prescribed*, and there are some women who should not have it (for instance, those who have had breast cancer).

High doses of oestrogen given over a long period of time are convincingly linked with an increased resk of gallstones and cancer. This link appears whether the oestrogen is synthetic or natural. (Premarin, made from the natural urine of pregnant mares, is one popular brand name.) This is why doctors prefer women to take them only for a certain number of years.

HOW MUCH DOES IT COST?
A year's supply of artificial oestrogen currently costs about £2, but doctors prefer to prescribe natural oestrogen, which costs about £9 a year – a much smaller sum than might be spent on the sleeping-tablets and antidepressants which are handed out to menopausal sufferers as a matter of course.

NHS MENOPAUSE CLINICS

Aberdeen: Gynaecological Endocrine Clinic, Department of Obstetrics and Gynaecology, Aberdeen University, Foresterhill, Aberdeen AB9 2ZD (☎ Aberdeen [0224] 23423).
Belfast: Samaritan Hospital (Dr J. F. O'Sullivan), Lisburn Road, Belfast BT9 6AD (☎ Belfast [0232] 41316).
Birmingham: The Menopause Clinic, Professorial Unit, Women's Hospital, Queen Elizabeth Medical Centre, Edgbaston, Birmingham B15 2TG (☎ 021-427 1377).
Brighton and Hove: The Menopause Clinic, Department of Obstetrics and Gynaecology, The Lady Chichester Hospital, New Church Road, Hove, East Sussex BN3 4AG (☎ Brighton [0273] 778383).
Durham: Department of Obstetrics and Gynaecology, Dryburn Hospital, Durham DH1 5TW (☎ Durham [0385] 64911).
Edinburgh: Gynaecological Out-Patients, Royal Infirmary, Department of Obstetrics and Gynaecology, 39 Chalmers Street, Edinburgh EH3 9EW (☎ 031-667 1011).
Glasgow: Gynaecological Clinic, Glasgow Royal Infirmary, Rottenrow, Glasgow G4 0NA (☎ 041-552 3535).
Leeds: MRC Mineral Metabolism Unit, General Infirmary, Great George Street, Leeds LS1 5EX (☎ Leeds [0532] 32799).
Department of Obstetrics and Gynaecology, Women's Hospital, Roundhay Hill, Jackson Avenue, Leeds LS8 1NT (☎ Leeds [0532] 665121).
Liverpool: Gynaecological Clinic, Women's Hospital, Catharine Street, Liverpool L8 7NJ (☎ 051-709 5461).
London: The Menopause Clinic, Department of Obstetrics and Gynaecology, Chelsea Hospital for Women, Dovehouse Street, London SW3 6LT (☎ 01-352 6446).
The Menopause Clinic, Dulwich Hospital, East Dulwich Grove, Dulwich, London SE22 8PT (☎ 01-693 3377).
The Menopause Clinic, Department of Gynaecology, St Thomas'

Hospital, London SE1 7EH (☎ 01-928 9292, extension 2262).

The Menopause Clinic, Department of Obstetrics and Gynaecology, King's College Hospital, Denmark Hill, London SE5 9RS (☎ 01-274 6222).

Merthyr Tydfil: Department of Obstetrics and Gynaecology, St Tydfil's Hospital, Merthyr Tydfil, Mid Glam. CF47 0SJ (☎ Merthyr Tydfil [0685] 3401).

Nottingham: The Menopause Clinic, Department of Obstetrics and Gynaecology, City Hospital, Hucknall Road, Nottingham NG5 1PB (☎ Nottingham [0602] 68111).

Nuneaton: Department of Obstetrics and Gynaecology, George Eliot Hospital, College Street, Nuneaton, Warwicks CV10 7DJ (☎ Nuneaton [0682] 4201).

Oxford: Department of Obstetrics and Gynaecology, John Radcliffe Hospital, Headley Way, Headington, Oxford OX3 9DU (☎ Oxford [0865] 64711).

Sheffield: University Department, Jessop Hospital, Leavygreave Road, Sheffield S3 7RE (☎ Sheffield [0742] 29291).

PRIVATE MENOPAUSE CLINICS

Birmingham: The Menopause Clinic, 10–12 Leahurst Crescent, Harborne, Birmingham B17 0LG (☎ 021-427 6525).

Blackpool: Menopause Clinic, 48 Whitegate Drive, Blackpool FY3 9AL (☎ Blackpool [0253] 32647).

Bristol: Brook Advisory Centre, 27 Richmond Hill, Clifton, Bristol BS8 1BA (☎ Bristol [0272] 36657).

Edinburgh: Menopause Clinic, Royal Scottish Nursing Home, 9 Drumsheugh Gardens, Edinburgh EH3 7RW (☎ 031-225 3881).

Glasgow: The Bellgrove Clinic, 556 Gallowgate, Glasgow G40 2PA (☎ 041-554 7157).

Liverpool: 31 Rodney Street, Liverpool L1 9EH (☎ 051-709 8522).

London: The Menopause Clinic, 152 Harley Street, London W1N 1HH (☎ 01-935 8868).

The Menopause Clinic, 56 Harley Street, London W1N 1AD (☎ 01-580 1143).

The Menopause Clinic, 56 Anerley Park, London SE20 8NB (☎ 01-778 8027).

The Menopause Clinic, 9 South Road, Twickenham, Middx TW2 5WU (☎ 01-977 6099).

The Menopause Clinic, Grantham Centre, Beckett House, Grantham Road, Stockwell, London SW9 9DL (☎ 01-733 6191).

Marie Stopes Memorial Clinic, 108 Whitfield Street, London W1P 6BE (☎ 01-388 0662).

Southport: The Health Centre, Churchtown, Southport, Merseyside PR9 7LT (☎ Southport [0704] 24411).

Newcastle: Nuffield Clinic, Osborne Road, Newcastle upon Tyne NE2 1JP (☎ Newcastle upon Tyne [0632] 815331).

'WOMEN'S OPERATIONS'

Granny was sinisterly mysterious about 'women's operations'. This is what they are, and very boring reading it is, unless you're about to have one.

DILATATION AND CURETTAGE (*D & C*)

The vagina is dilated and the lining

of the womb is scraped clean of polyps, fibroids or other adhesions. Often used as a treatment for excessively heavy periods and performed under an anaesthetic. It's a very minor operation: you don't normally stay in hospital for more than two nights.

REMOVAL OF POLYPS, FIBROIDS AND CYSTS

These are lumps of different shapes and sizes. A *polyp* is a protruding growth from the mucous membrane which may appear in the vagina and uterus (or anywhere else). It may look, like a knob on a stalk (a tiny mushroom).

A *fibroid* is a growth of muscle and fibre tissue which may be harmless but which can be malignant (cancerous).

A *cyst* is a closed cavity usually containing a liquid or semi-solid material (like a gumboil). Cysts can grow to any size and are probably harmless although they may be uncomfortable. They can be removed by piercing the cyst and releasing the liquid, or by surgery.

Old wives' tales' cysts are *never* smaller than an egg, orange or grapefruit.

VAGINAL PROLAPSE

A number of things can go wrong with your sex organs, as they can with any other part of you. Sagging and looseness of the vagina can be caused by overstretching in childbirth to the point where you can hardly feel a thing during intercourse – and neither can he. This may be associated with depression (no wonder) and can really spoil your sex life.

To correct vaginal prolapse you have a general anaesthetic and the surgeon cuts a strip out of the front and back of your vagina, then sews you back to standard size (like putting a dart in a sleeve).

You may be in hospital seven to twelve days but should come out what might delicately be described as several sizes smaller.

UTERINE PROLAPSE

Vaginal prolapse can also be associated with uterine prolapse. This is when the ligaments holding your uterus (womb) up in your abdomen become stretched and the womb falls down against the muscle floor between your legs. If you have a bad case of uterine prolapse the womb may actually hang outside your vagina by some inches.

Uterine prolapse can obviously cause great discomfort and sense of heaviness. Both vaginal prolapse and uterine prolapse may cause slight incontinency (involuntary pee) because you have less control over your bladder muscles.

Uterine prolapse is usually corrected by a hysterectomy (see next) or it can be corrected by surgically tightening the uterus ligaments (in which case you do not have to have your womb removed).

HYSTERECTOMY

This is performed for several reasons and often brings great relief from ill health and discomfort.

Hysterectomies are common operations. In 1973 (the latest year for which figures are available) 62,900 women in England and Wales had hysterectomies. Of these the great majority had their wombs removed but their ovaries left intact.

The only reason for removing ovaries is evidence of disease such as cancer or some pelvic disorders. Removal of the ovaries before the menopause will cause premature menopause but HRT will usually relieve the more unpleasant effects of this abrupt change (such as hot flushes, night sweats, depression and irritability). After a hysterectomy you cannot have a baby.

FIBROIDS

Some women develop a continuous problem of fibroids which cause uncomfortably heavy periods. Apart from discomfort they can cause anaemia, exhaustion and general dragginess. Your doctor may recommend a hysterectomy.

CANCER OF THE CERVIX OR WOMB OR A PRE-CANCER CONDITION

A cervical smear may show that you have a pre-cancer condition, or cancer of the cervix or womb.

If the condition is pre-cancerous you can have a simple operation in which the surgeons remove a small portion of your cervix to *prevent* cancer development. If cancer has developed, you will be advised to have a hysterectomy.

Doctors promise that a hysterectomy should make no difference to a woman's sex life (or her man's) although you won't feel the penis against the cervix. Sexual relations should be possible within two to three months – sometimes earlier. For some people sex is more enjoyable because pregnancy is impossible.

A hysterectomy is a major operation and it can take some women up to a year to feel really strong and fit again. However, some women feel fit within six months and many notice the benefits immediately.

The ignorant old wives' tale to the effect that you've lost your womanhood, femininity, etc., is just a lot of rubbish.

MASTECTOMY

This is removal of a breast, usually because of a malignant cancer growth. The operation is neither fatal nor shaming and needn't leave a disgusting mutilation, just a neat scar. Plastic surgery can provide a false breast but most patients simply wear a specially made-to-order padded bra (swim suits are also available). Splendid ladies, such as ex-US president's wife Betty Ford, and Mrs Happy Rockefeller and Shirley Temple have publicized their mastectomies, instead of hiding them, so you can see that this operation is neither fatal nor shaming.

SEX AND THE MENOPAUSE

'The menopausal woman . . . is likely to become frigid or alternatively overwhelm her husband with her demands. Homosexual tendencies will become manifest, she may take up masturbation and seek romance she has never known, and soon will no longer be able to know . . . She will also know a mad desire for prostitution. Her dreams will be peopled by erotic fantasies and she will fall in love with one young man after another . . .' – Simone de Beauvoir

Difficult to decide what's going to happen to *you* with such an amazing range of options. But does that really happen in Brighton or Glasgow? Or anywhere else? Can your sex life really change so drastically? Are you really going to lose interest in the whole ridiculous performance, or are you going to amaze your children by turning into a nymphomaniac and chasing the milkman?

Many sexual myths have been clobbered during the last twenty years. One of them is that your love

life goes off and you become less sexually attractive during the menopause. In fact, the menopause brings positive advantages. A woman can enjoy a new sexual freedom once she no longer fears pregnancy (although that's not such a menace today) and has any period problems under control.

Children become less of a responsibility and take up less of your energy when they don't barge in wanting ice lollies or bang on the bedroom door demanding to know why they've been locked out. You may have more time and energy to enjoy a new rising-moon of romance and excitement, because your love life can certainly get better and better. Elizabeth Taylor at forty-four said of her new husband, 'He's the best lover I ever had.' So there's hope for all of us.

Women who continue to have a good and active sex life can:

Age more slowly.
Look better.
Live longer.
Show least physical evidence of the change.
Enjoy sex more.

There's no such thing as being too old for sex, but you certainly can go through a temporary phase (at any time of life) of feeling worried, ill, exhausted and therefore off sex. This is only natural. On the other hand if you are 15 lb overweight and looking it, losing it can make a *lot* of difference to your love life – not only are you less embarrassed when cavorting naked, and stop turning the light off, but you actually feel more agile, energetic and *sexier*.

In Midlife you *may* experience a couple of minor, physical changes when you're making love. Your contractions (if any) may not be as strong as in earlier years but you can still have as many orgasms as ever. However, *after* the menopause, vaginal lubrication diminishes, which can lead to the problem of dryness, soreness and sometimes pain. This is easily avoided by using a lubricant. Get an odourless, tasteless, sterile cream such as KY Jelly (from Boots). *Don't use beauty creams*; and avoid using what happens to be in the medicine cabinet, such as Vaseline, which is very sticky: you can end up glued together and completely exhausted.

The chances are that you may feel sexier in your forties than you did in your twenties: women may be at their most responsive in Mid-life. Unfortunately (or you may think otherwise) Nature has arranged for men to be most sexually active in their late teens. This doesn't necessarily mean that any spotty teenager is an amazing stud. It might mean that he masturbates incessantly and climaxes in thirty seconds.

Middle-aged men get fewer orgasms (one for every two acts of intercourse, rather than invariably) but they can go on longer without ejaculating, if that's what you want.

A recent British study of men and women aged between sixty and ninety-three found that 54 per cent were still sexually active, including one in four of the over seventy-fives. (In case you suspect they were boasting, modern surveys always contain hidden checks to test validity.)

The message from scientists and surveys is that sex gets better the more you practise it, and the more you get, the better it is for you, and the more you do it, the more often you *can* do it. If you get in the habit of making love regularly and don't get lazy about it you are more likely to retain your sexuality into old age.

To stay attractive, strong and energetic, the sex experts of the Western world, Masters and Johnson, suggest *regular* intercourse, once or twice a week. Use it or lose it is the message.

'Getting into the habit' doesn't mean always doing it in the same place and the same time every week but the ancient British custom of Friday-night-after-steak-for-supper is not to be sneezed at.

But will you still attract men and how much will it matter? In fact, it's not your attraction that may go, it's more likely to be your self-confidence. The birthday with a zero ending is generally the one that starts you worrying.

But this is a self-fulfilling expectation: if you *expect* to get less attrac-

tive then you will, because so much of 'attraction' is invisible – charm, vitality and that carefree don't-give-a-damn attitude.

What is unattractive in a woman is anxiety about her looks, too much make-up, total self-absorption, bitterness and tension (feelings that are not restricted to Middle Age).

And of course it's very middle-aged to lie about your age. Not only is it pathetic, but you will undoubtedly get found out fast.

In fact, you should be able to attract just as many people as you have done in the past (if that's what you want). You are *not* a woman who is 'still attractive', you are an attractive woman. It sometimes helps if your spouse can *see* that you can still attract, but don't bother to flirt to do this, it's far more devastating not to.

As writer Jilly Cooper has said, 'A jaunty woman can go on having fun until she's 100 . . . and the menopause is but a short pause between men.'

THE MALE MENOPAUSE: DOES IT EXIST?

We were brought up on the myth (another of Life's Little Lies) that women age faster than men. Whereas women deteriorate with age, men were actually supposed to *improve* in a distinguished sort of way, like chateau-bottled claret. Physically this doesn't seem to be so any more (just look at the men in your neighbourhood who are losing their looks).

Contrary to what we were led to expect, men can start looking pretty moth-eaten soon after thirty. Often they're too complacent to do anything about it, and occasionally there's nothing they *can* do about it. They start to go bald (and that can put on twenty years in two); they don't look after their skin so it looks as if someone's been cleaning the car with it for the last twenty years; then the neck disappears in a fleshy roll and lots of them start to look five months pregnant, backwards, forwards and sideways. As far as losing their looks is concerned, men certainly have as much to worry about as women.

And lately there's been talk of a male menopause. Obviously a man isn't going to go through 'the Change' but the male menopause or Midlife Crisis is neither a myth nor a joke.

Men certainly experience a decline in sex hormones due to ageing. The difference is that these hormonal changes are generally much milder and much later than in women.

If there is a sharp drop in a man's hormone level, then he may show some of the same classic symptoms as a menopausal woman, namely:

Symptoms of the body
  *Insomnia.
  *Hot sweats.
  *Headaches.
  *Cold feet.
  *Palpitations.

  Eventually there will be:
  *Skin dryness.
  *Loss of muscle tone.
  *Brittleness of bone.

  Symptoms of the mind
  *Irritability.
  *Bad temper.
  *Lethargy.
  *Exhaustion.
  *Restlessness.
  *Nervousness.
  *Rapid swings of mood, from euphoria to gloom.

*Depression (particularly if his chances of promotion are fading).
*Indecision.
*Unpredictability.
*Instability.
*A failure of nerve (a different sort of cold feet).
*PANIC.

What is *really* meant by the male menopause is a state of mind, rather than a state of body (as it is with women). This period of Midlife Crisis can, of course, seem like a second adolescence, with all the accompanying moodiness and discontent (*see* 'Is there a Midlife Crisis?' *opposite page*).

As with a woman, the big fear is of losing his sexual attraction, which can lead to desperate over-compensation. Any female in any office knows that at a certain age a certain sort of chap will pursue *any* girl who is young enough in order to prove that he is still irresistible to the girls.

A man often reacts to his anxieties with exhaustion and loss of libido. He may not want sex and he may not be able to get an erection (although both these effects can also be due to overwork, business responsibilities, physical illness or prescribed drugs, such as tranquillizers).

At this point a lot of men start worrying that their sex drive is disappearing. And that leads to thoughts of impotence (there are no British studies, but over 20 per cent of American men over fifty worry enough about impotence to consult their doctors).

Only a small number of men (one estimate is less than 2 per cent) experience a genuine physical (as opposed to mental) climacteric due to a sudden drop in hormone output. Fortunately they can be helped, as much as women can, by hormone therapy. Treatment is available on the NHS with injections of testosterone (the male hormone) or Pro-viron tablets which can restore good spirits, energy and feelings of good health. Pro-viron is a hormone tablet that is used to help sub-fertility but there's no doubt that many men who are put on a course of such tablets feel generally better and sexier, although Dr Eric Trimmer, editor of the *British Journal of Sexual Medicine*, says that the relationship between hormone levels and libido is doubtful.

It can be a grave problem if both partners suffer physical and mental changes at the same time, particularly if the woman is told that her physical problem is 'all in the mind' and the man (whose problem *is* in the mind) seeks to prove that *he* has no problem, by taking to expensive gymnastic clubs, young secretaries and embarrassingly juvenile shirts.

IS THERE A MIDLIFE CRISIS AND, IF SO, WHY AND WHEN?

It's unlikely that anyone can get through life without some sort of identity crisis. It might start suddenly when you wake up one morning wondering who you really are and why you're here, or where you went wrong, or what's the point of going on. Or it might creep up on you as a slow realization of futility.

Some people experience this turbulent time in their teens. Some signposts are: swings of mood from elation to anxiety, hostility to the rest of the family, a negative, resentful, jeering attitude to society, and inflexible high ideals with a consequent all-pervading feeling of inadequacy. Standard teenage behaviour in a nutshell, some mothers may think glumly.

A Midlife Crisis is *also* a major period of growing up, which we all know doesn't automatically stop when you get the key of the door, or even the key of the executive washroom. In fact, some people aren't adult by the time they're ninety.

However, the theory of Midlife Crisis is that most people reach a critical stage of personal development between the ages of thirty-five and forty-five and the transition stage may last several years. This theory was put forward by Professor Elliott Jaques of Brunel University after he had analyzed the lives of over three hundred historically famous musicians, writers and artists. He noticed that creative capacity may suddenly burst out or dry up during this period and that nearly all the subjects of his study drastically changed their work after their Midlife Crisis.

A creative person certainly stops getting ideas and dries up if he loses his nerve and self-confidence and starts to question the validity of what he's doing, instead of just getting on with it. These are three classic symptoms of the Midlife Crisis. And, of course, it isn't just one simple crisis:

the whole roof tends to fall in at once, and then it starts to rain.

Symptoms can be some or all of the following: the loss-of-youth crisis; the loss-of-looks crisis; the loss-of-health-and-fertility crisis; the sex crisis; the religious crisis; the marriage crisis (this can be especially turbulent if the partner is *also* going through a Midlife Crisis); the creativity crisis; the personality crisis; the am - I - a - Mum - or - am - I - Queen - of - the - Hearth - or - am - I - a - Nothing crisis.

Midlife Crisis occurs when something inside you forces you to examine yourself and society and to re-evaluate your one and only life. You suspect that the aims you were aiming at and the life you have been brought up to lead simply don't work according to the rules that you were taught.

The resultant slow splintering or fast fracture of personality can resemble a hellish game that seems to be played in an endless pit of snakes with no ladders. The snakes are self-doubt, self-loathing and self-destruction and the rest of the family will find them very difficult to put up with.

During this period, when you may be at your most uncertain, other events may happen to influence the increasing development of personality. These might be personal events (such as bankruptcy, job loss, divorce or death) or impersonal events (such as a war, a train crash, inflation or North Sea oil).

Anyone who has been through such a period knows that you generally totter out of the tunnel as a better person. A successful Midlife Crisis should result in genuine self-awareness, self-sufficiency, indepen-

dence and contentment. It should mean less pressure and competition and lots more freedom and fun. (Bet you can't wait.) This may only be achieved at great expense in terms of money, spirit and shame, but it can be even more expensive *not* to have a Midlife sort-out.

American writer Gail Sheehy believes that men and women continue to develop through a series of predictable crises until the age of fifty. She believes that each passage of life (however painful) can be used to develop the full personality. What is so comforting about her remarkable book *Passages* is that she demonstrates the *predictability* of the crisis periods. Somehow your problems are less painful if *everybody* is having them. If you are in one of those dreadful Biblical seven-year spans of disaster to the point that you're wondering what happens next and when the locusts are coming (or even WORSE, like Job you have a plague of boils), it is almost cheering to read that 'a sense of stagnation, disequilibrium and depression is predictable as we enter the passage to midlife . . . Each passage is a shell to be discarded and then followed by a period of tranquillity. Times of crisis, of disruption or constructive change are not only predictable but desirable. They mean growth.' Happily she adds, 'Coming out of each passage we enter a longer and more stable period in which we can expect relative tranquillity and a sense of equilibrium regained.'

She also makes another particularly interesting observation. There is a constant tug-of-war in one person between the safe feeling of being one of a group (especially a group of two) and the wobbly wish for the freedom of individuality. Of course the price of individuality is separation.

She labels as the 'Seeker' that separate, adventurous, curious and possibly selfish part of an individual. The cosier 'Merger Self' involves less risk but has no possibility of individual growth.

Also hovering inside everyone's head is the 'Inner Custodian', the phantom parent, the reproachful, inescapable conscience that you *weren't* born with but that was implanted by the do's and don't's of parents, customs and society. The 'Inner Custodian' is what gives you the illusion that someone always has – and always will – look after you.

During a Midlife Crisis these three are whirling round in your head. You should emerge with the Seeker in control.

The thinking woman

Before this book was started a group of girls, all under twenty-two, were asked what Middle Age is and when it starts. They were adamant that it had little to do with age and a lot to do with mental attitude.

'Middle Age, it's this navy blue aunt, upholstered like a sofa, with a pink, corseted, inflexible mind; she can't go on a picnic without a thermos . . .'

'Middle Age is when your mind closes and ceases to develop, when you shut your mind off from ideas and concepts. A shut mind is the start of death, you know . . .'

'It's when you're unwilling to try new things and have fixed ideas . . . you think they're always right . . . everything has to be rigidly planned . . . everything has to fit neatly into place. No disruptions, no overgrown gardens, nothing to upset your little schedule . . .'

'There was a girl who was at school with me and she's middle-aged already; but her parents were always middle-aged, you see.'

'Quite often I've found that much older people of sixty plus can be far more flexible and tolerant and understanding. They're not upset about things and they encourage you. I don't mind getting older and I don't mind being old but I hope I'll never be middle-aged.'

Everyone wants to look their best and many women are prepared to put a lot of money and effort into overhauling their beauty schedule and smartening up their wardrobe from time to time. But very few women regularly overhaul their most valuable possession: have you ever thought of smartening up your brain? Perhaps you have. Scott Fitzgerald drew up a study plan of reading for his mistress which they called *College of One*. Perhaps you have similarly drawn up reading lists or gone on holiday with *Das Kapital*, *Ulysses*, a hunk of Proust, or even *War and Peace* (the only one of that lot that ever gets finished).

For all *we* know your mind already runs Mercedes-smooth on oiled wheels, like that of Mrs Stitch in

Scoop who could not only do ten things at once but was also a ravishing beauty and punctual as well. But there may be several good reasons for drawing up your own swift plan for getting your mind to work faster and better.

Curiously enough, although it's everybody's greatest asset, you are rarely directly taught at school to use your mind. They may teach you to climb a rope, use logarithm tables, endlessly practise the piano. But you're not taught to speed up your learning power, improve your memory, think creatively, make quick decisions, find out the facts for yourself, take part in a discussion and make up your own mind instead of, parrot-fashion, accepting other people's opinions.

Why should you want to improve your brainpower? First, you might need it, more than your grandmother did. Today more homes need a second income, more exciting jobs are available to women and more women are having to get along on their own. The divorce rates are higher. Women often find themselves leading a life for which they weren't properly prepared or equipped. But not many women prepare for these statistical possibilities – they prefer to rely on the Magic Ostrich method of survival ('If I don't learn to look after myself, then I'll never have to . . .' 'If I can't manage on my own then he'll never leave me . . .').

We laugh to hear that at the first British girls' boarding school they learned reading and embroidery and were only allowed to read the Bible. But only twenty years ago girls at finishing school were seriously *taught* in a *class* how to get out of a low-slung sports car without showing their knickers and instructed in umbrella drill (how to hail a taxi with, how to lean gracefully on, how to defend yourself with, how to use as an accessory, like gloves). But even today when a beautiful twenty-one-year-old girl has come top of the honours degree list in mechanical engineering at Imperial College, London, parents are advised by ACE (the Advisory Centre for Education) to send their daughters to coeducational schools if they want to study science, because the equipment will be better if there are boys around.

It's also a sad fact that some men still habitually belittle women's intelligence – particularly if they're married to them. It is extremely hard not to be affected by the opinion of your nearest and dearest, no matter how affectionately or jokingly it is expressed. There's still a lot of unrealized old-fashioned indoctrination which can make a woman shy of using her wits to her best advantage or make her doubt whether she has any wits left.

By the time she reaches the late thirties, even a conscientious and devoted wife may feel that a spot of mental stimulation might be a better investment than beauty treatments to enrich the family togetherness by making sure that she understands what they're talking about. (It can be far harder to keep up with the children than with the Joneses.)

You are undoubtedly cleverer than you think. Don't be put off by people who tell you that ten thousand of your brain cells rot every day. You still have more than enough to be an Einstein (several thousand million) and very few people use more than a tiny bit of their brainpower.

You start off with amazing power.

Think how clever a baby is when it learns to speak. Somehow, in order to do so he has to have an understanding of rhythm, music, physics, the relationships between words and their integration. He has to exercise his memory and creativity and finally get around to logical reasoning in order to say, 'Dad-dad-wanna-see-Gangan'. You learn amazingly fast until you're five (which is why it's iniquitous that there are so few nursery schools for three-to-five-year-olds) and after that the mind continues to develop until you're twenty.

You may have heard that your brainpower starts to decline from then on, so if you haven't mastered Chinese or the mysteries of nuclear fission by then, you never will. However, the latest research on growth of intelligence doesn't agree.

For instance, your vocabulary is likely to grow until you're in your fifties and won't drop until you're over seventy. Some intellectual abilities improve with age when people get into a more stimulating environment (which may be why American studies show that women's problem-solving abilities *improve* between forty and fifty).

Women's intelligence scores drop behind those of men in the thirties (it's all that Dad-dad-wanna-see-Gangan) but catch up a lot by the fifties. In fact, it now looks as though a lot of old incorrect theories about drops in intelligence were due to women working in unstimulating surroundings. Studies have proved that older workers show increased intelligence if moved on to interesting, new tasks.

It is true that older people show a consistent decline in ability to perform complex tasks at speed but working at their own pace they get the same results as younger people. Older people also compensate by working more economically than the young. They seem to use less data, less energy and make better use of other people's abilities. Otherwise there are enormous variations, which increase with age and ability. In fact, sociologist Michael Fogarty has pointed out that up to 60 per cent of the best work in history, literature, philosophy, science and the arts has been achieved by people over fifty.

Brains, like the rest of your body, need exercise, recreation and plenty of nourishment – both physical and mental. Physical nourishment means eating a balanced diet. You should *always* eat protein for breakfast – a slice of Cheddar cheese or a boiled egg – and possibly (after age thirty-five) supplement it with large, regular doses of vitamin B. Some doctors are sceptical about this and only give a vitamin injection (such as Parentrovite) as a booster after flu. If this treatment is going to benefit you, *you* will notice a marked improvement within a couple of hours of the injection.

Brain exercise is logical thinking, recreation is imaginative thinking and games, such as bridge or crossword puzzles. The mental nourishment your brain needs is a reasonable dose of facts, problem-solving and a study of the work of people whose interests are yours but whose performance is better. (This is what stretches you.)

The quickest way to get your brain back in trim is to work out your own quick *Concentrated Brainpower Course*. Don't feel foolish. Don't be put off by a bit of leg-pulling. Don't be put down. Don't think you're not clever enough. Lots of academics are very stupid; they do nothing positive or creative and often prevent other people doing so. A lot of stainless-steel brains can't be relied upon to wash up properly, let alone raise a family, and lots of women turn out to be creative thinkers, in spite of a dull school record.

DESIGNING YOUR OWN SELF-IMPROVEMENT COURSE

> *'Your little head*
> *Your little ears*
> *Your eyes that shed*
> *Such little tears*
> *Your little mouth*
> *Oh God, how sweet*
> *Your little hands*
> *Your little feet*
> *Your little voice*
> *So sweet and kind*
> *Your little soul . . .*
> *Your little mind.'*
>
> Anon.

The natural way to learn is to pursue your own interests and see where they lead. In nature, they lead either to your advantage (and the survival of the fittest) or to catastrophe (better pick the right mushroom, the right river, the right cave). In traditional schools children learn not what intrigues them but what other people think ought to interest them and we all know children are often bored by this arrangement, but they have very little say in the matter and no alternative occupations or obligations.

Adults wouldn't accept such bossy treatment and adults don't (indeed can't) stay on any course that isn't carefully related to their particular interests, rate of learning, time available, resources and commitments, both financial and family.

About the only way to find a course that is entirely suited to you is to design it for yourself. You can then suit it to your timetable, to your previous experience and your present resources.

This doesn't prevent you from including in your programme a set course at a polytechnic, for instance, or even a stay at a residential college. It just means that you have to consider the ways in which you are most likely to learn effectively and make good use of all the free teaching aids around you such as your local library and any museums or art galleries, radio and television as well as what *you* can afford to pay to borrow or buy books, cassettes, records, correspondence courses or a complete programmed learning text in book form.

Be realistic. Decide what time you can spare each week then halve it. Set yourself a rough timetable – then halve the amount of work you hope to achieve in it. Carefully plan to reward your progress every step of the way.

You have to find out what is the best way and time *for you* to learn. It may be between midnight and 1 a.m., it may be a half hour at midday or the whole of Monday evening. Some people seem to soak up information on buses, in the garden or even in the bath, some can't. What matters is that you find one that suits *you*.

Start by deciding what you hope to achieve and how long you're prepared to take to get there. Adult drop-outs generally don't fail because of lack of ability but because they don't realize that success takes *time*. (NOBODY is an overnight success. What some people get is overnight *recognition* of what they may have been doing for years.) If you want to succeed, plan to do so from the beginning and only start something that you have a real chance of completing.

Check your *time, resources, working conditions, motivation, rewards* and a *personal first-aid kit* for disheartening moments.

The best possible first-aid kit is an encouraging and *interested* partner, who can sometimes decide for you when you've had enough and need a break, who can spur you on, who can be very gentle or very tough with you when you think you'll never finish, who can point out what a lot you have achieved so far and remind you how you got over your faint heart or exhaustion last time you felt that way. It's also easier for someone else to distinguish whether you really have a work problem or whether you're just depressed or tired for other reasons.

Mothers can be marvellous, so can some mates, so can *one* good friend who knows what you're trying to do and your children can sometimes be very encouraging (although not always and not all the time).

Anyone working alone needs this sort of encouragement because you can't pace yourself or compare notes with anyone, so it can be a lonely business. Painters know this, so do poets, pianists and writers.

Most adults underestimate the *time* that study takes. After a few weeks they realize that it's going to take longer than they thought and that they can't fit it comfortably into their free time. Whereupon, instead of readjusting their aim, they abandon their objective altogether. This can make someone feel despondent, or inferior or a failure – even though what she had set herself was clearly,

for her, *an impossible task*. So be pessimistic when guessing the time in which you can study and the amount you might accordingly achieve. If you think it's going to take a week – allow a fortnight (accountants call this the contingency factor). And remember that your original guess didn't allow for you to feel tired or anyone else to be ill, or for the washing machine to break down. The less you expect of yourself, the more likely you are to succeed. So don't set your own failure traps.

After all, you can always go *faster* if you find that you learn some things easily; you can always skip bits of your course where it covers something that you already know. Adults' learning speeds vary much more than those of the young because, on the whole, the young don't know anything else, whereas you will find that you have little surprise pockets of information that you thought you'd forgotten years ago and that now suddenly reappear. Overall, however, adults are slower than the young. Don't give up because your tiresome bright child did some test (correctly) much faster than you. You will get there.

RESOURCES need not be a problem but it depends what you're preparing to study. The minimum you can manage with is likely to be a pencil and notebook, a concertina file (with about thirty partitions) that you keep away from the rest of the family, and access to newspapers, journals, books and any other necessary teaching aids.

MINIMUM WORKING CONDITIONS means a *quiet* room or a corner of one, with a table and a good light, where you can work without interruption in tolerable comfort. If you can't get this at home, try working in the local library where it's always luxuriously warm and hushed.

Interruptions are particularly distracting to adult learners, a condition that is more difficult as time goes by. It is hard to regain your concentration and get back into a studying mood.

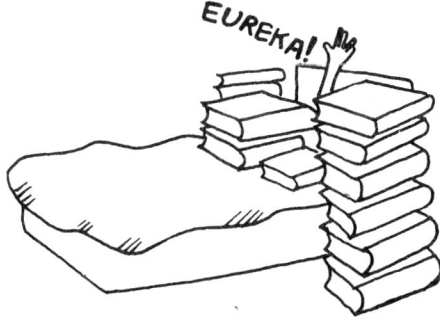

Discomfort is a perpetual distraction in itself, so you *must* be warm and comfortable. Wearing a quilted dressing-gown may be a good idea. Winston Churchill did a lot of work sitting up in bed. It's not a bad idea to go to bed at 6 p.m. once a week in order to study, especially if it's difficult to get away from the family. (If you can't keep them out of your bedroom for a couple of hours you're never going to get anything done.)

You may have to change the system at home somewhat to get the time, resources and working conditions you need (*see page 91* for how to change the system). But don't forget that *you* may have to change too.

You'll learn much quicker if you can see the overall programme ahead of you. If you choose to follow a standard course, read the syllabus, which will define what you are supposed to know or be able to do at the end of the course, and ask for the section objectives of the course, which should briefly show how each section relates to the main objective.

If you design YOUR OWN PERSONAL SELF-IMPROVEMENT COURSE you must also decide on a syllabus and section objectives. Whether you're designing your own course or following a standard one (or slotting in both together) try to begin by reading only one good general book on the subject you want to study (ask your local librarian to suggest one). Read it through once, not trying to remember anything, then look at the list of contents and use it to block out the structure of your course (a list of contents is generally the *structure* of the book) and you can use a contents list to decide on your *section* objectives (sometimes the contents are listed in separate sections).

Some good introductory books are:

Art History: *Civilization* by Kenneth Clark, John Murray/BBC Publications, 1971.

Biology: See General Science.

Crafts: *Golden Hands*, the part work series published by Marshall Cavendish Ltd. Re-issued regularly. Also in bound volumes by Book Club Associates, 1978. (Try your local library.) *The Penguin Book of Sewing* by Julian Robinson, Penguin, 1973. *Everybody's Knitting* by Kirsten Hofstätter, Penguin, 1978.

Conservation: *Only One Earth* by Barbara Ward and René Dubos, Penguin, 1972. *Silent Spring* by Rachel Carson, Penguin, 1965.

English: *A Short History of English Literature* by Ifor Evans, Pelican, 4th ed. 1976. (A classic introductory book: superb.)

General Science: *The Ascent of Man* by J. Bronowski, BBC Publications, 1976.
Guide to Science 1: The Physical Sciences by Isaac Asimov, Penguin, 1975.
Guide to Science 2: The Biological Sciences by Isaac Asimov, Penguin, 1975.

History: *A Short History of the World* by H. G. Wells, revised by Raymond Postgate and G. P. Wells, Penguin, 1965. (A bit old-fashioned but does its job.)
A Shortened History of England by G. M. Trevelyan, Pelican, 1959.
Kings and Queens of England edited by Antonia Fraser, Futura, 1977. (A really good little crib.)

Music: *A Short History of Western Music* by Arthur Jacobs, Pelican, 1972.
A History of Western Music by Christopher Headington, Paladin, 1977.
Introducing Music by Ottó Károlyi, Penguin, 1965.

Philosophy: *A History of Western Philosophy* by Bertrand Russell, Allen and Unwin, 2nd ed. 1961.
Learning to Philosophize by E. R. Emmet, Penguin, 1970.

Politics: *Voters, Parties, and Leaders: The Social Fabric of British Politics* by Jean Blondel, Penguin, 1974.
International Politics by Joseph Frankel, Penguin, 1973.

Psychology: *Psychology for Everyman* by Larry S. Skurnik and Frank George, Penguin, 1967.

Sense and Nonsense in Psychology by H. J. Eysenck, Penguin, 1958.

Psychiatry: *A Layman's Guide to Psychiatry and Psychoanalysis* by Eric Berne, Penguin, 1969.

YOUR PLAN

Any journey into the unknown is easier with a map. A map of the country and the cities shows you your overall general direction and the distance you have to go, so you can work out roughly how long the journey will take.

A map shows you how you're going to get from A to Z with a structure that can give you some idea of the difficult parts of the journey: you can see that a winding road full of hairpin bends is going to take longer than the straight stretch on the M1. The route map you draw up to get from town to town by one road or the other can be compared to the *structure* of a study course. Structure design principles are the same whether you're carving a six-foot marble statue, writing a book, or planning a wedding reception. It shows the overall picture ahead of you, then breaks it down into manageable portions of work.

Make sure that each section you study relates to your course framework. A formal course is likely to follow some logical pattern (a chronological sequence if you're studying history or English literature). Provided you have a strong enough structure you can risk wandering up a secondary road to study the sections which interest you most.

For instance, if you're studying sixteenth-century British cookery, this alone is your *plan*. Your *structure* consists of the different sections put into some sort of linked order. These might be:

1 Ingredients from land and sea (fish, fowl and meat).
  Herb garden (borage, rosemary for remembrance and also for lamb).
  Cellar (wine, cider and beer).
  Still room (jams, jellies and preserves).
  Kitchen (sauces, pie crusts and sweetmeats).
2 Utensils.
  Preparation (methods).
  Cooking (methods).
  Serving (styles).
3 Menus and recipes (ceremonial food, some famous meals).
4 Dietary range for different groups in different areas (feed Queen on wing of fowl; breast to Lord Chamberlain; potage for peasant).
5 Poisons (illnesses associated with diet or beauty preparations – lead and mercury).

With this firmly in your mind and timetable, you can start wherever you like, at whatever interests you most, which might be the history of the two-pronged fork, a selection of syllabub recipes or a nasty little paragraph on what they did with larks' tongues.

Some people who are allergic to formal courses get better results if they decide on an initial structure then proceed to other areas of study *after* they have become curious about how it all fits together. This is one of your freedoms when designing a course for yourself.

A good general introduction to a subject can be read critically, so that you start asking questions about it. Make notes of anything you want to know more about and jot down criticism and questions.

For example, whatever you start learning, the experts use some technical words that you won't understand. What do they mean? Find out and develop your own glossary (perhaps at the back of your notebook).

YOUR MOTIVATION

Doing something that you enjoy can still mean hard work whether it's gardening or glass blowing. Keep yourself interested, perhaps by starting with the interesting bits (*see* 'Your plan') but also:

SET YOUR OWN TARGETS

The ultimate target is completion of the course or success in the exam, but decide on in-between targets at regular intervals and put a date on them. A formal course may include regular essays and exams. If not, *you* set yourself these interim targets. For instance, to write a page of notes once a week; to review them once a month; to reach a certain stage of work by a certain date. It's important to realize that you will undoubtedly misjudge your times when you start but *do not reallocate them*. You will then, after a bit, be able to see that your work takes twice as long as you guesstimated or five times, or whatever, and you will then be better able to assess your own capability. (In other words, continue to guesstimate, but multiply the result by two or five or whatever.)

A page of notes can be made more interesting for you if you think of it as intended for an audience ('What I found out' about Chopin, hotel catering, Roman jewellery, or whatever would interest your branch of the Townswomen's Guild).

Your targets should be realistic: not impossible and not a walk-over.

You should *expect to reach them*; this is very important.

WIN YOUR OWN PRIZES!

The traditional sticks-and-carrots learning principle of rewarding good behaviour and punishing bad is still unbeatable, so offer yourself some rewards and punishments. Make sure the reward is something you would really enjoy: a large slice of chocolate cake or a day out. Reserve large prizes for major efforts (say, the end of every section), but have *plenty* of small prizes on the way.

GO ON YOUR OWN VOYAGES OF DISCOVERY

Use the questions you noted down from your introductory book to pursue special lines of *original* inquiry. For instance, this might involve visiting a churchyard to check the spelling of a name on a tombstone, trying to milk a cow straight into a jug (the traditional way to start a syllabub), or growing your own wortbane.

You will probably have to give rewards to yourself. But you'll know you have really caught alight when the rewards become intrinsic – meaning that you'll start looking forward to every moment you can spare to get on with your study. It becomes a reward in itself.

POST THE SIGNPOSTS

Signposts are reminders of where you have got so far and how it all relates to the grand design, so, before you start, add to your structure some 'logical' signposts – headings and subheadings to show where you start and complete each section. Have signpost days or an exercise session when you summarize where you have reached and what is still ahead, and check that you aren't wandering off on too many fascinating side roads. Or try a critical review of each section and your own performance. (These may provide opportunities for giving yourself a few *more* prizes.)

PLAN FOR SPACED LEARNING

You will probably get on best if you plan for regular, short, concentrated periods of study, rather than for a crash course. Crash courses sound so appealing and dynamic but too often they do exactly that – crash. You need time to link all newly acquired information to things you already know and you need *more* time to consider its meaning and relevance.

PLAN EACH LEARNING SESSION

At each learning session aim at a basic pattern of INPUT: PRACTICE: FEEDBACK.

★ Input – learning something new.
★ Practice – making use of what you've learned.
★ Feedback – checking that you learned correctly.

In a well-run formal course, this is automatically done for you in four main ways. A lecture or reading assignment should be followed by *discussion* or a *question period* (both of which mean that you have to think about the new material, express your ideas and have them checked by the instructor). *Writing essays or completing questionnaires* (which the instructor then corrects) has the same effect.

If you're out of practice you should expect to spend about twice as much time on practising and working over the information as you spend on absorbing new information.

WHAT CAN YOU DO TO PRACTISE ON YOUR OWN?

Your own practice time can include:

1 Writing notes.
2 Writing notes about how you can use what you have learned.
3 Selecting material for a one-page article or a short speech.

If you're lucky enough to have someone to discuss it with, this can be a great help. A critical teenager is splendid for asking what's the point of it all or questioning the meaning of this and that, and demanding why you are making so many assumptions. In fact, this is one way to stop you treating him/her as a child (which is what they're always moaning about) and start transforming him/her into a valuable training aid.

HOW DO YOU PROVIDE YOUR OWN FEEDBACK?

After taking notes, or discussing the subject, you are bound to be left with some small points about which you were uncertain or perhaps huge gaps in your new knowledge. In a personal self-help course, checking up on these matters is what constitutes feedback.

Don't think that feedback is a little extra chore you can do when all other inspiration fails. It is an essential part of the learning process.

One of the advantages of studying in later life is that you are more likely to appreciate this point than you would have been in your youth. As you grow older you get increasingly meticulous about getting information right, because you have learnt from exasperating experience that:

1 It is important to be absolutely correct, and
2 It's even more important not to be incorrect.

Once older people learn something, it generally *sticks*. And they need to get it right first time because they have relatively greater difficulty in correcting errors.

On Open University courses or on correspondence courses you submit papers to a tutor, and so have the benefit of working at your own pace, at times of your choosing, while still enjoying the valuable feedback function which a teacher can supply.

DEVELOP YOUR OWN TEACHING AIDS

Not for nothing do primary schools set children to making model Norman forts, it's an experience none of us ever forgets (not only the Norman building but the agony of cutting up miles of thick cardboard with blunt scissors and getting glue in your hair).

You will have a much more enjoyable time when you design your own charts, diagrams and models. They'll provide a relief from study and can be pinned up (get a scarlet felt pinboard from Ryman's) or kept in the file as another way of reminding yourself how much you have achieved so far. Don't worry about your artistic abilities; it's to help *you* remember and understand, not to hang in the local art gallery. Don't spend too much time on it; perfection isn't necessary.

MAKE USE OF ALL THE OTHER TEACHING AIDS YOU CAN FIND

These are any outside material that relates to what you're doing. Find out what books, radio or television programmes, recordings or programmed texts are available to help you. For example, if you're studying a language on your own, look at the Linguaphone records and courses and see if your local polytechnic has relevant sessions in a language laboratory. Or whether there is a neighbouring French au pair to practise on. Tell other people what you're doing and you'll be surprised to find how often they provide useful snippets ('I cut this bit about lemon syllabub out of the evening paper . . .' 'Here's a two-pronged fork I found on the junk stall . . .').

Learning from a variety of sources has several advantages: it keeps you interested, it stimulates your imagination and it helps you remember, because the ideas reach your brain in several forms.

AIM FOR REPETITION

You have probably noticed, what with note-taking and review sessions and making charts and diagrams and telling the neighbours, you're likely to have gone over some of your material a good many times. *This is what you should aim at*. Repetition, especially with variety, and in ways that stimulate your thinking, is fundamental to thorough learning.

COMPETITION

You aren't trying to do anything faster or better than anyone else, whatever their age. You are learning something for your own sake. Ignore competition.

How to make *more* friends and influence *more* people

'With the best will in the world "they" cannot possibly do everything and look after everyone all the time. The alternative is self-help . . . an essential element in our free society . . .' — Prince Philip

The one thing you would expect a national government to have is a long-term, overall, responsible view of the future of the country. Unfortunately, the British parliamentary system ensures that the party in power is primarily concerned to stay there, so short-term popular measures take priority over long-term national planning. (See any pre-election budget to prove this.)

As modern society gets more complicated and life gets slower, more frustrating and exasperating, you can feel that you're floundering through a sea of grey treacle towards an island of buff forms.

As the Welfare State gets increasingly cumbersome, expensive and INEFFICIENT, indignation and resentment sometimes burst into protest against an example of injustice (as in some housing allocations), callous neglect (as in some baby-battering cases), or a bit of senseless bureaucratic steam-rollering, such as running a motorway through a contentedly built-up area.

Such situations led to the explosion of *voluntary pressure groups* during the sixties and the growing development of voluntary community work such as Shelter and Age Concern.

The old-fashioned Lady Bountiful concept of a voluntary job as 'charity' work is now seen as citizen survival work.

Traditional voluntary work, such as the Red Cross, the WRVS and St John Ambulance Brigade, is now run professionally (for instance, the Women's Institute has one of the best public relations offices in Britain) and much of it involves training.

There are other big new growth

areas in voluntary work. One example is the very successful *sympathy-and-support groups* such as the widows' rehabilitation club CRUSE, Alcoholics Anonymous, Gingerbread (the association for one-parent families) and the Compassionate Friends, an organization for parents who have lost a child.

These groups were founded and are run by people who have been so overwhelmed by their own unhappy experiences that they want to help other people in the same boat. Such people have the vital requisite – they know what it feels like – but they also use modern body- and mind-therapy methods, as well as old-fashioned friendship, generosity and human warmth to overcome some of the problems, loneliness and alienation of modern society.

The conservation groups, such as the Friends of the Earth, the National Trust and the Conservation Society want to preserve our irreplaceable natural resources, to reduce pollution and waste and to improve the quality of life in our towns and countryside.

They are concerned about the government's failure to predict and prevent the tidal course of disaster that is heading our way unless *somebody* does

something to solve the problems that we are currently creating for ourselves: proposed motorways that threaten to strangle the country; pollution of air, earth and water and food that kills animals, birds and fish and quietly debilitates citizens; high-rise housing blocks that lead to delinquency, depression and suicide.

Another fast-growing area of voluntary work is *international relief* carried out by groups such as Oxfam, Save the Children, LEPRA and Amnesty, which are very efficiently organized and dynamically promoted.

Working for one of the organized *political parties* or for a *trade union* is possibly the most useful (for you) unpaid work you can do. It will bring you into contact with the most interesting and influential people in your area. You will all be able to start inflicting your views on the rest of the world and do something about your opinions instead of just airing them over the After Eights. And it's one sort of unpaid work that will bring you into contact with a lot of men – unlike most other voluntary work. Political and trade union work (women are remarkably lax about the latter) is organized, disciplined and hard (so it's extremely good rehabilitation training before going back to work full time) and it can sweep over you like a tidal wave.

You'll be so needed so fast by so many new friends that you won't have time to feel shy or have worries, doubts and regrets.

There is obviously plenty of important and interesting voluntary work to do, and helpers are urgently needed – but why should you do it?

You may of course want to help other people (even if you've already got lots to do) or you want urgently to protect your interests, if the proposed motorway seems about to bisect your own front garden, but there are many other (sometimes unexpected) rewards that accrue to those who do voluntary work.

You meet nice people. It's a very good way to make *real* friends, not just social encounters for coffee and chat. A cheerful camaraderie can develop from an afternoon spent envelope-stuffing or cutting up sandwiches for the disabled children's trip to the seaside. You may also meet well-known people who take an interest in your project. Many entertainers, such as Jimmy Savile, Frankie Howerd, Frankie Vaughan and Vera Lynn, enthusiastically do voluntary work (and are far more approachable than you might think, if you write). So do influential local people, such as Lords Lieutenant, mayors and MPs.

HOW TO FIND VOLUNTARY WORK

You may already know what organization interests you; it may be one that has already helped you. The London Borough of Islington has about five hundred volunteers working with the local Social Services Department, half of whom were themselves previously clients of the social services. Alcoholics Anonymous and Weightwatchers are entirely run by those whom they have helped.

Organized voluntary work is now less class-conscious and less age-conscious. Marion Ede of Birmingham CAB says, 'We have some lovely grannies, very nice businessmen, students, housewives, young shop assistants, factory workers and one shop steward who's marvellous at dealing with difficult people.'

If you don't know what sort of self-help work and neighbourhood-based groups are available in your community, contact your local Volunteer Bureau (look up in the Yellow Pages: they are quite often not listed under 'V' in the telephone book, but under 'G' for Glasgow Volunteer Bureau or whatever). Volunteer Bureaux have been set up all over the country since 1971 to coordinate local voluntary work with the abilities of local volunteers.

They work in a way similar to an employment agency, and can tell you about everything that's going on in the community. Skilled interviewers chat to you, ask one or two questions, take a few notes of what you want and try to find the work that would most interest you.

The interviewers have personal contacts with all the voluntary agencies: they know who to ring up, and will probably make an appointment for you with any organization of your choice. They will cheerfully understand if you say you don't like hospitals, don't want to get too involved with one person or can only spare two hours a week. They can be really imaginative when offering you different possibilities. For instance, a widowed, part-time researcher in Birmingham with previous teaching experience, free mornings, a car and the problem of personal loneliness was offered a choice of four sorts of work (quite near her home): with priority children in inner-ring playgroups; emergency driving for hospitals; probation work with young offenders; or work with CAB. Each job needed extra training, which was offered free. The interviewers make a point of telling you that if you are not happy with the work that you choose, they will happily offer you something else.

If you aren't near a Volunteer Bureau try the local Council of Social Service (again, look under the name of your town) or telephone the social services department of your local authority. If none of this is fruitful, write to the head office of the national council of whatever organization interests you. They will refer you to their community work division.

Before you volunteer, quickly work out what you have to offer (see the end of this section) and what you won't be able to tolerate. For instance:

Hospital work needs firmness and you had better not be squeamish. You may work with demented geriatric patients, feed helpless patients or take others to the lavatory. You will work with people who are in pain and people who are dying.

Work with the disabled or mentally handicapped needs people who are prepared to work one-to-one and this also applies to probation work.

Old people's visitors need patience and they must be good listeners; good talkers drive the old people mad because *they* want to do the talking (about themselves).

People who don't want to get too personally involved or feel that the above work may distress them too much can be of more help with *reception work, telephone enquiries, regular driving jobs* or *office work* such as *typing* and *book-keeping*.

People who want a real challenge and who don't mind a tough job are welcomed to work in night shelters for alcoholics, drug addicts, meths

drinkers or all-round down-and-outs.

What no voluntary organization wants is people who don't like rolling up their sleeves and getting on with it, people who have to be waited upon and people who come *solely* for their own benefit. People often get far more out of voluntary work than they put in but people who join merely to work off their neuroses and problems are no use. Voluntary work is no quick cure for clinical depression.

Many people wonder why there's any need for voluntary workers, when you consider the wealth that is poured into the Welfare State. But the Deputy Commissioner-in-Chief of the St John Ambulance Brigade said: 'Taxpayers' money cannot be used to employ people in the many time-consuming tasks that are amongst the most important in true welfare – visiting the lonely, comforting the bereaved, helping the aged, the infirm and mentally subnormal of all ages. And most important and time-consuming of all – just sitting and listening.'

It is now government policy to encourage volunteers to collaborate with trained social workers. The 1968 Seebohm Report on the reorganization of the social services stressed that among the general public there is a rising expectation (if not demand) that the personal social services should cope with all social problems. Consequently, says the report, 'It will be more and more necessary for local authorities to enlist the services of large numbers of volunteers to complement the teams of professional workers.'

Anyone can see the dangers of this happy theory. The professionals fear that the volunteers will upset their wage claims and working hours, as well as threatening the number of available paid jobs. They also fear that volunteers will meddle with difficult cases that they haven't been trained to handle efficiently.

The volunteer risks being irritated by rules and regulations and having to refer to professionals instead of getting on with the job. If you're working with professionals, remember their understandable anxieties and be prepared to learn from them. After all, it's all supposed to be in a good cause.

EASING YOUR WAY BACK TO WORK

Another bonus of doing unpaid work is that it can be a painless, uncompetitive way of re-entering the job market. You meet – however briefly – the local important people. Often, they're the ones who know of plum jobs on offer, through their connections with the local Chamber of Commerce, the Rotarians, the Round Tables and the local council.

Voluntary work has often been the route by which a timid woman has found out how much more she can do than she thought and then suddenly found herself in a good job. For instance, Anne Wood, who started the Federation of Children's Book Groups (of which she is now the National Chairman), had been a secondary-schoolteacher who only wanted to interest her neighbours in getting good books for children available locally. She was subsequently made children's book editor with a paperback company, so her voluntary work led to a dream professional job.

You may not want a job but want to widen your horizons in other, more flexible ways.

GETTING A TRAINING

Many forms of voluntary work now automatically give you a free training, which can often prove useful in other spheres of life later on. *The National Childbirth Trust* will consider suitable lay people to help mothers prepare for childbirth. This can be most exciting and rewarding work. *The Marriage Guidance Council* gives you a training that includes how to interview, how to be a group leader, some law, some medical training and some training in handling psycho-sexual problems. The *St John Ambulance Brigade* gives you first-aid training. *CAB* give part-time training, spread over six months, in community advice and how to find your way around the Welfare State.

GROWING SELF-RESPECT

Helping other people in the right way can not only be a wonderful way to break out of despondency or depression, it can also be a wonderful way to forget your own problems or get them in perspective by seeing how small they are compared to those of other people. Self-pity disappears; doing good is good for you.

WHAT ARE THE DRAWBACKS?

Just one cautionary word. Voluntary work can consist of direct work (actually wheeling the trolley round the ward or driving the OAPs up to see Derek Nimmo), or it can consist of organizing other people to do the grass-roots work. Both sorts of work are important and both have their frustrations.

BE PATIENT

By definition, voluntary work is full of volunteers, most of whom have strong, emotional views of what needs to be done and how it should be done. What they are worst at is applying personal self-discipline in order to achieve the objective of the group. The result can often be a lot of wasted time and effort, a good many arguments and altercations if everyone wants to do everything a different way. You must put up with this. Try not to mind about it. Remember the commitment and enthusiasm.

If *you* really do have good constructive ideas start *asking* why it's done this way and not that way, then you'll either get thrown out or put on the committee.

BE RELIABLE

Voluntary work is a commitment in some way greater than that of paid employment. People come to rely on you (not only your fellow workers but also those you are helping). If you let them down there won't be anyone else to replace you. So you must be reliable.

DON'T ALLOW YOURSELF TO BE PUT UPON

If the work is always piled upon you, but never a word of thanks, then say that you think you will have to stop. Whereupon you will be pampered for a bit. People will bring you cups of coffee and offer to drive you home.

BE TIGHT-FISTED

Voluntary work is not just work you give free. It can be extremely expensive for you. Take it for granted that even if you can claim any expenses they will not cover your costs (unless you're a local councillor, in which case you can do rather well). But always *ask* for your expenses to be paid, rather than say that you can't afford to carry on.

BE FIRM

If you're any good at your job you will be under constant pressure to do more. You have to learn to say no, however heart-rending the appeal. One way to get round this is to decide for yourself in advance that you only have *x* spare hours a week. Never, ever, do more. Never accept any further work on the spur of the moment.

Don't even do it for a panic situation, such as an election. In voluntary work there is *always* a panic situation somewhere. If you offer extra time, do so well in advance and stick to your bargain. Otherwise you risk your home being over-run by envelope-stuffers, bald car tyres from chauffeur work, an astronomical telephone bill, a mutinous family and old-fashioned exhaustion.

WHO NEEDS YOU? WHERE? WHAT FOR?

*Work that could be done in the evening.

CHILDREN AND YOUNG PEOPLE

Pre-school playgroups
*Adventure playgrounds and play projects
*Children's homes
*Baby-sitting
Non-teaching help in schools
*Toy library for handicapped children
*Youth clubs

THE DISABLED

*Driver/escort

Wheelchair pusher
Clubs and day centres
Holiday homes (residential)
Shopping
Riding clubs for the disabled
Paraplegic sports centres

THE ELDERLY
Driver/escort
Social and lunch clubs
Old people's homes
Decorating and gardening
*Friendly visits

HOSPITALS
Trolley shops
Mobile libraries
Arranging flowers
*Ward helpers
Private radio programmes for patients
Out-patients' clinics (as hostess or guide)
Beauty treatments
*Children's playgroups

MENTALLY HANDICAPPED AND MENTALLY ILL
*Social clubs, day centres and hostels
*Baby-sitting
*Friendly visiting
*Psychiatric wards
Holiday camps (residential)

PEOPLE WITH SPECIAL NEEDS
*Teaching non-readers (adults and young people)
*Teaching English to immigrants
*Helping social workers in befriending people with problems
*Prison visiting (befriending offenders)

ADVICE AND ACTION GROUPS
*Citizens Advice Bureaux (interviewers, receptionists)

Consumer and shopping advice centres
*Samaritans
*Marriage guidance
*School welfare
*Family planning
*Committee work for charities

MONEY-MAKING PROJECTS
Flag selling
Charity shops
Jumble sales, bazaars and swap shops
Sponsored walks, swims, etc.

EVERYBODY, IF YOU HAVE THESE SKILLS
*Typing
Sandwich making/catering
*Poster design
*Sewing and knitting
Interpreting

WHAT HAVE YOU GOT TO OFFER?

Before you telephone a Volunteer Bureau, work out what you have to offer and jot it down.

Then decide:

1 What time of day are you available?
2 Do you want to work alone or in a group?
3 Do you have any special skills or hobbies which volunteer organizations could use (chess for instance)?
4 How far can you travel? Could you help in your own home?
5 What resources can you offer?

RESOURCES

Time
Morning/afternoon/evening

Weekdays/weekends
How often can you help?
Regular/occasional

Space
Space to work at home
Space to hold meetings
Storage space

Equipment/facilities
Car
Other transport (bicycle, old pram,
shopping bag on wheels)
Telephone
Typewriter
Dictating machine
Pocket calculator

Skills
Typing
Interviewing
Driving
Writing
Designing/making (anything from
lavender bags to the Chancellor of the
Exchequer in effigy for Bonfire
Night)
Teaching
Nursing
Publicity
Accountancy
Cooking
Making arrangements

Any useful personal qualities, such as:
A sympathetic manner
A good talker
A good listener (very, very
important)
A good telephone manner
Patience
Efficiency
A methodical approach
Not easily upset
A good memory
A good temper
Imagination

Common sense
Health

HOW TO RAISE MONEY FOR CHARITY

One of the best ways to help voluntary organizations is by raising money. But it isn't easy. You can laboriously collect old newspapers, mixed rags, milk-bottle tops or salvage and you'll find yourself with a great deal of rubbish that takes an enormous amount of storage space. Then nobody seems to want to come and collect it from you and transporting it to the depot can easily cost more than it's worth.

If you must collect, ask for valuable items: pure wool (difficult to find these days, except on a sheep), old car batteries, bits of lead piping and brass, forks and spoons, so long as they're not stamped BR . . .

The drawback to organizing a flag-day type of collection is that you need an awful lot of people and an awful lot of tins (the return per head is quite small). Standing on a corner and rattling a collection box is not only wildly embarrassing for the first time but very expensive in the long run (because you never again pass a collector on a corner without putting something in her box) and you have to get police approval in advance.

There's a booklet of official rules which covers public performances, raffles, bingo and lotteries. Everything is in it except guessing-the-weight-of-the-cake, because this involves *skill*, not chance. Get the rule book from the National Council of Social Service, 26 Bedford Square, London WC1B 3HU; ☎ 01-636 4066.

Any asset that you possess can be hired out for charity, whether it's an ability to perform simple conjuring tricks, a rod on the River Trent for a day or a box at the Albert Hall. Carols at Christmas can still raise a lot if you're not too early and you sing well enough (a descant is good for an extra 30 per cent at least).

In the summer, however small your garden, you might arrange a garden party. (Try for Wimbledon fortnight, when it rarely rains, and avoid the first week in August, when there's terrific competition.) You might organize an event that's safely under a roof, such as a bazaar, a jumble sale or a bring-and-buy, or a swap-shop sale (but if it's under your roof watch out for petty pilfering).

Home-made jams (especially with a rather amateur label) are wildly popular and chutney even more so; home-made cakes, with rather wobbly icing to prove their authenticity, are almost as sought-after as home-made wine, for which you can run a guess-the-weight-of-the-bottle competition (skill).

There are many ingenious variations of home industry and selling. One fund-raiser in Camden, London, got £600 by writing to local artists and asking if she could sell a picture for them and donate the 20 per cent gallery fee to charity. She then gave a cheese and wine party in her garden, asked everyone she knew who seemed likely to buy a picture and charged them 50p entrance fee.

Another woman charges a small sum per head for bring-and-buy sales combined with really luscious luncheons in her own home which are really delicious and have become famous in the neighbourhood as an annual event that *really* raises money for the Red Cross. She gives them in October, selling objects that make good Christmas gifts. She says that you have to persuade people to give you quite expensive things, a little silver photograph frame as well as babies' bootees, but it's often easier for someone to find something they don't really need (such as a photo frame) lying around the house, rather than junk.

Another woman sells *good* second-hand clothes, with her bedroom as the swap shop. For every item you bring, you get 50p knocked off the price of anything you buy. Half the money goes to charity, half goes to the original owners and everybody has a terrific time.

A crafty refinement of money-raising is to telephone all your friends and say, 'Will you send me a cheque for £1 [always state the amount] if I *don't* ask you to help me organize a jumble sale, plus an extra 50p if I *don't* ask you to help me clear up afterwards?' Clearing up after a jumble sale is easily the worst part, especially if it's your garage. Arrange in advance for the local rag-and-bone man to be there at the end and buy the lot off you.

Another good idea, on the principle of not-doing-it-yourself, is sponsorship of walks, digs, swims, climbs by schools. Once a year, in Hong Kong, the Governor and Chief Secretary walk sixteen miles to the Peak and back in torrid heat. Find someone equally chic to head your walk and get the local newspaper to photograph it. In this case the sponsor (anyone who pays *not* to do it) chooses what to pay, say from 2p to £2 a mile.

If you have a lot of friends who can afford it, one simple way to raise money seems to be to nobble one celebrity for a charity luncheon and then ask everyone else, by thick-card, gilt-edged invitation and charge so much per plate. You mention the charge in a separate letter so that the invitation on the mantelpiece grandly reads:

The pleasure of your company
is requested at a luncheon
given by Mrs Mileva Medway
to meet the Earl of Doogoodie.

Funnily enough, much the cheapest way to raise money is simply to ask for it from the right people. These are people whose charities you have supported in the past (morally obliged to help *you* now), people who sell things to you, people you know (be careful not to ask too often) or people whom *they* know: 'Lord Bloggs, who is on our steering committee, has suggested that I write and ask you if you could possibly make a small contribution to the Accrington Brass Band Benevolent Fund. If you wish, I would be happy to visit you and explain the reason for our special drive to replace the trombone . . . etc. etc.' Leave it to the recipient to decide what is a 'small' contribution

(his small may be your big, although you can't rely on it) and he may pay up in order to avoid seeing you.

Always mention a target. *Always* try to add some extra incentive such as 'Lord Bloggs has promised to double the sum if we raise £X'. *Always* tell people what you're going to do with their money. *Always* record contributions you receive so that if you ever apply again, you can mention that they were kind enough to help before.

Always try to get local official support of doctors, hospital committees, local council or whatever group is relevant. *Always*, when sending a duplicated letter, add a few personal words and sign them yourself (all the grandest people do this). Never have a stamped signature. *Always* give value for money and thank anyone who helps at all. *Never overdo the blackmail*. There's nothing more irritating than going to a luncheon for which you've paid through the nose and then having a collection box rattled under it.

If you want to give money to a charity regularly, consider doing so by deed of convenant because this means that you give far more than you send. You fill in a form (which the charity will post to you), on which you agree to pay, say, £5 a year for seven years. Each year the charity will send you a form to sign which enables them to reclaim the income tax (at basic rate) on the amount you gave. So £5 out of your taxed income becomes worth £7.58 to the charity if the basic rate of tax is 34 per cent.

To register any group to which you belong as a charity, go to the Charity Commission and ask for their regulations (Charity Commission, 14 Ryder Street, London SW1Y 6AH;

☎ 01-214 6000). They will help you to interpret the regulations and if you meet their conditions you apply to them to be registered. The main advantages of registration are that you can reclaim tax on gifts made out of taxed income, and apply for money from funds reserved for charities.

The main disadvantages are that you aren't supposed to campaign for your cause; you can't engage in any activity for profit and you can't apply for money from those funds which specifically exclude charities. If you break these rules you risk being prosecuted and if you're found guilty you have to repay all the income tax you claimed on money gifts. Some registered charities seem to get away with a lot of activities which look like campaigning or profit-making but the risk is there. If you want to check up on any charity, The Central Register of Charities is at 57 Haymarket, London SW1Y 4QX; ☎ 01-214 6000.

HOW TO GET HELPERS

The second most welcoming move you can make on behalf of a charity is to produce people. Once you've run out of friends, and friends of friends, you can write to the editor of the local paper, explain what you're doing and ask for volunteers.

You can telephone the news editor of the local paper, magazines or radio stations and ask if you may tell a reporter about it (try to get him to visit you; provide some photogenic idea, such as the prize of your coming raffle – Queen Victoria's rose bowl – held by the local beauty queen).

You can advertise for helpers in the local paper-shop window.

You can print posters and leaflets asking for helpers. Leave them in the library, on notice-boards, in shops or post them through the neighbouring letter-boxes.

You can perhaps take a stall in the market-place or put up a bridge table in a supermarket or large store (ask permission first from the manager) explaining what you're up to.

If you get any offers of help, take them up immediately and enthusiastically. Cheer people along and make it *fun* for them – don't just shove a pile of leaflets at them to get on with, or you'll never see them again.

Ian Bruce, director of Volunteer Centres, says: 'It is just as necessary for a volunteer to get what he wants out of the organization as it is for the organization to be helped. What many people want is company, so start by making sure that they have it from the beginning and that they know what they're supposed to be doing and make sure that they are doing work that is interesting and worthwhile for *them*, as well as useful to you.'

WHO DO YOU WANT TO HELP?

Addresses are on pages 86–90.

Campaigners: Fawcett Society (the Women's Movement); Fair Play for Children Campaign (a national umbrella organization which coordinates voluntary groups involved in play leading for children of all ages); Campaign for Nuclear Disarmament (CND); Patients' Association.

Children: Pre-School Playgroups Association; Child Poverty Action Group; National Society for the Prevention of Cruelty to Children; Children's Country Holidays Fund; National Association of Youth Clubs; The Girls' Brigade; Girl Guides Association; Cub Scouts: Local Scout Association; Association for Jewish Youth; Federation of Children's Book Groups.

Conservation: The National Trust; The Victorian Society; Friends of the Earth.

The Deprived: Shelter; Child Poverty Action Group; local authorities who need volunteers to teach people to read and write, and to teach immigrants English.

The Desperate: The Samaritans.

The Disabled: Central Council for the Disabled; Disablement Income Group (which works towards a decent pension); Winged Fellowship Trust (which organizes holidays).

Everyone, About Everything: Contact your local Citizens Advice Bureau (CAB).

The Ill: The WRVS; National Association of Leagues of Hospital Friends who provide comfort and friendship.

Those Who Need Medical Help: St John Ambulance Brigade; British Red Cross Society.

The Married: National Marriage Guidance Council (NMGC).

The Mentally Handicapped: The National Association for Mental Health; the National Society for Mentally Handicapped Children.

The Miserably Poor: Oxfam; Christian Aid.

Old People: Help the Aged; Age Concern; the WRVS; Task Force (in London); Simon Community Trust (London); Institute of Home Help Organizers.

Prisoners and ex-Prisoners: National Association for the Care and Resettlement of Offenders (NACRO); The New Bridge; Apex; local council social workers.

Special Medical Groups: Royal National Institute for the Blind; National Society for Autistic Children; National Deaf Children's Society; Association for Spina Bifida and Hydrocephalus; Spastics Society; Multiple Sclerosis Society.

Watchdog Organizations: Consumers' Association; National Viewers' and Listeners' Association.

Women's Organizations: The big, all-purpose charity run by women is the Women's Royal Voluntary Service (WRVS). It undertakes thirty different categories of social work, has 45,000 specially trained members on call for disasters. In 1350 hospitals, the WRVS organizes canteens, shops and other services. It runs twenty-eight residential homes for old people, organizes living accommodation for ex-Borstal boys and a holiday home for tired mothers. It provides mobile shops for old peoples' homes, mobile library services for the disabled and house-bound, and in some districts laundry services for the sick and elderly. It runs over 2500 luncheon and/or day clubs for the disabled, carries over 15 million meals a year for local authorities and provides holidays for thousands of children. The WRVS is marvellous.

BECOMING FAMOUS

Voluntary work can help you to develop an identity of your own, apart from your family. In fact, you might suddenly discover a *new* you. You may suddenly find overnight that *you* achieve local fame as a result of your idea on the children's crossing scheme or the garden-sharing scheme. It's often little local jobs such as these that lead on to bigger jobs in the community at decision-making level (and perhaps even paid).

Baroness Serota was once a part-time social worker with the Hertfordshire Council; Lady Plowden trained as a secretary, was then a housewife, started voluntary work and ended up as chairman of the Independent Broadcasting Authority.

Furthermore, you will be amazed by the total inertia of all around you (especially when it comes to envelope-addressing) and if you are prepared to give up a lot of your evenings, your star will shoot up like a sputnik, simply for want of anything or anybody to hold you back.

Working for fame alone is, of course, a dangerous substitute for self-confidence and self-approval. You only recognize and accept your own worth if it is proved by the applause and approval of other people. But doing helpful, important work and having other people acknowledge it as such is not neurotic and is good for everybody (so remember to hand out bouquets as well as accept them).

Plenty of people are school gover-nors, members of area health authorities, councillors, JPs and MPs. So why not you?

How do they do it? How did they get there? Where did they start? By doing some humble routine work to begin with, that's how. They were then interested enough to give more time, get more involved in organizing which led to policy-making. And on the way they probably spotted the strings and started to pull them sensibly.

If you join an appropriate voluntary organization and quickly make your mark as a humble but active member then it's very likely that you could be put up for, say, the Community Health Council, the watchdog of the health services in your locality. This might easily lead to even more important community work, which could lead to work that is often of real importance to the nation. And this *can* happen amazingly fast. Small local consumer and pressure groups can overnight be transformed from a local irritant to one of the country's saviours and subsequently recognized by the Establishment as such.

HOW TO BE A PARISH COUNCILLOR, A SCHOOL GOVERNOR/MANAGER OR A JP

The requirements aren't so different, whichever you'd like to be.

To become a parish councillor you need two nominations, a proposer and seconder. You are elected within your parish by a ballot every three years (you can go on being re-elected for as long as you like). To stand a good chance of being elected, you will need to have one or more of the following qualifications:

1 To have lived locally for some time (it's not often that a newcomer gets elected).
2 To hold (or to have held) a job of value to the community – such as teacher, doctor, builder or newsagent.
3 To do active work for a local organization such as the British Legion, Meals on Wheels or a play group.

Parish councils usually meet monthly or bi-monthly, and discuss such matters as keeping rights of way open, getting adequate lighting in the area, getting enough playground space and *commenting* (only) *on planning applications*. It's a non-political job and that's an attraction to some people. Parish councillors have almost no real authority as local governors, but they can be influential in deciding matters that affect their community. For example, they can protest about the effects of local by-laws (whether or not to close a right of way, perhaps). One active parish councillor says that she does it because she likes to know what's going on and she feels that she is sometimes at her most useful when *stopping* inappropriate community decisions.

The way to become a borough councillor or a member of the county council is generally through your local political party. After your quota of stamp-licking and door-to-door canvassing you can offer to stand for local election and whether or not your offer is accepted will be decided by the local ward groups. You then have to stand for election. You get paid £11 a day for council work, which may sound handsome but it can be a twelve-hour day.

Local government reorganization, as well as much other recent legislation, has greatly increased both the amount of work required of councillors and the number of council committee meetings that are held. If you take your work seriously, you should expect to be at committee meetings *at least* four nights a week and put in a good deal of homework on law and accounts and reports.

Councillors who don't bother to do this are in danger of merely agreeing with the council officers, because they sound knowledgeable and convincing, or disagreeing with them merely 'on principle'. This might explain some of the current problems of local government.

Many MPs had their first taste of the Power Game as a borough councillor. And such a respected position carries an awful lot of clout in the community and in later business life. You learn a lot and, who knows, you might end up as mayor!

For background knowledge, many local education authorities hold evening classes in local government – but the best way you can learn is by going to your local council meetings. You can find out where they're held and you can also get any necessary specialized books from your local library.

Just belonging to a local political party should quickly teach you how the system works and the leading political parties have training sessions for their members.

How do you *become a school manager* of a primary school *or a school governor* of a secondary school or comprehensive school? Most governors are appointed by the local education committee (and quite often they are members of it). Many schools now want to get parents involved in running the school to which their children go. (A growing number of schools also have pupil governors, elected by the sixth form.) Parent governors are usually picked by the parents' group, such as the parent-teacher association (PTA). Different local education authorities have different ways of choosing their governors. In some areas they have one governing body for *all* their schools.

You might be proposed by a councillor, who either belongs to the same political party as you do, or who knows you and your proven interest in education and schools. You can always approach a member of your local education committee to suggest that you are proposed. DON'T JUST WAIT TO BE ASKED.

It's not as difficult as you might think to *become a Justice of the Peace*, dolloping out justice at least twenty-six times a year in your local Magistrates' Court. There are about 20,000 JPs at work in England and Wales today and one-third of them are women. If you are appointed, you have to take an oath that you will fulfil your obligations in Court.

You are trained. You don't have to make decisions without guidance, because the Clerk to the Court (who is legally trained) is always there. Be prepared for plenty of hard work, plenty of interest, plenty of boredom (the bulk of the work is motoring offences).

The Lord Chancellor appoints about 1500 JPs a year in England and Wales. Their names are put forward by 100 special local committees who are advised by area panels. How do *you* get on the list? Ask the Clerk to the Justices at your local Court for an application form and the name and address of the secretary of your local area panel. It helps to be recommended to the area panel by someone of local importance or a local organization who can vouch that you would do the job properly.

The Magistrates Association says the JPs are selected primarily on personal merit (no Os or As needed!). You can't be appointed if you are over sixty or have a criminal record. You don't get paid as a JP but you can claim various allowances. Allowances are meant to be fixed at such a level that nobody is deterred from becoming a magistrate because they couldn't afford to be away from work. At the same time it is meant to be a voluntary service and not an easy way to make a living.

You can claim for loss of earnings, either the amount of loss actually incurred whilst you were on your magisterial duties or a fixed sum (currently £10.75 for an absence of more than four hours, whichever is the less). You can also claim for travel from your home to the Courts or on magistrate's work and a subsistence allowance if you have to be away from home for any length of time. For example for between twelve and sixteen hours you can currently claim £7.14. If you are away overnight you can claim £18.72.

There are no lay magistrates in Northern Ireland. All the Magistrates Courts are conducted by stipendary magistrates who are trained lawyers. In Scotland, many JPs are local councillors acting *ex officio*. But some names are put forward independently. If approved, they are appointed by the Secretary of State for Scotland (not by the Lord Chancellor).

BEING HONOURED

It's always interesting to know why and how people get on the Honour's List. Some jobs seem to attract honours more than others, for faithful work, especially in the Civil Service, the Armed Services and perhaps the *Daily Mirror* (but not the *Sun*). It looks as if you have to be quite high in the right organization, or else be terribly lowly (tea lady, unpaid, for twenty years).

Certain of the established voluntary organizations seem to be more honoured than others, whereas a lifetime's devotion to a cause that is mysteriously unpopular with the Establishment will get you nowhere. On present showing, the Friends of the Earth are unlikely to get many honours for dumping truckloads of empty bottles on the doorsteps of soft-drink manufacturers (although ecology *is* getting smarter).

UNPOPULAR GOOD CAUSES
★ Anything cranky.
★ Anything militant.
★ Anything to do with young academics.
★ Anything that attacks the TUC, the Law Society or the Road Lobby.
★ Anything that is run by the young, the poor, or the underprivileged.
★ Squatters (they're about as anti-Establishment as you can get).

OKAY GOOD CAUSES
★ A well-established group.
★ Any group with a royal patron.
★ Political work with the leading parties (preferably doing dog's-body, personal work for the most influential person in your area).

★ Local political work (say chairman of your local Conservative Party).
★ County council work rather than district council work.
★ Any group with a strong professional backing such as doctors or lawyers.
★ Hospital work.
★ Anything publicly supported by old academics.

Anyone can write to the Prime Minister and nominate somebody for an honour – but you need the backing of an influential person or organization to give the nomination any weight.

Another sort of honour and recognition of hard work done for the community is an invitation to a royal garden party. Three of them are held every summer at Buckingham Palace and one is held at Holyrood House in Edinburgh. Naturally, few people work for their community merely hoping for such an invitation, but it is cheering to think that the work of even the humblest helper may be recognized by the highest in the land. Her Majesty the Queen has made it clear that she wants people from all walks of life to have the opportunity to attend. There is a rough total of over 30,000 guests each year, and the guest list is changed annually.

ADDRESS LIST FOR VOLUNTARY WORK

Action Resource Centre, 4 Cromwell Place, London SW7 2JJ (✆ 01-584 0438).

Age Concern England (National Old People's Welfare Council), Bernard Sunley House, 60 Pitcairn Road, Mitcham, Surrey CR4 3LL (✆ 01-640 5431).

Greater London, 54 Knatchbull Road, London SE5 9QY (☏ 01-737 3456).

Alcoholics Anonymous, PO Box 514, 11 Radcliffe Gardens, London SW10 9BQ (☏ London Region Telephone Service: 01-351 3344; Central Service Office: 01-352 9779; Publishing: 01-352 5493).

Amnesty International, Tower House, 8–14 Southampton Street, London WC2E 7HF (☏ International Secretariat: 01-386 7788; British Section: 01-242 1871).

Apex Charitable Trust, 31–3 Clapham Road, London SW9 0JE (☏ 01-582 3171).

Association for Jewish Youth, 50 Lindley Street, London E1 3AX (☏ 01-790 6407 or 01-790 9938 or 01-790 0016).

Association for Spina Bifida and Hydrocephalus Ltd, Tavistock House North, Tavistock Square, London WC1H 9HJ (☏ 01-388 1382).

British Council for Rehabilitation of the Disabled (REHAB), Tavistock House South, Tavistock Square, London WC1 (☏ 01-387 0166).

British Leprosy Relief Association (LEPRA), 50 Fitzroy Street, London W1P 6AL (☏ 01-387 7283).

British Red Cross Society, Joint Committee of the Order of St John and the, 6 Grosvenor Crescent, London SW1X 7EH (Headquarters) (☏ 01-235 7131).

Campaign for the Homeless and Rootless (CHAR), 27 John Adam Street, London WC2N 6HX (☏ 01-839 6185).

Campaign for Nuclear Disarmament (CND), Eastbourne House, Bullards Place, London E2 0PT (☏ 01-980 0937).

Central Council for the Disabled, 25 Mortimer Street, London W1 (☏ 01-637 5400).

Child Poverty Action Group (CPAG), 1 Macklin Street, London WC2B 5NH (☏ General Enquiries: 01-242 9149).

Children's Country Holiday Fund, 1 York Street, London W1H 1PZ (☏ 01-935 8373).

Christian Aid, Headquarters, 240–50 Ferndale Road, London SW9 8BH (☏ 01-733 5500).

Citizens Advice Bureaux (CAB) Service Ltd, (Greater London) 31 Wellington Street, London WC2E 7DA (☏ 01-240 0910).

Commission for Racial Equality, Elliott House, 10–12 Allington Street, London SW1E 5EH (☏ 01-828 7022).

Community Relations Commission, 15 Bedford Street, London WC2E 9HX (☏ 01-386 3545).

Community Service Volunteers, (Social Service, Education) 237 Pentonville Road, London N1 9NJ (☏ 01-278 6601).

Community Work Division of National Council of Social Service, 26 Bedford Square, London WC1B 9HH (☏ 01-636 4066).

Compassionate Friends, The, 50 Woodwaye, Watford, Hertfordshire WD1 4NW (☏ Watford [0923] 24279).

Conservation Society, National Office, 12a Guildford Street, Chertsey, Surrey KT16 9BQ (☏ Chertsey [093 28] 60975).

Consumers' Association, 14 Buckingham Street, London WC2N 6DS (☏ 01-839 1222).

Council of Social Service for Wales, Crescent Road, Caerphilly, Mid-Glamorgan CF8 1XL (☏ Caerphilly [0222] 869224).

Disablement Income Group, Attlee

House, 28 Commercial Street, London E1 6LP (☎ 01-247 2128).

Fair Play for Children Campaign, 248 Kentish Town Road, London NW5 2AB (☎ 01-278 5150).

Family Planning Association, 27–35 Mortimer Street, London W1A 4QW (☎ 01-636 7866).

Fawcett Society, The, 27 Wilfred Street, London SW1E 6PR (☎ 01-828 4966).

Federation of Children's Book Groups, The Mustard Pot, Fairwarp, Uckfield, East Sussex TN22 3BT (☎ Nutley [082 571] 2632).

Friends of the Earth Ltd, (Conservationists), 9 Poland Street, London W1V 3DG (☎ 01-434 1684).

Gingerbread, 35 Wellington Street, London WC2E 7BN (☎ 01-240 0953).

Girls' Brigade, The, Brigade House, Parsons Green, London SW6 4TH (☎ 01-736 8481).

Girl Guides Association (Headquarters), 17 Buckingham Palace Road, London SW1W 0PT (☎ 01-834 6242).

Help the Aged, 8–10 Denman Street, London W1V 7RF (☎ 01-493 6515).

Institute of Home Help Organizers, 4 Spences Lane, Lewes, East Sussex BN7 2HE (☎ Lewes [079 16] 4555).

International Planned Parenthood Federation (IPPF), 18 Regent Street, London SW1Y 4PW (☎ 01-839 2911).

LEPRA, see British Leprosy Relief Association.

London Council of Social Services, 68 Chalton Street, London NW1 1JR (☎ 01-388 0241).

London Housing Aid Association (SHAC), 189a Old Brompton Road, London SW5 0AN (☎ 01-373 7276).

MIND, see National Association for Mental Health.

Minority Rights Group, Benjamin Franklin House, 36 Craven Street, London WC2N 5NG (☎ 01-930 6659).

Multiple Sclerosis Society, 4 Tachbrook Street, London SW1W 1SJ (☎ 01-834 8231).

National Association for the Care and Resettlement of Offenders, (NACRO), 125 Kennington Park Road, London SE11 4JJ (☎ 01-582 7172).

National Association of Leagues of Hospital Friends, 44 Fulham Road, London SW3 8HH (☎ 01-584 7713).

National Association for Mental Health (MIND), 22 Harley Street, London W1N 2ED (☎ 01-637 0741). 111 Mycenae Road, London SE3 7RX (☎ 01-858 4849).

National Association of Youth Clubs, 30 Devonshire Street, London W1N 2AP (☎ 01-935 2941).

National Childbirth Trust, The, 9 Queensborough Terrace, London W2 3TA (☎ 01-229 9319).

National Council of Social Service (Incorp.), 26 Bedford Square, London WC1B 3HU (☎ 01-636 4066).

National Deaf Children's Society, 31 Gloucester Place, London W1H 4EA (☎ 01-486 3251).

National Marriage Guidance Council, Herbert Gray College, Little Church Street, Rugby, Warwickshire CV21 3AP (☎ Rugby [0788] 73241).

National Society for Autistic Children, 1a Golders Green Road, London NW11 8EA (☎ 01-458 4375).

National Society for Mentally Handicapped Children, Pembridge Hall,

17 Pembridge Square, London W2 4EP (☎ 01-229 8941).

National Society for the Prevention of Cruelty to Children (NSPCC), National Headquarters, 1 Riding House Street, London W1P 8AA (☎ 01-580 8812).

National Trust for Places of Historic Interest or Natural Beauty, 42 Queen Anne's Gate, London SW1H 9AS (☎ 01-930 0211).

National Viewers' and Listeners' Association, 42 The Drive, London E18 2BL (☎ 01-989 6006).

New Bridge, The, St Botolph's Church, Aldersgate Street, London EC1A 4EU (☎ 01-606 3692).

Northern Ireland Council of Social Service, 2 Annadale Avenue, Belfast BT7 3JH (☎ Belfast [0232] 640011).

Oxfam (Head Office), 274 Banbury Road, Oxford OX2 7D2 (☎ Oxford [0865] 56777).
(London Area Office), 4 Replingham Road, London SW18 5LS (☎ 01-874 7335).

Patients' Association, The, 335 Gray's Inn Road, London WC1X 8PX (☎ 01-837 7241).

Pre-School Playgroups Association (Headquarters), Alford House, Aveline Street, London SW11 5DH (☎ 01-582 8871).

RADAR, see Royal Association for Disability and Rehabilitation.

REHAB, see British Council for Rehabilitation of the Disabled.

Royal Association for Disability and Rehabilitation (RADAR), 25 Mortimer Street, London W1N 7RJ (☎ 01-637 5400).

Royal National Institute for the Blind (RNIB), 224 Great Portland Street, London W1N 6AA (☎ 01-388 1266).

Royal Society for the Prevention of Cruelty to Animals (RSPCA), National Headquarters, Manor House, The Causeway, Horsham, West Sussex RH12 1HG (☎ Horsham [0403] 64181).

St John Ambulance Brigade, National Headquarters, 1 Grosvenor Crescent, London SW1X 7EF (☎ 01-235 5231).
London District Headquarters, 29 Weymouth Street, London W1N 2DR (☎ 01-637 4105).

Samaritans, The (London Branch), St Stephen's Church, 39 Walbrook, London EC4N 8BP (emergency number ☎ 01-629 2277).
(General Office Adminstration), 17 Uxbridge Road, Slough, Berkshire SL1 1SN (☎ Slough [0753] 32713).

Scottish Council of Social Service, 18-19 Claremont Crescent, Edinburgh EH7 4HX (☎ 031-556 3882).

Scout Association, The, Baden-Powell House, 65 Queensgate, London SW1 (☎ 01-584 7030).

SHAC, see London Housing Aid Association.

Shelter National Campaign for the Homeless Ltd, 86 Strand, London WC2R 0EQ (☎ 01-836 2051).

Simon Community Trust, 129 Malden Road, London NW5 4HS (☎ 01-485 6639).
47 Milmans Street, London SW10 0DA (☎ 01-352 2242).

Spastics Society (Head Office), 12 Park Crescent, London W1N 4EQ (☎ 01-636 5020).

Task Force, Clifford House, Edith Villas, London W14 8UG (☎ Director's Department: 01-602 2627; Information: 01-602 1469).

Victorian Society, The, 1 Priory Gardens, London W4 1TT (☎ 01-994 1019).

Voluntary Work Information Services, 68 Chalton Street, London NW1 1HJ (☎ 01-388 0241).

Volunteer Centre, 29 Lower Kings Road, Berkhamsted, Herts HP4 2AB (☎ Berkhamsted [044 27] 73311).

Winged Fellowship Trust, Holidays for Disabled, 64 Oxford Street, London W1N 0AH (☎ 01-636 5575).

Women's Aid Federation (National), 51 Chalcot Road, London NW1 1LY (☎ 01-586 0104).

Women's Institutes, National Federation of, 39 Eccleston Street, London SW1W 9NT (☎ 01-730 7212).

Women's Royal Voluntary Service (WRVS) (Headquarters), 17 Old Park Lane, London W1Y 4AJ (☎ 01-499 6040).

Improving the system at home

'To achieve the actual equality of men and women within the family is an infinitely . . . arduous problem. All our domestic habits must be revolutionized before that can happen.' – *Trotsky*

You can't get a quart out of a pint pot. If you want to do something more interesting than housework (and many women don't) then you have to drop some of the less interesting things or get someone else to do them.

If you can't get or afford or don't want paid help, the logical solution is to use the people who make the work in the first place because, if nothing else, they then might not make so *much* work. Obviously you don't expect anything of a tiny baby, but it's amazing how *old* a tiny baby can become, and how helpless it can remain even at fifty.

If you have a wonderful, helpful mate then you need no further assistance, but if you haven't and you feel that housework is getting you down, then you may want to know HOW TO GET YOUR MAN TO HELP without having a mutinous, resentful, spiteful, frigid saboteur on your hands – or even worse, in someone else's arms.

Real partnership in marriage is still a newer concept than racial equality. Marriage expert Dr Jack Dominian has pointed out that the tremendous tensions involved in adapting to the inevitable are a major factor in the exploding rate of divorce and remarriage. This is evidence that the problem of modernization of marriage *exists* and will continue to exist until solved.

The old order could no longer stand; the new order is still evolving. Social attitudes have changed remarkably quickly and women have come a long way since 1973 when the *Sunday Times Review* – *on its front page* – put as the twelfth of twelve tips to help the working wife, 'An automatic washing-machine is very useful'. A helping husband wasn't included in this list but tacked on to it, as an afterthought.

Yet by 1977, when two in three women were working full time and more were working part time, the *Sunday Times* was running a series on taking the stress out of marriage in which the husband had the star part, his home-helping role being seen as the key to a happy family.

How do you get one of these paragons who will love, cherish and clean up? It's not so difficult as you might think, but if he's not helping by now the first obstacle is possibly not him but *you*.

DO YOU RECOGNIZE A BIT OF YOURSELF?

Get a drink, put your feet up, then search deep into your heart and soul to check whether *you* are making too much work for yourself, whether any of the following obstacles are difficulties of your own making.

1st MOLEHILL

Many women are anxious to preserve the mystique of housework, how long it takes and how difficult it is (the Housewife-as-Brain-Surgeon Syndrome). A woman like this doesn't really want her man to help because then, suddenly, this Big Important Job would dissolve into a bit of routine cleaning and he might wonder what she's been *doing* all these years.

2nd MOLEHILL

Many women feel that they don't *deserve* any fun unless everything is impeccable at home (impossible, of course) so that no one can accuse *them* of neglect or not having care-worn hands (the Martyred-Mother Syndrome).

3rd MOLEHILL

Many women have unnecessarily high standards, feel the need to show that they can do three things at once and schedule their day with bossy bustle, as if they were running a hospital (the Superwoman Syndrome). Like hospital patients, the family of a woman like this may sometimes feel that it might all run better without them.

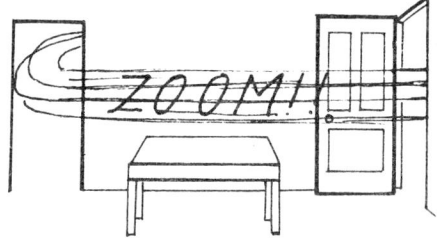

4th MOLEHILL

Some women have low, but fussy, standards, that quietly irritate the whole family. This was once described by an exasperated husband as the 'Valance Factor', after his wife has spent the whole of Saturday shopping for bed valances because an unexpected guest was coming to stay instead of joining him on a long-planned motor rally. Other indications of the Valance Factor (making life uncomfortable by excessive attention to home-making) are coasters, doilies, too many ornaments, over-elaborate table-laying, and fragile furniture that looks as if you had better not sit on it.

5th MOLEHILL

You may be suffering from a spot of *Corset Conditioning*. This is not something you can sweep aside: you are stuck with it for ever. But once you recognize it, you can avoid it, like puddles in the road.

★ Were you taught that a husband works and thinks and earns money and makes big decisions ('Your father's always right, dear')?

★ Were you taught that a wife runs the home and children without any of these worries ('A woman's place is in the home')?

★ Did your father ever change a nappy or know how to mix a feed?

★ Did your father do *any* of the jobs listed in 'How Does Your Man Rate as a Home-Maker?' (*see page* 97)?

If you answered yes to either of the first two questions and no to either of the second, then you have probably been corset-conditioned.

Another variation of corset-conditioning is mother-in-law innuendo, now dying out, thank Heaven. Beware of such guilt-creating, slave-making, sink-chaining phrases as, 'He's always sent his shirts back to me.' 'He's looking a bit *peaky*.' 'He doesn't look *happy*, to me.' 'We made our *own* fun in my day.' Most lethal of all and always delivered with an irritating, indulgent, knowing smirk, 'Men are little boys at heart.'

But little boys are very capable (Boy Scouts, stamp collecting, washing other people's cars). Little boys can help a lot and enjoy it; so can big ones.

6th MOLEHILL

Many women think, 'Oh, it's no use asking one of the children, it's quicker to do it myself'. When her husband does something to help (perhaps slowly, perhaps through lack of practice) she says, 'Here, give it to me.' This is a short-term solution and a very, very serious molehill. She is more concerned to get some job completed than to train her children to be self-sufficient. She is cutting her help off short, in more ways than one (the Castrating Housewife Syndrome).

Such ladies must earnestly remember (possibly over a second drink) that they owe it to their children and to future generations to do as little housework as possible.

IF A CHILD COULD DO IT, WHY NOT LET IT?

Novelist Margaret Drabble (among others) thinks that it is a mother's duty to see that her sons are taught at home how to look after themselves. She has said that mothers are irresponsible if they allow their sons to grow up unaware of the most basic acts of survival and that this perpetuates the system against which many women bitterly complain.

'I no longer find it touching or amusing when men say they do not know how to boil an egg, I think it damn silly,' she said in *The Times* and added, 'If a man, presented with button, needle and thread, cannot work out how to combine them, he is unfit for any form of higher education.'

Naturally, children don't like being used as a convenience to run errands simply because they are *there* (that's why they creep off with an apple and hide). They don't like being taken for granted, any more than you do. And they don't like their own odd interests being thought unimportant, any more than you do.

Children like comfort; they like order; they like to know what to expect and where they are; they like routine and they like you to be part of it (children are little men at heart).

They like to be given interesting jobs and be shown how to do them well. They like to be appreciated, praised and see immediate rewards after the job is finished, not next Christmas. They also like a bit of real responsibility and can generally be persuaded to do housework if they see the logic of it. ('It's *not fair* if everyone makes the mess but only mother clears it up.')

If you think what bits of housework you like and what bits you don't like you'll get a fairly good idea of what might interest children and what you had better not try. At this early stage of improving the system at home aim to hand over the *pleasant* jobs and keep the unpleasant ones for yourself. Remember that your main aim *for the moment* is merely to do *less* work while keeping everyone happy.

If your personal problem is molehill 2, 3 or 4, teenagers can be a very great help and a truly wonderful example, because they are superb at doing nothing without feeling guilty. This may infuriate you at first, but it is a true gift and you should cultivate it yourself, according to their ethic. Because they are always doing something more important and enjoyable when faced with a job (even if it's sleeping) their immediate questions and comments are right to the point.

Why do it anyway?

Why should I?

Why shouldn't I?

Surely it doesn't have to be done *now*?

I'll do it when I feel like it.

Would it be such a *great tragedy* if it didn't get done?

Violence breeds violence, you know.

A two-week Teenage Training Course in Attitude to Housework can make you feel better and more rested than a fortnight in an expensive health farm, and both parties may moderate their view of what is necessary.

One of the few advantages of getting divorced is that you haven't been corset-conditioned to Expectations of Divorce. Nobody told you from childhood how divorced families should behave themselves. Barbara Cartland hasn't yet written about it in depth. So you use your common sense and sort out your assets, your priorities and pretensions amazingly quickly (first to go is the Valance Factor) and then share out the housework among those who are there to do it on logical lines. You take far more notice of what the children want and think – which is probably unusual (to put it mildly) but may also be more logical and sensible than your own traditional method of running a home.

HELP COULD BE LYING NEXT TO YOU

Of course, your biggest potential source of help is your mate. How helpful he is depends on:

1 His age (the older he is, the bigger your problem).

2 His corset-conditioning and subsequent marriage expectations (possibly as unrealistic as yours).

3 His experience – what he did after leaving home. If he did National Service, you've got a head start (they iron particularly well), especially if he did any camping. Carpenters, gardeners, electricians, mechanics and sailors can be marvellous home helps. Academics

are the worst. They view housework as beneath them and they're
ruthless and clever enough to make
you wish very soon that you had
never asked them to help in the
first place.

Because of their corset-
conditioning, most husbands have
very firm views on what they can be
seen to be doing. A study of dual-
career families in the 1976 Rapoport
Report showed that *even* in these
families women are still firmly
regarded as *totally* responsible for the
home organization. Even in these
households men didn't see themselves as *sharing* responsibility for the
home, but *helping*. They had kindly
decided to help their wives at home.

It is in this situation that you get
conned stupid. If you both work full
time it may be important for you to
emphasize loudly that he helps in the
home because he does not want the
responsibility of running the home.

This situation generally suits both
parties. It is the managing director's
job at home that the Queen of the
Hearth wants to keep, it's the managing director's job that a husband
doesn't want. A man wants a home
where he can relax and put his feet
up, because *she's* in charge. He wants
to be able to wipe his mind clear on
leaving home and spend his day concentrating on his work and nothing
else. This might affect a wife's outside interests in one major way:
she can't usually take a job that
involves much travel, overtime or
odd working hours (useless to protest, we are dealing with fact, not
theory).

According to the report, most husbands are very tough indeed about
the demarcation lines of a work

agreement and very critical of any fal-
tering in the housewife's role. Even
where couples with full-time jobs *had
agreed to run the family jointly*, the
women did more at home than they
had anticipated and the men preferred to have an irritable, overworked
wife rather than take on any more
work themselves.

Strangely enough, there was no
problem with the children.

In these families, both parents
expected their children to be independent and competent and housework was equally shared out between
boys and girls. These children are
going to grow up without the traditional hang-ups listed here and will
probably *really* share the housework
with their permanent sexual partners,
whether or not they are married.
Today, there seem few problems
about sharing housework with your
mate, *provided you are not married*.

TOEING THE KING KONG LINE

Another interesting discovery
revealed in the Rapoport study is that
both husbands and wives have *identity
tension lines*. A husband's identity
tension demarcation line marks the
boundaries of the touchy zone where
he *thinks* being manly/masculine/
macho begins and ends. Every man
has a different set of illogical taboos.
Some King Kongs can wash the car
but not the nappies; some will make
breakfast but never the bed. Your
man's identity tension demarcation
line has nothing to do with logic but
with his corset-conditioning. However much he loves you and intellectually approves of any new development, emotionally he's at the mercy
of the Old King Kong in him.

People accept things intellectually
long before they accept them

emotionally (daughters-in-law, for instance). Once a man realizes that his wife isn't getting a fair deal, he *may* want to help her to enjoy her life more. But naturally he doesn't want to enjoy his life less. Equality is much easier to accept if you are getting, not giving, and identity tension lines are an indicator of this situation.

So observe and recognize them (even if he can't); remember and respect them; and realize that asking him to do what *he* considers to be not King Kong work may well get you nothing except perhaps a primeval clip across the ear. If you want to keep him, have a quiet life and get your own way to a reasonable degree.

Never underestimate his King Kong line.

Here are a few popular chest-thumpers (Aaaaarghrorr!):

1 The wife may earn – but not earn more than the husband.
2 The husband must not actually work *for* his wife in any way.
3 Both must consider her work as play and not real.
4 However competent at work, the wife must appear submissive at home.
5 Some work is illogically but fiercely labelled *woman's work*. This might be waiting in for a plumber or repair man; dealing with any hired help (cleaner, babysitter) or serving the pudding.
6 Some work is fiercely labelled *man's work*, such as dealing with insurance, stockbrokers, central heating (especially the boiler), any non-household machinery (especially the lawnmower or the car, but not the bikes), taking the dog out at night or carving the primeval haunch of lamb.

WHAT MEN WORRY ABOUT

There is probably a surprising gap between what he knows he ought to think and *says* to you and what he complains about when he lets his hair down in the pub.

The things a man may really fear if his wife suddenly starts earning or develops an absorbing interest or is suddenly besieged by local newspaper reporters are:

★ *Lack of attention* ('It's as bad as having a baby again').
★ *Lack of interest* (subtly different) ('She doesn't listen to me any more, she's full of her own affairs').
★ *Lack of support* ('In my field you have to entertain a lot but now *she's* taking a course in psychology').
★ *That he may have to share the chores* ('You can't sit down peacefully for five minutes without being asked to *do* something' . . . 'Next thing, she expects *me* to take the kids to school').
★ *That spontaneity will go and system will take over* ('Now I can't ever bring a few people back home without telling her in advance' . . . 'I can't just ring up and tell her to meet me any more').
★ *Rivalry* ('All I hear about now is her peak potential and whether she's hitting it').
★ *That he will lose sole-breadwinner status* ('Mind you, I'm glad she got it, but it's not as if we *need* the extra money').
★ *That she will expect him to pay her taxes* ('Then they sent me this tax form. I told her, "I'm damned if I'm going to pay your taxes" ').
★ *That she will over-exert herself* ('And then at night, she's too bloody tired . . .').

HOW DOES YOUR MAN RATE AS A HOME-MAKER?

This questionnaire is for couples who both work outside the home.

	Always	Sometimes	Never
GENERAL ATTITUDE			
Does he do any of the domestic work?	+50	+30	−50
Does he do housework *regularly*?	+50	0	0
Can you rely on him to do the job properly?	+50	0	0
Can you ask him to help in an emergency or when you're exhausted and will he do it willingly?	+70	+20	−50
Is he likely to offer?	+150	+20	−30
LOOKING AFTER LIVING CREATURES			
Does he help with the children?	+150	+50	−100
Does he take or collect them from school?	+50	+30	0
Does he look after the pets?	+30	+10	0
TIME-CONSUMING AND ESSENTIAL TASKS			
Does he shop for food (try for this because it's so good for the height of the housekeeping allowance)	+30	+10	−0
Does he cook in the evening?	+200	+70	0
Does he cook twice a week, regularly?	+50	+10	−50
Does he cook at weekends, or all Sunday?	+50	+10	−50
Does he wash up?	+150	+70	0
BASIC SWABBING			
Does he deal with the laundry?	+30	+10	0
Does he tidy and dust?	+50	+30	0
Does he clean windows?	+30	+20	0
Does he look after a car or bikes?	+30	+10	0
Does he clean the bathroom?	+30	+10	0
Does he clean the kitchen?	+30	+10	0
Does he clean floors?	+60	+40	−30
Does he spring-clean (wash walls, etc.)?	+75	+50	0
MAINTENANCE WORK			
Does he decorate?	+25	+10	0
Does he look after the garden?	+25	+10	0
Does he do carpentry, electrical or plumbing work?	+25 for each +100 extra for all three	+10 for each	0
Does he ask what the hell do you think he is, a daily help?	−70	−10	+10

HIS RATING

He gets high marks for showing that he loves you, for helping regularly so that you can rely on him for time consuming jobs and jobs that are considered traditionally feminine.

He also gets high marks for work that needs strength. These days, it needs more strength to scrub floors than to do such traditionally manly work as sitting on a bulldozer and pulling the levers.

The potential top marks for the impossible Superman is 1200.

The lowest possible rating for the very turgid, lazy or rich is −350.

If your man scored 400 he's an average, decent fellow.

If your man scored 600 he is to be cherished.

If your man scored 800 he is a real mate.

If your man scored 1000 what are *you* doing?

Now try marking yourself. If your score is the same as his, you really *are* equal partners.

Find out if your man is worried about any one of those fears and try doubly hard to make sure he needn't worry. But watch out for one spiteful remark that indicates you are in the deep waters of illogicality and likely to be torpedoed: 'It's not that I mind for myself, but I can't stand seeing the children neglected.'

There are a couple of other points to remember before launching your spring (cleaning) offensive. Trotsky didn't ask you to overturn the system overnight. Take it easy, one chore at a time.

Don't believe a word that other women tell you about their perfectly adjusted husbands who dust impeccably or their lovers who leap up and bring them breakfast in bed.

Don't be depressed or browbeaten by the more truculent, aggressive Women's Libbers in your neighbourhood. *They* are not living with your husband. *You* are dealing with fact, as well as theory.

THROW AWAY THE APRON

Some items of apparel, such as chastity belts, whalebone stays and cycling bloomers, have a deep significance, far beyond their usefulness.

So, temporarily, hide every apron you possess. Boiler suits are a working garment acceptable to the male, so are jeans. If you want to protect your clothes while doing the housework either change them or tie a tea towel around your waist. Later you might introduce the unisex navy blue striped butcher's apron.

THE HAPPY FAMILY ACTION PLAN

There is a great deal of difference between keeping a house clean and running a home. Nobody can tell you how to run *your* home because everyone and their circumstances are different, but there is unlikely to be one living woman who would claim that her system cannot be improved.

If you feel like trying to improve your home system by spreading the work load more evenly, there are a few basic principles which can be used to help a group of people to work happily together. These principles have been successfully applied by different groups of different sizes, ranging from early Christians to pioneer settlers and modern factory workers.

No one's suggesting that you start to run the place like a factory (*you* are doing something more difficult) but the following Happy Family Action Plan is based on these principles.

It is important to stick to the eight main points, although every woman's plan will obviously differ, according to her situation. You may wobble off the new system from time to time, you may have flare-ups or even full-scale rows, but keep checking back to the eight main points of your plan.

Move slowly and carefully, pause whenever necessary, but *never retreat* and make it clear that THE OLD ORDER IS GOING TO CHANGE.

Often the whole family prefers a new system, once they know *what* it is and *why* it is and see where they will each fit in and how they will each benefit.

In industry the action plan would be:

1 Decide your *objective*.
2 Decide your *resources*.
3 Define *tasks and priorities*.
4 *Consult* everyone concerned and make sure that they agree to the final plan.
5 Jointly *allocate jobs* so that everyone contributes, using special skills where they exist (worker participation).
6 Make sure that everyone in the team realizes the *importance* of everyone else's contributions, as well as his own.
7 Jointly decide on a *time plan*, to check your progress.
8 *Reward results*.

That doesn't seem very difficult, but it depends what your objectives and resources are. A factory can decide what it wants to make (bull-dozers or canned beans) and then use people, material and machinery to make it. This may be a fairly straight-forward objective compared with yours.

Your objectives might be:

1 To keep everyone healthy, confi-dent and friendly.
2 To keep everyone fairly clean and well fed.
3 To make sure everyone in the fam-ily gets what they want and wants something worth having.
4 To make sure everyone in the

family is responsible about re-lationships, money and work.
5 To make sure that the family work is shared by the whole family.

This is a pretty ambitious target compared to cans of beans, especially if your family includes people that any factory manager in his right mind would send straight home – anyone under six, too old, too ill, or irres-ponsible. What is more, the factory workers are paid and they all troop off in the evenings, giving the manager a sixteen-hour daily breather. (Cheer yourself up with these thoughts when your new system doesn't leap into smooth operation overnight.)

WHAT ARE YOUR RESOURCES?

You + Them = The family

What's important here is that the sum is greater than the parts. A fam-ily working together is better equip-ped to face the world (separately or together) if it has learned to work as a group. This is one of the most impor-tant things you can teach your chil-dren at any age.

DEFINE THE TASKS

And so build up the family work-list:

1 The list of *easy self-support tasks* that everyone over eight can do for themselves, such as clean bath, wash up after personal snack, empty own wastepaper basket and make own bed. These can be done to personal standards (which they will be anyway).
2 *Routine responsibilities* (*see* 'How

Does Your Man Rate as a Home-Maker?', *page 97*).

3 *Special responsibilities* such as care of garden, pets, bicycles, boats, clothes and office work (insurance, bill paying, etc.). These are generally seasonal responsibilities and don't come at you, three times a day, like washing up.

4 *Entertaining and special celebrations* such as birthdays, Christmas and Easter, the annual holiday treks and visits from your/his family and friends.

Quite possibly it makes you sag at the knees just to read the list. Quite often men don't realize what a lot is expected of their wives until *they* read the list. Quite often, there is an immediate change when this happens. Some things get done more efficiently (the kitchen gets a hatch, the refrigerator alters its position and new shelves appear). Some things don't get done at all (no longer does he bring six people back to dinner without warning, not unless he stops on the way and buys a take-away meal).

DECIDE YOUR PRIORITIES

What is essential, what you can live without, what isn't really worth the hassle.

DECIDE HOW MUCH TIME IS NEEDED *to do all the work*

Decide how many hours a week *you* are prepared to spend to keep the place clean and organized. Decide when you will do this work.

Decide how many hours a week help you want from each member of the family.

MAKE A WORK-SHARE LIST

List all the jobs to be done and share them out among the whole family. Don't think for one minute that your list will be acceptable. This list is planned to be thrown out (but when it is discussed, listen carefully to the reasons for rejection).

Some of the more deadly routine jobs are more fun if done in a group (such as all the cleaning on Saturday morning).

Try to get them to settle for routine self-support jobs and Saturday morning (starting early). Then *you* stick to that routine as well.

AN INTERESTING SCRAP OF AMMUNITION

In February 1977 a German court had to judge the compensation to be paid to a housewife injured in a car crash. The judges consulted the West German Housewives' Federation and the Food, Entertainment and Public House Trade Union. They concluded that a housewife should not be expected to work more than forty-six hours a week if running a small home with one child or fifty-five hours a week running a larger home and two children.

For this she should be paid *£345 a month*. After deducting the cost of her board and lodging, she should be left with just over £65 per week as personal salary.

NOW FOR THE CONSULTATION

How do you get your group together to explain that there are going to be changes? Armed with your two lists, you lobby them all beforehand so it's not a surprise, and then give them a marvellous meal. *After* the meal you say that you want to do less housework and produce your two family work-lists (the original long-string-of-everything list and the second one, sharing out the jobs among all the family).

You obviously won't expect everyone to agree enthusiastically that it's a terrific scheme and that they want to help immediately. Expect anything from yawns to rage. Someone might even jump up from the table saying, 'Oh, don't be so bloody silly!'

Keep quiet and stick to your guns. You can, privately, decide to lower your standards if they really won't help more. But right now ask your family *what their priorities are,* because *(a)* this helps you to decide what to do in your work time and *(b)* unless this is discussed with all of them *together* you have no hope of delegating efficiently. Managers in industry who impose their priorities on other people would simply have a strike on their hands and *you* could have a mutiny.

If (as is likely) you privately think that their priorities will lead to disaster, you can suggest what might happen, but then try it, all the same. It will be good for them and (in the long run) for you, *because you will have started to work as a group.*

Incidentally, *what you will see* at this family conference is:

1 How much your family value *you* and want *you* to be contented.
2 How much they are each prepared to put into getting a happy family life.

Now let's assume the worst: assume that *nobody* is prepared to help you. In this case, remember that you are *not* Lysistrata; you are *not*

Gloria Steinem and that politics is the art of the possible, even in the Women's Movement. So draw up a timetable for yourself (just like theirs at school) and allocate their priority tasks into the amount of time you have decided to contribute (at this point *your* priority task may be merely doing far, far less).

If they refuse to discuss priority tasks, say in that case you won't do anything that isn't vital until you are told what is required of you.

What you mustn't do is allow anyone to goad you into bursting into tears or showing anger, or losing your temper, even if they yell, sulk or don't eat any of your lovely meal. This is a showdown and you mustn't be psyched out by anyone's bad behaviour.

But start your new emergency routine immediately and then, one or two weeks later (depending on degree of stubbornness encountered), again lobby individuals with your family work-list.

Eventually you will either have a whole new lifestyle or a whole lot more help.

Reward results by praising twice.

Always, if possible, praise a job *when* it is done. Praise should *always* come before criticism, and that shouldn't pass your lips for the first three months, at least.

After a month, hold another consultation (another marvellous meal). This *must* sound as if progress has been made, and that you are very happy with what has happened (either they are starting to help or you are doing less, preferably both).

Read out everything that everyone has done (public praise and recognition in front of everyone else is heady stuff). Whatever happens, criticize *nothing* and praise as much as possible.

Then reward results. Depending on age and tasks it might be a night at the opera, a day's trip to the sea, a barbecue in the back garden. It's difficult to find something that everyone enjoys, so make sure that this is discussed and perhaps that each member takes it in turn to suggest or decide on a treat.

You must also show rewarding behaviour (not presents) perhaps as a result of your having the extra spare time to do it. Perhaps you could help a daughter to make a dress or test a son on his gunnery. (One mother painted a wooden, life-size tattooed lady on the back of an old door, for target practice.)

Then ask the family whether they think that anything else needs doing – and if so, who is going to do it.

Always decide on the date of the next magnificent meal after the praise and rewards but before the end of the feast.

Ignore difficulties, jeers and insults whether they come from your mate, your mother or your teenagers. Vary this plan according to your own problems – but stick to the basic principles, and you will get results.

THE REVERSE CRISIS

More freedom and less responsibility can be some of the advantages of being over forty but some women suddenly find themselves with *more* responsibility and *less* freedom – because there is an unexpected new dependant in the home.

This might be the result of a joyous event, such as a late baby or a marriage that brings stepchildren. But it might be a chronically sick husband, a handicapped child or an old, decrepit, senile relative.

However much you love an elderly relative, to have him or her suddenly dumped in your lap for ever can make you feel as tied and tired as the Ancient Mariner. You might also feel despondent, despairing and exasperated – as well as guilty for feeling this way.

Difficulties can increase as the old person becomes physically, and sometimes mentally, more frail. Odd, distressing habits can develop as a result of arteriosclerosis, which sometimes weakens the part of the brain that controls moral behaviour. This is why Gran can turn into a kleptomaniac and why Grandad starts pinching little girls' bottoms. This is also one of the reasons why old people can become unusually aggressive (like old Steptoe), selfish (about such minor things as getting the biggest teacup), super-critical (the tea is never right), paranoid (frightened of burglars to a ridiculous degree) and forgetful. Such behaviour can be difficult for the whole family (one small boy asked his father, 'Daddy, what are we saving Grandfather *for?*').

But there it is. According to the population predictions and the NHS resources, many of us will be obliged to look after an elderly semi-invalid. Today there are more than 9 million pensioners, and by 1991 there will be a 40 per cent increase in those aged eighty-five and over. Although patients are kept clean, fed and protected, NHS hospitals for old people are far below the standard that the average doctor would wish for *his* mother.

Faced with such a reverse crisis a

woman might have to change her life dramatically overnight. An established wage earner may have to reorganize hastily or chuck in her job and return home for good. Women who haven't had a paid job since their teens may have to go out to work. At home, there is more work for everyone.

The following advice comes from many people who have handled a reverse crisis. In spite of the similarity of the advice, their situations were very different. For instance, Barbara had her first baby at forty-one but managed to continue at work and won a major award for it. Francis was left to look after a retarded child of ten when his wife ran off with another man. Francis still makes first-class television documentaries. Stephanie's husband was a window cleaner who fell and broke his back when he was forty-two and is now paralysed from the waist down. Stephanie (who has a bad TB record) ended up as a successful, well-known book critic.

But they all had a tough time, and some bad moments, before getting the situation in hand. Their experiences show that, whatever the reverse crisis, the following actions are important:

1 Face the situation; don't refuse to think about it or hope it will go away. (But only if it has to be faced, don't be dumped with someone else's responsibility against your wishes.)
2 Get all the official help you can.
3 Reorganize your home routine and cut housework to the minimum (for how to do this see *Superwoman*).
4 Realize that it is not possible for you to run a perfect home, job and family *and* look your best. Nobody is Doris Day in real life (not even Doris Day). Sort out your priorities and then plod steadily on. Try not to waste time and energy worrying about a situation that you cannot (or do not want to) avoid.

Concentrate on essentials such as sleep, food, togetherness and apartness (this can be very important with an elderly relative).

5 Consider rearranging your rooms to suit the new situation. For instance, make your bedroom into a bed-sitting-room, make the sitting-room a teenage bed-sitter and make Gran a bed-sitter in the now-empty teenage bedroom. It's important to protect everybody's life and sometimes geography helps – *especially* with old parents or a late baby among the teenage stereo. Separation can add to togetherness.
6 Reconsider your situation as a whole. Is it better to get home help while you go out to work? To change your work so that you can work from home? To stop work altogether? To move somewhere smaller and cheaper?
7 If you are going out to work (whether you always have, or are going back to work after a baby, or just discovering the joys of Tipp-Ex after twenty years away

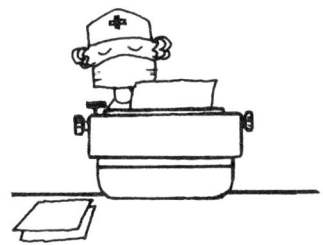

from the typewriter) plan what will happen in an emergency. The most likely threat to a smooth life is illness at home. (If you are the sole bread-winner, this is trebly worrying.)

Before it happens do decide what your policy is going to be if illness strikes the home, whether it is measles or flu.

What priorities do you give to the family and the job? Perhaps delegate the dentist visits and regulation hospital attendance but down tools for anything contagious such as mumps (which should meet with fervent approval from your boss).

When do you stay at work and get someone in to look after Gran?

Who do you delegate to?

Sort out your emergency plan, make it clear to any other resident adults, any home help and to your boss (don't make a big thing of it, in fact keep it as short as possible). Have a dummy run, like children with fire drill.

It's worth being prepared to spend a lot of money on your emergency plan, not for when it happens, but to leave you free of anxiety for the rest of the time. You might make a plan for emergencies with a neighbour or friend but try to avoid last-minute appeals to friends (it's asking too much of the friendship) and never allow help to go unrewarded.

Keep a list of emergency telephone numbers stuck on the kitchen wall and also a note about what to do in a possible emergency, when the old lady has one of her turns or where the fresh bed linen is.

8 *Don't take the family's problems to work with you*; compartmentalize the different parts of your life.

9 Make sure you get half an hour a day to yourself (preferably in the early evening), when you are sitting or lying down and *resting* (not learning German in the bath).

10 Learn your limitations. Don't ever take on anything, however alluring, outside your present responsibilities, because when the day dawns you probably won't have time to do it. Learn to say no, with no explanations.

11 Always double the amount of time you think it may take you to do any job that isn't routine. For instance, taking the washing to the launderette when the washing-machine packs up.

12 When you're on a tight schedule, always expect the unexpected, because there's never a day when it doesn't happen. And the day on which the washing-machine breaks down is the day that your son gets mumps.

13 If you have to look smart in your job, try keeping clothes for that alone. One glamorous fashion expert said, 'I have two separate lots of clothes: smart ones for the office that have to be dry cleaned and ones for home that have to be washable. I always change as soon as I get home so I can crawl around with the baby if I want to, but my office clothes stay good.'

14 Don't rely on your memory. Get a small, handbag-size notebook and develop your own system of notes and lists. Many women have a list of things to be done at home, another list for things to be done at work and a shopping list. It's also useful to have a big family diary which is kept in the kitchen,

for appointments and memory joggers.

LOOKING AFTER THE ELDERLY

Age Concern, the nationwide group that cares for the elderly, says that the problems they meet most often are those that concern money and housing. Other problems are when the family of the old person may be hundreds of miles away, for work reasons, or when the mother of the family can't give the old person all the attention that is needed because she is out, earning her living. Other frequent and upsetting problems are senility, incontinence, irritability and upsetting the rest of the family.

For advice on any aspect of care for the old, contact your local Age Concern group or write to head office at Bernard Sunley House, 60 Pitcairn Road, Mitcham, Surrey CR4 3LL (☎ 01-640 5431).

If you are caring for an elderly person see if the local hospital has a free clean linen service (the hospital provides the sheets for incontinent patients and you swap soiled sheets for clean ones).

It's also well worth asking your local welfare services for help. Don't ask for a health visitor, who is mainly concerned with the well-being of mothers and babies. Ask for a community nurse who carries out nursing duties in the home (but is usually called in to help people who have left hospital) or for a home help who will do cleaning work.

If the old person is ill or handicapped, you may need both sorts of assistance: the home help can visit regularly if you have to go out to work yourself or if you become too exhausted to cope with the situation; the nurse can advise you on special aid and equipment for nursing an old or sick person at home (you may be able to get these on free loan from your area health authority). There are many useful aids, ranging from bathrails and hoists to upholstered bedrests. One marvellous light little gadget has a magnetic hand on the end of a short walking-stick and is a great aid to the handicapped or bedridden for reaching things and picking them up.

For further information on aids for particular problems, write to the Disabled Living Foundation, 346 Kensington High Street, London W14 8NS (☎ 01-602 2491).

Partly because the oldsters are increasing so rapidly, gerontology has recently made great strides in caring for ageing minds as well as bodies. The basic rules are simple:

1 *Keep them active.* Give them small responsibilities, such as making morning tea. Don't get exasperated if they are slow or clumsy, which may well be the case. Just buy cheaper china.
2 *Stimulate them.* Keep them part of the family group, keep everyone talking to them (check the hearing-aid). An armchair in the sitting-room is far better than a lonely bed. (Watch out for this problem if you subdivide your family age groups into bed-sitters.)
3 *The opposite sex* cheers them up no end, as proved by placing old people in mixed wards. So encourage social life, outings and visits as long as possible.
4 *Deal with disorientation* the way the newscasters do, emphasizing the

facts: 'This is *Joan*, Gran, and *it's four o'clock* and *here's your tea*.'

IF YOU ARE A SINGLE WOMAN

It's particularly difficult if a single woman suddenly has to look after a dependent relative (it's much easier for a man to get home help) and there are 310,000 such women in Britain. According to the National Council for the Single Woman and Her Dependants (NCSWHD), the main problem is the loneliness, isolation and narrowing life that is almost certain as these women face the inevitable decline of their charges.

The Council advises such a woman to hang on to her job as long as possible, try to get an annual holiday, no matter how short, and try to protect herself financially. Thanks to the NCSWHD, since 1975 they have been able to claim the Invalid Care Allowance, which is £11.70 a week from November 1978 (compared to the £56 a week which is seemingly the lowest cost of keeping someone in a local-authority old people's home). Whether or not she works in paid employment, if she is receiving an invalid care allowance, the single woman will be credited with insurance stamps, which means that she will get a *full* pension when she retires.

The change need not be the sudden, unexpected care of an old parent. When her mother died, Margaret was eventually forced to give up her career in the Civil Service in Glasgow in order to look after her younger, retarded, forty-two-year-old sister Joan.

'I felt mother had worked for forty years, training her, and I couldn't just

waste that; besides I love her. I never considered putting her in a home but that decision has made a great difference to my life.

'I'd had a good pensionable job with good money and quite a lot of status, I'd been in the Civil Service twenty-five years and wanted to stay in it, so I got Joan a place in an adult centre. But it didn't suit her and getting her ready can take two hours if she has a bad day, so I had to get up very early and then pick her up at 3.30 p.m. I was finally asked to leave my job. I couldn't get another suitable job because I can't leave Joan for more than three hours; you see, she needs to be put on the loo, and she's now physically handicapped and has psoriasis: I have to sleep with her.

'They put me on unemployment benefit for a year, although there was a fight about it, because I couldn't take any job that didn't fit in with Joan. Nothing suitable turned up so now I am on reduced supplementary benefit, an attendance allowance and Joan gets her invalid allowance.

'I can hardly ever go out but I sometimes take Joan to a concert; my friends are very good with her – because she always has to be with us. I've tried to let the new situation interfere with my life as little as possible and I'm determined to keep up the club I organized and the show we do for charity. I have a full-time job here. I've had to come to terms with being a full-time housewife and nurse and being badly off financially but I would do it again, every time.'

Another serious problem can arise for a single woman who has always stayed home, or who has left her job, in order to care for a parent. If the parent dies without leaving a will, the family home may be sold, in order to divide the proceeds equally among the children.

It is vital that such a single woman has any financial arrangement for the future *confirmed in writing by a solicitor's letter*. There is no reason why an amicable verbal understanding should not be so confirmed and signed by all the people making the arrangement (the parent as well as the other children). Any unwillingness to put such an agreement in writing should be viewed with the utmost seriousness and pessimism. Many a devoted daughter has suddenly found herself without a roof over her head. Brothers and sisters can be very sharp (sharp enough not to be left looking after the old lady).

Do you sincerely want to work?

Not every woman wants to go out to work. Most women have happy fantasies of spending the afternoon curled up with *Gone with the Wind* in a home that is endearingly, comfortably, haphazardly and entirely paid for by someone else. These women do not want to take over the husband's traditional role; they do not want to be a new Independent Woman, paying her way and sampling new freedoms together with fatigue, nervous breakdowns, tax and divorce.

Who, given the choice, would?

If you're not already one of the 54 per cent of British women who are paid to work, then your main reason for wanting to go out to work may be to get a bigger family income because you've already cut your housekeeping budget to the bone and the mortgage rate has just gone up again.

But there may be other good reasons why you want a job in Mid-life. You might be lonely or you might feel the need for a more stimulating life. A 1977 survey showed that it was not only for money that two out of three British women over forty had taken a job. Some of them had been advised to go to work by their doctor, as a relief from the loneliness they felt at home or the boredom or the pressure of constant family responsibility – and nothing else.

Many happily married women can feel this way. But sadly, a lot of *un*happily married women have also lost their self-confidence. If you feel (or are told) that you're not a success as a wife, you tend to feel no good all round, and certainly incapable of trotting off to a job. But work can restore your self-esteem far more reliably and rewardingly than other diversions, such as cheap sherry or that milkman. You get friendly adult company, shared interests (whether it's hitting that sales target or swapping tales about the young ginger-haired copy-typist). It's comforting to be under a benevolent business umbrella where responsibility is shared and it's someone *else's* job to bring your tea, and to make sure you're warm, looked after, appreciated and paid.

Perhaps work outside the home

will give you a chance to use an undeveloped talent. What did you shine at in school? Painting? Acting? Making maps? Capacity is its own motivation; just because you *have* a gift you will want to use it and will regret not using it.

But consider the reasons you might *not* want a job even more carefully than the reasons for taking one. Check that a job won't jeopardize the things that make your home a home. Check that it won't upset your family or social life. Assess your true market abilities and the true financial value of a possible job.

Draw up your job-shopping list and then go out looking for opportunities. There are so many things that you have never tried and for which you don't need a neat jawline or waistline or even neat typing. Don't expect opportunities to come to you and when you see one – grab it fast with both hands.

TWENTY-ONE GOOD REASONS FOR GETTING A JOB (or a different job)

If a reason doesn't apply to you then ignore it. Otherwise, give yourself a grade for each answer as follows:

A if the reason is very important now.

B if the reason is important from time to time.

C if the reason is not really important to you.

1 The family needs more money.
2 It would allow your mate to take a different job or go for training.
3 You are taken for granted in your present job.
4 You think the family would value you more.
5 You'd like a break and more fun.
6 You'd like to feel more useful.
7 You are ambitious.
8 You would like to achieve something.
9 You'd like a bit more recognition.
10 You'd like some life of your own.
11 You want more out of life.
12 You'd like to meet more people.
13 You'd like to play more of a part in your community.
14 You'd like to be a member of a work-group instead of working alone.
15 If you don't get out you feel bored and depressed.
16 You feel restless; you'd like a new interest, a new enthusiasm, a new point to the working day.
17 You'd like further training and a new job might provide it.
18 You'd like to make better use of your talents.
19 You'd like to develop other abilities.
20 You want to use your training or education.
21 You'd like a personal income (or a larger one).

If you have over five As then you probably need a job or a change of job. If you have over eight Bs, then a suitable job (or training for one) would probably improve your life. If you have only a couple of Cs, then you're very lucky. Get back to *Gone with the Wind*.

TWENTY-ONE GOOD REASONS FOR NOT GETTING A JOB

Your situation	*Comment*
1 You have your home, love looking after and being in it.	Definitely back to *Gone with the Wind*.
2 You have children under five.	The best reason not to leave home, unless your doctor thinks otherwise.
3 Your children wouldn't like it if you weren't there when they got back from school.	Possibly a good reason to stay home, but check with 'Will it Upset Your Family If You Work?', *page 112*.
4 Your family needs you.	Not twenty-four hours a day.
5 You can't look after the family, the home and a job.	See 'Improving the System at Home', *page 190 onwards*.
6 You want plenty of time to pick wild flowers, read bedtime stories in the nursery, grow grand-children round the cottage door.	Don't we all? But look at the birth rate. Half of us are unlikely to be grandmothers.
7 At the moment you're still picking up the pieces after being divorced/widowed/ill.	You certainly shouldn't take a job until you feel you can handle it but a job might help you to get yourself together and take your mind off your problems. What does your doctor think? Perhaps a short TOPS training course would be a good idea.
8 You can do what you like when you please, at the drop of a hat.	This *is* one of the luxuries of not working.
9 You have plenty of interests, plenty of friends, plenty of ac-tivity and a contented husband.	Congratulations. Stay put.
10 You enjoy that 'Queen of the Hearth' feeling that you wouldn't get at work.	You obviously have a marvellous husband and appreciative children.
11 If you're sloppy or lazy at home nobody will know and if they *do*, they won't dare to complain. You are your own boss.	On the whole, you get out of life what you put into it.
12 You can stretch your husband's money twice as far.	But you have far more time in which to be tempted to spend it.
13 Your husband wouldn't like it. He would hate his wife to go out to work.	Why? Have you asked him? Are you sure? Are his reasons loving ones? Today's husbands are often thankful

– and show it – for a helping hand with the mortgage.

14 You're frightened that if you go out to work your husband will think you're competing with him, will go off with other women, will feel neglected, will make you suffer for it.

What does he think? Don't underestimate his manliness. Adult behaviour need not lead to adultery.

15 You've seen plenty of homes made unhappy by discontented absentee working mothers.

Why did they want to leave home?

16 You're always too tired.

As writer Jill Tweedie so truly said, '*Life* is tiring, baby.' Such a symptom doesn't always have a physical cause. You might well feel livelier in a part-time job. What does your doctor think?

17 You don't want an exhausting, dreary, boring job, thank you. You had enough of that after leaving school.

Things have changed since you left school. Jobs for women are now far better paid with better perks, in far better conditions.

18 There are no suitable jobs for you in your area.

Could you train for another enjoyable job? Check the TOPS courses at your local Job Centre and see *Superwoman in Action*.

19 You'd only get a low-status, low-paid job.

You may not only need a job for money and status. Again, check the TOPS courses.

20 You'd feel inferior beside all those self-assured, trained, beautifully made-up young girls.

Only if you behave in an unfriendly, inferior or superior way. Today the young are far more adult and understanding than they were twenty years ago.

21 You're too old.

Studies show that people in their forties, fifties and sixties are better than younger ones at altering their occupations. For proof get *Second Careers and Part Time Jobs* (50p) from the Over Fifty Club, The Elms, 26 Broad Street, Wokingham, Berks RG11 1QS.

There's one more big job consideration. The sad fact is that *it costs money to work*, so check whether you can afford to earn because:

★ You will undoubtedly spend more money on food (at least £250 a year according to a 1976 survey).

★ You may have to pay for home

help from after-tax money. Help in the office is tax-deductible but not help in the home; although it might be if the Chancellor of the Exchequer had to do the family washing.

★ You will probably spend more money on clothes and dry cleaning (allow at least £100 a year more for clothes and £15 for dry cleaning).
★ Fares cost a lot.
★ So do lunches.
★ Surprisingly, a lot of money goes on presents for neighbours or friends or elderly relatives who help you out with the children (at least £25 a year).
★ Sixty per cent of women in the 1976 survey lost wages when they had to stay at home because a relative was ill.
★ You may find yourself with the odd big expense such as a round of drinks, contributing to office presents or a taxi home.
★ *If* you're in employment you're taxed at source (PAYE) and you also have to pay your share of the National Insurance contributions. (So you make sure that you get your maximum welfare state benefits.)
★ Men can be very emotional and unrealistic about money. A fruitful source of marital disharmony can be what you do with your earnings. Of course you pay your own expenses and tax but if you become an earner it shouldn't mean that you are never, ever going to get a housekeeping rise, no matter what the inflation rate or how many rises he gets. It's just as well to sort these things out before you set foot outside the front door.

There are three main areas to which you might want to direct your taxed money.

Your personal allowance: This might be the same amount as your mate.

Family savings: such as a joint mortgage. Some of *your* money should go to savings as well as his.

The family maintenance fund: i.e. housekeeping, holidays, machinery – whether lawnmower or deep freeze. But see that your earnings aren't all dissolved in family maintenance, while his go towards building up capital in his name alone. Of course your husband would never do a thing like that, so see that you don't.

WILL IT UPSET YOUR FAMILY IF YOU WORK?

Of course you want to stay at home as long as your children and husband need you there but how long is that? Not a lifetime.

Dr Mia Kellmer Pringle is an authority on children and a passionate advocate of parental care. She has analyzed and reviewed hundreds of studies on child development and her conclusions also apply to adolescents.

She says that the prime needs of children are:

1 *Love* – the need to know that 'someone will go to unreasonable lengths just for your sake'.
2 *Concern* – enthusiasm, warmth and interest in their performance. Once a child is *certain* that he is loved and cherished, 'this satisfying experience is ever afterwards craved and so constitutes a powerful driving force'. So no wonder we all seek it.

What children need is this stability of affection and concern from *both* parents. Naturally, you're going to show your displeasure from time to time (especially with adolescents who can be particularly exasperating) but it must be made clear that this is a temporary reaction, and doesn't alter your basic feelings.

3 *Praise and recognition* – given more easily to small children than to adolescents. Praise is most useful when it is precise and comes from a knowledgeable, respected source.

4 *New experience and creative play* provided by caring adults. In other words, you should see that their spare time is happily, creatively occupied, not spent in front of the goggle box.

5 *Good adult models* on which to base their own standards and behaviour. To take an extreme example, one of the grave and less obvious dangers of staying with a wife-battering husband is that the little boys grow up to be bullies and the little girls grow up to be cowed grovellers, who can't stand up for themselves, and invite bullying in their turn.

6 *The chance to take responsibility.* Children develop emotionally when they are given responsibility. Too often a woman at home gives a great deal of responsibility to her husband but fails to hand it to her children. For instance, a child who isn't given a proper allowance, won't learn to handle money.

Because they don't take the trouble to *teach* properly and *delegate* properly and won't put up with the inevitable mistakes that beginners make, many mothers fall down on this part of parenthood (see 'The Happy Family Action Plan'). And if you've ever allowed your children loose in the supermarket with the week's housekeeping or in the sitting-room with a paint-brush you will understand the reasons only too well.

Everything that Dr Pringle states is important to a child's development can be provided by the mother who must (or wants to) go out to work and a father who already is at work.

Research shows that children of mothers who are working and enjoying it are more self-reliant, tolerant and ready to share responsibility than children whose mothers stay at home full time.

What seems to damage children is having a mother dutifully at home when she doesn't want to be at home all the time or alternatively having a mother who goes out to work when she very much resents having to go (some single mothers find themselves in this difficult situation).

YOUR ABILITY PROFILE

We all know that if housewives were hired for their abilities we would all be paid at the same rate as managing directors. A recent study even showed that women really *do* possess a special ability to guess correctly how other people will react (sometimes called intuition).

Most of us are probably worth far more than we think on the open market. But when it comes to selling these assets our nerve fails and we feel naked in the market-place.

One good reason for assessing yourself systematically is to sell yourself, but the other equally important reason is to reassure yourself.

To get the job you want, you must

know why you want it, and what you have to offer. This analysis is designed to summarize your assets and experience; it will give you your ability profile.

You can only learn from your own experience if you can thoughtfully and honestly review what has happened to you and understand why. This takes time, so allow a quiet evening for the following assessment.

Read all questions before scribbling the answers in your notebook.

1 LOOK FOR PATTERNS

★ What have you always been able to do easily (anything from making meringues to ends meet)?

★ What have you always found difficult (anything from making meringues to ends meet)?

★ What have you always been praised for?

★ What have you been rewarded for (as opposed to thanked)?

★ What have you been asked to do again?

★ What have you always been in trouble over (whether or not it has been your own fault)?

★ What sort of situations have usually gone smoothly for you (you can always attract plenty of men) and what situations have usually proved difficult (you can never land a permanent one)?

★ What sort of people do you always get on well with (anyone from tiny babies to intellectuals)?

★ What sort of people make you feel uneasy (homosexuals, successful businesswomen or your local brilliant Lady Antonia)?

★ What sort of social situations are *most* difficult for you to manage (parent-teacher evenings; rows with neighbours)?

Sometimes you may just have been lucky or unlucky, but a pattern that repeats itself, that you can see following through your early life, at school, in jobs and in your home and friendships is likely to indicate some abiding quality in you, some great strength (which you want to use) or great weakness (that you want to avoid). Don't try to conquer your great weaknesses overnight (certainly not when job-hunting) – just avoid them.

2 STUDY SOME CRITICAL INCIDENTS

(*a*) Think back to two situations, events or experiences in which you played a central part and which had an important effect on your life. What made you choose your job, where to live, who to marry?

(*b*) Now think of a family problem (when the boiler blew up or Granny came back with typhoid) or a community emergency (the day when the caterers didn't turn up for sports day or when the street flooded).

(*c*) Think of two situations which you handled well and two which you handled less well (or even downright badly).

Write down the situations and ask

yourself the following questions about (*b*) and (*c*):

★ How much of the original crisis was really due to me (probably the one consistent factor)?
★ What abilities did I use, or fail to use, that contributed to the final situation?
★ Did I stop and think or did I just dash into action?
★ Did I deal with the other people well or badly?
★ Did I keep calm, keep my head and generally behave creditably? Or the reverse?
★ Was I clear about what needed to be done to resolve the situation? Did I do it?

3 COMPARISONS

Your potential employer will compare you with other applicants when he's trying to decide who should be offered the job. Never show off but never underrate yourself with that misleading, exasperating British understatement that should have disappeared with Ealing films.

This exercise is to help put yourself in perspective. You will impress an interviewer if you can give him reasons why you believe you are good at certain things – especially if you *sound* objective. To practise, write down your best abilities or achievements (not necessarily business ones) and try to give some reason for claiming them. For instance:

What are you good at?
'I'm very good at organizing things.'

'I'm good at putting people at their ease.'

'I play tennis well.'

How can you tell?
'I'm always asked to take charge of the school jumble sale and the Oxfam sponsored walk.'
'Hostesses always put me with difficult guests; people pour out their problems to me.'
'I was second in the local club tournament, although none of us was tried for the county.'

4 GET A FRIEND TO HELP

If you can't think of anything you're good or bad at and never got near club tennis standard in anything, two kind but candid and objective friends may help. Don't ask how they see you as a person but whether they would hire you and, if so, what for and why, and what evidence are they using for their judgement.

5 THE QUESTIONNAIRE

Now complete (in pencil, so you can rub it out) the questionnaire on pages 116–17, put a cross in the appropriate column and rate yourself on each ability. Give yourself:

A rating of 1: if you think you are bad.
A rating of 2: if you think you are rather below average.
A rating of 3: if you think you're comfortably average.
A rating of 4: if you think that you are rather above average.
A rating of 5: if you think you rate amongst the top 10 per cent of people you know.

Jot down in your notebook one good proof of anything that you seem very good or very bad at (the 'How you can tell' column). It's as important to see your weaknesses as it is to know your strengths and use them.

	YOUR TALENTS	Assess yourself on this 5-point scale				
		1	2	3	4	5
1	Your ability to understand rules, procedures (e.g. income tax)					
2	Your ability to understand ideas					
3	Your ability to be analytical					
4	Your ability to be constructive, think of alternative courses of action					
5	Your ability to interpret facts and ideas to others					
6	Your ability to see new opportunities					
7	Your willingness to try new ways of doing things					
8	Your creative and innovative ability with ideas and methods					
9	Your ability to understand and work with figures					
10	Your ability to understand and work with words, rather than figures					
11	Your ability to express yourself by: (a) talking					
	(b) writing					
12	Your ability to organize: (a) things					
	(b) events					
	(c) people					
13	Your ability to plan, to draw up a realistic timetable					
14	Your ability to keep things tidy					
15	Your ability to make friends					
16	Your ability to keep friends					
17	Your ability to listen genuinely to others					
18	Your ability to talk and express what you have to say, simply and clearly					
19	Your ability to amuse and entertain others					
20	Your ability to make life interesting for other people					
21	Your ability to make things run smoothly, get people to work together					
22	Your ability to persuade people to do things that they don't want to do (whether it's eating spinach or paying a debt)					
23	Your ability to assess how people will behave and react					
24	Your ability to support and protect people (loyalty)					

PROFILE

YOUR TALENTS	Assess yourself on this 5-point scale				
	1	2	3	4	5
5 Your ability to face tricky situations, to discuss constructively 'difficult subjects'					
6 Your ability to lead people					
7 Your ability to work on your own					
8 Your ability to work with a group					
9 Your ability to put others' needs first					
10 Your ability to accept responsibility: (a) for yourself					
(b) for things					
(c) for other people					
11 Your conscientiousness					
12 Your punctuality					
13 Your ability to resolve a nasty, simmering situation even if it means having a row					
14 Your ability to be flexible: to change direction, change opinions, change your habits					
15 Your self-reliance: (a) in making arrangements					
(b) in forming your own opinions					
(c) in making your own decisions					
16 Your ability to be a self-starter, to do something on your own initiative, by yourself					
17 Your ability to keep a place clean					
18 Your ability to maintain order and follow routine					
19 Your ability to keep to agreed plans					
20 Your ability to work hard, with concentration					
21 Your physical ability to work long hours, if need be					
22 Your persistence and tenacity					
23 Your ability to overcome obstacles					
24 Your ability to reach high standards					
25 Your ability to get facts right					
26 Your ability to finish a job properly (that last vital heave)					

To see your ability profile, join the crosses together with a pencil. It's surprising to see the highlights (the 5s) of what you have to sell. On no account show it to any employer because you don't want him to notice what you're bad at.

YOUR JOB-SHOPPING LIST
(how *you* can assess *them*)

By now you should know whether you want a full-time or part-time paid job (40 per cent of the British female labour force works part time; there's a lot of it about) or an unpaid serious outside interest (the WVS or badminton). You can decide whether you want to work inside or outside your home and whether or not you need further training or to be trained from scratch. So, if you feel like it, draw up your job-shopping list (see opposite). Use the list whether you're taking your first job, changing your job or going back to work after a break.

Let your eye wander idly down it and then jot in your notebook:

1 What is ideal.
2 What is acceptable.
3 How important this is to you: very important, not much or not at all.

For instance, when considering how many hours a day you want to work, what is *ideal* might be two hours, what is *acceptable* might be five hours and this is *very important* because you want to get things ship-shape at home before everyone comes rushing back after work. Or perhaps instead of 5 à 7 you prefer matinées.

Having sorted the job list out, *don't indulge your prejudices*, which are undoubtedly as deep-rooted as the corns on your little toes. Check for any twinges such as:

★ I won't work for a woman
★ I won't work outside the centre of town
★ I won't work where there isn't central heating

★ I won't work in a dingy office
★ I won't work for charities/schools/doctors/accountants/salesmen
★ Routine office work is boring
★ And so on

When you get your job, you can use this list to check that all important points are covered in your contract or letter of employment. Never, never take a job without one or the other, dated and signed. Never, never assume that you will get *one item* that isn't in the letter or contract – not a tea mug or a telephone, not a desk or use of the office bicycle, let alone a place in the car park.

If, at a later date, you want to argue about what was agreed and what wasn't, you will need:

1 A letter or contract of employment (the employer is legally required to give you a written statement of certain of the most important terms in your contract of employment within thirteen weeks).
2 A written job description from your employer.
3 A clear, written statement of the company policies on pay, promotion, training and benefits. Many large firms deal with these things in an employees' handbook.

HOW TO LOOK FOR A JOB

1 *Look everywhere*: Job centres; PER; National Advisory Centre on Careers for Women; advertisements in national daily and weekly, local, specialist and trade press; billboards. (The more precise your ability profile is, the more you'll be able to look in the right places.)

JOB SHOPPING LIST

WORKING CONDITIONS
Hours of work:
  per day
  per week
  shifts
  overtime

JOURNEY TO WORK
Time
Convenience
Cost

HOLIDAYS PAID
Extra time off permitted unpaid

REWARDS
Pay
Pay increases
Pension
Other financial benefits
Sick pay
Luncheon vouchers
Medical treatment
Perks, such as expense account or company car
Chances of advancement in job
Chances of promotion

ENVIRONMENT
Nearness to shops, lunch places, recreation (park, swimming-pool)
Attractive surroundings
Cleanliness
Orderliness
Attractiveness
Quietness of place of work
Warmth/coolness

JOB SATISFACTION
Does it use your training/qualifications?
Is it in an area in which you are already experienced?
Is it in an area that might interest you?
Is training offered on the job?

Will you be using your mind?
Might it be boring?

RELATIONSHIPS WITH PEOPLE
Sort of work-group (working alone; small group; large group; changing situation)
Your position in the group
Skills with people that you would use
Opportunities for developing your social life

HOW YOUR BOSS BEHAVES
Delegates a lot
Delegates little
Gives you precise instructions
Works closely with you
Leaves you on your own
Expects total devotion at all times

STRESSES AND CHALLENGES
Job security
Fair appraisal and promotion
Range of jobs to tackle
Meeting challenges, deadlines
Maintaining accuracy

DEGREE OF RESPONSIBILITY
For others
For equipment
For safety, security
For the firm's money

PEACEFULNESS, RESTFULNESS
Routine
Excitement
Travel possibilities

MOTIVATION
Job seems to be valuable/useful
Job is in line with your conviction or beliefs
Job is in line with your long-term objectives

Write to any organization that particularly interests you and ask if it has any suitable jobs and can send you some literature (enclose a S.A. *large* E.). You may get an interview and you may get filed as someone to bear in mind for a future job. One large insurance company recently ceased recruiting from universities when it discovered that better-quality candidates were applying *direct* to headquarters.

2 You can also advertise yourself in the local paper.

3 *Read advertisements carefully.* Don't apply if you're obviously hopeless in a major requirement (e.g. profound knowledge of company law). But don't be deterred if you're somewhat too old or somewhat underqualified.

4 *Always have a go* at what looks possible. Norman Page (who organizes courses at Manchester University for women returning to employment) says that women are too timid when applying, because they fear failure. Men have become more accustomed to it, right from the first time they asked a girl to dance and she said no, with a bored look.

5 *Don't be frightened of failure.* Of course you won't get every job you apply for. You mustn't think that it's all a big competition: it's more important to try to match yourself with a suitable job. You may enchant your interviewer but still not seem the most suitable person for that particular job.

6 *Use every application and every* *interview* to learn how to present yourself, how to describe your experiences and what sort of questions you're likely to be asked next time. Undergraduates sometimes try to be interviewed by all the relevant potential employers who visit their university, just to get this sort of practice.

7 *Remember* that it often takes quite a few jobs *to find out what you don't want*: an incessant telephone; an inconvenient journey to work (not necessarily long, but three changes of bus in twenty minutes); working for more than one boss (neither of whom will agree who is the more important); sitting alone all day in a room with only a filing cabinet for company.

8 Before you go to an interview, it's as well to write a list of what you want and what you don't want. (Use the job-shopping list.) You may then remember to check all the things you *do* want and not agree to conditions that you *don't* want ('Some of the keener staff sometimes work through the lunch hour').

FIRST, TRY YOUR JOB CENTRE

Whether you want training or a job you should find a similarly encouraging attitude. Job centres are now pleasant places to visit, in fact some of them look like international hotel lounges – a very different image to the old-fashioned labour exchanges that they are replacing.

There's a self-service system from which you can pick a selection of jobs. Having selected one, you go to the Job centre receptionist, who will arrange a job interview for you or, if you would like job guidance, he can make an appointment with a trained employment adviser. He can also introduce you to the occupational guidance officer, if you don't know exactly what sort of job you want and would like to talk it over with two trained assessors.

If you need special training the occupational guidance officer can direct you to one of the marvellous free TOPS training courses. TOPS will train almost anyone – or retrain them. There are over 600 TOPS courses and if they haven't got the one you want, then they'll consider paying for you to take it elsewhere.

Many of the women training in TOPS are middle-aged mothers who want a new, more exciting job with an absorbing future and the chance to make more cash. The government wants to encourage such women to train for decent jobs – or better jobs, if they are already working.

You will be *paid while you train*. At time of writing the amount varies from £25.70 to £41.80 a week *tax free* plus perks that can include fares or petrol allowance, midday meal allowance and allowances for dependents if you have them (a non-earning husband can qualify as a dependent). This may mean that while you're training you can afford to pay *somebody else* to look after your home.

Depending on what training you choose, the course can last from three weeks to a year. Previous qualifications may be useful but they're not necessary. You just have to take a simple little entrance test to check that you can read, etc.

Many women take a TOPS secretarial course either as a refresher course to get a senior version of

their current job or because they know they'll probably always get a well paid job as a secretary or personal assistant with hours to suit themselves.

Many women take a TOPS course because they're bored by their present job. Perhaps a filing clerk wants to be a plumber, or start silversmithing, or repairing grandfather clocks or taming lions. A secretary who had to move to the country with her husband took an accountancy course so that she could travel round different farms (as it suited her) doing their book-keeping.

Once trained, such ladies have no problem getting customers. Housewives especially flock to any woman who starts to operate in the traditional male rip-off areas. Anyone who has failed to understand how half an hour's work can result in such a huge bill might be delighted to employ a female television repairer, electrician, plumber or garage mechanic.

Women are also becoming lorry drivers, they are welding on Clydeside, doing construction work and many other of the traditional male jobs that, surprisingly, don't need much strength. If you can carry two shopping bags (especially when pregnant) you can certainly operate a fork-lift truck or bull-dozer (really exciting work this) and do it sitting down. And, of course, you must legally be paid a man's wage for it.

Once you have paid enough Class 1 National Insurance contributions you qualify for unemployment benefit should you be sacked. You get some unemployment benefit as soon as you have paid in the equivalent of twenty-five times the lowest weekly contribution (currently £1.14), and have full unemployment benefit when you have paid in the equivalent of fifty times the lowest weekly con-tribution. It might be better to sit at home being paid for it, than just sit at home.

If you want a professional, techni-cal, scientific or managerial job go to PER (Professional and Executive Recruitment). Some people claim to have found PER inefficient, but it finds as many jobs for people as do private agencies. PER has a computer-operated system to select the sort of jobs that you might care to take. They have over 20,000 vacancies including overseas jobs, in the Middle East and the Near East. Again, if you need a special training course, PER may well have one or find one for you.

PER will also present you to pros-pective employers and tell you what salary you should be asking for. They also publish a useful employment market review called *Reward* that comes out three times a year. You can flip through it at a PER office or get your local library to obtain it.

No charge is made to you by TOPS, PER or Job centres.

PRIVATE AGENCIES AND ADVISERS

There are also old-established groups that for years have specialized in employment for women. If you have unusual problems and can't get a job in your area through Job centres, private agencies or answering adver-tisements in newspapers, technical magazines or on notice-boards, you might like to write to one of the fol-lowing organizations for *advice only* on getting a job in your area:

National Advisory Centre on Careers for Women, 251 Brompton Road, London SW3 2HB (☎ 01-589 9237), who are kind, understand-ing and very, very helpful.

The Over-40 Association for Women Workers, Grosvenor Gardens House, Grosvenor Gardens, Lon-don SW1W 0BS (☎ 01-828 2867).

The Over-50s Club Ltd, Mark House, The Square, Lightwater, Surrey GU18 5SS (☎ Bagshot [0276] 74622). This club also has some useful ideas in its inexpensive booklet *Second Careers and Part Time Jobs*.

Success After Sixty (the emphasis here is on office staff), 49 King Street, Manchester M2 7AY (☎ 061-832 7637) and 14 Great Castle Street, London W1N 8JU (☎ 01-580 8932).

Age Concern run regional employ-ment agencies through a number of their branches, so check with your local Age Concern branch.

WHEN A JOB GOES WRONG

Industrial Tribunals hear cases concerned with equal pay, redun-dancy, unfair dismissal, sex discrimination, racial discrimination, contracts of employment and other aspects of employees' rights (but not racial discrimination in Northern Ireland because the Race Relations Act doesn't apply there).

To find out whether you have a case on any specifically woman's issue (particularly the first four of that lot) read *Rights for Women* by Patricia Hewitt (published by the National Council for Civil Liberties).

You can find out how to appeal to a tribunal from:

★ Your local Citizens Advice Bureau (CAB)
★ The National Council for Civil Liberties (NCCL)
★ The Child Poverty Action Group (CPAG)
★ The Equal Pay and Opportunities Campaign (EPOC)
★ The Patients Association
★ A lawyer under the legal aid scheme.

To bring a case before an Industrial Tribunal, get form IT1 (called the Originating Application) from an employment exchange or Job centre or CAB.

You write a brief description of your case and send it to your nearest Industrial Tribunal (ask where it is when you collect the form).

The Tribunal will send a copy of your application to your employer. The employer has to respond, within fourteen days, with a form IT3 (Notice of Appearance) stating whether he is going to contest your claim and, if so, on what grounds. A copy of this IT3 is sent to you.

What happens at a tribunal? Industrial Tribunals are formal affairs although less so than a court of law.

You should try to get help to present your case, though you can represent yourself. Ask your trade union official or go to a solicitor who operates the green-form scheme (cheap, government-subsidised legal advice).

In Northern Ireland the Law Society has a scheme for providing free, or partly free, advice.

Otherwise, you can't get free legal representation before a Tribunal under legal aid, but a CAB may be able to get help for you from the Free Representation Unit, 3 Middle Temple Lane, London EC4Y 9AA. You must go to a CAB or law centre for this help, you can't apply to the Free Representation Unit direct.

The hearing may go roughly like this.

The person bringing the case is the Applicant, the party that's being accused of bad behaviour is called the Respondent and either of them can have a legal representative, instead of speaking for themselves. The Tribunal itself consists of a legally qualified chairman and two lay assessors.

1 The Applicant speaks first. She gives her address and occupation, then presents her case. She is then questioned by the members of the Tribunal and by the Respondent.
2 The Applicant may call witnesses, who can also be questioned by the Tribunal and the Respondent, and produce documents.
3 The Respondent then puts his case and calls his witnesses.
4 The Respondent and any of his witnesses can be questioned by the Tribunal or the Applicant.
5 The Respondent can make a final speech, summarizing his case.
6 The Applicant can make a final speech, summarizing her case.

7 The Tribunal discusses the case in private (the Applicant and Respondent may have to leave the room while this goes on).
8 The Tribunal gives its decision in public and both sides are entitled to know the reasons for the verdict.

ILLNESS OR INJURY COMPENSATION

A medical board assesses the effects of any injury you have suffered due to work (accident or disease). They also assess disablement pensions or gratuities; special hardship allowances; unemployability supplements; death benefits.

The local insurance officer then makes an award, based on the findings of the medical board.

To get your case heard, go to the local Department of Health and Social Security office (ask at your local CAB or library or post office for the address) or ask your doctor for the correct medical form, and fill in part 3, which is on the back.

SOME USEFUL ADDRESSES

Central Office of Industrial Tribunals England and Wales, 93 Ebury Bridge Road, London SW1W 8RE (☎ 01-730 9161).

Central Office of Industrial Tribunals Scotland, St Andrew House, 141 West Nile Street, Glasgow G1 2RU (☎ 041-331 1601).

Central Office of Industrial Tribunals Northern Ireland, Bedford House, 16–22 Bedford Street, Belfast BT2 7NR (☎ Belfast [0232] 27666).

The changing shape of marriage

The only thing that can be said with authority about marriage is that never before have so many people been studying it. Sometimes a lot of expensive research results in the discovery of something that any sensible woman could have told you in two minutes, sometimes the findings are surprising.

In Britain, the National Marriage Guidance Council says that the most causes of breakdown in normal marriages used to be:

1 In-law trouble
2 Money
3 Children

Now they are:

1 Desertion (or threatened desertion)
2 Sexual problems
3 Money

The Establishment has been forced to re-examine its attitude to marriage. The Church of England's Wedding Service Report, published in 1975, is more realistic about marriage, emphasizing that it is 'for mutual society, help and comfort and that the enjoyment of sexuality is not a grudging concession for the avoidance of sin and fornication'.

Nevertheless, marriage seems to be going out of fashion for the young. The figures have been dropping steadily since 1972, while the divorce figures have been zooming up. There is now one divorce to every three marriages (statistically that's either you or one of the neighbours).

The peak periods for divorce are before the family is established in the first decade of marriage, and then again after the first twenty years.

Statistically there is a great risk of marital breakdown in the forty-to-fifty age group. One study of marital satisfaction showed that companionship and affection were highest in the first four years of marriage and fell to a low point when the children were in their late teens. If this middle-years period was survived, companionship increased with retirement.

Some marriages are good, some are

bad and most, like the curate's egg, are good in parts. This has always been so. But one reason that the divorce rate may be going up so fast is that today you get a lot more marriage than your ancestors did.

Marital expert Dr Jack Dominian says that we haven't learned to cope with longevity in marriage. In Jane Austen's time all those neat marriages, on a firm financial basis, lasted an average of fifteen years, because people died very young. By 1911 the average marriage lasted twenty-eight years, but now that we are all living longer a marriage might last fifty years, if you don't divorce. It can be hard to keep up conversation after the 10,000th breakfast egg.

We have not learned to cope with some of the marital situations that our grandparents never knew. Two of the most obvious disaster areas for the middle-income groups are the Commuter Scene and the Company Executive Scene.

THE COMMUTER SCENE

Together, a couple choose a lovely country home with grass and trees. Husband commutes long hours to hectic, exhausting job in order to pay for it. High spot of wife's uneventful day is his evening return. This gets later and later and less predictable. He becomes increasingly tired and perhaps drinks more. Reproachful looks and burnt dinners dissolve into sour resentment and no dinner. Counter-resentment from husband under strain adds to collapse of the television-margarine-ad myth.

THE COMPANY EXECUTIVE SCENE

The other disaster-prone situation is when both partners start by being ambitious for him, but the wife quickly learns that the first rule of business is women and children last. She is expected to sympathize with his exhaustion because of jet-lag, expenses-luncheon-lag and entertaining - Arabs - at - the - Playboy - Club - lag. Her plans are often changed or cancelled at the last minute and she only sees him to eat scampi on her best behaviour at dreadful business

dinner parties. And perhaps the man who is Top God in the office doesn't like being expected to be human at home.

Some such women live with a quiet despair that is labelled 'depression', while others show a noisy despair often called 'nagging'. This bitterness and frustration can often seem irrational. Sometimes the bewildered husband doesn't understand her problem, sometimes he doesn't want to understand her problem, he is doggedly, enduringly, silent as part of his private survival blueprint.

One study showed that in such situations the children felt the lack of a father and wives felt a lack of shared life and support. Some of the wives got emotional support from the other wives, in place of their husbands, some of them couldn't cope, became unstable, took to tranquillizers and other drugs or tried to commit suicide.

Another study showed that the company executive wives who survive are either unusually placid ones, or the fiercely supportive ones who are ambitious at one remove and want to be the chairman's wife. The ones who can't take it are those who want companionship or intelligent women who resent being left with only the chores of marriage in exchange for giving up their girlhood/job/career ambitions.

CHANGING EXPECTATIONS

In both these situations, if the wife doesn't want the marriage to collapse, she may have to change her expectations, and so may he.

Sometimes, gradually over the years, both husband *and* wife change their minds about what they want. She wants what he's had and he wants what she's had.

A wife in her thirties may feel that she's losing her looks and her youth (and possibly her mate) while being tied to the home; she may be jealous of her mate having fun outside it. By the time she reaches her forties she may wish that she had spent more time in achieving something for herself, as well as a happy family (she feels this even more if the family *isn't* happy).

She may re-start the development of her own personality and find new, absorbing interests; or she may start to blame her partner for her seeming lack of success in life ('He held me back.', 'He didn't encourage me.', 'If it hadn't been for him . . .').

She may use her partner as a personal lightning rod to externalize her frustration. So long as she can blame the unhappiness and boredom of life on somebody else then she need not change her ways. Stale mate. But if a woman blames her husband for all her problems and failures and they divorce, her problems won't then disappear. She may even get a *new* set of problems (especially with a new mate). She still won't find the Real Her that she's hoping for until *she* stops wasting the only life she's got and starts doing things *for* herself and *by* herself. That is the road to self-confidence and self-respect.

It is often in her forties that a woman steps into the world again. On the other hand, a husband in his forties may want to retreat from it. He may feel that *he's* losing his looks and his youth (and possibly his job). He may resent being tied to the treadmill of work and regret that he chased after material goals instead of enjoying his own family. (Too late now, those magic Weetabix days are gone for ever and the children have beards.)

Another study of marriage expectations showed changes of needs in different phases. In the early years (up to age thirty), people valued love, understanding, mutual interest and respect. In the main child-rearing decade (thirty to forty) they valued teamwork, compatibility and mutual interests. Once forty-five was passed they settled for give-and-take, honesty, faithfulness, and absence of nagging, bullying and selfishness.

As you can see, the trend is for people to settle for less, to accept what they've got instead of what they were led to expect.

Many of the more realistic younger generation already know the differences between the myths and the facts of traditional marriage, which they find bogus. They are experimenting with different sorts of partnerships that are less pretentious and demanding. They are rethinking what they want of a permanent mutually supportive relationship – which is now their aim instead of marriage. They are guardedly groping for a new form of mating where it will be possible to keep the promises you make, because the promises won't be so impossibly

ambitious. (In other words, they still want marriage, but they're changing the name and the rules.)

Many of them are experimenting (more seriously than their elders give them credit for) with different relationships in communal living and in 'open' marriage, where neither partner promises sexual exclusivity.

Some of these relationships amount to trial marriages and can lead to a traditional marriage with children; sometimes they are short-term relationships, which are recognized as short but exclusive and important passages in the life of both partners (statistically the *average* life of an American marriage is seven years).

What's needed may turn out to be something more than living together but different to marriage. Perhaps there will be more 'contract' marriages (perhaps legally binding, perhaps for short-term relationships, with an optional, renewable five- or ten-year lease, or a longer lease if children are planned).

Undoubtedly the young of both sexes now know and understand more about the aims and feelings of the other. But although there's been a burst of publicity about the wicked indoctrinating shackles that the liberated woman has to burst asunder, not many people point out that men were also indoctrinated with similarly false (but different) expectations.

The big shift of emphasis in recent years seems to be that many modern men are now seeing marriage and the family as a much *bigger* part of their total existence while women are seeing it as not the *only* part.

Dr Dominian says that marriage is no longer needed for material and social security, but there is now more stress on personal development. Our requirements of a partner have definitely changed and this may be a good thing. 'We should see marital breakdown as the grinding of the gears as humanity changes up from one gear to another.' In other words, it may be a necessary part of our transition; analysis, experiment and rethinking that may lead to an improved society.

Dominian says that the ideal mate might now have his virtues listed in the following order:

1 Someone to help you develop your own interests and to encourage you to use your own talents; not someone that's going to be jealous and subtly sabotage them.
2 Someone to give encouragement and moral support.
3 Someone to help resolve your problems, both practical and emotional.
4 Someone you can talk to on a permanent basis. Someone you really care about, and whom you can trust.
5 Someone who will talk to you.
6 Someone to comfort you and quietly understand how you feel when Fate deals you this month's kick in the teeth.
7 Someone to totter into the sunset with.

A modern marriage is successful to the degree that both partners can give and receive this sort of emotional support. If two people marry and both are incapable of giving each other these things, then the marriage will fail.

Doctors Rhona and Robert Rapoport, who study family relationships, have some practical factors that add to the chances of a happy marriage. They are:

1 When a wife has a firm interest outside the home. Surprisingly, this makes it easier for a couple to communicate. The Rapoports found that in dual-career families the rows were not about emotional problems but practical difficulties.
2 When the husband has a job that doesn't exhaust him and doesn't prevent him playing his major part in his own home and family.
3 Personal privacy (perhaps a separate room each, not necessarily a bedroom). It's sometimes hard to remember what privacy was, after the last plastic duck has bitten the dust and the last football boot has been given to Oxfam.
4 When a husband and wife have a strong, shared interest. Anything from looking after his mother to dinghy sailing.
5 When a couple arrange to spend a reasonable amount of enjoyable, quiet time together with no one else around.

It's important to re-check these things in Midlife, because a relationship of two often has to be relearned after the busy years of bringing up a family.

You may want these qualities from your mate:

1 Someone to talk with when you get home.

2 Someone to care for.

3 Someone who cares about you.

4 Someone who provides company and friendship.

5 Someone who is interested in what you have been doing.

6 Someone to do things with.

7 Someone to share experiences with.

8 Someone to share expenses with.

9 Someone to share responsibilities with.

10 Someone who helps you keep things in perspective.

11 Someone with whom you can be grumpy and behave badly

12 Someone who stops you being selfish.

In fact, the situation may *not* be different.

Perhaps it is the same.

UT OF THE MARRIAGE

*en a relationship is soured by selfishness, these virtues may look very
ferent, for instance:*

Someone you have to listen to when you get home.

Someone you always have to worry about.

Someone who demands that you look after them.

Someone who insists you're always with him.

Someone who always wants to know where you've been, what you've been
doing and who with.

Someone you can't do anything without.

Someone you can't get away from.

Someone who wants money.

Someone who demands more and more of you.

Someone who constantly nags and criticizes.

Someone who only sees your bad side.

Someone who takes you for granted.

1aps it is your attitude that has changed.

LOVE ON THE ROCKS

The Church still thinks adultery is wrong, but many people think it's impossible to avoid and a few think it's unimportant.

If infidelity rears its ugly head in your marriage, it is important that you accept that there *are* affairs in marriage and that they don't necessarily mean the end of a marriage or personal rejection.

The really happily married rarely have love affairs partly because it's all such a sweat, it's too much trouble. Those bitter-sweet moments involve so many lies, such organization, the split-second timing of a commando raid and possible discomfort (back of the car, an impersonal borrowed flat). But there may be an indiscretion or two – the overnighter at a boozy business conference is all too easy.

How badly you feel if you discover that your mate is unfaithful is likely to depend on how you find out, the state of your marriage, the age of your children, with whom he's unfaithful and where and how he treats you while the affair is in progress. Whether the situation is handled successfully or not depends on whether the underlying reason for the affair is fully recognized and taken into account by the other marital partners.

Realistically, the two times when adultery is most likely to occur are early in the marriage or in middle age when a man becomes anxious about his looks, his sexual and business performance, all of which may be not as high as he had hoped.

A woman may also feel disappointed by life and she, too, may be frightened that her looks are fading, and that her future romantic opportunities will be few. Some women look for romance rather than sex, most men want the reverse. It is at this point that either of them might plunge into a passionate, disastrous love affair, which may rock a marriage, if not end it.

The main rocks are:

Rock 1: For rejuvenation and reassurance at the anxious time of menopause.

Rock 2: For the irresistible thrill of a series of spicy liaisons. You don't have just one of these little ego-boosters, you start a series.

Rock 3: For the terrific stimulation and thrill of a new pursuit, a new quarry; an exciting clandestine adventure; a glamorous, secret, irresponsible interlude in ordinary life.

Rock 4: To escape from some state of contained hostility in the marriage.

Rock 5: Relief from absence. If you go away for long periods (or he does) then you must expect that your partner might have affairs (and perhaps you will).

Rock 6: Friendship combined with opportunity.

Rock 7: A surprise to both the lovers.

There's a big difference between 'a love affair' and 'sleeping with other people'. A full-scale *love* affair can be far more threatening and hard to handle than the activities of a compulsive philanderer. A philanderer's compulsion can be almost like that of an alcoholic and it can be coupled with a real terror of losing his wife.

An illicit relationship that develops into love is never, in itself, entirely satisfactory because it cannot be a *complete* relationship. This can fragment the people concerned. In such a situation both wife and mistress are denied the full role of a loving partner, which is what a human being always wants if he or she really loves someone. This is the situation that really threatens a marriage (or two, three or four).

The experts at holding a marriage together in rocky situations are traditionally the French, traditionally supported by Church and Law. As the Roman Catholic Church doesn't recognize divorce, the wife, the husband, the lover and the mistresses concerned all know where they stand.

Nobody's basic security is threatened and nobody can build on false assumptions or hold out false prospects. There is something to be said for such a steady system, which allowed for the reality of marriage, as opposed to the myth. Certainly, the best sexually loving relationship may be when you are madly in love with your life's partner and never tempted by anyone else but not everyone seems able to perpetuate this state for forty years or more.

French women grow up knowing that, on principle, the sensible way to treat infidelity may be to turn a blind eye to it, on the understanding that they miss out as little as possible in every other department.

This attitude may be a very sensible way to handle Rocks 1, 2, 5, 6 and 7. Current counselling on Rock 3 tends to be on the lines: 'Remind him that you are *many* women in one: romantic girl, tempestuous gipsy, tempting sexpot, and so on.' Dressing up can be successful, surprising and intriguing when the marriage is happy, but if it isn't, then glistening black thigh boots and matching corselet are about as much use as Elastoplast on a broken leg (and possibly far more embarrassing).

If you've never seriously considered the possibility of your mate's infidelity what are your feelings likely to be if you find out that it has happened? Possibly some of the following:

★ Shock and disbelief.
★ A surge of possessiveness and jealousy.
★ Shame and humiliation: you are taking second place to someone else and someone else is taking your first place.
★ A sudden lack of security and self-confidence.
★ Rage, because you are being deceived, humiliated and made to lose face (it's *much* worse if other people know).
★ The theft of emotions that you thought were yours: affection, attention, concern and interest and FUN.
★ Material deprivation: you may feel cheated – and of course you always are – of your mate's time and money, the presents, the treats, the trips that go to *her*.
★ Indignation: especially if you had sympathized about all that overtime, the smoke-filled conferences, those boring, exhausting, long business lunches.
★ Indignation and mystification if the enigmatic She looks like the back of a bus (although you would feel much worse if she didn't).
★ Despair if she's younger than you and prettier.
★ Physical disgust, especially if

you're pregnant or he's old enough to be her father.

★ The nagging need to compare yourself to her, to know more about her, to understand how it could possibly have happened and what she's got that you haven't got.

★ An odd nakedness. He must have talked to this other person about you. The enigmatic She knows your little shared secrets.

What now makes the situation worse is that an unfaithful mate is no beauty treatment. Doubtless the enigmatic She is blooming like a peach, whereas *you* look a drained, pale, hopeless harpy. You can almost understand why he wants to leave you as, despondently, you peer in the mirror.

The depth, intensity and duration of these feelings will depend on how much of a two-faced, old-fashioned cad he's been and whether it's a serious threat or a single indiscretion at the conference ('There she was, lying naked in my hotel room. What else could I do?').

Your feelings will also depend on how you find out, what his reactions are when he finds out that you have found out, whether this happens accidentally or because someone else tells you or because She does. Worst of all is if he tells you himself, perhaps simply to hurt, or (really unforgiveable) to clear his conscience of pain and guilt or because he loves her and wants to tell the whole world, shout exultantly from the rooftops, at the price of your peace of mind. It's not so bad if he's telling you because his infidelity is about to be denied in the House of Commons.

If his or your reasons are variations of Rocks 3 and 4 then you may benefit from marriage counselling. The National Marriage Guidance Council is not a bad place to start. Its counsellors are far more realistic and experienced than your girlfriends and can refer you to experts if they feel that you need more help than they can give.

If his attitude is that it wasn't serious, then you had better explain that, to you, it is. It is not just 'a bit of fun' if it swipes away your trust in him.

If it slowly dawns on you that he's having affairs and he *likes* it and he doesn't give a damn about anyone knowing it, then you may find yourself coming to terms with his behaviour.

You start by giving an inch.

'I don't mind if it's not in England.' (Adultery begins at Calais.)

'I don't mind so long as it's not here in Reigate' (or wherever you live).

'I don't mind so long as it's not with my friends.'

'I don't care so long as it's not with my *best* friend.'

'I don't care so long as he doesn't make passes at my sister.'

'I don't care so long as he keeps away from the au pair.'

'I don't care so long as it's not in my bed.'

This is a basic reaction to philandering behaviour. You decide whether you're going to put up with it (and, if so, how?) or not (and, if so, what?). Your decision may well depend on your children, your social position, your home comforts, your present prospects if you stay, the grey uncertainty if you leave.

What if he announces that he wants to leave you? Either one of you gives way or you both stay and fight it out. Whatever happens, DON'T LEAVE

YOUR HOME, whether or not you want a divorce. If you choose to fight it out, your basic attitude might be to make life more agreeable if he stops his present behaviour and more disagreeable if he doesn't.

When such crises strike, the women who keep their men and rescue their marriage are not always the ones who behave with quiet dignity and acceptance – far from it! What often seems to happen to well-behaved ladies is that he leaves faster, with a free conscience and every expectation that she will be equally understanding about any maintenance.

The women who keep their husbands and steer round the rocks and finally reach the calm waters of the bay, often seem to be the ones who fight like tigers protecting their cubs.

SUCCESSFUL RESCUE NO. 1

Shortly after her fortieth birthday, an accountant's wife with three sons was told that her husband intended to marry someone else. For years she had scrimped and saved and bought her clothes second-hand for the benefit of his career. She sat tight. She didn't raise her voice or throw a thing. But she threw him out immediately, changed the locks (a locksmith will do it in an hour for a £10 tip) and within a couple of weeks she had a replacement, the rich, faithful, friend of the family who'd been around for years. The lover gave her sables for her birthday.

She telephoned her bank manager, just to keep him in the picture; the bank manager spoke to her husband 'just to sort out adequate temporary financial arrangements for the benefit of the children'. She refused to let her husband see his children and told him

on every possible occasion how unhappy he was making *them* (not her). He quickly realized that he couldn't have his cake and eat it, that he was going to lose his human investment of the past twenty years and that starting all over again was going to mean being *back* where he started twenty years ago – only he was twenty years older. She got another family friend to spell the message out. Within weeks the husband wanted to return on any terms. She turned him down and the lover gave her a mink for Christmas (can't help it if you think fur coats are immoral, that's what she got). After three months she relented and the husband happily moved back. The mistress quickly found another accountant; the lover is still heartbroken and wouldn't accept any of the presents back.

Very nasty behaviour on her part, you may think. On the other hand you may see her as a sensible, practical mother who successfully protected her home.

SUCCESSFUL RESCUE NO. 2

Shortly after her fifty-fifth birthday the wife of a titled, rich senior civil servant was told that he wanted to remarry. Her method of defence was to attack his respectability. Such people often like a quiet life so she gave him hell, as publicly as possible. She nagged him non-stop, she rang his office constantly to check his movements, she turned up in it to ask where he was and if he wasn't there she sat weeping in front of his desk. She got the name of the Other Woman and did the same thing in *her* office. She also telephoned the Other Woman's boss, incessantly.

She cross-questioned her husband

whenever she saw him and quickly spent a great deal of money on herself from their joint account. Then every ailment she'd had in her life suddenly reappeared, and she took to her bed. Her doctor said that her health might be suffering because of such thoughtless behaviour. She persuaded her married daughter to intercede with her father; her son told him that he was a heartless bastard. Every possible relative and friend was invited to visit her and was told what a swine he was.

The husband's reaction was totally dazed, as if he'd suddenly found a dangerous dog at bay in the bathroom. You would think that these methods would have driven him straight off to the Other Woman – but then he was going anyway. Eventually he couldn't stand the thought of any more public scenes, and neither could the Other Woman, who left him after six months of the above treatment.

This method may make a man stay with his wife but it's hard to conceive how it could make him love her again or what their future relationship would be like. A more respectable approach with a basically amiable, easy-going man may be:

SUCCESSFUL RESCUE NO. 3

This wife had been married over thirty-five years and lived modestly in a cottage in the country. Her husband was an actor and had had several previous affairs, to which she had turned a blind eye. But this time he wanted to leave her. She decided it would be useless to rage or make scenes. She just quietly stuck to her guns, and made sure that she was looking good, and so was the house and that the food was perfect. Although she felt suicidal, she didn't once let it show – and she didn't threaten it. She kept her dignity (very difficult); there were no tearful scenes, no reproaches, no 'you've had the best years of my life' or 'I can't manage without you' or 'I don't want to live without you'.

She acted as normally as possible and kept telling him that although he was in love and euphoric at the moment he would, in time, feel just as bored with his new lady as he now did with his marriage. Within a year, the affair had slowly petered out.

What did these three women have in common? They didn't lose their heads. They followed a thought-out course of action based on a shrewd knowledge of their men and what they really wanted MOST.

THINKING ABOUT A SPLIT

There are plenty of reasons, apart from open adultery, why a marriage might break up but they are often more difficult to pinpoint. And in this fast-altering world the reasons seem to be changing in importance. What used to be considered normal may be intolerable and what used to be considered intolerable is not.

Midlife is a time of reassessment, not only of what is slipping from your grasp (a lot of which you probably no longer need) but also of your recent and future development. Traditionally, a couple married, started a family and she then concentrated on the children while he concentrated on his job. Ideally, their interests came together again after the children left home.

But one American study of patterns of middle-aged marriages has identified five main types. In order of frequency they were:

1 *A state of controlled conflict* in which couples were careful to avoid open rows.
2 *A devitalized marriage*, based on habit, in which couples no longer had a real interest in each other, but stuck together for convenience.
3 A marriage in which the couple were *passively content* but not important to each other.

The two smaller groups of marriage types were more cheering. They were:

4 *Couples held together by a strong, common interest* – children, work or a hobby.
5 *Couples lucky enough to have a great range of interests in common*.

Sometimes a couple grow apart simply because their interests continue to develop differently and the couple are left with nothing in common. Sometimes one personality matures much faster than the other, sometimes one partner doesn't mature at all. Mental development isn't at the same rate for everybody and this can mean that, after many years, for no particular dramatic reason and through nobody's fault, a couple may be ill-matched.

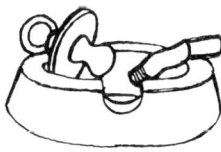

We all know cases of the tycoon with a good grasp of international affairs whose wife seemingly never listens to what he says, let alone understands it. She passively moves among his friends, mentally knitting. Sometimes she can be a bit spiteful ('We aren't good enough for your father's clever friends').

Sometimes the reverse is true and after bringing up the family a woman realizes that she is married to a man who is still emotionally adolescent.

Sometimes one partner gets fed up after twenty years of being used by the other partner to work out problems, such as unresolved emotional difficulties with a parent.

The genuine importance of the 1971 changes in the British divorce law was the recognition that it need be nobody's *fault* when a marriage breaks down. People don't stop developing when they marry and they grow at very different rates – sometimes away from each other.

On the other hand, some people seem prepared to live in what might seem to others an intolerable situation, because both parties have matured to a stage where they can accept that their partner's needs differ – sometimes drastically – from their own. One person's intolerable situation is another person's everyday life.

Unconventional situations include contented marriages and shared parenthood with homosexuals or bisexuals. Some such relationships continue as long as the wife/husband can come to terms with a mate who occasionally wants to make love to someone of his or her own sex.

Increasingly, it seems, provided that the basic relationship is valued, a woman is also prepared to put up (indulgently or otherwise) with transvestite behaviour such as frilly bras, lingerie, corsets, fishnet tights and make-up, all worn by him.

Following an article about such things, two women wrote to the *Observer* newspaper as follows:

> He is a homosexual – I knew that before I knew his name. The fact that this week I toast three very happy, fulfilling years belies a lot of the suggestions that we are dealing with the impossible . . .

> I found out that my husband was bisexual after only five months of marriage, although it should have been obvious from the start . . . We stayed together for two and a half years, probably, despite the turbulence, the happiest of my life. Our sex life was spectacularly good . . . he taught me how to enjoy myself.

Condoned sado-masochism in marriage ranges from simple bottom-spanking to the doctor who cut off his wife's toes, one by one; she filed a divorce because he wanted to remove one of her eyes (this couple have five children!). Some partners will tolerate urolagnists (peeing), coprophiliacs (shitting), and everything that *Forum* magazine has ever written about. (*Forum* has helped a lot of partners to understand deviation and put it in perspective in the context of a marriage.)

Conventional reasons for breaking up a marriage are no longer so strong; the quality of the relationship seems now to be considered far more important. With this new emphasis on relationship, some of the modern signs of a jagged marriage are not that

he slips in furtively with lipstick on his collar but when:

1 You feel lonelier when he's with you than when he's away.

2 If you're in serious trouble he's the last person you'd go to for help. You feel that he won't help you, whether or not he could.

3 You feel more constrained when he's with you than when he's out of the home. You watch your tongue more if he's there than you do with other people. You stop chatting if he enters the room.

4 The things that interest you must be cleared out of the way before he gets home and a telephone call from a friend abruptly ends as he steps inside the door. You can't behave naturally.

5 You realize that what you say to him is different from the way you act. 'Of course I care about being with you' when you arrange not to have a spare moment, in case you might be with him.

6 What *he* says to you is different from the way he acts to you.

7 You start squirrelling, almost without realizing it. You secretly save a tiny comforting bit of money in the teapot or the post office or the toe of your second-best boots (a good place). This can be a subconscious sign that you are preparing for a possible exit.

8 You don't want to discuss any real problem with him (for instance about the children's school progress or lack of it) because he will immediately criticize both you and them instead of being constructive and comforting.

9 You *can't* discuss any real problem with him. You try but for weeks he refuses to discuss it. As you talk

you get the impression that he can't *hear* what you're telling him. Or is it that he won't *listen*? Perhaps you're not putting it properly? Eventually you insist that the bills won't wait, the forms won't wait or little Polly's asthma won't wait. Perhaps you write him a note or try to discuss the problem with him via other people (his mother, brother, doctor, ex-girlfriend or man friend). They get nowhere.

Whatever way you look at it, you cannot escape the conclusion that there seems to be a breakdown in communication. Perhaps he won't communicate with you because he doesn't want the same relationship with you that you want with him. Perhaps he wants OUT.

You may go to a priest and *he* will say that if you both put each other first there will be no problem. With two totally logical, unselfish people that would indeed be so, but if that were possible in your situation, you probably wouldn't have needed to go to him in the first place. Such behaviour, if one-sided, is asking to be a doormat, a martyr or kicked in the teeth.

You might talk to your doctor, who will probably be sympathetic, who may give you tranquillizers, who may even tell you privately what he thinks of your situation. Perhaps he may hint that you must either put up with your spouse's behaviour and/or take a lover or separate. Your friends may give you the same advice in a rather more straightforward manner.

Your doctor may recommend you to a local Marriage Guidance Council or a psychiatrist or a sex counsellor. Your husband may refuse point-blank to go, until he's told (by an authority figure, not you) that this is a direct sign that he no longer wants a relationship with you (i.e. he's in the wrong). Alternatively he may go and refuse to listen to them. Or he may go and *pretend* to listen to them, in the guise of a logical, reasonable man of thought. He is unlikely to fool the marriage guidance experts: they can see through such behaviour, especially if it subtly tries to lay the blame at his partner's feet, instead of frankly discussing the situation. The NMGC say that a marital problem is not 'his' or 'hers', it's a *shared* problem.

If your partner refuses to recognize this then you have reached a sad state of non-communication in marriage and you may have to consider seriously planning a life on your own. Indeed, the decision may be forced upon you.

Naturally, the sort of bad behaviour that breaks up a marriage isn't confined to men. A wife can behave in the same sort of way for the same sort of reasons – that she's fallen madly in love, she's resentful or bored, she's got itchy feet or she sleeps around – or all of them.

WHAT TO DO WHEN YOU ARE FACED WITH A DIVORCE

Whether or not you ever consider divorce for yourself, or any friend or neighbour, you should know how to help someone who is facing it because it is now so common. Someone in a state of shock because of impending divorce may need practical help. Your neighbour probably needs no advice if she just runs her eye coolly over that grounds-for-divorce list (see later) and says, 'I'll take point 4'. But if she has suddenly been told that her husband has decided to have a point-4 divorce it can be a terrible blow, even if it wasn't exactly a surprise.

Draw up a *Practical Emergency Plan* involving, if possible, a minimum of eight calls:

Calls 1–3: Telephone three good friends and tell them briefly what's happened. One woman came back with her children from holiday to find a letter propped on the mantelpiece ('By the time you read this I shall be in Moscow') and not a penny remaining in the joint bank account. She told three key friends – a neighbour, someone in her office and her mother – to spread the news around and say that she didn't want to talk about it. She quickly had masses of support, masses of help and she had wasted little emotional energy, none of it in self-pity.

Call 4: Tell your doctor immediately. The anxiety and stress of a divorce can often make you ill without your realizing it (divorce rates second on the major-stresses-of-life list). You can suffer headaches, insomnia, pimples, boils, backache, slipped discs, high blood pressure or even a heart attack as the result of a looming divorce, so you must check on your health. You're going to need good health and vitality to get on your feet again.

Call 5: Telephone your bank manager, if you have one, and immediately tell him of your position.

Call 6: Visit your local Citizens Advice Bureau and get their Proceedings for Divorce (Form PIP). This is issued by the Family Division of the High Court.

CAB will also give you a list of solicitors in your area and they will tell you about the procedure if you decide to handle your own divorce.

Call 7: You should also immediately contact the Association for Independent Divorce which not only guides people who want to arrange their own divorce proceedings but also advises over marital breakdown and complicated litigation. They have a network of lawyers, tax consultants, doctors and welfare workers prepared to offer FREE consultations twenty-four hours a day. AID, 177 Peregrine Road, Sunbury-on-Thames, Middx TW16 6JJ (☏ Sunbury-on-Thames [093 27] 84990).

Call 8: Change the locks immediately (look in the Yellow Pages or ask the Police if you don't happen to know a locksmith). Install a peephole and a chain. You must know where you stand! He can no longer come and go as he pleases. Neither must anyone else.

YOUR HOME

If your husband leaves in any but a friendly manner, on no account leave your home *on any pretext*, or you may find that you and the children have nowhere to live.

If your husband leaves and the home is in your husband's name only, establish your right of occupation *at once* by registering a caution at the Land Registry (*see page 219*).

YOUR BUDGET

Before visiting your lawyer or bank manager, work out how much it will cost you to live. Do not guess, *check*. If you don't already know how much the family spends you will be amazed and horrified to find the total yearly sum needed to continue to live as you do.

The most important practical money step for you to take is to work out a *budget* and pay close attention to it. Check it with your bank manager.

Do your accounts monthly in future. You're in a difficult enough position as it is, without letting the bills pile up. As soon as you're sorted out, you may have a wonderful life – so long as you don't get into debt. Don't assume that your husband is responsible for paying your debts, and even if he *is*, he might not pay them.

The second most important step is to start saving. It's not so much what you're saving that counts, or how much you're saving; what's important is that you should have a tiny surplus rather than a tiny deficit.

LONELINESS

If you feel lonely and bewildered (as well you might) contact a self-help group, who will understand how you feel and may be able to help you. Contact the National Council of the Divorced and Separated, which has it's headquarters in Cambridge. The council has about sixty federated clubs throughout the UK to arrange events which people don't like to do alone – theatre, coach trips, dances.

National Council of the Divorced and Separated, 13 High Street, Little Shelford, Cambridge CB2 5ES (✆ Shelford [02204] 2544).

Association for Independent Divorce (AID), 177 Peregrine Road, Sunbury-on-Thames, Middlesex TW16 6JJ (✆ Sunbury-on-Thames [093 27] 84990).

WHERE TO GET LEGAL ADVICE

1 *The Association for Independent Divorce*, offer free legal advice (*see* Call 7 *on previous page*).

2 *Your Local Citizens Advice Bureau.* Some CABs provide free legal advice; if your local CAB doesn't, ask them to direct you to one that does. If the CAB can't help you, they can direct you to your nearest Law Centre, or give you a list of reasonable, reliable, local lawyers who operate under the Green Form Scheme. Under this scheme you can have up to £25 worth of free legal advice, depending on your means. At the time of writing, you must have less than £35 a week to spend on yourself and less than £400 in savings, to qualify for any free legal advice. The solicitor works out what you should get from tables prepared by the Law Society. (A snag for married women is that your husband's income counts as yours on this particular occasion, unless you are suing him.)

Some CABs have duty lawyers, who will see you at the CAB office. CABs provide an invaluable service by unravelling legislation for the harassed public: they can also advise you of your rights and how to enforce them. But CABs vary from place to place. Some are more efficient and cheerful and better staffed than others.

For a list of CABs that provide free legal advice (not all do) throughout Britain and of community lawyers who operate under the Law Society's Legal Aid Scheme, write to the Law Society, 113 Chancery Lane, London WC2A 1PL (✆ 01-242 1222).

3 *Neighbourhood Law Centres.* These offer bare-bones efficiency and will give you *free* legal advice. Law

Centres are intended to help people who could have real difficulty in finding or briefing lawyers so they are usually in 'less prosperous' areas. At the time of writing there are nineteen centres in London; three in Birmingham; one each in Liverpool, Cardiff, Newcastle, Doncaster and Merthyr Tydfil. They act as a sort of walk-in legal clinic and employ qualified lawyers to provide *free* legal services including preparing and presenting a case.

4 *Legal Advice Centres.* Not the same as Neighbourhood Law Centres. An Advice Centre gives you advice but cannot help you to prepare or present your case in court, or brief your solicitor.

Get an up-to-date list of Neighbourhood Law Centres and Legal Advice Centres throughout Britain from the Legal Action Group, 28a Highgate Road, London NW5 1NS (☎ 01-267 0048). The list costs 50p post paid.

5 The Legal Action Group publishes a bulletin on social and welfare law. It is a pressure group to promote better legal services, especially in deprived areas.

WHERE TO FIND A SOLICITOR

6 Write to the Law Society, 113 Chancery Lane, London WC2A 1PL (☎ 01-242 1222) and ask for a list of specialist lawyers in your area, and of lawyers operating under their legal aid scheme.

7 Look in the Yellow Pages under 'Solicitors'. Look up the lists of solicitors in the *Solicitors' Diary* in your local reference library.

8 Go to the nearest Magistrates' Court or County Court (look in the telephone directory under 'Courts') and ask for names of local solicitors.

9 Contact Rights of Women (ROW) which is a legal watchdog voluntary group of female solicitors, barristers and articled clerks who are lobbying for more equal laws for women and more equal opportunities for women in the male-dominated legal profession.

They want to hear of women's experiences (both good and bad) with the legal profession; all information is confidential.

They can send you a list of recommended lawyers throughout Britain and will answer straightforward, quick queries if you write or telephone them at 274 Gray's Inn Road, London WC1X 8BB (☎ 01-278 6349).

In marital cases, *don't* use a firm of solicitors previously used by your husband or a firm recommended by him or his solicitors. *Don't* go to a solicitor recommended by your women friends as sweet, fatherly, kind, understanding; sympathy can be very expensive. You want an experienced, efficient, ruthlessly unemotional, specialist solicitor.

Hiring a lawyer is like getting yourself a hired gun. On the whole, you want the best, fastest shot there is. No need to be unpleasant about it, you just want a quick, clean job and it's not so much that you want to be the winner, it's just that you want to make sure you're not the loser. A lawyer's aim is to win, win, win and it can't be repeated often enough.

Be cautious: self-protection should be an instinctive part of your survival kit and if it hasn't been to date, then you had better start developing it now, because you're going to need it – especially if you have children. There is no judge who knows the price of bread or shoe repairs. Never be naïve enough to assume that child maintenance will be adequate to maintain your children as they have lived to date. It will be far, far less.

You are likely to get more for your children if you use a lawyer.

Before visiting your lawyer you should know your own income and assets, if any. Check your *husband's income*, if you can, but this is quite likely to be impossible.

The first thing to ask your lawyer is how much it's going to cost. He'll probably say (at length) that he doesn't know because it depends on the work involved. Reasonable, but he is able to quote the scale of charges per hour on which his bill will be based. For his benefit as well as yours (because he wants to get paid) ask him to send you an interim note every time another hundred pounds is incurred. He should confirm in writing whatever financial arrangements you make about how much money is to be paid, for what and when.

In the case of a divorce by mutual consent (*see page 145*) you should both arrange in advance and in writing who is going to pay and how much.

Lawyers are supposed to sort things out, not stir them up. Nevertheless they can, in the course of their duties and without meaning to, cause trouble, stir up more hate than you would believe possible. A divorce is not a friendly action. Like marriage, it is a combination of sentiment and business. But whether you are getting divorced in hate or in regret, avoid sentiment at all costs (sentiment is very, very expensive).

Sentiment need not be tears and grief; it can be a determination to be civilized and unemotional, to be friendly, to incur as little unpleasantness as possible. Every divorcer probably thinks that at some time. But it is grabbing at a mirage and evading the issue. You're not bulldozing a marriage, you're clearing up the debris. It may be a very, very expensive mess for you if you let sentiment interfere for two minutes – the time it takes to lift the phone to *him* and say, 'Why can't we go out to dinner and discuss this sensibly?'

Unless you are having an in-regret divorce, unless neither of you has any possessions or children, avoid your husband until it's over. Plenty of time to be nice to him later.

It may be comforting to be in touch with your separated husband; it may be unavoidable if you live in the same home or if you have children, but it is dangerous to do so and you must remember this. Don't get in touch with him for minor practical reasons (you don't want to borrow his car that badly). In fact, once you've gone to a lawyer, don't see your husband, do not speak to your husband and, above all, do not *write* to your husband. Not so much as a postcard. Without realizing it, you might be blunting your lawyer's lance. Don't forget that the Law is not fair (as you judge 'fair'). It is just a set of rules and *you don't know them*. A simple, reasonable letter can contain twenty-four reasons per page not to send it.

Don't discuss any business aspects with your husband. That's what you have a lawyer for, like writers have an agent – to do the haggling. Remember that your husband has *studied* you, he knows exactly how to get round you. Remember that you needn't do anything that your lawyer suggests if you really don't want to.

What your lawyer expects of you is: (*a*) to pay him, (*b*) that you should sit calmly and without emotion in the chair in front of him, answer his questions clearly and provide him with the maximum evidence, (*c*) to be told the truth about your financial and sexual situation. He doesn't want any nasty surprises sprung at the trial by the other side. He won't throw up his hands and order you out of his office; he won't turn a hair; he won't tell *anything* to *anyone else*. He's heard it all before and it's not his business to judge, but to win.

Ideally, after meeting you, your lawyer would then like to lock you in a cupboard until the divorce is over, because then you can't get into any trouble that might upset the case, but few clients agree to this wise precaution.

GROUNDS FOR DIVORCE

Since the Divorce Reform Act 1969 nobody need be called 'guilty' or 'innocent' and the *sole* grounds on which a husband or wife can present a petition for divorce in England or Wales is that the marriage has broken down irretrievably. 'Adultery' and 'unreasonable behaviour' may be accepted as evidence that the marriage has broken down, but they are no longer in themselves automatic grounds for divorce.

The Divorce (Scotland) Act 1976 brought Scottish divorce laws approximately into line with the divorce laws of England and Wales with *minor* differences. Here they are:

England and Wales	**Scotland**
Ground 1	
Adultery, which is normally proved by the man and woman involved making written statements. You must also state that you find it intolerable to live with your adulterous spouse. To demonstrate this you must not have lived with him/her for more than six months (in total) after discovering the adultery.	Adultery must be proved by two witnesses not including the man or woman involved. (Their written statement is not acceptable.) You are assumed to condone your spouse's behaviour if you continue to live with him/her for more than three months after learning about the adultery.
Ground 2	
'Unreasonable' behaviour; usually interpreted as serious, actively damaging behaviour (physical and verbal cruelty; sodomy; drunkenness; unreasonable sexual demands; refusing to have sex or children).	'Unreasonable' behaviour may be passive as well as active, e.g. severe physical or mental deterioration.
Ground 3	
Desertion for at least two years. Your plea may be rejected if you live with another man or woman meanwhile.	Divorce on grounds of desertion by spouse can be accepted even if you live with another man or woman.

Ground 4
Living apart for two years continuously up to the time of the petition, provided both partners agree to a divorce.

The same.

Ground 5
Divorce after five years' separation immediately preceding the petition. One party to the marriage can obtain a divorce on this ground *without* the other's consent, unless the court finds that divorce would cause grave financial hardship and would be wrong.

Divorce after five years' separation is allowed without spouse's consent only in cases of severe financial hardship.

There are also *minor* differences in how the law is administered, as follows:

Difficult to get a divorce within three years of marrying.

You can apply for a divorce any time after you marry.

If your divorce is granted you get a decree nisi and you can apply for a decree absolute six weeks later, provided there are no outstanding financial questions or questions on the children's welfare.

Decree is granted when all questions have been settled and is immediately effective, but twenty-one days are allowed for appeal.

Orders regarding children cover custody (making the long-term decisions), and care and control (day-to-day care). They may be split, the parent with care and control sharing custody with the other parent.

One parent gets custody, care and control, the other usually has access.

Maintenance (*see page 149*).

In Scotland, maintenance is called aliment.

Northern Ireland
In Northern Ireland, divorce is still governed by the Matrimonial Causes (N.I.) Act 1939 and things are much more difficult. If you want a divorce you petition the High Court in Belfast and must prove one of the following:

1 Adultery.
2 Desertion for at least three years.

3 Cruelty (only accepted as a plea after three years of marriage).
4 Insanity for at least five years.
5 Sodomy, bestiality or rape (of the wife).

A Court in Northern Ireland can dismiss your petition if it concludes that you connived at or condoned the adultery or cruelty. An attempt at reconciliation might be interpreted this way: all that a husband need do after deserting you for three years is to say that he's sorry and pop back into bed with you and then pop off again for another three years, before repeating the performance. Of course a wife dare not risk this.

In Northern Ireland the Court can also dismiss your petition if it decides that you have colluded with your spouse to get a divorce. It will also dismiss the petition if it concludes that you are yourself guilty of adultery, desertion or delay in presenting your petition.

The only easy way to get a divorce (in England, Wales and Scotland) involves at least a two-year wait. At the end of those two years your mate may withdraw his consent which may mean waiting another three years until you qualify for the five-year/no-consent divorce.

Living apart is a relatively simple thing to prove. The other situations can be very difficult. For instance, you can't get a divorce on one single act of adultery. You have to go into a lot of detail (with evidence) in order to prove sodomy or rape (of you).

If you want a divorce on these grounds you will certainly need a lawyer. You should also use a lawyer if children, a settlement, money or property are involved because you can't possibly find your way alone through the legal maze.

Any British woman who has prepared for the possibility of divorce in a pre-marriage legal document is a remarkable woman indeed, although this is traditional in other European countries, such as in France. Considering the current strong statistical possibility of divorce it's a pity that before marriage people don't make prudent practical arrangements about what will be done with money, possessions and children should the marriage break up. However, this is now happening more often in Britian, not only with marriage contracts arranged by a solicitor, but also with living-together contracts, written and signed by both parties.

DIVORCING

What happens in a divorce court

Here are the bare bones of divorce procedure. Except in Northern Ireland this now consists basically of filling in a few forms and was described at the British Legal Association's 1977 conference as 'about as difficult as getting a television licence'.

If you're going to Court, then drop along and see someone else's divorce, the week before your own comes up, so you'll know what to expect (there's a schoolroom atmosphere, everybody looks dead bored, they drone on for about a quarter of an hour, which is all the time it takes to get a conveyor-belt divorce).

A: YOU FILE A PETITION

You deliver this by post or hand to the Divorce Registry at Somerset House, Strand, London WC2R 1LP (☎ 01-405 7641) or to any County Court with divorce jurisdiction. All forms and correspondence mentioned below go to the same address, addressed to the Registrar.

A different form is required for each type of petition. Make sure you get the right one, if you're doing it yourself. You need three copies, two of which go to the Court.

If you have children, you must also fill in a form setting out the arrangements (again, you need three copies, two for the Court) proposed for their future welfare. The judge must be satisfied about these arrangements otherwise he won't grant a divorce.

You must also take to the Court your marriage certificate. A photocopy is not acceptable. If you've lost it, get another marriage certificate from Somerset House, Strand, London WC2R 1LP.

If you are having a do-it-yourself divorce (see later), take a crossed cheque for £16 to the Court, made out to the Paymaster-General.

B: THE PETITION WILL BE SENT BY THE COURT TO YOUR SPOUSE

If he signs and returns the acknowledgement of service (allow a couple of weeks for this) and doesn't intend to defend the case you can apply to the Court for 'directions for trial'. Get the application form from the Court office.

If you're handling your case without a solicitor, ask the Chief Clerk to the Registrar of the Court when the next hearing of undefended divorces is likely to be and let him know that you're handling the case yourself. Ask him if there's anyone in his office who can check your petition before you finally present it.

The Registrar will then set the case down for hearing and will send you notice that this has been done. He will also tell you the date of the hearing or else tell you how to apply for a hearing date.

If your spouse wants to defend the case by filing an answer you should go to a solicitor at once because it will be a High Court case. It can't just be whipped through the County Court in a few minutes.

If your spouse agrees, and there are no children, you may be able to avoid going to Court by getting a postal divorce. You fill in two forms and a form of Affidavit or Evidence and swear to it before a Commissioner for Oaths (cost £2). Now you fill in another form for direction for trial and send it to the Court Registrar. If he's satisfied he will certify that you're entitled to a decree and the date of trial. The Judge will grant the decree without your having to go to Court.

C: FINANCIAL ARRANGEMENTS AND PROVISIONS FOR CHILDREN

These are made separately and privately, by the Judge or Registrar.

D: THE HEARING

When your case is heard (if you're not doing it by post) it will be heard in an open Court and you may have to give evidence. This can take as little as six minutes.

If the Judge considers the case proved and is satisfied about arrangements made for any children he will pronounce a decree nisi. This is not a divorce and you can't remarry until you have your decree absolute. You can apply for this six weeks after getting your decree nisi.

E: THE DECREE ABSOLUTE

To get your decree absolute, *you* have to apply (on yet another form obtainable from the Court office). ON NO ACCOUNT FORGET TO APPLY FOR YOUR DECREE ABSOLUTE.

DO-IT-YOURSELF DIVORCE

In London in 1975 – as soon as it was possible – one in six divorces were handled without a lawyer.

An uncontested divorce suit handled by a solicitor can cost each party several hundred pounds. A straightforward Do-It-Yourself divorce can cost from £16, the procedure is relatively simple, and this sum should include custody and access to children, conveyancing of property and maintenance.

For any legal advice, apply to AID, 177 Peregrine Road, Sunbury-on-Thames, Middx TW16 6JJ (☏ Sunbury-on-Thames [093 27] 84990). This is a non-profit-making organization which was formed in 1974 by a small group of people who had all suffered the humiliation, ignominy and bewilderment of traditional legal proceedings. They believed that divorce should be obtained in a cheaper, easier, happier manner. Not surprisingly AID branches are starting up all over the country and many are already established. As you can no longer get legal aid for an undefended divorce case, AID is badly needed.

Over 90 per cent of divorce cases are undefended by the time they reach the Court. But before that point there might have been much bitterness, resentment and disillusion, rows and threats as well as unashamed horse-trading.

There's no point in trying to get a Do-It-Yourself divorce unless you are both in agreement about everything concerning children, property and finance, and have sorted out all arguments, have got the decisions down on paper and are not going to change your minds.

If you have no children or savings, own nothing jointly, are both broke and incredibly civilized, then a Do-It-Yourself divorce should be no problem.

READ ALL ABOUT IT

You can get a free leaflet on Do-It-Yourself divorce from your local CAB.

You can get a free booklet from the Family Division of the High Court, Royal Courts of Justice, Strand, London WC2A 2LL (☏ 01-405 7641).

Other good books include *On Getting Divorced* (published by the Consumers' Association, Caxton Hill, Hertford SG13 7LZ, price £2.25).

On Getting Divorced is a step-by-step guide covering such questions as 'What are the grounds for divorce?', 'Who is going to be the petitioner?', financial provisions, child custody arrangements and carving up the matrimonial home.

It shows you how to write your petition (with examples) and how to file your petition. It tells you what documents are needed, what the Court procedure is, how to swear an affidavit and what will happen if you actually get to Court (it's no longer always necessary to go to Court). The time schedule even reminds you to apply for your decree absolute, and the book finally covers variation and enforcement of payments (which may be necessary to get the payments actually paid, increased or decreased).

There is also *Action in Person: How to Obtain an Undefended Divorce*. This covers the grounds for divorce, legal jargon, Court procedure, children, the home and money arrangements. It also provides the necessary forms and tells you how to fill them in. You can buy it from a bookseller or direct from Oyez Publishing Ltd, Dept OB, FREEPOST, London SE1 4PU (£6.75 including postage).

Although it's slightly out of date you might also get a very clear guide, *Divorce without a Solicitor* by Thomas Porter, a former naval officer (happily married to the same wife for over twenty-five years) who was horrified to see what happened when a close friend got a divorce. Anyone who can read can understand this book. It's also a *method* of handling your own divorce, a set of divorce forms is sent to you with the book, and if you want, the author will fill them in for you, for a small extra charge.

Divorce without a Solicitor costs £3.50 from Millstream Publications Ltd, Mill Lane, Burley, Ringwood, Hampshire BH24 4HR.

CAB can also help you to file your petition. You can apply for the forms from the Solicitors' Law Stationery Society, PO Box 55, 237 Long Lane, London SE1 4PU (☎01-407 8055).

MAINTENANCE WON'T MAINTAIN YOU

In Britain, there's no such thing as alimony and lawyers wince if you use the word (although in Scotland there is aliment). The correct term is main-tenance, and it is awarded as the Judge considers appropriate, taking into consideration who, in the family, has got the money and who needs it.

Don't think you are automatically entitled to maintenance. The Courts are supposed to take into account:

1 *The total family assets*, including the potential earning power and capital of the wife as well as the husband and even any possible future inheritance. The Court may discount *some* of the wife's capacity to work if it is thought reasonable that she shouldn't work (for instance, if she's looking after her *young* children).

In these days of sexual equality it's by no means certain that a husband always pays maintenance to his wife. She might have to pay regular maintenance and/or a lump sum *to* him. For instance, a female clerk working for a local authority had divorced a layabout husband and was *afterwards* left £8000 by her father. Her former husband (unemployed) immediately sued for support – with success.

The Court will also consider any pension, insurance or other future benefits that either party may lose as a result of the divorce. Already, in Germany, a widow's pension is split between *all* the wives of the deceased, according to the length of their marriage to him. At the moment, in Britain, the general rule is that the latest wife gets all the pensions and any previous wife gets nothing, even if she stuck to him (or stuck him) past the Silver Wedding. It's worth noting that recently a few women have successfully challenged this disgraceful rule.

2 *The financial needs and responsibilities of each party*. For instance, if the husband, by now, has another woman and children to support, the Court will take into account that he cannot support you as well as before because he just won't have enough money. This means that the Court gives preference to a current family rather than a discarded family and is realistic, if unfair, because it's pretty certain that that's what the father is *going* to do.

3 *The contribution of each marriage partner*. If the wife doesn't earn anything the Court takes into account her contribution in looking after the home and family, and any physical work she has done to improve the home.

4 *The age of the couple and the length of the marriage*. A woman of over forty-five who's been married for a long time and who has had children will get more than a young, childless woman. The Court also considers that it may be harder for an older woman to get a job.

5 *Physical or mental disability* of either party is also supposed to be taken into account.

As a result of pondering all this, the Court may order either you or your husband to provide for the other out of income or capital. If you have no money or assets (still the standard situation for the majority of British women) the Court may order your husband to make 'periodical payments' to you during the divorce proceedings. (You can't claim this payment until you instigate proceedings, so do that first.) Once the divorce is through you may receive one of three kinds of permanent provision:

1 Maintenance for a set length of time. This ceases on your husband's death or on your remarriage. At any time either of you can apply for the amount to be varied.

If you are repaying a mortgage on a home, try to get some of your payments *specifically earmarked for mortgage payments*. Then, if you need to claim extra benefits from the State, you do not have to declare this money as part of your income (*see page 227*).

2 The husband may have to secure his wife's maintenance by transferring assets to trustees, who can use the capital for the wife's benefit. If you remarry, you lose your rights to this.

3 A lump-sum settlement. The Court can order one partner to give a lump sum to the other outright (it may be paid by instalments). This sum cannot be altered and it can't be affected by the husband's or wife's death or remarriage. The Court can order the sale of property or assets in order to raise the sum. Again, the man can claim from the woman. In one instance, a wife had three children and they lived in a £10,000 house that she had inherited from her father. Her husband (with no assets) successfully sued for maintenance so she had to sell the family home and move with the children into a flat, in order to provide money for her husband, as ordered by the Court.

A lump sum is in many ways the most satisfactory form of maintenance settlement because it frees both partners of all responsibility and both parties know where they stand. Lawyers like lump-sum settlements on the bird-in-the-hand principle. Of course it is only possible where a partner has money, property or assets.

If you are a young, healthy, earning woman you may not be given maintenance for yourself, even if you keep the children. But on no account fail to obtain a peppercorn allocation (a nominal sum around 5p) because this entitles you to ask for the Court to vary the financial provision if your circumstances change for the worse. If you don't do this you can be in the gutter while he's a multi-millionaire, but you won't get another penny in maintenance for yourself.

ROW (Rights of Women) urge women completing their own divorce forms to claim for everything about which they are in doubt, because later it is much easier not to take the money than it is to get what you unexpectedly need, but did not ask for at the time.

Get your maintenance order registered with the Court at the time it is granted. You can have it registered at the County Court or with a Magistrates' Court.

Ask for registration with a Magistrates' Court because there are more of them and they will probably be more convenient to get to if you have to complain about arrears of maintenance.

Get any maintenance agreement you reach by negotiation with your ex-husband drawn up as a deed, and witnessed and signed.

This gives it the standing of a legal contract which the Courts can enforce.

You can always go to Court to ask for a private agreement to be varied (some women don't know this) but your case may be harder to prove if the agreement was not drawn up as a deed.

Maintenance orders are enforceable throughout the European Economic Community and indeed in any country with which Britain has a Reciprocal Maintenance Order Agreement. But it's not easy to enforce Maintenance Orders in Britain.

First you have to take him to Court and the Court has discretion as to *when* it will hear the case (he may have to be several payments in arrears before a Court accepts that he is defaulting). Then the Court must consider his salary and liabilities; they may order him to pay off the arrears in very small amounts over a very long period.

A Court can make an Attachment of Earnings order. This means that his employer deducts the amount he should pay you out of his salary, and pays it into the Court, which then forwards the money to you. But you'll be lucky to get it. Attachment of Earnings orders are not much used because the ex-husband can simply skip his job.

This is one of the reasons for the strong movement to have maintenance of divorced wives and children paid by the State and the husband's contribution then deducted by the State from his income tax. After all, the State pays maintenance anyway if the husband defaults on payments, because the wife claims supplementary benefit.

CHILDREN

There are two matters to consider with children in a divorce: who's looking after them and what money is available. Two different orders are made for children, one concerning money and the other concerning custody, care and control.

Custody is the right to make major decisions regarding method and country of upbringing, education, religion and holidays.

Care and control is the daily looking after of children. Until recently, a woman who lived with her lover (however long and however sedately) was generally considered by the Courts to be an unsuitable person to bring up children. Your chances of getting care and control and custody of your children are unlikely to be affected, these days, by your extramarital relations, unless the wife is a lesbian, when everyone will behave as if she's got leprosy.

Generally, both parents have joint custody and the mother has care and control, but there is no reason why the husband shouldn't have care and control, while the wife shares custody. The ratio of one-parent families headed by a father is one to five, and is steadily increasing.

Children need a lot of money, and they like their comfort and an orderly routine. Sometimes it can be less harassing for the children and the mother if the father has care of the children, while the mother has full visiting rights on weekends and holidays. Then, instead of a non-stop, seven-day-a-week struggle to make ends meet, together with all the physical and mental exhaustion of doing so (which doesn't make for good mothering), an overburdened mother might have two happy full days at the weekend with her children and possibly contribute towards their keep, if she is earning.

Many mothers react with indignation to this idea but in some situations *it can be better for the children's wel-* *fare* – which should count for more than anything else.

Whoever has care and control, there will be the question of *access* for the other parent. Unless there are really good reasons why your children should not see their father, make access as reasonable as possible, or you are depriving your children of their father. And try to make the meeting as cheerful and comfortable as possible. Wet afternoons in the zoo or park are not conducive to happy fathering.

Always stick to the arrangements you've made and be punctual. Don't use your little bit of power to mess up their outing. Don't tease your ex – it will only exasperate him but it may disturb the children deeply.

CHILD MAINTENANCE

Unless the mother has means, the father is generally liable to provide for the children until they are eighteen or until the end of their full-time education (up to age twenty-one). The Courts will award what appear to be very tiny sums, however rich the husband. Private school fees, which he may pay in addition, won't cover school extras, which can be horrendously high.

If the mother is earning and the father isn't (or chooses not to do so) then she has to pay for the children; she might be entitled to supplementary benefits and help with rent and rates (*see page 237*).

MAINTENANCE AND TAX

Whatever your financial arrangements, you must know whether your maintenance and any maintenance for your children are being paid *gross* or *net* of tax.

A *If maintenance for yourself is paid gross* (which happens if the payment is a 'small maintenance payment' or if the payer is abroad or has no income for the year in which payments were made), you will have to pay tax on it at earned income rates (before April 1978, maintenance above a certain limit was liable to the investment income surcharge!).

B *If maintenance for yourself is paid net* and you don't have any other income, you may be entitled to a tax rebate. You won't be able to claim before the end of the tax year but it could mean that in due course you get a handsome extra sum, although it has been known to take up to six years to claw it back from the Inland Revenue, which doesn't help today's grocery bill.

C *Your tax situation is also affected* by whether your children's maintenance is paid gross or net. After April 1979, as a single parent, you will have a personal tax allowance (currently £985 a year) and an additional tax allowance of £550, which brings your tax allowance up to that of a married man.

Each child, whatever his age, has a personal tax allowance (currently £985 a year). If his maintenance is paid gross and is above this amount, you will have to pay tax on the extra.

If a child's maintenance is paid net you may be able to claim a tax rebate.

Under the arrangements for small maintenance payments, child maintenance of up to £52 per month (or £12 per week) per child can be paid

gross, if it is paid in accordance with a Court order.

If you are the parent caring for the child this won't affect your tax position or the child's.

Maintenance and tax is headache country where expert advice can save you hundreds of pounds, whether you receive maintenance or pay it out. Go to a divorce lawyer (*not* an accountant and *not* just any old lawyer, you need a specialist). Or go to your local Inland Revenue office. Some local Inland Revenue Offices are better than others at dealing with tax and divorce, but every office can help you through the Revenue's own tax guides, and their help is free. One good London office is the Inland Revenue office at Colquhoun House, 27 Broadwick Street, London W1V 2AE (☎ 01-734 1696).

Here are some useful points:

1 Ensure that all payments are made in accordance with a Court order. Never make any voluntary extra payments (though you may not mind receiving them). Only payments under a Court order can attract tax relief.

2 Check that you know exactly what you should receive (or pay) for each period (week/month/year). This helps with your personal budgeting. Check that it *is* paid (you can do this at a glance if you open a separate bank account for these payments only).

3 Check with an accountant or local Inland Revenue office whether you are eligible for tax rebates (whether you're paying or receiving maintance). If you are, get your tax returns in as quickly as possible. (All tax repayments seem to take at least twelve months; don't give

them a chance to take twenty-four months.)

4 Remember that university grants are based *on the income of the person who houses and cares for the child*. (Your ex may be a millionaire but your child's maintenance grant is still determined by *your* income, if you are housing and caring for him.)

5 If you are receiving maintenance, get your lawyer to negotiate for you and your children to be left something in the payer's will, to offset the effect of possible sudden loss of maintenance on his death.

A FEW OTHER THINGS

PROPERTY AND ASSETS

(Check: pension, private income, shares, property, jewellery.)

Assets are split between you. If she has just inherited some shares or Gran's cottage, then he can claim half (and vice versa). Sometimes during the strain of a break-up one spouse will privately persuade the other to hand over assets ('Have a glass of champagne darling . . . and sign here'), but the Courts can overrule such agreements. In fact, the Courts are required to ensure that the final settlement is as fair as possible. They should look closely at any private agreements you have reached between you over assets and they have to be satisfied about any conditions you have agreed to concerning children.

THE COURTS CAN OVERRULE ANY PRIVATE AGREEMENT YOU MAKE, perhaps when under emotional stress (possibly induced by champagne). Mr Justice Balcombe exercised this power in July 1977, when he disre-

garded the transfer of the wife's joint interest in the former matrimonial home to the husband and awarded her a lump sum. He said that the Court should look with circumspection at any transfer of property made by one spouse to the other without the benefit of independent legal advice and with no value being given by the other spouse.

If you are awarded the home as part of a settlement make sure that your lawyer legally confirms with the other side that there are no outstanding debts of any sort such as overdue mortgage payments, outstanding estate agents' or other bills, rates, rent, electricity or gas bills; or that, if there are, payment of these is taken into account in the final settlement.

PERSONAL POSSESSIONS

Division of personal possessions can be a relatively small but dangerous emotional point at which a so-called civilized divorce suddenly explodes into hysteria and you're back at square one ('But that was my *grandmother's* desk'). It's not only shared property that causes trouble or even valuable property, it's *desirable*, beloved property. A good way to handle such a situation is to find the intrinsic (not sentimental) value of everything that you're fighting about (get a valuer to do it if you can't agree). Check what the total financial value is, and then think about how important each item is to you. Offer to pay the appropriate amount for items which have great emotional significance for you.

Another good way to divide the property is simply to hold an auction between the two of you for everything you're fighting about. Hold it with pretend money but the difference between His pile and Her pile should be paid up by the biggest debtor in real money or allowed for in the settlement.

YOUR WILL

After a divorce, change your will, if you've made one. It would be really galling to get run over and have him get everything. If you haven't made a will, do so. If you want to do it on your own see page 196. If you want your lawyer to do it, make sure you know beforehand how much he will charge and make sure it's in writing. When making a will don't forget to name the people that you choose for your children's guardians and don't forget to ask them before you do it.

It seems unfair when you're so short of money that you have to pay still more money on further little legal trivialities but the dreary little trivialities are worth the charges, whereas the big production number is apt to be where everybody loses out (except the lawyers).

SEX AND DIVORCE

In England and Wales, if you are divorcing your husband for anything except ground 3 (desertion for two years, *see page 144*) then any adultery on your part cannot affect the grant of the decree.

With ground 3 your husband could claim that he did not desert you for the whole two-year period, that he tried to come back but could not because of his aversion to your behaviour. It's then up to you to prove he is lying, which could be very difficult.

If there is going to be a battle over the children, then your husband may try to prove that you are unfit to have them because of your immorality.

You must tell your solicitor what you really have been doing so that if necessary he can defend you against exaggerated aspersions or, alternatively, work out how to make your lifestyle sound entirely normal and reasonable.

Sleeping with your ex during the divorce or the nisi period or later certainly happens; in fact a *lot* of divorcers seem to do it. This might be because:

1 You want to seduce him, just to prove that you still can.
2 He wants to seduce you, just to prove that he still can (especially if you've just got cosily organized with someone else).
3 You both might feel territorial rights. It might be partly possessive, partly an ego trip, partly, because you're missing him, partly because of the panic of being alone, or you might just be feeling randy.

It doesn't *necessarily* complicate things legally (unless you are divorcing in Northern Ireland) but it can make you feel far more mixed up, confused and bewildered than you would believe possible (especially if it also means that you're being unfaithful to somebody else).

He might say he wants it so that you can get back together again. Consider whether he's telling the truth. Even if you do sleep with him it doesn't naturally follow that you will be reconciled. Consider 2 and 3 above.

Remember that if he seriously wants you back then (*a*) he would not restrict his attempts just to getting you into bed and (*b*) going to bed with him won't settle all the background grievances, although it may set the scene for doing so.

HOW TO TREAT YOUR HUSBAND

Try not to see him (it's not generally very difficult). The less you see of him or anyone connected with him, the quicker you will get over it.

Don't expect any help from your husband. He didn't help you, did he? He hurt you. Don't personally ask him for help; if you want it, ask reasonably, through your lawyer. If he won't give it through a lawyer, he is unlikely to give it to you. Don't risk a humiliating rebuff.

If he causes trouble (such as physical harassment) deal with it immediately and firmly through your lawyer. Don't make any threats – *do it*, without talking about it, whatever it is. Never try to bluff him. He knows you, remember? Nevertheless, he will successfully bluff you.

Try not to provoke or be drawn into angry scenes with him. Try to ignore him politely. Remember that what your husband does or whom he goes around with is no longer any of your business. If anyone tells you something upsetting, because they think you ought to know, be laconic. Tell them you'd rather not talk about it *and don't*. There is nothing like a divorce for bringing out the best in you, or showing up the worst. The choice is up to you.

Of course you won't worry about any of this if *you* were the errant spouse.

HOW TO TREAT THE CHILDREN

Of course children are unhappy when their parents divorce but they may be even more unhappy if their parents don't divorce and they are in the midst of bickering, rows and unhappiness. They are often also confused and embarrassed, especially if they are used as scapegoats. What you can best do for your children is to treat them as normally as possible but to be with them as much as you can manage. Let them see as few emotional scenes as possible and tell them as soon as the divorce is definite. Be brief and calm: point out a few immediate advantages, however shallow. Children can be blissfully shallow.

Don't overburden children with responsibility ('You'll have to be a big boy and look after Mummy now') and, however much of a rat he's been, however noble you've been, however terrific any other male you produce – bear in mind that your children only have one father and *he can't be replaced*. You should in no way, openly or covertly, try to deprive a child of its father. You should in no way try to persuade a child that its father is a double-dyed villain or rat. (You will, of course, if only by grimly tightening your mouth, snorting cynically or addressing sarcastic remarks to the ceiling.)

Children can easily pick up the vibes if you even *think* unpleasant things about him, so try not to, for their sake and for yours. And don't let your parents or relatives taint this saintly atmosphere. You don't need sympathy that badly.

YOUR ATTITUDE TO THE WHOLE MESS

You should have a proper period of mourning for your marriage, as you would, say, for your grandmother, but after that you should try not to dwell on it in a morbid manner. You have been bereaved, your marriage has passed away. Now life must continue. But don't think that you will get over it, and don't pretend to yourself that you have done so. Years afterwards you may still feel real physical pain at the accidental thought of it and it's unrealistic to pretend otherwise.

Everyone has to grope their own way through a divorce and the only people who can really help you are the experienced ones. If you need support, contact the National Council of the Divorced and Separated, 13 High Street, Little Shelford, Cambridge CB2 5ES (☎ Shelford [022 04] 2544). If you don't want to talk to strangers, try to talk to one or two (not more) other divorced women who look to you in good shape and are not bitter or twisted or smashed every evening by 6 o'clock. They may well have felt what you're suffering, have also felt rejected, humiliated and a failure. But now they seem wiser and more tolerant or you probably wouldn't be seeking their advice. You may need their reassurances that there's daylight at the end of the tunnel.

Only tell your close friends *once*. After that, as a topic of conversation, it's boring. Never discuss your divorce with men who ask you out for the evening. It's pointless, embarrassing for others and furthermore, it shows you in a worse light than you think.

Don't expect your joint friends to side with you; you shouldn't expect them to side with anyone. Don't be surprised if they take your husband's side. They can't know all the details; don't tell them. Grit your teeth, for-give them for their ignorance and ignore them politely or shut up.

Once you've made your vital telephone calls, if you feel that you can't cope – don't try. Go to bed. Concentrate on crying your eyes out. Keep it up for a whole day, then try to stop because it doesn't improve anything, especially not the eyes.

Try to do something pleasurably physical and exhausting every day, such as going for a long walk or long swim. Try not to take tranquillizers. Try not to drink.

Because *you* are the one who has to sort out your mess, find out where you stand financially, perhaps take over the full burden of the children and decide what you're going to do with your life. Nobody else can do it for you, however much you weep, wail, drink, eat, smoke, complain, sleep around, don't sleep at all, wring your hands helplessly or flutter your eyelashes at lawyers and accountants (very expensive this).

Don't feel that you've failed as a wife or a woman or a human being. It takes two to tangle; realize that it wasn't you that failed, it was the marriage.

Don't feel guilty.

Don't blame yourself.

Don't blame him.

Don't blame her, that grasping scheming bitch.

Don't build a funeral pyre of hostility.

Remember that every time you rage against your ex-mate, you're wasting more of your life and energy on him. It's pointless and it won't change anything. Remember that every dirty trick he plays should make you even gladder that you are no longer lumbered with him.

Spite rebounds and bitterness

doubles and redoubles (especially when you are vulnerable). Try not to be bitter, particularly if you have reason to be, because it poisons your life and will show very fast on your face. Bitterness makes you look older, uglier and gets you nowhere, and it certainly doesn't attract men.

Don't waste time on revenge – you're not a Sicilian peasant. Remember they were *not* the happiest years of your life, otherwise your marriage probably wouldn't have broken down; perhaps the happiest years are about to come, whatever your age.

Don't waste another minute. Be determined that from now on you may not have so much money but you're going to enjoy life far, far more. You are now FREE. You can stay up all night or you can stay in bed all Sunday. Supper can be a cheese sandwich in bed or a glass of wine in a bubble-bath; never again will you have to check what he wants to do – it's what *you* want that counts.

Don't be frightened of being alone; it's just that you're not used to it. Being alone is not necessarily being lonely; far from it.

Don't see yourself as tottering along, bravely picking up the pieces. See yourself as being on the brink of a marvellous new way of living, with much, much more time to devote to yourself.

Get out and get around. Forget about men and start thinking about people; try a little voluntary work and you'll meet lots of people and find how much better off you are than you thought.

If you have parties, don't pair off the sexes and mix age groups. The more informal your first parties, the less stilted and strained they (and you) will be.

Do one thing you positively enjoy every single day, whether it's eating an apple or telephoning someone you really like. Go out, just to enjoy yourself, once a week, preferably with a friend. It doesn't really matter whether you enjoy yourself or not, the point is that you are not withdrawing from society, staying home and brooding. Try not to be alone yet and not to be a bore.

On the other hand, don't try to do everything at once, as in the magazine 'why not' columns (why *not* sew a sampler, dye your hair green, take up karate, learn Eskimo and hike to Katmandu?).

But you might check the local evening classes (*see* 'The Thinking Woman', *page 60*) and check *Time Out* to discover how much the cheapest route to Katmandu actually does cost. And you might start a piggy bank here and now with 5p pieces towards it.

Expect sudden overwhelming waves of panic, rage, terror and inadequacy. In such moments of self-doubt, telephone one of your sensible, divorced friends to be reminded of the reality.

Expect a sex problem. Don't be

worried if you feel not only dazed from the neck up but dead from the neck down as well. You can't expect yourself to go on functioning as normal when you're in a situation which is *not* normal and which is causing you great anxiety. Wait until you don't confuse sex and companionship with proving something to yourself.

Along with other things, a divorce is a personal and sexual rejection. This is a great blow, and do not try to kid yourself otherwise. *Expect* to feel this way and you are less likely to make a fool of yourself and have awful morning-after regrets. Try to avoid doing anything that would shame you to yourself; it isn't worth it.

Don't rush out and have an affair with someone just to prove that you still can. Of course you can. Don't rush out and remarry for the same reason or to irritate your ex or just because you're so grateful that someone asked you or because you can't stand dealing with things like insurance, or because you want to be looked after. These are not good reasons for getting married.

You don't need to find a man at the moment, but you may need to find yourself and learn to *enjoy* your own company. The world has probably changed since you married, so has morality, so have aims and attitudes. So has the female situation. Get out there and prepare to have a good time. Think not of yesterday or tomorrow, but only of today.

A SUDDEN SECOND FAMILY

The generation that is growing up at the moment in Britain is the first to accept divorce as part of the background to life. So it's not nearly such a stigma for today's children as it was twenty years ago.

If, after a divorce, you marry again, you may find that you metamorphose overnight from lone ranger into mother-of-three and have to take a shock course in treading the delicate path of a stepmother.

But if you are suddenly transformed overnight into mother-of-three-*more*, it's not nearly such a problem, providing you keep a balanced view of the situation.

Of course you may have to discard a second set of unrealistic marriage expectations (all eight of you skipping to the zoo, hand in hand).

You may have gloomy forebodings that are directly based on your empirical knowledge of the natural inclination of your children to play up just when you desperately need their good behaviour.

You may fear that his (large, tough) children will tear out the throats of your (quiet, well-brought-up) children.

In fact, children will be people, so there are bound to be the odd scraps. But the children of a remarriage are often very pragmatic, very practical and very relieved. Basically, they hope that it's going to be a better all-round deal for everybody.

The situation is easier if both sets of children are in similar age groups because you will be dealing with the same emotional problems at the same time and can, more easily, all understand each other's difficulties. General harmony will also depend on careful handling of all the children's property, rights and privacy.

If you're marrying someone with children, you are not marrying a person but a family. You can't afford to think of his children as tiresome additions that you must tolerate. They are part of the person you love. They are not nuisances; they are a part of the whole situation that you have settled for, even if they only appear at Easter. (This is not to say that you let his kids walk all over you.)

These other small people that he loves may regard *you* as a usurper – and you are. Aim at friendship and treat them as adults. Never think of yourself as their mother, never ask them to call you 'Mummy' or 'Mum'; Christian names are more natural and less of a land-mine.

Respect the relationship he has with his children and expect him to want time alone with them. Realize that his children may well see you (with reason) as successfully taking their mother's place. Your children may see *him* as an interloper, especially if they have struggled alongside you to survive a death or divorce.

You are likely to be very defensive about your own children and so will he be about his. Do not be disappointed if they don't like you. They may do in time but expect a long haul. What they will eventually acknowledge is your continued good behaviour. Don't order anyone around and try not to criticize their awful behaviour; they may well be unconsciously testing you.

If, occasionally, you have twice as much family to cope with, try not to get resentful because of the extra work. If they are old enough, try Improving the System at Home (*page 98*), which is usually easier with any children other than your own because they are, by definition, more objective. Don't allow yourself to be overworked; martyrdom is bad for relationships. Make an effort to organize and delegate the extra workload, consulting as you go.

You would be very unusual if you weren't, sometimes, unreasonably, wildly jealous of the first Mrs X for all sorts of silly reasons and perhaps quite a lot of sensible ones. She shared a part of his life; he probably can't talk about that part, and certainly not think of it, without referring to her. It is a credit to you if he feels that he can mention her when her name naturally occurs, although he must realize that if he makes a remark like 'Helen used to add those marvellous little fennel seeds to the French dressing' it may be flung back at him.

Remember that he chose you for good reasons. But he also chose his previous wife for good reasons. There must be something good to be said in her favour or else he's a rotten picker. Which would you prefer?

Be generous and be silent about her because he will always notice and resent your sniping, however subtle. *He* is allowed to bitch but you are not. You may not get good marks for behaving well but you will certainly get bad marks if you don't.

Try not to be jealous if your children immediately take a shine to Mrs X or any of her family. Be thankful for cheerful relationships.

However unreliable and irritating the first Mrs X may be about holiday dates, always try to offer a reasonable selection, well in advance and *in writing*.

Try not to resent Mrs X's financial arrangements. His legal and moral priorities may be to her. You knew this beforehand. What now happens to the two of you (or more) is nothing to do with the ex-Mrs X.

Don't be in too much of a hurry to establish a new order. Introduce your changes very gradually. Try not to redecorate; leave the monograms as they are; don't mind about the photographs; don't tear loving dedications out of books. Remember who is the *present* Mrs X.

Feeling sad

'Who's afraid of growing up? Who isn't? For if and when we do begin the process of re-examining all that we think and feel and stand for, in the effort to forge an identity that is authentically ours and ours alone, we run into our own resistance. There is a moment – an immense and precarious moment – of stark terror. And in that moment most of us want to retreat as fast as possible because to go forward means facing a truth we have suspected all along: we stand alone.' – Gail Sheehy in *Passages*.

Midlife is Unknown Territory for which no one has prepared you and the upheavals of Midlife can be as big an upheaval as having your first baby. But you don't get any pre-natal counselling, either to tell you what to expect or to guide you through the woods and across the water jump.

This has always been true of the Midlife period but particularly today, when we are living much longer, change is coming faster, while there are many more social upheavals in Britain and the world in general (the oil crisis, inflation, teenage violence and the altering of morality, to name but a few).

Middle Age is often a crisis time for marriage, family and career. Your father-in-law comes to stay for ever. Someone whom you love dies. Your children leave home and you start to worry about *their* training, jobs, love affairs and money. You may face loneliness or – even worse – clutch at straws in order to escape it.

Anyone finds such major changes upsetting, disturbing and depressing. Such situations can arouse strong feelings, none of them agreeable. Any violent and destructive reactions are understandable. But no one warns you to expect these changes of feeling or else, mistakenly, they are attributed to the menopause.

It's important to expect and recognize such emotions and understand why they happen because then you can handle them far more easily. Unrecognized, such feelings can exhaust and destroy you, or upset your judgement and lead to actions that you will regret, such as running off with a Spanish waiter.

A feeling that many women experience in later life, although it's difficult to notice and then analyze, is a vague feeling of emptiness, a flat sensation that nothing hopeful lies ahead. Some women wonder, 'Is that all there is to my life?' Some women feel that they have been cheated, that they were encouraged in expectations that (they can now see) will never be fulfilled. They were fed a set of romantic myths and now realize that they were untrue and unfair, and that life is not a bed of roses.

Retrospectively, they feel misled by their parents and teachers, although these people probably did the best they could (or what was considered best at the time). And at eighteen *everybody* believes that life is a bed of roses so you wouldn't have listened to them anyway.

Possibly the only major way in which a woman may have been misled was in being brought up to believe that she would *always* be someone else's responsibility and that someone else would *always* look after her, so that she is frightened, resentful and unprepared if self-sufficiency is forced upon her.

Once you know what your reactions and feelings are likely to be after an upsetting event, you should be able to handle yourself better. So several months after any difficult time sit down and check your feelings for:

★ Bitterness
★ Anger
★ Resentment
★ Jealousy
★ Humiliation
★ Depression
★ Loneliness
★ A sense of loss
★ Grief
★ Futility and uselessness
★ Agitation
★ Fright
★ Despair

People often deny such feelings or refuse to face them, because they are not part of their picture of a nice person, as taught in Sunday school. But we all have them, to some degree, and unless you face them you won't be able to recognize and control destructive impulses or compulsions. So they escalate. Bitter at forty, spiteful at fifty, sour at sixty and after then who cares?

So try to reassess your feelings and attitude to the upsetting event and get them in perspective. Check:

★ What happened.
★ Why it happened – in simple situational terms, not plonking the blame on someone. Not 'Why did he have to die and leave me in this mess?' But 'James didn't take out life insurance with the mortgage because he didn't expect to get killed in a car crash at forty-seven and I left all that boring paperwork to him; I wasn't careful enough to check on what was happening at the time.'
★ What is happening now.
★ Why it is happening.
★ What might happen next.
★ How important is it? The most important thing in your year or your life? Something that happens to many people or only a few?
★ Can you do anything constructive about the consequences?
★ Can anyone else help you?

FEELING LONELY

'You're very much alone if you work in the theatre, regional touring is a very lonely business. You need courage and guts to fight it and fight it you must. You have to keep busy. You can't just let it swamp you.' – Actor Edward Fox.

And yet actors always radiate self-confidence and seem to live in a busy world of talent and charm. Actors, commercial travellers or international businessmen are always meeting people and always on the move, but they are often lonely, because loneliness isn't necessarily the result of being alone.

You can feel very lonely in a crowd, while possibly the worst sort of loneliness is when you're lying unhappily next to someone whom you're supposed to love.

Of course, everyone feels lonely at times, particularly the successful. They are striking out in unknown territory: there is no one to ask the way, no one to check an idea with, no one to share the strain or the responsibility of being ahead of the crowd or the one soldier in the army who *isn't* out of step. Ask any really successful politician, impresario, tycoon or writer what it's like up there and they'll say, 'Well, it can be a very lonely business.' (But of course you don't believe it.)

Loneliness at times is part of the price you pay for individuality, for developing your own self, by yourself. We all know the joy of togetherness, the cuddle of mother and baby, the oblivious bliss of lovers in the grass, the craven strength of a gang, the uplifting group support of the family, the team or the school.

In spite of all that you are *basically* always alone and should therefore be capable of surviving alone. In the end, the only person you can rely on is yourself, so you had better be sure that you are reliable (self-reliant) and then being alone is unlikely to mean being lonely.

Anyone can see that a lighthouse keeper might be lonely, although such loners are generally people who are not isolated, but in isolated situations. Someone who chooses to be a lighthouse keeper probably does so because a life of solitude is just what he likes. He is happiest when by himself with the lonely sea, the sky and the birds, his Desert Island Discs, his books, his bottles and his special tins of ginger or jars of strawberry jam.

People tend to think of the lonely as being alone but the Women's Group of Public Welfare produced a study on loneliness and found that the loneliest people of all are:

1 Young mothers confined in suburban houses with small children.
2 Young mothers bringing up children in large cities, especially in high-rise blocks.
3 Single parents who get little relaxation and cannot share their responsibilities.
4 Mothers with mentally or physically handicapped children who are confronted with a much longer and more severe period of isolation than if their children were normal (perhaps for life).
5 Students, who perhaps are overworking and young people in city bed-sits who have left home to find work and excitement.
6 Disabled adults.
7 The mentally ill, especially the elderly.
8 Those leaving hospital.
9 Those leaving prison.
10 The divorced and the widowed.
11 People who can't find jobs or who have been declared redundant.
12 People who retire and then move away from the place where their friends and relatives are.

SITUATIONAL LONELINESS
You might find yourself in a lonely

situation that you haven't specifically chosen. You may live isolated from the community in the middle of nowhere. You may have just moved into a new area, home or situation where you don't know anyone. Your job may prevent your meeting people. You may be travelling about all the time, like a pop singer or a television repair man. You may be so overworked that there isn't time to talk to anyone. (Industrial studies show that these are the people most likely to get left out and feel isolated within a business.)

Situational loneliness need not be a problem if you can just make *one* effort to join a club or meet people, although it's not always simple. A shy listener wrote to broadcaster Jimmy Young, 'It's not so easy to alter a situation that you've grown into gradually. If you live alone for a long time, you can get to the stage where you don't even talk to other people, where you almost can't.'

If you are lonely only because you have no opportunity to meet people, then this can be easily remedied. Visit your public library, where you'll find lists of the local activities and jollifications pinned to the notice-board. Go to evening classes, telephone your nearest clergyman, Women's Institute or CAB and just say that you're lonely. Ask CAB to suggest one or two voluntary organizations that you might join. Or advertise in specialist magazines for local birdwatching, photography or painting friends.

For people who want a simple sort of friendship there are forty-six clubs in the National Federation of Solo Clubs (for the widowed, divorced, separated and single). The Federation also runs a postal club to put you in touch with other people by letter.

For membership, write to: National Federation of Solo Clubs, 7–8 Ruskin Chambers, 191 Corporation Street, Birmingham B4 6RP (☎ 021-236 2879). Membership costs £20 for twelve months. You can also place an advertisement in the Federation's newsletter which is published each month.

If you are very shy, how about choosing a pen friend? Write, enclosing a stamped addressed envelope, to: Pen Friends, International Friendship League, Peace Haven Hostel, 3 Creswick Road, London W3 9HE (☎ 01-992 0221).

Tony Lake, a psychologist who once worked for the computer dating agency Dateline, realized that four important reasons for loneliness are shyness, inability to communicate, personality and social circumstances. Lake set up Wavelength Society, 73 Grosvenor Street, London W1 (☎ 01-409 0152) as a contact group to help lonely individuals deal with these problems.

LONELINESS CAN BE FATAL

As any disc jockey or Samaritan knows, loneliness must be taken seriously. Loneliness doesn't sound dangerous but in fact it can kill you.

American Dr James Lynch of the University of Maryland found a surprising relationship in the death-and-marriage statistics of American men between sixteen and forty-six. Bachelors living alone died much younger than married men from stress-linked causes such as cirrhosis of the liver, heart disease, lung cancer, car crashes, strokes and suicide.

Dr Lynch also found that the lonely (single, widowed and divorced) spent much more time in institutions that ranged from mental homes to prisons (where there was an average of twenty-three bachelors to one married man).

LONELINESS AS A PERSONALITY PROBLEM

Not all loneliness is situational, it can also be the result of personality problems. Aggressive, defensive and prickly people are sometimes shy but they are sometimes ill. Ideally, you learn to form relationships when you're a child in your own home. If you are deprived of the opportunity to do so at this important stage (because you have no home or your parents don't have any time for you or they don't have any friends themselves), then you may have a tough problem, because if you are not taught, by example, the habit of loving and trusting and succeeding with others when you're young, you may never get the knack.

Some unfortunate children pick up clumsy, unsuccessful ways of interacting with other people, so they do not form good relationships and continue, through life, to repeat their early mistakes. Eventually they cease to believe in the existence of love and friendship. They are unable to trust anyone, for fear of being rejected or abandoned and may finally retreat into a private, frozen hermit's cave, where at least they know who they hate and are no longer worried by repeat performances of failure.

Even in the happiest homes people have to *learn* how to form new relationships. We have all seen likeable children metamorphose into disagreeable adolescents when they first set foot alone into the outside world. They are trying to find their identity in strange, new surroundings and it's

like moving into a new town, miles away. They have to put their past life behind them and organize new friendships. They are gingerly putting a toe into unknown water to test the social temperature and they are not entirely certain that the toe won't get bitten off.

One result of such anxiety may be that they become hypercritical of their parents, their brothers and sisters, the neighbours and anyone else in sight. If you introduce them to anyone with whom they might have something in common (same age, interests, background, opposite sex) then that is the *one* person into whose eye they're going to spit. They develop enormous passions for people who, to you, seem unsuitable: large louts and supercilious henna-ed females who ignore you. They develop an exasperating phoney veneer of sophistication or disdain (no wonder they attract such ghastly friends). Their manner may seem calculated to shock or to make other people feel inferior.

Teenage behaviour has always been so and the psychological clue to it is that they don't really know and haven't yet worked out who they are, what they can do and what or whom they want. In a nutshell, their problem is that they feel they are not good enough for other people.

Exasperating though this is, never worry about such behaviour. It is merely exploratory and normal, so long as it doesn't persist.

However, such confused behaviour in a lonely adult might well indicate a personality problem that needs expert help from a psychiatrist (obtainable on the NHS, via the local GP, though you may have to wait a long time).

Be very wary of a stranger who immediately tells you that he's lonely. There may well be good reason for his sad state. Especially in modern city society there are a lot of nutters around who seem, on first acquaintance, to be normal. But somehow they've had a run of bad luck that seems to have lasted for the whole of their life to date. Such people are to be avoided because, at best, they can often upset *your* equilibrium. They can be like the drowning man whom you jump in to save, but who gradually drags you under. Do not act like a Samaritan before carefully checking on family and background, or, at worst, say the police, you might end up strangled.

On the other hand, someone you know slightly may ask for your help because he or she is lonely, perhaps after some sad event. You whizz around, arranging introductions and parties and club meetings and involvements in the hospital bazaar. But nothing comes of it all. Some months later he or she again asks your help, so you go into a similar routine. And again nothing happens. You realize that such a person may be lonely because they are not prepared to put enough into relationships; they want immediate large returns of love on their initial small investment of time. But love and friendship take a lot of time to establish, especially as you get older.

SHYNESS

Adults who feel that they're not good enough for other people generally describe themselves as shy. They find it painful to go out for a cup of coffee and going to a party can take real courage, because they are so afraid of looking and feeling a fool.

They are so afraid of feeling inadequate that they may behave as if they *are* inadequate. They are either tongue-tied or say a lot of damn silly things that they don't mean.

Veteran American actor Robert Cummings says that what you have to do is remember one thing: that *everyone* is shy. Then you can walk into a room with a big smile and start talking to the nearest person, having decided beforehand what to say. Something as simple as, 'What do you do?' or 'Where do *you* come from?' is an excellent start to a conversation,

much used by Royalty. The Duke of Edinburgh once said that people are often nervous before he enters a reception and he understands that, but no one ever seems to think that *he* might be nervous, about to enter and talk to a roomful of strangers. 'It's a very lonely business approaching the door and knowing that everyone inside is probably as nervous as you,' he said.

Rudyard Kipling wrote that it took him nearly all his life to realize, when he had to meet a group of new people, that they were probably as shy as he was, and more likely to feel *friendly* towards him than otherwise.

A lot of people are particularly shy of speaking to someone who attracts them. If you like the look of the tall dark man by the window, you may feel so shy that you immediately move to the opposite end of the room. But what you *should* do is to march up to him with a smile, start your friendly behaviour and then, after a short conversation, move away to get a drink or to talk to someone else. He may or may not come up to speak to you again. This is not 'making a dead set at him'. It is showing interest. It is daft *not* to show interest in people who interest you but only, as you may have been charitably taught, to people who may be in need of you or who ask you to dance before anyone else. That way, you end up with the wet and the weedy.

HOW TO MAKE FRIENDS

Getting on with people is a real social skill, and you have to learn it. Some people are lucky enough to learn it at home. The children of ambassadors have a terrific drilling in it. They are taught how to get on with anyone who turns up in the embassy drawing-room, no matter what age, size, shape, colour or creed. They are not taught to say a few stiff words about the weather, they are taught to put a stranger at his ease, never to embarrass him and always make him feel welcome.

Such skills amount to a knack that can be learnt. Painfully shy students can be taught in a few confidence-building sessions how to enjoy a party. However, you have to keep in practice. If you get rusty, you'll lose your self-confidence, so if you find yourself in an isolating situation, put out your community feelers fast. If you move home, don't wait until you've got the place straight, get socially embedded before you get the curtains up. Go and borrow a bottle of milk or a ball of string from your neighbours – something that they're likely to have and that you are likely to remember to return.

But be cautious. One of the problems, when going to a new area, is finding out who you *really* want to know and whom you had better avoid while getting to know everyone. The trick is to be friendly with everyone – yet keep your distance while you do so.

In loneliness, by definition, the only healing factor is other people. What you have to do is to work *slowly* towards the right ones. Here's how to do it.

When you meet someone:

1 Smile, and look pleased to see him (or her). Imagine you are seeing someone you dearly love, unexpectedly.
2 Take care of him and his comfort ('Come in and get warm, you must be frozen'). Offer food and drink if appropriate ('Would you like a cup of tea? Or a hot rum toddy?').
3 Help him to talk to you. Openers are:
   *Something you have in common (the difficulties of making a journey, the goddam weather, something in today's newspaper);
   *Something of general interest that anyone can talk about (the Queen, food, the cost of living);
   *Something easy to understand

(not British policy in Rhodesia or Ireland);

*Something in which he's been a success;

*Something small that you can praise: he got to the meeting on time; he's arrived looking marvellously well; you like his tie/jacket/jeans/haircut (men like to be told they look nice as well as women). Never say 'You look exhausted' or he will immediately feel it or, worse still, start telling you why.

4 Ask him something about himself (always a fascinating topic) provided you *really* feel interest, instead of acting it. You can do this with increasing perception, the better you know someone ('How did Thursday go?', 'How did they react to your ideas?', 'What eventually did you decide to cook?').

5 Don't talk about yourself; except as it relates to him. If you have a triumph to report, attribute it in part to him ('I'll never forget that marvellous advice you gave me', 'I wouldn't have thought of it without you') or show how it helps *them* ('I'd like to introduce you to these people, they will love you'). Never mind if he immediately attributes any success you may have to himself. What does it matter?

6 Really *listen* to another person's answer on anything important. Don't just keep the conversation going or think up more clever questions while nodding your head intelligently. Show by your reply that you have listened, are interested in and understand his point of view.

7 Never talk about yourself in a way that shows you are richer, cleverer, better educated, luckier, morally more admirable, a better goldfish-hunter or salad-dressing-mixer than the person you're talking to. This is putting down and putting off (although a lot of men still think it's a good way to impress a woman). If a woman lets on that she has a higher salary or a lower golf handicap, then it shrivels him. However, he's happy to hear that she's a gold-medal skier, if he doesn't ski.

8 Once he starts talking, look for opportunities to praise (technically, this is called 'stroking'). You can be lavish so long as you're genuine and base each bit of praise on a fact he has given you.

Mindless praise is 'Your speech was marvellous'. Mind you, he'll accept even that, but it's better to be specific: 'I thought that the best part of what you said was . . .'

9 Continue to take care of his practical problems. Remember to fill his glass up or remember not to do so, if he's driving.

10 All the other points are easy. But this one is the step that counts and it requires concentration. A 'good listener' (one who always gets her man and never comes across the tongue-tied) *doesn't just listen*. Her secret is that she gives confidence to the talker, through a deep genuine interest in what he's saying. You will know you're properly reaching this point when you hear yourself saying something that *shows* you have been listening, such as: 'Well, you obviously enjoy getting wet/having a row/a quiet life/excitement' or 'You're

obviously good at dealing with people/figures/gambling.' Pick out what he's *good* at. Don't be brilliantly clever at immediately seeing where he went wrong.

11 Forget that you, yourself, could do with a bit of technical stroking. You're more likely to get it in this way than if you show off or stay silent. But praise is vital to development (although not everybody knows this, including quite a lot of schoolteachers). If somebody never praises you, ask yourself if his (or her) standards are too damn high for anyone to reach or if he's so damaged that he *can't* give affection.

With this treatment almost everyone begins to thaw and you see the best side of them. That doesn't mean that you'll always like what you see, but whatever the outcome you will have practised your ability to be likeable.

What makes the difference between this being a happy encounter, the flexing of a social muscle, and the start of a real friendship is often whether you are more interested in the other person than you are in yourself, whether you have time for the friendship (relationships, like plants, need nourishing) and your ability to project genuine unaffected warmth as opposed to the professional good humour of a publican. This skill also takes some practice. The easiest way to learn it is to watch someone else do it – one of those charmers of whom people say, 'A chat with Felicity makes me feel as if I've been sitting by a warm fire' or 'When I leave Felicity I always feel *better*' or 'Felicity is so *cosy*.'

Take those eleven steps slowly.

You don't want to overwhelm the next Independent candidate that stands on your doorstep . . . but, come to think of it, why not?

DEPRESSION ISN'T ONLY THE BLUES

A cut finger is not described in the same way as an amputated arm, so it's a pity that the same word – depression – is used to describe temporary gloom on a rainy day as well as a prolonged suicidal mood.

Depression used to be called melancholia. It is a recognized illness that can affect as many as 4 per cent of the population every year. Many more women than men unsuccessfully attempt suicide and the predominant cause is unhappiness about a man. Peak hours for suicide are between midnight and 3 a.m. and townsfolk outnumber country people by twelve to one.

One of the difficulties of depression is that it comes on gradually and *physically* it doesn't show (except, of course, in your whole demeanour) so it can easily look to an inexperienced onlooker as if depression is self-willed and self-induced. 'Snap out of it!' you are told. 'Pull yourself together!' But you are only told to pull yourself together when you can't.

Sometimes there is an obvious reason for depression. Between 50 and 60 per cent of women suffer from post-natal depression. Further causes of depression for women are widowhood, divorce or the daily glare at each other over the breakfast porridge, which can easily result in deterioration of health and sometimes death.

One study showed that the

bereaved were seven times more likely to die within a year or two of the death of a spouse than others in the same age group who had not suffered bereavement. This increased risk of ill health and death continues for at least three years after the bereavement.

Some less obvious unhappy episode might start a snowball condition of depression, especially if you are physically run down. Perhaps one day you feel unable to cope, perhaps there is then a series of tiresome mishaps that you handle clumsily. You may be thoughtless or impatient with other people so they snap back at you; you overreact – you've had a bad day.

But perhaps the bad days continue, if you are unhappy, overworked or under stress. You may find yourself in a downward spiral of increasing self-perpetuating failure and distress, and are understandably downhearted and depressed.

But that isn't what it looks like to other people. From the outside you merely look disagreeable. You stop laughing, then you talk less. You seem increasingly lethargic, you can't be bothered, you start to look unkempt (the dirty-bra-strap syndrome). Your world narrows, because meeting people becomes more of an effort and it gets harder for you to go out.

You finally abandon all social activities. You prefer to be alone, you decide that you are a loner and that other people are tiresome. After frequent rebuffs your friends may fade away. Your family's patience may last longer but you also seem to care less for them and increasingly pick rows or ignore them. They may eventually find it too depressing to be with you

(you pull them down) and avoid seeing you, in self-defence.

A depressed woman may clean an already clean room, very slowly. Or she may sit, apathetic, in a chaotic room and do nothing at all. Everything is too much effort and she feels too exhausted to do anything.

A pathologically depressed woman is withdrawn, she doesn't smile, she keeps still, sits and stares. She may do stupid things, throw away her embroidery or sell her favourite dress for next to nothing. She may order goods that she can't pay for. One woman ordered two Rolls-Royces in an afternoon (she had no money); one booked a world tour and one bought a grand piano on impulse.

Inside she may be anguished and feel worthless; she feels that there is no hope to life and no end to it. At this point she has lost all her self-confidence, she feels personally worthless and may also experience a terrible sense of panic. By now it's obvious that there's something seriously wrong – she is ill.

Many famous people have suffered in this way. As a matter of fact, depression can often be one of the reasons for their fame – striving to prove their worth, to prove that they are worth loving and cherishing. Throughout his life, despite triumphs and world fame, Winston Churchill suffered these periods of deep dejection, known to his family as Black Dog.

A person who has been cruelly and constantly rejected in childhood can probably never get enough of such reassurance (via applause) in adult life. For instance, the beautiful Jennie Churchill was a selfish mother to the young Winston. She took London by storm and dazzled her son, but she gave him no steady, reassuring affection.

A predisposing factor of depression is that you are not loved enough in childhood. If you feel you are not loved enough in adulthood, depression can close in like a wet fog.

Some people try to avoid depression by becoming workaholics. 'As soon as I stop doing something constructive, I feel as depressed as a wet Bank Holiday,' said one fashion tycoon. 'I feel agitated, I can't stop and I don't want to stop, because I know I'll feel much worse if I do.'

Some people try to ward off depression with jokes that are too painful to take seriously. Some famous comedians suffer from depression; perhaps the best known was Tony Hancock who committed suicide at forty-six.

Why do people increasingly suffer from serious depression and why do five times more women get it than men?

The reason can be *physical*. Premenstrual tension at *any* age can produce depression. This is very common and a sign of it is water retention, so if you tend to put on 6 lb once a month and get impatient and bitchy, see your doctor about it (or go to a menopause clinic, *see page 50*).

Some doctors think that a similar imbalance in hormones contributes to the sudden post-natal depression from which a lot of women suffer. One theory is that this occurs because the body has been producing an unusually large amount of progesterone (Nature's tranquillizer) during pregnancy, which may be why so many expectant mothers feel well, tranquil and happy. The progesterone level drops at birth.

Up to 60 per cent of women get post-natal depression (the baby blues), with tears, exhaustion, and general inability to cope. Up to 10 per cent get bad post-natal depression, which can mean hallucinations, violence towards the baby and suicidal tendencies. One woman in 200 has a mental breakdown and one woman in 500 is hospitalized for serious depression. They may need psychiatric supervision for as long as two years after the birth.

It is easier for the father to spot post-natal depression than it is for the mother herself and the earlier it is treated, the better. The personality change is not permanent.

The hormone imbalance at the menopause can certainly be a contributing factor to depression.

Anything that contributes to physical exhaustion will undoubtedly contribute to depression. Heavy menstrual periods may mean that you are short of iron and therefore anaemic; such a woman's mood may improve dramatically within eight hours if she takes iron tablets, which are absorbed by the body extremely fast.

The reason for depression might be *mental stress or exhaustion*. Overwork is depressing, as demonstrated by the high-rate of suicide among students. The depression that derives from *stress and mental exhaustion* may well be offset by large doses of vitamin B complex (Orovite pills or Parentrovite injections) which are also good for treating depression after flu or a cold that you can't seem to shake off.

The aftermath of a family crisis with which you have had to deal, or moving house or looking after a very old, querulous person or a very young bawling person can be depressing. The aftermath of failure (especially after tremendous effort) is depressing; so is a public humiliation, deserved or otherwise.

Many women were brought up to believe that marriage was their career. So if she has an unsuccessful marriage, a woman may feel that she has a failed career as well as a failed relationship. Her man goes out to work, she is stuck at home, she feels isolated and the classic symptoms start. She may blame her husband, but it's hardly his fault if she has insufficient inner resources to fall back on.

Many women feel depressed if they have been acting a traditional (passive, docile, Welsh-farmhouse Earth-Mother) feminine part that they don't really feel. If she stays at home to be the perfect twenty-four-hour-a-day mum, an intelligent trained woman may feel exhausted, on edge and snappy – and *then* feel guilty because according to some child specialist, who has never been potty-chained, she ought to be feeling fulfilled.

Some depressing factors are environmental. People often feel exhausted and depressed after a long, grey dreary winter (as opposed to an exciting, snowy one). Doctors' surgeries overflow in a cold sludgy February.

Possibly the fastest way to get depressed is by living with depressing people. Because it's catching – worse than measles. If your flat-mates wallow in depression – move out fast. You *cannot* help them, only a doctor can.

What can a doctor do? Since the seventeenth century medicine has recognized that depression is a serious illness and a doctor can certainly help you if you feel unable to break out of a depression by your own

efforts. He may prescribe an anti-depressant such as imipramine (proprietary name Tofranil) to jolt you out of your depression, or a tranquillizer, such as diazepam (proprietary name Valium), to calm you down if you're over-anxious.

Another drug for treating recurring depression is lithium. It has been used as a long-term *protective* drug to cut down the number of attacks.

Twelve married middle-aged women on a cake-factory assembly line were interviewed on loneliness. They were all happy as larks in their brown gingham dresses and little frilly caps. They sang as they stuck cherries on cakes. All twelve of them were on tranquillizers and so was the factory nurse (although none of them was aware that the rest were 'on pills'). They had nearly all gone back to work at the suggestion of their doctors, because they had felt so isolated, alone and depressed at home.

If you are prescribed pills (*see* 'Drugs', *page 274*) make sure that you know how your depression has been diagnosed, why you are getting drugs and how long you can expect to keep taking them. It may be a few weeks, six months or possibly a year.

Your doctor may suggest that you go out and meet people and have fun. Of course, this is the last thing you *want* to do if you're depressed; you may feel like spitting at him but he's likely to be right.

Don't necessarily accept a doctor's advice if it doesn't *feel* right, if it doesn't fit you, if he doesn't seem to understand what you're talking about or if he doesn't sympathize with you. The doctor who really understands you is the one who puts his feet up on his desk and said, 'Tired, exhausted and depressed? That's exactly the way I feel myself. Let's have a cup of tea.'

A controversial treatment for depression that has been in use for many years (although it is not fully understood by the medical profession) is electro-convulsive therapy (ECT). Treatment is by electric shocks through your skull after you have been given an anaesthetic: a small amount of electricity is passed through the brain and produces a convulsion. Treatment is repeated perhaps twice a week for three weeks or longer. One possible side effect is temporary memory loss; there can be other unpleasant side effects. ECT can have a good effect, bad effect or no effect. Most important: in general, you should certainly never be given it unless *you* agree to it.

WOMAN BITES BLACK DOG (HOW TO HANDLE DEPRESSION)

Treat depression as seriously as you would a broken leg. As everyone knows, who has been in this state:

1 You can recover.
2 Once you have suffered badly from depression you must always be on your guard because it may recur and must be stopped at the outset.

Different people develop different preventive measures but they will be variations of the following:

1 Fix your lifeline. If you haven't got a loving partner, if you haven't got Leonard Woolf right beside you, alert two relatives or friends who know you well enough to be able to reassure you

and are sufficiently fond of you to do so. If you really are friendless, contact Depressives Associated, who have many groups around the country. Their head office is at 19 Merley Ways, Wimborne Minster, Dorset BH21 1QN (✆ Wimborne [0202] 883957).

The danger sign is when you can clearly see that the black dog is coming, but already feel too apathetic to do anything about it. This is when you need your lifeline.

2 Whether or not you are on your own, you must eat, sleep and *not drink*. All the problems are compounded if you get exhausted, overtired and hungover, because practically everyone feels depressed in this situation.

3 Regular exercise has a physical effect on the body that counteracts depression.

4 Get away and keep away from places that depress you, especially if it's home. Just put your coat on and step outside the front door. *Then* decide where to go, if only for half an hour.

5 Normal chat *outside your home* is very important, because you need to make a bit more effort than you do on the telephone, even with banal subjects over a cup of coffee with a cheerful neighbour, or with the librarian (not on a Saturday morning) or the greengrocer (ditto).

6 Prepare *A Seven-day Energy Plan* for when depression strikes. Don't think you can't afford it. What you *can't* afford is to have depression. Many amusements are cheap, so is a bus ride, followed by a walk back, so are libraries and museums. So is a

transistor radio. Not everyone sees Jimmy Young as a Lifesaver, but even if he gets you into a frenzy, well you're no longer

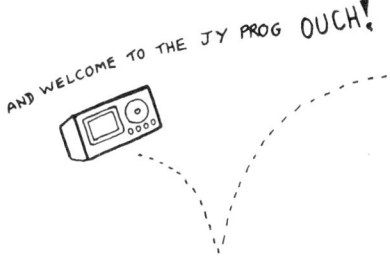

apathetic, are you? Now write and *tell* him what you think of his recipes.

Gardening, sewing, photography and embroidery are soothing, satisfying and reassuring occupations, so is dressmaking. Not necessarily for yourself: anyone who does simple dressmaking or gardening for friends is never short of a friend.

7 Don't *think* after 10 p.m., especially not around dawn. Anxieties and problems are magnified after 10 and multiply after 3 a.m. Write down your worries if that gets them out of your system. Your notes will probably look over-agitated in the morning ('Connect spies with shoplifting. . .drop some Pelicans. . .improve on H. G. Wells. . .') in which case *keep them* to remind you, next time you feel that way, how pointless it was to worry.

8 Make an enjoyable ritual of going to bed. Don't wait until you're too exhausted to unbutton yourself. Have a hot drink in a pretty cup; nice music; a warm, scented bath; a clean fluffy towel; clean pretty sheets; lots of plumped-up pillows; a pretty nightgown. It doesn't really matter if it takes you all evening to get ready for bed. It's better than spending all night unable to sleep.

9 In the morning GET UP, have a cold shower if you can bear it, do your exercises and have your favourite breakfast.

10 Then GET OUT. What you do after that doesn't much matter.

THE CALAMITY SPIRAL

There's quite a lot of scientific evidence to prove that the better you look, the more self-confidence, success and fun you'll have. Studies indicate that attractive people can apparently get away with mediocre performances, whereas the plain ones have to produce better work. And we all know that when you look better, you feel better, you sparkle more, you perform better and you also have more fun at parties.

We all have our off-days but no one who hasn't had a clinical depression could understand why film star Shirley MacLaine in her mid-thirties had a few off-*years*. She neglected her appearance, put on 25 lb and looked 'dour and frumpy'. 'I wasn't working at the right things, I was depressed, I hadn't looked in a mirror for months . . . My self-esteem had disappeared and so had my sense of humour.'

The Calamity Spiral is very common. Some women have been up and down it several times. This is how it goes:

PHASE 1
You feel tired all the time for no good reason. In fact there is probably a

good reason, which may be financial, or a worry, or a loss, or an unhappy love affair, or some *minor* rejection.

You start to neglect your appearance and surroundings.

You gradually give up things – you stop going out, seeing people and start to get sloppy (not making the bed, wearing dirty underwear, not putting on make-up).

You put off things – it's too much trouble.

You feel listless and aimless. Perhaps you eat to console yourself and the pounds creep on. Perhaps you gradually neglect your appearance, apart from basic cleanliness, because you're too busy looking after other people or finishing up their Farex.

PHASE 2

You notice that you're not looking or feeling good. You give up in the head.

You resign yourself to looking scruffy, being not-happy; everything seems too much. (This is the woman-in-a-dressing-gown stage.)

You get minor irritating illnesses and become prone to minor accidents. You can't get rid of a cold, you fall off the kitchen stool, you cut yourself with the kitchen knife.

You look worse, know it, and are depressed. When a woman loses confidence in herself it very quickly shows in her face.

You may tend to slump, which doesn't help your figure. Letting muscles droop causes body stress, which can add to physical and mental strain. By now you feel exhausted quite often and may even slip a disc.

PHASE 3

Other people notice, don't understand and give you much negative feedback (at first kind, then exasperated).

People notice that your work starts slipping. This is when you really lose your self-esteem, when everybody confirms to you your poor opinion of yourself.

You rapidly reach the point where *you don't care what you look like,* because you don't much like yourself. You lose your self-esteem and this is the danger point.

PHASE 4

Major calamities start to occur. You get sacked/your husband talks of leaving/you think of suicide. Sloppy little habits turn into positive neglect. The problems spiral. The worse you look, the worse you feel, so the worse you look. From here it's very easy to slip into a case of clinical depression, which can be difficult to escape without professional help.

PHASE 5

Self-destruction. You are now your own worst enemy. You insult your friends, goad your husband to the point of leaving, you're deliberately rude to your boss, you mishandle an important meeting and you take impulsive, insane decisions. You may even attempt suicide.

And it all began with feeling a bit off colour and doing nothing about it.

Some of the most attractive women in the world have been down the Calamity Spiral. If you've got someone to help and encourage you, you can fight your way back, quite quickly, with your own crash programme.

If you can afford it the very best thing to do is to put yourself in the hands of experts and visit a *reputable* health farm for ten to fourteen days. The main therapy (which is hardly ever mentioned in articles about health farms) is that from the moment you enter the door you are taken care of, like a baby, by kindly professionals. You cannot duplicate this atmosphere by staying in bed and dieting on lemon juice for a fortnight, although you might, by going home to mother for a *quiet* rest *in bed*.

Shrublands or Forest Mere are used to people who just manage to totter in and flop. You'll be cosseted in comfortable surroundings, have your diet taken care of and terrific body and beauty treatments (which really work) will be arranged for you. It's amazing how quickly you start feeling restored. You don't have to meet anyone else but the other residents who are often very interesting. Perhaps a prime minister, perhaps a travel editor, perhaps a dynamic duchess who needs a rest (but the pop stars generally stay in their bedrooms the whole time).

Before going to a health farm always check with your doctor that your body is fit enough to cope with fasting (if you want to slim) and don't think that this is ridiculously unnecessary. A health farm is not for those who are not healthy.

Health farms cost from £75 basic a week (at time of writing) plus VAT and service. If you can't afford one, try to arrange some other trip on which you can be looked after and organized, but also stimulated. Perhaps a week at summer school, a study holiday, an activity holiday, a sports holiday or pony trekking. An all-in, sight-seeing coach trip can also be stimulating – if organized by someone else.

Activity holidays and holiday tours can also stimulate your mind, and give you rest, relaxation and a chance to get your vitality back. They are also a good way of meeting people. Find out more about them from the British Tourist Authority (addresses are at the end of this section).

There are many weekend or midweek courses. For example: two-, three- or four-day courses in yoga, bridge, chess, collecting antiques or learning a craft. These are held at an old Sussex rectory, and there are many other similar courses all over the country. Get a list of what's available in your area from your local library or, if you want to get farther afield, ask your travel agent for the recommended British Tourist Association list.

The idea is to provide you with something stimulating in totally different surroundings, *where you are looked after*. If you feel really tired and jaded, try to get a longer break. Take a cheap, holiday two-week course. There are many holidays planned for walking, rock climbing, nature watching, pony trekking, jewellery making, or similarly absorbing pursuits. Get details for a list of holidays in guest houses published by the *Countrywide Holidays Association*.

The Field Studies Council runs nine centres where you can attend a range of courses on the environment, from local folklore to archaeology and the landscape. For example, a week's residential landscape-painting course (for beginners as well as advanced painters) in the heart of the Constable country at *Flatford Mill* costs £39 at time of writing.

Loughborough University Summer Programme has a famous annual programme of activities for everyone from the under-fives to the most brilliant technologists. You can choose from highly scientific or technological courses or there are lots of creative and general studies courses. (There's also a crèche for your under-five-year-olds.)

University Holidays Ltd offer bed and breakfast (for a weekend) or weekly terms in single study-bedrooms on university campuses all over the country. If you take children with you, *Holiday Fellowship Ltd* has family centres all over Britain and also abroad and arranges excellent activity holidays. They specialize in painting, archaeology, bowls, bridge, geology, golf, music and almost anything you want to do, at centres all over the country. *The National Park Study Centres* include one in the Lake District National Park where you can learn about flora and fauna. To check the wide range of study and activity holidays available in this country and abroad, get the British Tourist Authority's publication *Holiday Courses* (12p plus postage) or write for *Study Holidays* from the *Central Bureau for Educational Visits and Exchanges* (85p plus 15p postage) or get details of holidays available in the North from the *Scottish Institute of Adult Education*.

The point is to get right away from your normal surroundings, meet new people and do new things. When you return, start to rebuild yourself and your environment. (Buy new bra, wash it, make bed, etc.)

If you can't afford to go away, you can do what Shirley MacLaine did – and invent your own Crash Course, picking what you need. It won't be so easy, but you can probably do it if you live alone or have an encouraging mate or friend. Shirley enrolled at a gym, jogged seven miles a day, went on a diet and didn't look up until she was a size 10 again. She thinks it's important to have definite short-term and long-term targets, 'otherwise it's difficult because of the day-to-day problems and seductions'.

'It needs a lot of discipline to work up your self-esteem. You need to be flexible with yourself and rigid with others. You need a little time each day, just for yourself, to spend doing something that will make you feel better. You mustn't feel guilty about being selfish, because you'll be much better company, and a much nicer person to be with, if you feel refreshed and alive.'

At first, try to do all your self-improvement with other people, because their interest will help to regain your self-esteem and, paradoxically, stops you thinking about yourself.

Doing something with other people is also a good way to get out of a 'can't be bothered' slough of despondency. Exercise classes, yoga, transcendental meditation and Weightwatchers are also ways to beat the Calamity Spiral. Weightwatchers costs about £1 a week; TM costs about £35 a course (£15 if you're a housewife or student and nothing if you can't afford it).

Check with your local library to see if there are any keep-fit classes run by your local council such as recreational gym, toning-up classes, dancing or sport. They'll also tell you where the nearest yoga, TM and Weightwatchers classes are. There may also be special meetings for the elderly or handicapped.

Go to your local sports centre (find out where it is from the library) and see if you can take up any sport you enjoyed at school, or try a new one, such as squash.

Being active and getting away from your home is the best way to fight off the blues and depression, and to improve fitness and health. It is the first step back to feeling confident and looking good again.

ADDRESSES
Write for brochures to:

Shrubland Hall Health Clinic, Coddenham, Ipswich, Suffolk IP6 9QH (☏ Ipswich [0473] 830404).

Forest Mere Hydro, Forest Mere, Liphook, Hampshire GU30 7JQ (☏ Liphook [0428] 722051).

Loughborough University Summer Programme, Centre for Extension Studies, University of Technology, Loughborough, Leicestershire LE11 3TU (☏ Loughborough [0509] 63171).

University Holidays Ltd, Borehamgate House, Sudbury, Suffolk CO10 6BD (☏ Sudbury [0787] 76111).

The Holiday Fellowship Ltd, 142–144 Great North Way, London NW4 1EG (☏ 01-203 3381).

The National Park Study Centres, The Principal, Loschill Hall Study Centre, Castleton, Derbyshire S30 2WB (☏ Hope Valley [0433] 20373).

The British Tourist Authority, Queen's House, 64 St James's Street, London SW1A 1NF (☏ 01-629 9191).

English Tourist Board, 4 Grosvenor Gardens London SW1W 0DU (☏ 01-730 3400).

Scottish Tourist Board, 23 Ravelston Terrace, Edinburgh EH4 3EU (☏ 031-332 2433).

London office: 5 Pall Mall East, London SW1Y 5BA (☏ 01-930 8661).

Wales Tourist Board, Welcome House, High Street, Llandaff, Cardiff CF5 2YZ (☏ Cardiff [0222] 567701).

The Central Bureau for Educational Visits and Exchanges, 43 Dorset Street, London W1H 3FN (☏ 01-486 5101).

The Scottish Institute of Adult Education, 43 Melville Street, Edinburgh EH3 7JF (☏ 031-226 7200).

The Old Rectory, The Fleet, Fittleworth, Pulborough, West Sussex RH20 1HU (☏ Fittleworth [079 882] 306).

Countrywide Holidays Association, Birch Heys, Cromwell Range, Manchester M14 68U (☏ 061-224 2887).

The Field Studies Council, Information Office, Preston, Montford, Montford Bridge, Shrewsbury SY4 1HW (☏ Montford Bridge [074 371] 674).

Dale Fort Field Centre, Haverfordwest, Dyfed SA62 3RD (☏ Dale [064 65] 205).

The Drapers' Field Centre, Rhyd-y-Creuau, Betws-y-coed, Gwynedd LL24 0HB (☏ Betws-y-coed [069 02] 494).

Flatford Mill Field Centre, East Bergholt, Colchester, Essex CO7 6UL (☏ East Bergholt [020 629] 283).

Juniper Hall Field Centre, Dorking, Surrey RH5 6DA (☏ Dorking [0306] 3849).

The Leonard Wills Field Centre, Nettlecombe Court, Williton, Taunton, Somerset TA4 4HT (☏ Washford [098 44] 320).

Malham Tarn Field Centre, Settle, North Yorkshire BD24 9PU (☏ Airton [072 93] 331).

Orielton Field Centre, Pembroke, Dyfed SA71 5EZ (☏ Castlemartin [064 681] 225).

Preston Montford Field Centre,
Preston Montford Hall, Montford
Bridge, Shrewsbury SY4 1DX (☎
Montford Bridge [074 371] 380).

Slapton Ley Field Centre, Slapton,
Kingsbridge, Devon TQ7 2QP (☎
Torcross [054 858] 466).

SORROW, GRIEF AND
REGRET: A SENSE OF LOSS

You don't feel a sense of emotional
loss when you lose your purse or your
wallet is stolen or you lose money on
the stock market or gambling; you
feel irritation to a small or appalled
degree. You only feel a sense of emotional loss if what has gone is a part of
your life; not your driving licence but
the irreplaceable snapshots in the wallet, not the expensive bit of stolen
jewellery but your grandmother's
little engagement ring. They are of
sentimental value and what you feel
for that loss is bereavement, to a small
or great extent.

Grief is a private part of life, not
given much public expression and not
always recognized. The Victorians
dealt with grief by ostentatiously recognizing it and surrounding it with
ritual. Today, grief has become
embarrassing and can make onlookers feel uneasy. Although the quiet
dignity of sorrow draws respect and
silence, the tears of grief are embarrassing in public. We always apolog-
ize for showing grief in the office or
consulting-room or at a solicitor's
(I'm . . . all right, I'll be . . . all
right in a minute'). We are still taught
to disguise and deny grief, unless
someone has actually died – and even
then people tend to tell you to pull
yourself together, after initial sympathy.

You may feel sorrow and grief to
a lesser degree after quarrelling seriously with a close friend or your
child. You anticipate what it would
be like to lose the relationship; you
long to restore things as they previously were. You may feel a deep sense
of loss, of deprivation, of bereavement.

You may also experience this sense
of loss if you lose a job, a home, a
lover, a dog or a limb.

Regret and guilt are the most
immediate feelings when mourning a
person. You think of all those times
when you chose to do something
without them, when you could have
made them happy but didn't, when
you made them unhappy and didn't
much care, when you could have gone
to them and didn't. When you didn't
tell them what you wanted to say,
when you didn't tell them – although
it would have been so easy – that you
loved them. When you didn't even
show it.

Then when you think you're over it
all you pick up something in the
kitchen that he found or she made, or
the sun comes through the curtains in
the bedroom like it used to, or you
smell fresh coffee or peaches and
blankets and suddenly the stabbing
pain is piercing your heart again.

In the best of lives, by the time you
get to the middle, there are a lot of
happy things to remember and a lot of
things to regret. You regret not only
what has happened, but a lot that
didn't. The child you didn't have, the
career you didn't have, the good
times you never had, even the books
you now suspect you never will read.
Sometimes it's not the things you've
done that you regret (however awful
some of them may have been) but the
things you didn't try. This feeling of

regret, of having 'missed out' is also a form of bereavement, a sense of loss.

It can show itself in physical and unexpected emotional ways. These may be:

★ Nervousness
★ Trembling
★ Fear
★ Headaches
★ Insomnia
★ Nightmares
★ Loss of appetite
★ Inability to work well

and above all a general persistent fatigue.

All these symptoms were found in a study of widows. Some of them suffered psychosomatic illnesses that were physical expressions of their feelings: breathing difficulties ('I can't say (gasp) *what I* (gasp) feel'); vomiting or inability to eat ('Food is not what I need'); and agitation, which is a classic symptom of searching for what has been lost.

Other reactions to loss can be excessive smoking or drinking, a dramatic gain or loss in weight, creeping dependence on drugs, endless daydreaming.

Young widows seem to suffer more than the elderly, because they have been deprived of their marriages whereas the older widow has had a more complete experience (and is also likely to have fewer dependents and more money).

SIGNS OF A MOURNING CHILD

It's hard enough to deal with your own feelings but very often sorrow and bereavement may be felt just as keenly by a child. A child can mourn a person, a parental divorce, a home, a lost friend, a lost scholarship or a lost place in the football team.

Whatever a child does, assume that he or she is experiencing great grief. He may appear callous, unconcerned, or casual. He may go skating on the day of the funeral and apparently be unaffected. Recognize this for what it is: shock and denial.

Expect odd childish behaviour (regression) and expect the child to demand a lot of your attention. You can also expect tantrums, nightmares, sleeplessness, bed-wetting (in boys) and a noticeable decline in school work, until the loss is accepted, which *may* be as long as two years.

It seems that regret must be acknowledged and loss accepted. The loss of a child's childhood, the loss of a love, the end of a rotten marriage or a good one.

GETTING OVER IT

We can postpone grief but not escape it. Far better to accept it than deny it. Better to recognize what's happening and mourn adequately than to postpone and suffer more severely later. Widows who postpone grief suffer more than others from the physical symptoms already described.

Realize that you may never *totally* recover; a part of you has gone for ever and don't let anyone deny it. But one day you will enjoy life again and will perhaps be able to remember with pleasure, instead of only with pain.

Don't think of mourning as self-indulgence. Never deny the past, especially the good bits. Allow yourself the dignity of sorrow. Respect your feelings: don't try to drown them in drink or smother them in tranquillizers.

Don't underestimate the value of rituals. A requiem mass or a memorial service is often more consoling than a funeral because it takes place later.

You might have to get right back to work a day or two after the funeral. This can be a good thing because it gets you back into your normal routine and gives you something else to think about. However, it can also postpone the mourning cycle and, although you apparently function normally, your reactions may see-saw alarmingly or you may overreact with unexpected violence to a relatively small, depressing event.

A rude telephone operator can bring a lump to your throat and the effort of getting to the office on time can exhaust you before the day starts. You may sit down and cry if the milkman has no change, if you're asked to do a little extra work, are mildly rebuked at the office, or if you lose 50p.

Don't be surprised if small incidents upset you. Realize why they occur and make allowances for them, rather than pretend that they don't or shouldn't exist. It is a comfort to know that such feelings are normal, that they will pass in the normal order of things, and that you can help yourself, so long as you don't deny your feelings of bereavement.

This period of gradual acceptance is a recuperation period. It's important to realize that it may last longer than you think.

Don't stay at home alone. Don't withdraw from life. Get out and meet people (any people) and try to be nice to them, even when you least feel like it. Say something pleasant to the bus conductor, smile at the sour supermarket check-out girl.

A bereaved person runs a great danger of inventing a vicious circle of unpopularity (so does anybody who is depressed).

THE BEREAVEMENT TUNNEL

Whether it's a slight sense of loss or appalling grief, when you suffer from bereavement after a death it can be a great consolation to recognize the symptoms; you are less likely to feel bewildered, disoriented or frightened by your own feelings.

When you feel as if you are in a never-ending black tunnel (which is, of course, the Valley of Despair) the shock waves may hit you in the following order, to a greater or lesser degree.

1 *Numbness, shock.* This is what happens in extreme injury. There is often a merciful release from pain. Mortally wounded men on the battlefield often cannot feel pain. This is why some widows cannot cry and often seem to be amazingly collected, almost unfeeling. They are anaesthetized by shock. They *can't* yet feel. They may even do very practical things, such as cooking the Christmas turkey or writing to the

How to lose friends and influence

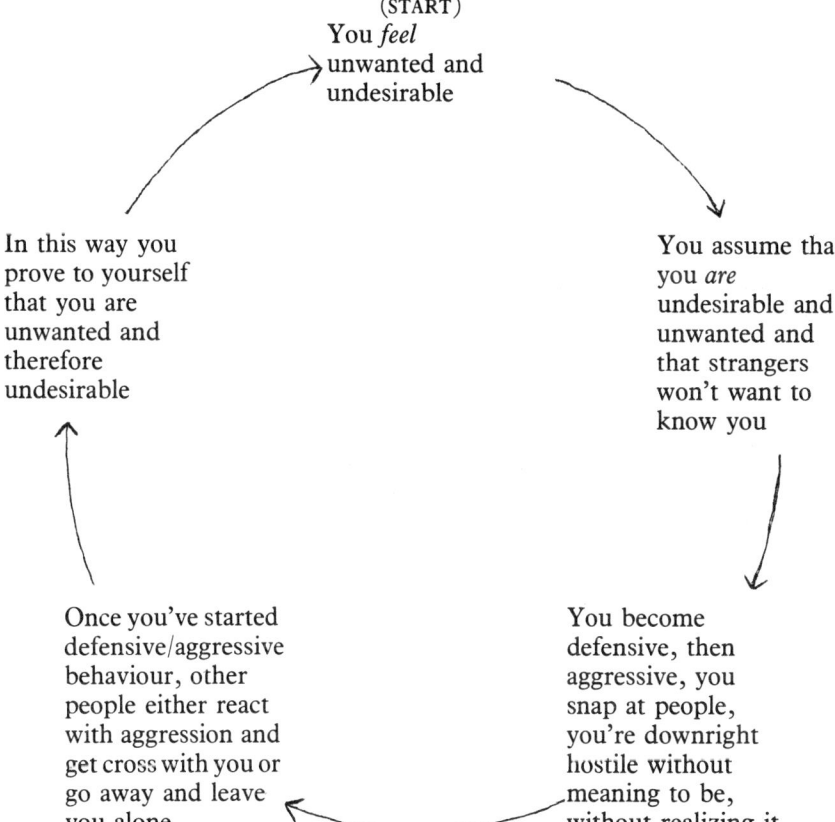

(START)
You *feel*
→ unwanted and
undesirable

You assume that
you *are*
undesirable and
unwanted and
that strangers
won't want to
know you

In this way you
prove to yourself
that you are
unwanted and
therefore
undesirable

Once you've started
defensive/aggressive
behaviour, other
people either react
with aggression and
get cross with you or
go away and leave
you alone

You become
defensive, then
aggressive, you
snap at people,
you're downright
hostile without
meaning to be,
without realizing it

---

family lawyer.

2 *Disbelief, denial.* It isn't true, it hasn't happened, I'll wake up in a minute. God wouldn't let it happen, he never would, not to me. I haven't done anything to deserve it.

3 *Physical pain.* Your heart may really ache.

4 *Protest, resentment, anger, bitter-* *ness, indignation.* How dare He do this to me! How *can* He? I did all I could. It's not fair! I didn't cheat. I can't be expected to put up with this. Why should I? I've done so much good. (Well, I haven't done much bad . . . Well, I've done less than most.) What *more* does He want? Why did it have to be me?

5 *Frustration.* Who can I talk to

now? Who can I do things with? Who can I share things with? Who knows my past, my jokes, my fears? Who am I supposed to spend Christmas with? Just *what* am I supposed to do now?

6 *Guilt, regret, shame.* The most difficult adjustments are those which have to be made by a widow who has constantly quarrelled with her husband but cannot now make amends, or who may feel guilt because she genuinely wanted him to die (or thinks that she did). On the other hand, devoted, distraught wives can invent guilt situations ('I didn't feed him properly when he was ill', 'I should have been with him more', 'I must have neglected him or he wouldn't have died').

7 *Bewilderment and disorientation.* Things are meaningless. All I've done is futile. Nothing in life makes sense. What *is* the point of life? Is this all there is?

8 *Acceptance.* I know I won't wake up. It *has* happened. This is how it's going to be for evermore. And I can't alter it.

9 *Sadness.* (Tears at this point). The life I knew is over. It's gone for ever.

10 *Humiliation.* This can take many forms, often imaginary ones. Many a widow realizes that, as well as losing a mate, she has also lost her social and financial position at one swipe. She is no longer the mayor's wife, or anyone's wife.

You can also sorrow and feel deeply humiliated over a broken love affair. A love affair proves one is lovable. A broken love affair seems to prove that one isn't.

11 *Emptiness, depression.* I am nothing now. I am worth nothing. Nobody cares about me. Nobody ever will again. I don't care. This feeling can deepen to:

12 *Despair.* Collapse of the will to live. The stage when life is the enemy and death is the friend. A deepening of emptiness to the exclusion of all other feeling. There never *will* be any light at the end of the black tunnel. The future is dreary and meaningless, and you don't even care. Suicide is most likely at this point.

13 *Idealization of the loss.* The good is remembered and exaggerated and the bad is blanked out. It's important to get over this stage, first in order to form new relationships and secondly because it's bad for others. It's very difficult for children to live up to an idealized father, it's easier for them to be able to joke with you about his idiosyncracies.

14 *Picking up your life and dusting it.* This is the recuperation period. You accept that your situation has changed, that you have to make your way in the world, that there's a great deal of work to be done. Some people react too quickly to this feeling and make drastic changes that they later regret, such as selling a home.

15 *New relationships become possible.*

You realize that you're not alone in the world, that other people have bad times, that other people need you, that you had good times before you met him and will again, although he's gone and so is the Siamese-twin situation of being half of a loving couple with him. Life never *will* be the same again, but there can be a different life. (This is the situation that Queen Victoria would never accept.)

HOW TO GET OUT OF THE TUNNEL

To get over a loss, a death or a departure:

Step 1 *Accept your grief.* It is normal to be in shock for a while and you may feel numb, unable to believe what has happened. You must believe it. It has happened and you *are* strong enough to survive.

Step 2 *Feel the pain.* If you are to heal, you must experience the hurt, the misery, the desolation. You don't have to wallow in endless self-pity – just accept your feelings. They won't overwhelm you, and you must not bottle them up or pretend they aren't there.

Step 3 *Be angry.* It is natural to rage against fate, society, the person you have lost, the person who's walked out on you or even people who have nothing to do with the situation. So scream, kick the wall, throw things, release your aggressive resentment in sport or housework. Don't be destructive. Don't cut your hair off, yell at the post-man, kick the dog or shake the baby until it rattles.

Step 4 *Don't expect too much.* A quick recovery is possible but unlikely. For every two steps forward, expect to take one back.

Step 5 *Forgive to forget.* Resentment, bitterness and hate corrode your soul, show in your face and in your conversation. They can wreck your life. You will not be free until you can stop feeling wronged. However:

Step 6 *Keep feeling.* For a long time you will still burst into tears when you are unexpectedly reminded of your pain. Even thinking about how it hurt will still hurt a bit. That's OK. Don't deny it. Feel it to the full.

Step 7 *Rest.* Take it easy. Don't rush around like a demented worker bee or social butterfly. Go to bed early, get up later. But don't overdo it: rest is necessary, slumping into total lethargy is not.

Step 8 *Ask for help.* However difficult, ask neighbours, relatives and acquaintances. Try not to be stiff, prickly or proud. You would do the same for them.

Step 9 *Be reasonable.* Expect the Demon Doom to descend at times when the rest of the world is happy – weekends, holidays, Christmas. Deliberately plan cheering activities for those times, or else go away.

Step 10 *Be realistic.* The past won't return. Don't allow false hope.

(Fantasies prevent healing.) Invest your thoughts (and any energy) in the present and in small, constructive activities (see further on).

Step 11 *Eat properly*. No dieting for the moment. Your body needs proper nutrition to heal. Think of your loss as a physical wound. Take vitamins, don't eat junk food, eat a balanced diet (*see page 38*).

Step 12 *Look after yourself*. If you had a physical wound you'd be a pampered invalid. Emotional pain is just as debilitating. If there's nobody to pamper you then take care of yourself: indulge your whims (if you think you can't afford it, remember you can't afford *not* to).

Buy yourself something lovely.

Invest time and money at the hairdresser or beautician.

Read a good book (or a bad one might be better).

See a good film or play.

Have a bathful of luxury with delicious soaps, bubbles and scents.

Wear your nicest clothes and lingerie.

Make yourself a delicious hot drink, last thing at night.

Have your breakfast egg in a pretty egg cup on a dainty tray.

Buy flowers for yourself.

Subscribe for a year to a glossy magazine.

Step 13 *Count your blessings*. Change is the rule of life, and as you get better you will see that the good life you had before your loss has not been totally destroyed.

Step 14 *Remember the distant past*. You used to enjoy lots of things, didn't you? Try reviving your old interests, possibly even ones from your schooldays (when you were contented without whatever you have just lost).

Step 15 *Accept the future*. Welcome new people, open your mind to new interests, new ideas, new places.

Step 16 *Slowly start picking up the pieces*.

Give yourself another small treat. A plant, a kitten (a goldfish isn't demanding enough), a window-box. Something that you have to look after.

Get a small aim. Embroider a cushion. Redecorate a room. Finish a book. Gardening is marvellous therapy, so dig, dig, dig (someone else's garden, if you haven't got one). If you have a garden, redesign it, completely, on paper, just as an exercise.

Offer to do little jobs for friends. A bit of shopping, a bit of baby-sitting, nothing very demanding, nothing very responsible.

Ask someone you know to do something minor with you. Go out and have fun is what the doctor orders and it's very, very difficult to force yourself to do it but it works.

So take a trip to the nearest stately home or museum: something that demands a bit of activity, not passive entertainment in a seat.

Take a boat on a lake, a bus to the end of the line, a *daily* walk in the park, a Hovercraft to France for the day.

Step 17 *Go away alone* for an activity weekend – *doing* something such as pottery or painting in a group. Don't risk a wet weekend alone in a hotel lounge in Bournemouth (*see* 'The Calamity Spiral' *page 175*).

Step 18 *Welcome the New Year.* Give yourself a pat on the back. You have weathered the worst of the storm.

Step 19 *Stay free.* Don't dive into another emotional relationship straight away, however miraculous it may seem if one turns up. Rest your emotions as well as your body.

Don't risk asking a man friend out (or in) until you can do so without worrying about it in advance.

Don't take a new demanding job or new responsible work or any big new commitment or move home until you – and those who care for you – feel that you have fully recovered and won't crack under the strain. But, if you can, go back to work as soon as possible, even if you don't feel like it.

Step 20 *One morning you will wake up feeling cheerful.* You will not be able to remember exactly how unhappy you were, only that you *were* unhappy. When that day comes, AS IT ALWAYS DOES, congratulate yourself on a successful survival.

HOW TO BE SURE THAT YOU'RE OUT OF THE TUNNEL

It is not at all unusual to think that you have recovered from bereavement or depression when you are still suffering. This can be dangerous: you may take hasty, wrong decisions and harm your life and relationships.

If you tick more than five of these symptoms you are still in a state of loss and bereavement.

Incidentally, you are far more likely to notice or admit the conditions described at the top of the list than the much more serious ones at the bottom.

1 Do you feel permanently tired, or does tiredness suddenly come over you – a sense of heaviness almost like a blanket?

2 Are you prone to tiny accidents? Have you sliced off the top of a finger, dropped a glass, spilt milk on the carpet?

3 Do you feel that you are losing your looks?

4 Do you suddenly forget what you were talking about?

5 Are you under-eating or over-stuffing? Or over-drinking? Or smoking?

6 Is it difficult to talk to your friends casually?

7 Are you becoming more easily bored?

8 Have you been feeling unusually inadequate, self-conscious, shy or awkward?

9 Does any normal action seem as much effort as wading through treacle?

10 Are you more sensitive, touchy or irritable than usual?

11 Do you suddenly fly into tempers?

12 Do you feel unusually angry about anything in particular?

13 Have you been tempted to shoplift?

14 Do you feel constantly guilty about anything?

15 Do you regard other people with unaccustomed shyness, fear or suspicion?

16 Is your concentration weak?

17 Do you constantly worry about things that are unlikely to happen (like getting sacked or the house falling down) or get churned up by insignificant trivia, such as the newspapers being delivered late?

18 Do your nerves feel raw?

19 Have your movements slowed down slightly, as if you were sleepwalking?

20 Do you still burst into tears, or feel that you would cry if you had to speak *one word* to anyone?

21 Do you feel helpless and despairing?

22 Do you feel there's no point to life, no hope, no future?

23 Do you feel a physical pain in your breast, or do you feel breathless, or as if your mind is screaming inside your head?

24 Do you feel numb or constricted?

WHAT TO DO WHEN SOMEONE DIES

You'll probably suffer from shock after the death of someone close to you. At its most usual and merciful this brings a numbness of feeling and temporary inability to appreciate all the implications of what has happened.

Fortunately, the practical part of your mind will continue to operate normally, because you're going to be so busy tending to all the bureaucratic necessities, that you'll hardly have time to mourn.

Expect to behave in a way that you had not expected. You may be briskly efficient, you may not shed a tear, you may find you've done or said some really stupid things – it doesn't matter. Don't accuse anyone of being heartless or mercenary, don't wonder why other people seem peculiarly unmoved or seem to be stealing the silver. Shock takes different forms. DO NOT CRITICIZE ANYONE ELSE'S BEHAVIOUR.

What you should do is:

1 Tell your doctor, if he doesn't know already.

2 Other people to inform after a death are:
   (*a*) the employer
   (*b*) the trade union
   (*c*) the bank
   (*d*) the family solicitor.

3 Try not to be alone. Friends are glad to help, but they often don't want to intrude, so you may have to ask for company.

4 Look after your health. You can't do anything for yourself, or anyone else, if you fall ill. So keep warm, eat light but nourishing meals and take any pills prescribed by your doctor (take tranquillizers, if he says so).

5 Don't neglect your physical comfort. Light the fire, draw the curtains, check that there's bread, butter, eggs and milk, basic food and drink.

6 A death must be officially registered within five days of the event. The person doing the registration must take the deceased's National Health Service card and a medical certificate of death to the Office of the Registrar of Births, Marriages and Deaths *in whose area the death has occurred.*

The registrar will want to know: date and place of death, full name and address of the deceased, age and occupation, date and duration of marriage, they will also want their National Insurance number, if possible.

You will be given one free copy of the certificate of registration of death; you will probably need more. You need *official* copies (not photostats) to claim social security benefits; to make claims on life assurance policies and when settling your husband's estate. Currently the charge is £1.45 for each extra copy. Get a couple more than you think you will need.

You will also be given a certificate of disposal, which you need before you can make any funeral arrangements.

If you want a cremation, there are extra forms to complete and you need two cremation certificates signed by different doctors (because after cremation no one can call for an autopsy).

For straightforward practical advice on these problems read *For Widows* by June Hemer and Ann Stany, published by Virago.

7 Funeral expenses are far, far higher than you imagine. The funeral director will advise you on comparative costs of different styles of burial but you must remember that death is his *business*, and it is to his advantage that you spend as much as possible. *You* will be in no state to shop around for coffins. You just want the best for your beloved, whatever it costs. But the best is not always the most expensive (in fact, the most expensive can be

nauseatingly vulgar). The simplest, least expensive funeral will probably be from the Co-op (according to *Which?*).

8 Money (especially immediate cash) is often an urgent problem for a widow. Of course she won't want to think about it, but she should claim *any* social security benefits to which she may be entitled as soon as possible. She may be entitled to receive *a death grant* (£30) to help meet costs incurred at the time of death. She may also be entitled to *a widow's allowance* which is a National Insurance benefit paid for twenty-six weeks after the death, to help a widow adjust to her nasty new financial circumstances.

9 If a widow is hard-pressed for money, she may be able to claim *supplementary benefit* as well as help with rent, rates and mortgage repayments.

Go to CAB for *advice about money entitlements*. They can help you immediately or direct you to such saviours as the Money Advice Centres (in Birmingham and Sunderland) which advise on all financial matters but *specialize in debt counselling*. Birmingham Money Advice Centre, The Birmingham Settlement, 318 Summer Lane, Birmingham B19 3RL (☎ 021-359 3562) and Sunderland Money Advice Centre, Guild of Help, 4 Toward Road, Sunderland, Tyne and Wear SR1 2QG (☎ Sunderland [0783] 72895).

10 After her first grief has passed, a widow may want to take a short TOPS training course in order to get a job. It is not generally realized (and no one goes out of their way to point it out) that IN THE

FIRST SIX MONTHS OF WIDOWHOOD she is entitled to the TOPS support grant of (at time of writing) from £25.70 to £41.30 a week (depending on her circumstances) AS WELL AS HER WIDOW'S RESETTLEMENT PENSION. This might mean an extra *free* £1000, so it's well worth pursuing.

11 If money that you would normally consider an extravagance can help to ease your burden at this time, then be extravagant: a nurse, a baby-sitter, taxis, help with cleaning and sorting clothes or papers, anything that eases your path is a good investment, because you are under great strain.

12 Wives should always know where their husband's relevant private papers are kept. It is very distressing to have to search for these papers at such a time. They may be needed in dealing with:
   (*a*) the insurance company
   (*b*) the Inland Revenue and PAYE
   (*c*) claims for post-war credits
   (*d*) the Department of Health and Social Security (DHSS)
   (*e*) claims for social security and supplementary benefits
   (*f*) the landlord
   (*g*) the building society
   (*h*) hire-purchase firms
   (*i*) the children's school (if they are in private schools he may have made special arrangements for paying fees).

13 After the funeral (or even before it, if you are alone or lonely) contact CRUSE, Cruse House, 126 Sheen Road, Richmond, Surrey TW9 1UR (☎ 01-940 4818). CRUSE is an organization for widows and their children which was set up to cushion the shock of widowhood. It is run with the aid of a government grant and was started by a doctor's wife, Margaret Torrie. Her book *Begin Again* (published in paperback by Dent at £1.95) is the best possible help that can be given to a widow.

CRUSE is *not* a social organization, although of course everybody has been through the same experience and is in the same boat so there's a strong feeling of comradeship. Their simple, sensible leaflets are very practical about money matters, including widow's allowance, what you can claim from the DHSS and how to do it.

Some women who marry young have developed in the shadow of the husband and have preferred this to taking their own part in the community. A woman can become similarly over-dependent on her husband when the marriage has been a secure and loving one after an unhappy childhood or adolescence. She may never have had to develop many areas of her personality or become a fully responsible adult. The death of her husband can leave such a woman uncertain about who she is or what she is or who she wants to be or what she wants to do.

Margaret Torrie says many a widow realizes too late 'that she has been over-dependent in her marriage in order to build up her man's self-confidence, or that the embellishment of the home to the exclusion of shared community interests has left her with nothing but *things*. Death has a painful way of revealing true values.'

CRUSE is also for women who may find it difficult to readjust, who often haven't enough money and who may feel lonely. Many such women retreat into their homes and the aim of the organization is to help them practically and emotionally to build up a new life. They can also help with such practical and painful matters as what to do with personal possessions, such as clothes, tools and hobby equipment.

The National Association of Widows was started by June Hemer in 1971, as a pressure group to work for reform of taxation of widows. NAW work has now extended beyond campaigning and they offer practical advice and personal support through their branches. They have seventy-three branches throughout England and Wales and two in Scotland, and are opening more. A difference between them and CRUSE is that CRUSE help is provided by professionally trained staff; although NAW has professional advisers, its helpers are volunteers and are all widows themselves.

Write to NAW headquarters, Stafford and District Voluntary Service, Chell Road, Stafford ST16 2QA (☎ Stafford [0785] 45465) for information and the address of your nearest branch, enclosing a stamped, addressed envelope.

WHAT IT FEELS LIKE TO BE A WIDOW

'Widows were other people, not me. Dry and old. That's what you think, until it happens to you. *My immediate reaction* was a feeling of total loss. At 2.30 I was happy and at 3.30 I was alone. He was gone, it was too enormous to grasp and I dared not think about: I shut that part of my mind.' That was what thirty-one-year-old Evelyn felt when her husband fell off a cliff and died instantly on their holiday.

'Then you realize you are alone, no one else can cope, nobody can do it for you. So I tried to grope at the future even in the first few hours. One of my thoughts was that we had no life insurance to cover the mortgage. We'd *talked* about it but neither of us had got down to it. Within the first few hours I did a quick guess at my financial position, which was awful, with two schoolchildren, then I forgot about it for a day or two. Does that sound callous? I think you instinctively behave when confronted by death as you do in life. I didn't dare collapse; to say I couldn't cope would have been more horrifying than dealing with the funeral.

'The letters of condolence are a great, great comfort, especially if they include praise, something genuinely nice about the dead, rather than sympathy, however great. And you love hearing any little story that you didn't know about him: you thirst for this. The letters confirm that your sorrow is for good reason, that this was a person who was valued by others, and the letters can be read and re-read for months afterwards.

'You have to deal with practical problems much earlier than you hope, and they can *seem* overwhelming. I had been a schoolteacher before I married, I'm methodical and quick to learn, so it wasn't too hard to take on the responsibilities. I'd been used to dealing with bills and household affairs. I knew what was insured and what wasn't, what we owed and what assets we had. I had my own credit card, and we had a joint bank account and a joint mortgage. Although the mortgage wasn't insured and James hadn't made a will, I still had immediate access to money, and this proved to be vital, because you aren't able to get a *penny* out of your husband's account. This is one good reason for having a joint current bank account on which both signatures are honoured.

'Everything is suspended until the will is "proved", and before this is done you may have to have your home and your possessions professionally valued. This can easily take six months. Your executor can apply to the Inland Revenue for permission to release a bit of the estate, pending tax decisions, so that you can pay your grocery bills, but even that takes weeks.

'Next came a period of detachment, of extraordinary serenity, which lasted *for about six weeks*. It was during this time that I tried to get work. I pursued work single-mindedly. I must have seemed very hard to some people, but my children understood that we needed the money. I built up a tough, brisk business veneer so that people would not refuse me work because they thought I might break down, although nobody did, of course. I had to convince myself that I could work because I *had* to work.

'I had so much to do in this period that I never had time to think, except at night and then I was so dog tired that I slept. I always refused Valium, except for the very first night, because I wanted to have all my wits about me. I ate and drank very little.

'*From two months onward* there were cracks in my veneer. Out of the blue would come the tears that I couldn't shed at the beginning, when there was too much to do. What depressed me most was just the fact of

being a widow. Widows loathe being called a widow. It means half a person, with something lacking. In losing a husband, lover and, above all, a friend you feel you have become a second-rate, incomplete person. So, the last thing I wanted to do was meet other "widows", other half-people. I wanted to be with WHOLE people, who would help me back to sanity and a normal life again.

'I can't remember feeling self-pity, but I suppose I did. It hit me like a brick when I went to places we knew well, when I came home and the house was empty, or just walking down particular streets in Manchester and even catching a train. Anyway, I would suddenly be overwhelmed by emotion. I learned to control the lump by concentrating on making my throat and stomach rigid.

'*After about six months* tears would still hit me suddenly when I was enjoying myself, when I was with happily married friends or after my first big job, when I couldn't tell him.

'I often felt bitter for James, about what he was missing, but I didn't feel bitter for myself and I wasn't really *depressed*, although I was sometimes in despair. This felt as if I was falling into an abyss, when the realization that I would never see him again suddenly hit without warning – again, and again and again. But I learnt that it never lasted too long.

'I also learnt that grief lingers much longer than you think. At six months, a year, you think you've coped. The first anniversary of the death is important because you can never again say "a year ago *we* did this". I reckon it took two years to heal my wound and to become a whole person again after being chopped in half.

'The important turning point in my widowhood life doesn't sound important at all. It was deciding, entirely on my own, to paint the front door a different colour. Then I re-arranged the house. It was painful but it was a physical way of recognizing that I was going to start a new life.'

Where there's a will . . .

We are none of us here for ever. Many people don't make a will because they fear that it's tempting Fate, or for reasons of conceit (it would mean recognizing their own mortality), pig-headedness, spite or ordinary, everyday fecklessness – because they just haven't got round to it. (Often a married woman just doesn't think it is important that *she* should make a will.) But it is. Everybody should make a will, even if you think you have nothing to leave. There are endless legal complications if you don't do so. Generally speaking it is foolish and irresponsible not to make a will.

'It's not morbid or mercenary, it's *necessary* if your family is to survive financially; unfortunately few people in their twenties or thirties take these things seriously,' said Anna, who had been widowed at twenty-seven and whose husband hadn't made a will.

WHY YOU SHOULD MAKE A WILL

1 The money will go where you want it to go.
2 It can be much cheaper (in legal fees and tax and bank charges) for your survivors if you leave a will than if you die intestate.
3 If you don't make a will your affairs will take a long, long time to settle, and your estate will attract maximum capital transfer tax. A *search* for the (non-existent) will then has to be made, at the request of a solicitor, before intestacy is accepted, and *letters of administration* are granted.
4 You may be able to avoid tax. Even if you don't care what happens when you are gone (to where the Inland Revenue can't touch you) it seems a shame just to hand it over to them if it can be avoided.
5 We can't always predict bereavement but some things are certain and doctors think that anticipation (advance acceptance that immortality is impossible), can strengthen you against a blow, such as the death of your mate. It's a *very* sensible idea to discuss seriously the emotional and practical aspects of what one would do if the other died, and such conversations, such joint plans and preparations made together can be a great source of comfort to the survivor when the situation occurs.

WHAT HAPPENS IF YOU DON'T MAKE A WILL

You will die 'intestate', which means that:

A widow (or widower or other relatives) will have to find two guarantors who will stand surety for the estate in perpetuity against the possibility of a will ever being discovered in which the lot is left to a cats' home.

If you die intestate your spouse (if you have one) will get all your personal possessions plus the first £25,000 if there are children, plus the income for life on *half* of what is left. (The capital reverts to the children on the death of the spouse.)

The children inherit the other half and this may not be the ideal situation for a widow. £25,000 isn't as much as it sounds when a cottage can cost over £40,000.

Where there is an intestacy, the law also restricts the ways in which the capital is invested for the widow (or widower) or children. The trustees have to put it in 'safe' investments such as government bonds or securities, rather than dashing Stock Exchange speculations. In fact one of the basic rules of trusteeship is: never speculate.

If you have no children your spouse will get the first £55,000 and *half* of what is left after that. The remainder goes to your blood relatives, which might be aunts you haven't seen for years (if ever) and didn't like much in the first place. Anyone in Timbuctoo or Scapa Flow who can claim to be related to you (and it's amazing how they turn up in battalions) is *entitled to grab a share* of your house, factory, sweetshop or racehorses.

If a man leaves no will in Scotland (even if he isn't a Scot) the position for his widow may be even worse, because she's entitled to even less. If there are children she may *only* be entitled to the value of her home up to £15,000, £5000 worth of furniture and cash of not more than £2500.

A single woman with no children who dies intestate automatically has her estate divided between her parents or (if they are dead) her brothers and sisters, or (if they are dead) her nearest blood relatives (that bunch in Timbuctoo).

If your grandparents are dead and if you have no living relatives who are descended from them, *your property will go to the Crown* (who can get along by themselves, without the benefit of your life savings). It's surely better to leave everything to friends who have helped you, to a charity or to someone who will get this amazing surprise one day and bless you for ever.

HOW TO MAKE YOUR WILL

Drawing up a will incorrectly is even worse than not making one (especially if it hasn't been signed and witnessed properly) and the lawyers will have a lot of expensive extra work. *It is a false economy to try to draw up your will by yourself* – especially if it's not very simple.

A solicitor might charge from £15 to £50 for drawing up a straightforward will. When you make the appointment to see the solicitor ask for a breakdown of his charges:

1 The basic minimum.
2 His hourly charge.
3 (After discussion of contents) how many hours are likely to be involved.

Make your will as simple as possible (it will be cheaper to make, and cheaper and easier for your executors to do what you want).

On no account buy one of those ninepenny printed forms in a stationer's shop. You might unintentionally land your family in terrible trouble, simply because one sentence is wrongly worded for *your* situation.

There's no all-purpose formula and one sort of form can't serve for fifty-five million people.

Write your own draft will on plain paper in your own words, *before* going to the solicitor. Don't try to use legal jargon; you'll get it all wrong.

Unless you're playing the Victorian great aunt game (getting maximum care and attention by being secretive about your will, and dropping heavy hints to your loved ones to keep everyone in line) then it might be a good idea to discuss your draft will with the major beneficiaries. They might have queries or suggestions which would eliminate any misunderstanding or squabbling afterwards.

Keep your will simple and clear. Avoid subclauses. Be precise. *If you insist on making your own will, make it as simple as possible.*

The simplest possible will would read as follows:

I Susan May Carr revoke all previous wills. I appoint my sister, Isabel Elizabeth Carr of 17 Smith Street, Chelsea, to be the sole executor of this will and leave to her everything that I own.

Date

Signature

Signed by Susan May Carr in our presence and by us in hers and each other's. [This sentence is called an attestation clause and is important. Don't leave it out.]

1st witness's signature, name in block capitals, occupation* and address*.
2nd witness's signature, name in block capitals, occupation* and address*.

*This will is then legal in Scotland.

Also, in Scotland, if your entire will is handwritten by you, and signed by you, you need no witnesses.

Another important point is that *no one who's going to benefit from the will* (or the spouse of any beneficiary) *is allowed to witness a will.*

Do not alter your will, or cross anything out, or mark it in any way. Instead, write a supplementary instruction (called a codicil). It must be dated, signed with the attestation clause and witnessed in exactly the same way as a will (although the two witnesses needn't be the same). If the addition isn't straightforward, make a new will.

A will should always be dated and, if possible, be on one piece of paper, with no typing errors or alterations.

(Alterations are assumed to have been made *after* a will and are therefore ignored.)

Never leave the back of a will blank. Draw a line right down the page so that nothing else can be written, and initial and date it at top and bottom. There must be two witnesses to this also. The three signatures should all be signed at the same time, with *all three people present together*. A blind person must not witness a will.

A later will doesn't automatically revoke an earlier one (which is something else that a lot of great aunts get wrong), and more than one will can lead to muddle, so if you make a new will you should always *personally* tear up or burn the earlier one as well as writing in the new will, 'This will revokes any previous wills'.

In your will you should:

1 *Appoint an executor* (perhaps two or three).
2 *Revoke previous wills*.
3 *Appoint a guardian* for any children under eighteen. It is usual to appoint the surviving parent *plus someone else*.

If you and your husband Ben both expire in the same instant in a car crash and have not named an appointed guardian the local authority's children's department will assume responsibility.
4 *Specify what you want done with your body* (cremation, burial or medical research). Let the appropriate organization know if, like Lady Churchill, you leave your eyes to science. That kidney is going to be no good if it's two weeks old and six feet underground.
5 *Name bequests* (gifts).
6 *Name legacies* (money).

7 *Dispose of the residue*. When you have made specific bequests (flat, the car, brooch, your books, and any specific sums of money you wish to leave to special people) you leave the 'residue' to some named person – that is, the remainder of your wealth and property after the other bequests have been made. This person is known as *the residuary legatee*.

Effectively, the costs of the estate – capital transfer tax, funeral expenses, legal costs – come out of the residuary legatee's part, so make sure that you leave him enough money to pay them.

Unless you specify something different, if your child, Jeremiah, dies before you, then Jeremiah's children (if any) would get Jeremiah's share of any legacy in any will. If anyone, other than your children, who is mentioned in your will dies before you, the diamond tiara destined for them simply goes to swell the 'residue'.

If the residuary legatee (say it's husband Ben) dies before you, then this results in what is called a *partial intestacy*, if you have named no alternative residuary legatees.
8 *Add the thirty-day disaster clause:* 'I bequeath the residue of my estate to my husband Ben, if he survives me by thirty days' (this is in case you are both in the same car crash).

Always give an alternative to the main benefactors of your will in case they die before you, with you or within thirty days of your death.

Lawyers and the money columns in newspapers show gruesome imagination when it comes to the possibility of your dear ones dying before you. They will not only suggest that you think about the possible plights of your unborn children's unborn children but cheerily ask you to imagine a cataclysmic family accident (an aeroplane crash is their favourite example) that instantly kills the man of the family but leaves his loved ones lingering on for a bit. The wife (you) dies of serious injuries twenty-nine days after her spouse, and the children go into comas of differing duration: the capital transfer tax will then be horrendous.

So it is a good idea, if you are leaving most of your estate to your spouse to say, 'I bequeath the residue of my property to my husband (or wife) if he (or she) survives me by thirty days' (two quick deaths in succession mean that capital transfer tax isn't paid at the higher rate applicable to the joint estate).

9 *Give an alternative residuary legatee* (brother Albert).

10 *Give a second alternative residuary legatee* (sister Jemimah).

A FEW FURTHER POINTS

When making a will, you should not only decide who's going to get what (and who isn't, ho-ho) but what really will happen if you suddenly die in an accident. (Perhaps with your mate.) What cash will be immediately available for the following six months? Will it be easy to get at? Who will deal with the funeral? Who will look after the children?

If you leave your property outright to A, you cannot specify that after his death it should then go to B. For instance, if a wife leaves her property to her husband she can't add that after his death it is to go to the children. (Unless it is left in a trust.) Only *he* can decide what will happen to what will be *his* property.

One way to avoid minor alterations to your will is to leave a sum of money (anything from £50 to £50,000 or more) for your executors to distribute in accordance with your wishes, as listed in a separate letter. This has the advantage of enabling you to change your mind over minor legacies.

You should review your will every five years so that when the sad event happens people who no longer exist will not stand to inherit property that no longer exists, and your executors will not curse you for ever.

Before making a will list what you own, and where it is, and your entitlement (documents that prove it belongs to you). For instance:

* House at 325 Regents Park Road, London NW1. Deeds with Nationwide Building Society guaranteeing mortgage. Reference number BZ47029ZOQB173.
* Aquamarine and pearl necklace. In my deposit box at Barclays Bank, Piccadilly, London W1.

You could draw up a possessions list in this order, before going to the solicitor:

Your name in full
Date and place of birth of self and children
Married at (if applicable, *all* marriages)
To
My home is at
My business is at
My will is with (name and address of bank, etc.)

A copy of the will is with (names and addresses of solicitor, trustees, beneficiaries, etc.)

My bankers are (if more than one list each separately, giving name and address)

(if necessary) My solicitors are (if more than one list each separately, giving name and address)

My accountant is (name and address)

At this date I own the following property:

* The freehold/leasehold of (if more than one, list each separately) The deeds of the property are at My mortgage is

* My other loans are (if more than one, oh dear, list each separately)

* My business is (details of stud farm, secretarial agency, etc.; if more than one, list each separately) I own —— shares in it (details of shares)

* My investments in stocks and shares, bonds, premium bonds are (list at date of will, although they may easily change within a short period) My share certificates are deposited with (bank or stockbroker)

* My insurance policies are (if more than one, list each separately) Beneficiaries Agent or company Policy number Policy is at Date on which premium started Date on which premium expires Amount of insurance Regular premium payment

* My pension/pensions are as follows (if more than one, list each separately) Pension number Personal contact(s) re pension Telephone number and address of contact

* Details of other income may be obtained from (agent, accountant)

* Details of other possessions (patents, copyright of writing or designs, etc.) may be obtained from (agent, accountant)

* Details of people and firms who owe me money are in

* My personal possessions are (clothes, furs, books, pictures, furniture, silver, jewellery)

* Add further details of any other valuables, such as cash in a deposit box

Date

Signature

WHAT TO DO WITH YOUR WILL

If there's anything further to say, anything about hoping that the children will always support each other and *not* sell the miniatures before you're cold, any final wishes, put them in an ordinary letter headed 'To be read with my will'. Put this letter in the same big buff envelope as your will (and mark it 'My will' so it doesn't get thrown away or accidentally torn up). Keep the top copy of the list of possessions and the top copy of the will in a safe place (safest is the bank) with, perhaps, a copy of both at your solicitor, and a copy of both in your home (so you remember what you did). Keep it where you keep the birth certificates, etc., not in a secret drawer that no one can find. Whether or not you let your beneficiaries see your will, make sure that they all know where it is. Tell your executors and trustees (in writing) where your will is kept, and where the copies are.

If you leave your valuables or your deeds with your lawyer, he can hang on to them, should you ever query his bill, and threaten to sell them if you don't pay. Better to keep your deeds and will safe in the bank.

After anyone's death, you can get a copy of his will, once probated, from Somerset House where yours, too, will be filed after your death, for all to see.

To simplify things for your survivors you might well put in that same big buff envelope one copy each of *What to Do when Someone Dies* and *Wills and Probate*, two excellent paperbacks published by the Consumers' Association (Caxton Hill, Hertford SG13 7LZ). Then, provided they are not in comas when the time comes, your benefactors and executors will know how to cope with your final bureaucratic rites.

WHEN TO MAKE A *NEW* WILL

Make a new will if you get married because marriage automatically revokes a will (except in Scotland). Husbands and wives should always discuss their wills when they marry, especially if they are business partners.

Widows or widowers who are remarrying should ensure that the new will makes sufficient specific provision for existing children.

Separation and divorce do not automatically revoke a will, in which case you may want to make a new will so that the swine/cow doesn't get his/her hands on your money. (But if you die intestate, your divorced spouse can't get his/her claws on a thing.)

You should also make a new will if

you have another child, or if a child or legatee or executor dies, or their fortunes change (one daughter marries a millionaire and another an impoverished artist).

HOW TO CUT PEOPLE OUT OF YOUR WILL

For women, one harsh fact about middle-aged divorce is that if your ex-husband remarries, you automatically lose any rights to his estate, *including any rights to his occupational pension*, which may be substantial. You also *lose the exemption from capital transfer tax (see page 203). These benefits are immediately, automatically transferred to his new wife*.

In Britain today, it is almost impossible completely to cut out of your will your present husband or wife, or an ex who has not remarried, or one of your children (even if illegitimate), or someone who is no blood relation but who has been treated as a 'child of the family' – anyone, that is, who is or has been a dependant and has a claim to be provided for.

The courts in Scotland have for many years overruled wills that failed to provide for immediate dependants. The Inheritance (Provision for Family and Dependants) Act 1975 brought English and Welsh court practices into line with Scotland.

People who can apply to the Court include a surviving spouse or a former spouse who may be awarded reasonable provision. The Court takes into account the person's age, the length of the marriage and the contribution made by her (or him) to the welfare of the family, as well as that person's income and earning capacity. Children can also apply in certain circumstances: sons who are under age or, if older, who are incapable of maintaining themselves; daughters who are unmarried, or, if married, are incapable of maintaining themselves or of being maintained by a husband.

Mistresses are increasingly claiming a portion of the estate under the 1975 Act. Anyone can claim if, immediately before the death, she was being either wholly or substantially maintained by the person who has died.

BUT in some circumstances a widow or children can claim back property (such as a house) which has been settled on a mistress. In fact, any property (even if jointly owned) that the deceased had given away within six years before death can be claimed back under the 1975 Act.

EXECUTORS

Always ask permission beforehand if you are going to name someone as your executor. *Always* try to refuse if someone asks you, because it can be a horrendous job. To stop fraud or mismanagement or simply mistakes, it is safer to have more than one executor. Choose at least one executor who is a staunch and sane friend. Choose at least one executor who has business or accounting or legal experience.

An executor should allow *at least* eighty hours' work to wind up an estate.

What an executor does is:

1 Arrange your funeral.
2 Carry out your wishes, expressed in your will and any accompanying letter.

3 Act as your legal representative, collecting assets, paying debts and taxes, distributing what is left as you desire.
4 Swear the executive oath before a commissioner for oaths.
5 Obtain probate (see later).
6 See to the distribution of the estate once probate is granted.

A will used to be read aloud after the funeral, but this doesn't always happen today. If it is thought necessary an executor can read the will.

Executors' duties can be very complicated and can involve coping with lengthy, tedious enquiries and harassing legal details. They may also involve helping your family, who may be very upset or unable to cope or be uncooperative.

The most tedious of the executor's tasks is getting probate. Probate is a written declaration from the Family Division of the High Court that your will is accepted and registered at the Court.

But the executor can't apply for probate until your estate has been valued and the value accepted by the Inland Revenue. The capital transfer tax has also to be assessed and the tax (or a very substantial part of it) must be paid by the estate.

Your executor then applies to the Court for probate. To do this he has to lodge the original will, the application for probate, the cheque for the probate fee, and the cheque for any outstanding capital transfer tax with the Probate Registry. He then receives the probate certificate, and is free to carry out the will according to your instructions.

You will spot at once that this procedure ensures that your will is not even accepted as valid until the

Inland Revenue has been paid its share of your estate. It is difficult to use any of your assets until probate has been obtained. This is why it is very important to leave your dependants something to live on whilst the executors are wading through the legal treacle.

If you like, you can choose one beneficiary only and make him the sole executor, then he can choose his own advisers. Husbands normally appoint wives, and vice versa, but it's generally a good idea to appoint someone else as well, who can do the practical work. After all, your spouse may be too distraught to start briskly filling in forms and applying for probate and getting a copy of the *Stock Exchange Daily Official List* on the day you die (to check the share prices).

You can appoint adult children or a close friend or godparents (youngish ones are best bets for obvious reasons), or you can appoint the bank or a solicitor but the last two are likely to be *extremely* expensive.

All the big banks, such as Barclays and National Westminster, have special executor and trustee departments. The bank is not a bad idea in some special circumstances, for instance, when a widow is making a will in favour of small children or taking over when an existing trustee dies. The bank is always there; it never dies or gets mumps, or is too busy or in St Tropez. It knows all the procedures; it's efficient and it can generally be relied on to see that any money is cautiously invested, which is especially useful if you are setting up a trust.

The bank can also help you organize your affairs so that you incur the minimum capital transfer tax. It is a safeguard against negligence and fraud. It also means that you probably won't have a problem in borrowing the money to pay the estate duty (*all* the dead person's assets are generally frozen – *every penny he has in the bank* – unless you have a joint account) until probate is granted and it isn't granted until *after* the capital transfer tax is paid to the Inland Revenue, remember.

The question of immediate cash availability for the survivors may well be vital. Arrangements for the provision of available cash for some months is extremely important for paying funeral and living expenses. If the wife has no access to a bank account, then arrangements should be made in advance for this eventuality.

WHAT YOU COST TO WIND UP

The bank is safe but *it is not cheap.* Banks charge a percentage of the estate, the size of the percentage depending on the size of the estate. At the time of writing, the Midland Bank is charging 5 per cent on the first £25,000 of an estate, 3 per cent on the next £75,000 and 2 per cent on anything above £100,000. Barclays Bank is charging 5 per cent on the first £50,000, 3 per cent on the next £50,000, 2 per cent on the following £150,000, and 1 per cent on anything above £250,000. These are maximum charges which may be reduced if the estate involves very little administration.

If you set up a trust in your will and appoint the bank as trustee, they will charge an annual management fee. The fees are calculated half-yearly as a percentage of the total value of the trust. The charge varies from 0.5 per cent every six months at Barclays to 0.15 per cent every six months at the

Midland. But the banks have additional charges for managing trusts, including charges for investments and withdrawals. Look at the details in their brochures.

If you appoint a solicitor as an executor he should prepare the will. And he will insert a clause enabling him to charge normal professional fees for his legal work in administering the estate. For dealing with an estate, the solicitor's fees are unlikely to be under £150. They are paid from the residue. Where the gross estate is worth over £2000, charges recommended by the Law Society for the guidance of solicitors (but not statutory) are on a sliding scale: 3 per cent of the gross up to £10,000, 2½ per cent of the gross up to £50,000, with lower rates above that. These charges will apply when the administration of the estate is not particularly difficult nor particularly easy. So, an estate consisting of a small house and a bit of savings probably will attract a solicitor's bill of £500. ('Gross' is the total value of the estate left. 'Net' is what's left after tax.)

If the list of possessions and the estate is in good order, and the will is simple then you probably won't need a solicitor as an executor. If the executors are efficient friends who will do the work for nothing (or very little) then there is no bank charge or solicitor's fee to pay. This could save £1250 on a £50,000 estate. A non-professional executor is only entitled to charge when he is authorized to do so by a charging clause in the will. So you must leave the executor who proves your will a sum of money to cover his expenses. Probate charges, including Court fees, may be charged to the estate. Court fees are charged as follows: £12.50 for an estate of £5000,

thereafter £2.50 for every £1000 up to £1 million. So, on an estate worth £50,000, the Court fees will be £125.

CAPITAL TRANSFER TAX

Includes tax payable on death. You now have to pay tax when you give away capital, whether you are alive or dead. But you pay *more* tax on capital handed on at death or within three years of death than you do on any given away during your lifetime and you can arrange your will to reduce the amount paid after death. So it is important to understand this tax.

HOW TO ESTIMATE YOUR CAPITAL TRANSFER TAX LIABILITY

Capital transfer tax is arranged on a sliding scale, like income tax, so that the more you leave the larger the proportion due in tax.

Parliament alters the rate from time to time, but from 26 October 1977 up to £25,000 would attract no tax. The Inland Revenue claims 10 per cent of the next £5000, 15 per cent of the £5000 after that and so on. The bigger the estate the higher the tax percentage until, if you happen to be leaving over £2,010,000, 75 per cent of it will go in tax (theoretically).

If you know the approximate value of your estate you can work out roughly what the capital transfer tax might be, from the accompanying table.

However, capital transfer tax *is not charged* on death in certain cases. No tax is charged on money or property left to a spouse – however large the amount. This may account for a lot of chic, geriatric marriages and is certainly one good reason for getting

Table of capital transfer tax charged on death

To get the total figure check column A for your total value (say, £40,000) and then look across to column D to see the *total* maximum tax payable (£2250). If you leave a total of £60,000 worth of property it will attract a maximum of £7750 capital transfer tax.

COLUMN A Value of estate	COLUMN B Rate of tax in each band	COLUMN C Maximum tax in each band	COLUMN D Total cumulative, maximum tax on an estate that reaches this band
Capital transfer tax payable on the first:			
£0 to 25,000	0%	£0	£0
Tax payable on the amount between:			
£25,000 to 30,000	10%	£500	£500
£30,000 to 35,000	15%	£750	£1,250
£35,000 to 40,000	20%	£1,000	£2,250
£40,000 to 50,000	25%	£2,500	£4,750
£50,000 to 60,000	30%	£3,000	£7,750
£60,000 to 70,000	35%	£3,500	£11,250
£70,000 to 90,000	40%	£8,000	£19,250
£90,000 to 110,000	45%	£9,000	£28,250
£110,000 to 130,000	50%	£10,000	£38,250
£130,000 to 160,000	55%	£16,500	£54,750
£160,000 to 510,000	60%	£210,000	£264,750
£510,000 to 1,010,000	65%	£325,000	£589,750
£1,010,000 to 2,010,000	70%	700,000	£1,289,750
Tax payable on any amount above:			
£2,010,000	75%		

married instead of 'having a relationship'.

You can leave your entire estate entirely free of tax to *registered* charities (check whether or not the charity is registered with the Central Register of Charities, 57 Haymarket, London SW1Y 4QX; ☎ 01-214 6000) or your favourite political party (who's making the tax rules, then?), provided that no one combo gets more than £100,000. You can leave your paintings and other collections to a public museum or library free of tax.

You can avoid capital transfer tax at death by being generous in life. On the following gifts made in your lifetime there is no tax:

1 £5000 upon marriage to each child. £2500 to your grandchildren, nephews and nieces upon marriage. £1000 to friends upon marriage.
2 Gifts up to a total amount of £2000 a year or £4000 in any two-year period.
3 Gifts totalling not more than £100 per person per year to any number of people.
4 Gifts which can be shown to have been made from your income and not your capital.

Apart from these four annual exemptions, you can cause to give away up to £25,000 without attracting capital transfer tax. Gifts up to and including 26 March 1974 come under the previous legislation on death duties. Gifts within three years of your death are added back into your estate on death. The amount of capital transfer tax payable on death depends on the total value of your estate.

Everything you own has to be valued. Any value your heirs put on it has to be approved by the Inland Revenue before they can find out for certain what tax is due. Getting Inland Revenue approval of the valuation is a preliminary to getting probate. (The poor executors may have to rush around visiting estate agents, jewellers, furriers, accountants, etc.)

Capital transfer tax always has first claim on the estate. Next any legacies or gifts are paid, followed by payments to the trustees (those banks and solicitors), then the residue.

Getting probate can take a long time, through no fault of yours or your heirs. But this does not stop the Inland Revenue charging interest on the amount that will eventually be paid. Interest starts six months after the death. Currently, the interest charge is 6 per cent per annum for overdue capital transfer tax on death (compared with the 9 per cent interest charged on all other overdue taxes).

An exception is the tax due on land and houses. This does not begin to attract interest until a year after death, unless your heirs sell the property before then (so it may be worth waiting a year before selling).

You can also avoid or reduce capital transfer tax on your estate by:

1 *Putting your home in joint names.* The valuation for tax on a jointly owned house is that of a house *without vacant possession*. This is greatly to the advantage of the surviving owner as a house valued without vacant possession may be worth about one-third of the value of the same house *with* vacant possession. (Of course, if the joint owners are married, the survivor wouldn't pay tax anyway.)

2 *Setting up a trust.* One way of reducing capital transfer tax, in the long run, is to set up a trust. You can set up a trust in which the income benefits your heirs but they cannot dispose of the capital because you want it to go to the succeeding generations. If you do this, tax is payable on the capital for the trust when you die, but is not payable again on the same property when your beneficiaries die.

Money is also often left in trust for minors or adults who cannot be relied upon to manage affairs as you would wish.

Appoint your trustees very carefully. If you appoint members of your family or a friend, pick a tough nut because they are likely to be involved in thankless disputes with the beneficiaries about investments (when to buy and sell them) and release of capital. (Sons have even been known to sue their fathers over trustee disputes.)

If you appoint a firm of solicitors as trustee the beneficiaries will almost certainly find them extremely slow and obdurate and their fees will cut a large hole in the trust income (perhaps even, eventually, *eliminating* it). A bank is a better bet (and probably more experienced). For their charges see page 202.

You can take out a life assurance policy to cover capital transfer tax, but don't forget that tax will be charged on the payout from the policy. So unless you are leaving everything to your spouse, make sure the sum insured by your policy is sufficient to cover the CTT on the policy as well as the estate.

Your heirs can take out a bank loan to pay the tax; the interest that they pay on the loan is free of tax (so it's better to do this than be charged 6 or 9 per cent by the Inland Revenue).

Your heirs can also avoid paying interest on tax by making a payment *on account of tax*, when the interest becomes due.

Your home

(How to get it, how to keep it)

If you already have a home, well that's wonderful, but in case a cloud ever crosses your sunny sky, you might like to check how much you know about your home and your rights to stay in it.

IF IT IS RENTED, you should know *who* rents it, from whom and on what terms. You should know whether the lease is *a joint lease, in both your names* or *only in his name*. You should know where the lease is. You should see the documents and check whether your name is on them.

You should know whether it is a protected or an unprotected tenancy or a restricted contract.

You should know how much the rent is, how it is paid, to whom it is paid and how you can prove it.

You should know what your responsibility is if any payments aren't made and what is the position if he suddenly dies or you break up the week before your silver wedding anniversay (has been known).

IF IT IS OWNED, you should know whether the property is freehold or leasehold, if it's leasehold how long the lease has to run, and where the deeds are to prove ownership (they should be with the building society or whoever gave you a mortgage or the bank – not a solicitor – and you should have a photostat copy in your important documents file or drawer or strong-box, in case the original goes up in smoke). You should also know whether you are entitled to buy the freehold of a leasehold property.

IF YOU'RE BUYING ON A MORTGAGE, have you got an insurance policy that pays off the unpaid portion if *one* of you dies?

Is the sum insured *all* that would be owed on the mortgage, or only half of it?

Is it a joint mortgage? In this case you are fully responsible for paying the instalments if *he* doesn't (whatever the reason, death or desertion). If you pay *all* the instalments and he doesn't pay one, with a joint mortgage, he will still own half of it (this can happen if A and B marry, A guarantees the mortgage and B doesn't pay his half of it).

What is your mortgage number and the address of the organization that you mortgaged the house to?

IF YOU WANT TO OWN YOUR OWN HOME

It's never too early and it's never too late to think about buying your own home and you would be very wise to do so because:

1 Rents creep up inexorably with the cost of living.
2 Although mortgage interest rates may fluctuate, the capital sum lent remains the same or reduces even though the value of the home increases.
3 There is full tax relief on the interest of the first £25,000 of a mortgage loan. (This could be called a government gift.)
4 That first small mortgage payment secures the use of an asset worth thousands of pounds.
5 If you're extravagant by nature it is also an unavoidable self-discipline to save (instead of spend) in order to build up some capital.
6 It is one of the few ways to increase your capital without paying capital gains tax upon the sale. (So long as the house is your principal residence)

★ *Remember that the first five years of a mortgage are the worst* (this can be a very cheering thought).
★ Remember that if you are desperately behind-hand on payments you can consider having lodgers to help.
★ If the house is to be a family home then remember to take out a mortgage protection policy, which immediately pays off the mortgage should you drop dead.

Whether you are buying or renting, consider your home with an eye to future alterations in your plans. This may be the patter of tiny feet or a big job in Kuwait.

So ask yourself:

1 Can it be let (or sublet) easily?
2 Can I rent out (sublet) a room or two?
3 What are the rates?
4 Has it got a service charge? Is it pegged or can it be put up, and if so, by how much?
5 What will the maintenance be? (Treble what you decide.)
6 Is local public transport good?
7 Is it near the shops?
8 Are there good sports and entertainment facilities nearby? (Swimming-pool, tennis courts, library, etc.)
9 Is it near schools?
10 Where can children play?
11 Is it near open space? (Park or playground.)
12 Has it got a garden or balcony (vital)?
13 Is it too isolated?
14 Is it noisy?
15 Is it damp?
16 What is the outlook? (Sunny south or bleak north-east.)
17 Will it qualify in any way for an improvement grant from the local council? (This can be as high as £2500.)
18 Could I look in a cheaper locality? Houses in the north-east of England cost about 50 per cent less than similar houses in London which means that you could get twice as nice a house for the money. (They sell for 50 per cent less too. For investment, buy as up-market as you can.)

Remember that if you let or rent out a room, this counts as earned income and the profit (earnings after expenses) qualifies for tax. It also means that when you sell the house the period during which you let it (or part of it) will attract some capital gains tax (in proportion to the period when you did not let it).

The same thing happens if you use part of your house for a business and deduct expenses relating to it from your income when making your annual income tax return. The tax is then in proportion to the *size* of the bit used for business.

Incidentally, if you take over someone else's lease on a house or a flat and you have paid a premium for fixtures and fittings which is more than they are worth (key money, in fact) you can quickly get them valued and will then be entitled to recover the excess money from the vendor for *up to six years after* you have moved in. It is a criminal offence to demand or to receive such premiums.

So if you decide to buy, what are the alternatives?

1 *Buy a home of your own* with some capital, a mortgage or some other kind of loan (*see page 211*).

If you are in a great hurry you may be able to buy *a home on a short lease* very cheaply. You will probably get an option to renew the lease (though probably at a higher price) but this might give you a breather while you look around or collect some more money.

You might not be able to get a normal building society mortgage on a short lease, but you might get the money through a bank or an insurance broker. You will probably have to pay a high interest rate and have good collateral or a good guarantee.

2 *Share a purchase with others.* This can create problems of its own (particularly lack of privacy) although it can also ease loneliness and mean help with children. You can do it without much trouble if you are living with someone of the opposite sex (building societies are very permissive, provided you keep up the payments and call him a fiancé) but they are not keen on two entire families sharing one property, especially if they are both headed by women.

3 *Form a Housing Association in order to buy and develop an existing property cheaply.* You can form an Association and get financial help in buying and developing a property if you can find at least six other people to start it with you. You need like-minded, determined people. (Watch out for people who describe themselves as being 'really motivated', which can mean endless talk and not much action.) You have to be registered as a Housing Association and it helps if you have some suitable property in mind before applying for registration.

Go to *The National Federation of Housing Associations,* 86 Strand, London WC2R 0EG (✆ 01-240 0604) to check that you are meeting the conditions for registration. They will say if your group is likely to get money for your purchase and property development, either from *your local authority* or from the *Housing Corporation* (Maple House, 149 Tottenham Court Road, London W1P 9LL). You have to be registered at the Housing Corporation, a government body, and it will cost you £100. But once you are registered you can get a lot of help:

(*a*) You may be able to get a mortgage

to purchase your property from your local authority.

(*b*) You may be able to get a grant of up to 40 per cent of the purchase or development price through the Housing Corporation.

(*c*) You may find it easier to get a grant for renovating your property.

(*d*) You can get a grant towards the management costs of running your property.

The amount and kind of help you get depends on the sort of Association you form. There are basically two sorts, Co-ownership and Co-operative.

In a *Co-ownership* Housing Association you and your partners put up some of the mortgage money and the Housing Corporation gives you a grant towards the rest.

The Housing Corporation is now trying out a scheme for helping Co-ownership Associations. An association can get a mortgage for 50 per cent of its property purchase price. The Corporation will then give the association a grant for up to 40 per cent of the remaining amount and lend it the last 10 per cent. Your association repays its 50 per cent mortgage on the terms agreed with the building society and also repays the 10 per cent loan from the Housing Corporation, usually over a very long period, say forty years.

If you form or join such an association, you live on property that you and your partners choose, at a modest rent (your 'rent' is made up of your proportion of the mortgage and loan repayments).

If you leave the association you get a lump sum representing your proportion of the increase in value of the property since you joined. If you die, you can leave your stake in the property to your heirs and they can take over your tenancy.

Once the mortgage or loan is repaid you can live in the property rent free and you can hand this benefit on to your heirs. So you actually buy a home for only 60 per cent of its purchase price. But what *you* can do with your part of the property is restricted, by the association and by the Housing Corporation, because the land on which the property stands is taken into public ownership and administered by the Housing Corporation permanently.

In a *Co-operative* Housing Association you and your partners do not put up *any* of the original mortgage money.

Your mortgage and grants come from your local authority or from the Housing Corporation. You have to repay the mortgage and you do not get any money if you leave or the property is sold, and you cannot leave it to your heirs.

What this deal amounts to is the accommodation of your choice for as long as you choose to stay there, at a modest rent.

Don't waste time forming a Co-operative Housing Association if you can get yourself accepted as a tenant in an established Fair Rent Housing Association which has property you would be happy to live in.

4 *Join a commune* or some other specialized community. This is a voluntary arrangement between like-minded people. Very few people are really suited to community life because you need the self-denial and patience of a saint, great tolerance for other people's children, dogs and

stereos, and, *above all*, you must not mind about lack of privacy.

Community life can be enjoyable for the right person or family, but you must be prepared to live in the community, let the community help to bring up your children, and make decisions about how you all live. Relationships tend to change and couples often split up but contented members say that the support of the whole group more than compensates for this. Prepare to give up rigid attitudes, jealousy, the right to explode from time to time and most material goods and conventional feelings.

A good example is *Lifespan*, based at Townhead, a village on the Moors fifteen miles from Sheffield. This is a successful commune with around twenty members of all ages (including some couples with children) who live in a row of terraced houses they have converted themselves. Everyone works in the gardens, helps with the building work and running the cooperative whole-food shop.

GETTING A MORTGAGE

Having found your dream nest, the next problem may be how to pay for it.

Whether or not you can get a mortgage or home loan often doesn't depend on *you* at all. There are times when the building societies and banks are eagerly looking for customers; there are times when (often for political reasons) the government 'suggests' that the building societies and banks should strictly ration their loans. They're then supposed to give preference to first-time buyers (for vote-catching reasons).

How much you can borrow depends on the type of property and the area it's in; your financial situation (any savings, any income); and who you borrow from.

How much you pay regularly depends on whether you arrange a fixed-interest loan or a loan which goes up and down (or up and up) in line with interest rates charged on other kinds of loans. You may get a mortgage from one of the following:

1 Your employer. Some will give a mortgage or help with it. If you're a clerk in a bank you may easily get a mortgage ranging from only 2 per cent to 5 per cent fixed-interest payment.
2 The building society you've been investing with.
3 Other building societies.
4 An insurance company. You will also have to take out an endowment life insurance policy (*see page 215*).
5 The local authority in the area where you want to buy.
6 An American bank. Citibank (branches in the telephone directory) is one American bank which is now offering mortgages in the UK. The mortgages are long term and you don't need to take out life insurance, but the interest rates are high.

To get a mortgage, enlist all the professional help you can. Has your solicitor/bank-manager/accountant or (most likely) your insurance broker any connections with a particular building society or contacts with someone else in the trade? How did your friends get *their* mortgages? Ask everyone you meet from the hairdressers' assistant to the newsagent. The most unexpected people may themselves have a really good mortgage deal and (consequently) a good contact.

If you save with one particular building society, NEVER, NEVER ASSUME that means you will automatically be able to get a mortgage with them, even if your financial position is good. This myth is building-society propaganda.

You will have to shop around for a mortgage. Before starting to visit them, telephone different building societies and compare their terms (addresses and telephone numbers are listed in the Yellow Pages).

The cheapest mortgage is a straight repayment mortgage through one of the big building societies, such as Nationwide or Abbey National. You can get it yourself, by approaching your local office of the society direct.

This is the sort of mortgage that your professional advisers may suggest that you won't be able to get (or try to dissuade you from taking) because they don't get *their* cut of *your* money. But *try*. And don't just try at one branch. Tour the High Streets and check at *different* branches (never telephone: always ask to see the manager) because they each have their own allocations and one branch may have committed it but the next one may not have done.

With building societies you will have the best chance if you are buying a new (or relatively new) self-contained, three-bedroomed house or flat which needs little renovation or maintenance. This sort of property will also be the easiest to resell, since prospective buyers should themselves be able to get a mortgage easily.

Local authorities (because of their different priorities) will often give mortgages on terms different from those of a building society. For instance, they may give priority to council tenants or children of council tenants. They may give preference to people on their rehousing waiting-lists. They may be specially prepared to help the homeless, the potentially homeless and unfortunate people who do not fit into any of the traditional categories.

Local authorities generally charge higher interest rates than building societies.

Whenever you want to borrow money consider the motives of the lenders, because this might influence your approach to them.

Building societies are subject to strict controls in order to protect the interests of the people who save with them. They will lend you money if you have a *steady job*, a *regular income*, some money for the *initial deposit*, which may be from 10 to 20 per cent of the total purchase price. (The initial deposit needn't be savings. You may have borrowed it from a bank or Aunt Mary.) The society may also want *collateral*. This is something of value (apart from the actual *property* being mortgaged) that they can actually hang on to (such as the deeds to Aunt Mary's house) until you have paid off your mortgage.

Naturally, nobody discriminates against women any more (not if they are likely to be noticed) but the building societies want very firm assurances that you can repay the money from regular income.

Local authorities are influenced by *the type of property* they have in the locality, their *obligations to the ratepayers* and the *length of their housing waiting-lists*.

Whereas a building society is interested in mortgages on 'safe' modern properties a council is interested in mortgages on properties within its locality. You may well get a mortgage on an old but structurally sound building from the local authority when you could not possibly have got it from a building society. Some local authorities don't mind helping you to acquire a property with a sitting tenant, though they may have rules about the proportion of the house that you yourself will occupy.

One or two local authorities have found a toe-in-the-door way round the problem of people who haven't got a high income or any savings for a deposit. They let you half-buy and half-rent your home. (In Birmingham this is called the Half-and-Half Mortgage Scheme.) You half-own the house from the beginning – and the combined half mortgage and very low monthly rent is MUCH less than a normal mortgage. You can take over the full mortgage whenever you are able to do so, or pay it off in a lump sum if you get an unexpected legacy from poor Aunt Mary.

Don't expect to get a mortgage from a building society for the full amount you need. Building societies generally think that a borrower ought to stake some of her own cash in the house being mortgaged. However, you may be able to borrow the difference from another source if you can put up some good security such as a life insurance policy or stocks and shares.

Normally a building society will only lend a proportion of what *its* surveyor says that the house is worth (regardless of the fact that you may be paying perhaps £2000 more than that). However, a local authority, if it has the cash, may give you a 100 per cent mortgage on an inexpensive property. At present, in London, this means one not costing more than £15,000.

The amount that a building society will lend you depends on your ability to repay out of your regular income. A society is usually only interested in the sole income of the borrower but may take account of the joint income of husband and wife (or man and fiancée).

A building society loan will usually be two and a half to three times the value of the *sole income*. On £3000 a year you could expect to borrow from £7500 to £9000.

On a *joint income* of, say, £5000, of which the man earns £3000 a year and the woman earns £2000 a year, the building society loan will usually be two and a half to three times the man's income *but only one-quarter to one-half of the woman's income*. (Wake up, building societies! Ever heard of the Pill?) In this instance the loan available on the joint income of £5000 would range from £8000 to £10,000.

But if a man (or theoretically a single woman) earns £5000 by himself, he can probably borrow £12,500 to £15,000 on it!

However, you *may* be able to find a society which will offer a loan up to the full value of the wife's salary.

A mortgage can take several months (at least two) to arrange. Fortunately, it usually takes that long to arrange all the other details of a house sale so that normally the money comes through just when it's needed. If there is any delay, though, you may be able to get a bridging loan from your bank, which will hold the property deeds as security until the mortgage society coughs up the purchase price.

TO GUIDE YOU THROUGH THE MORTGAGE MAZE . . .

. . . here's a brief exploration of different sorts of mortgages. You need to know the differences in order to decide what sort of mortgage will suit your pocket and circumstances, whether you need life insurance, what's the cheapest mortgage (probably an option mortgage direct from the building society for someone paying no tax) and what's the most expensive mortgage (a mortgage linked to a with-profits endowment policy).

OPTION MORTGAGE

Tax relief is no good to you if you don't pay income tax. An option mortgage is the best mortgage for people not paying tax for some reason (on supplementary benefit, on very low income, or with a very good accountant).

Most mortgage repayments qualify for tax relief but this sort doesn't. Instead the government gives the building society a special subsidy to keep the interest rate down. The idea is that the amount you pay each month for an option mortgage should be the same as if you had an ordinary mortgage and got full tax relief on your payments. However changes in interest and tax rates make this very difficult to achieve exactly.

CAPITAL REPAYMENT MORTGAGE

This is the most popular type of mortgage. Each year you pay the same amount of cash to the building society (usually in monthly instalments). Out of that the society takes the interest due on the amount of the loan outstanding at the beginning of the year and uses the rest of the money to reduce the amount of the loan. So at the beginning of the next year you have less loan outstanding on which to pay interest and more of your payments go towards reducing the loan, and so on until in the last year your payment clears off the loan completely.

The dispiriting part of the arrangement is that for a very long time almost all your payment goes in interest and it looks as though you're never going to get rid of that £10,000 capital debt. But this has its good side, because you get tax relief only on the interest that you pay, so the more interest there is the less the taxman takes from you. You can claim tax relief for the interest only on the first £25,000 of the loan.

You should also take out a mortgage-protection life insurance policy which costs from £2.00 a month per £10,000 borrowed (you get a small amount of tax relief on the premiums).

The examples that follow assume monthly repayments and interest at 10 per cent: the current rate is always liable to change.

Example A. A 35-year-old woman

takes out a £10,000 mortgage repayable over twenty-five years, assuming interest at 10 per cent, monthly repayments are £83.33. Tax relief at 33 per cent is worth £27.49. When this is deducted from £83.33 it reduces the payments in the earlier years to *£55.84 a month*.

Tip: If you have a pocket calculator (quite a big one) and understand the mathematics involved you could try working out the true rate of interest in the last three or four years of your mortgage, bearing in mind that you reduce the debt monthly but the building society charges you a whole year's interest. (Use the calculator and the society's end-of-year statements to check this *is* how they calculate the interest.) Depending on what the rates of interest are on suitable alternative investments, there may be a point when it is financially sensible to pay off the mortgage, if you have the cash available, rather than invest the cash to earn less interest than you are paying the building society. Remember to include your personal taxation position in your calculations. In 1979, most people coming to the end of a twenty-five-year mortgage are paying off an original loan of much less than £5000 and this calculation is unlikely to yield them enough profit to pay for the pocket calculator. But in years to come, timing the mortgage payoff correctly could make a noticeable saving.

WITH-PROFITS ENDOWMENT MORTGAGE (LINKED TO LIFE INSURANCE)

This type of mortgage is mainly for people who can afford a large outlay each month: you need to be earning over £5000 a year to consider it. It is

MORTGAGE DIAGRAMS
An Endowment Mortgage

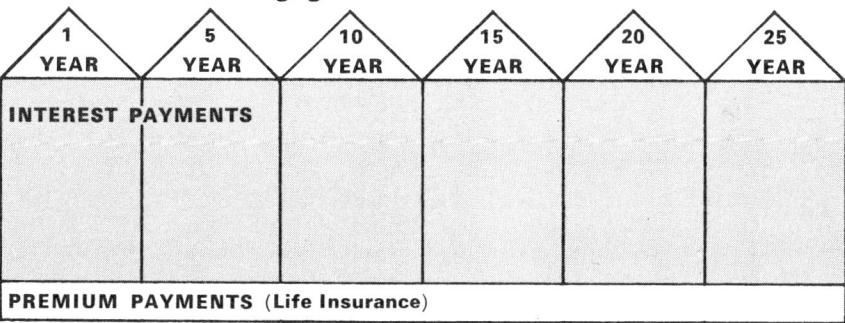

A Capital Repayment Mortgage

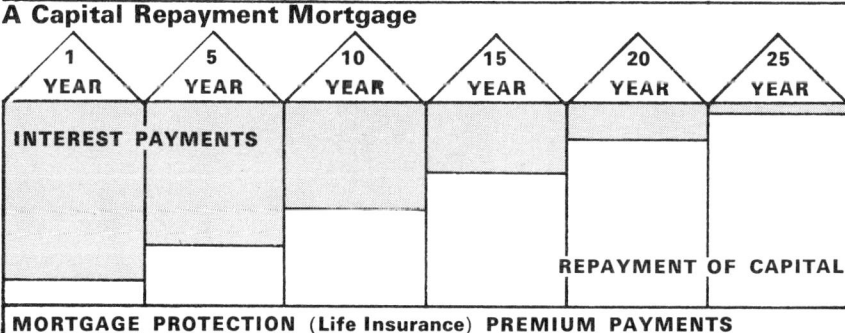

linked to a life insurance policy that is big enough to pay off the mortgage in a lump sum and also buys a share in the profits the insurance company has made from investing the premiums. So you have some extra cash at the end (you never know exactly how much profit there will be).

With this policy you merely pay the interest on the loan of the capital, throughout the period. You repay *none* of the capital each month. So you can claim tax relief on the whole of your mortgage payments, or on £25,000, for the whole twenty-five years.

You also pay a premium on the life insurance, on which you also get tax relief of half the basic tax rate. This relief also has to be claimed on your income tax return.

Example B. A 35-year-old woman takes out a £10,000 with-profits endowment mortgage over twenty-five years at 10 per cent interest.

Interest on the loan after tax relief is £55.83 each month. The insurance premium could cost an additional £34.80 per month, or just under £29 after deducting tax relief of about £6 a month. Total payment after tax relief is *£84.84 a month*.

The advantages are:

1 If the mortgage payer dies, the mortgage is then paid up in full by the insurance company. But (in the example given) this protection for a loan of £10,000 costs £417.60 gross a year.
2 You get two lots of tax relief (on the mortgage interest and on the insurance).
3 You end up with a house and some extra cash (it should not be less than £17,000 in the example quoted above), on which *you don't pay capital gains tax*.

The disadvantages are:

1 To pay out such a lot of money you need a large, regular income.
2 There's more bureaucratic hassle to reclaim two lots of tax relief.
3 Building societies charge an extra $\frac{1}{4}$ to $\frac{1}{2}$ per cent interest on loans linked to endowment policies.
4 It costs much, much more per month than a capital repayment mortgage.
5 It's an expensive way to buy capital.
6 It can be very difficult to transfer this mortgage if you want to move to a larger house or have been posted to a different part of the country. You may have to SCRAP this deal (whereupon you lose a lot of the accumulated cash-in value of the insurance policy). Or you may find yourself left with an expensive insurance policy and no house.

Never think that you will stay in your new home for the full period of repayment. The average mortgage lasts between seven and eight years. So before taking out a mortgage check the rules of *your* building society (they all have different rules) to see whether you will have to *pay a penalty* if you pay off your mortgage before the end of the term. The penalty can be as high as three months' additional interest – which can be £650 on a £25,000 property, which is a lot of money to pay for nothing.

Tip. Agents will persuasively and persistently try to sell you with-profits endowment mortgages because they get high commission rates on them.

LOW-COST WITH-PROFITS ENDOWMENT POLICY

This fairly recent idea is advantageous to most taxpayers. Monthly outlay is cut as low as possible – but you still get tax relief on interest and insurance payments and you get a tax-free cash bonus at the end – though not so large as with a full with-profits endowment policy.

The scheme works like a with-profits endowment mortgage except that you have an endowment policy for only half the size of the loan and use the bonus to make up the rest. You also have an ordinary life insurance policy which pays the other half of the loan if you die before the end of the mortgage term. Your monthly payments cover the insurance premiums and the interest on the loan so you get tax relief on both premiums and interest. On past performance the endowment policy bonus is more than enough to pay off the loan so you will get a cash sum at the end.

Example C. A 35-year-old woman takes out a £10,000 policy repayable over twenty-five years at 10 per cent interest. Monthly repayments after tax deductions are £55.83 a month. The cash bonus after twenty-five years should not be less than £3000.

This is not a big bonus for paying £10 a month extra over twenty-five years (totalling £3900) but the main advantage is the life insurance cover, which costs £900 over twenty-five years in this example. (Of course this is a *very* rough reckoning, not allowing for interest or inflation on the extra sum for life cover.)

Remember again to check whether there is a penalty clause if you pay off the mortgage early.

NON-PROFIT ENDOWMENT MORTGAGE

This works on the same principle (the payments you make cover interest on capital, repayment of capital and life insurance premiums), but you get no cash at the end, just the money to pay off the mortgage.

Oddly enough, premiums on this type of policy will probably be *higher*

ANATOMY OF A LOW-COST ENDOWMENT POLICY

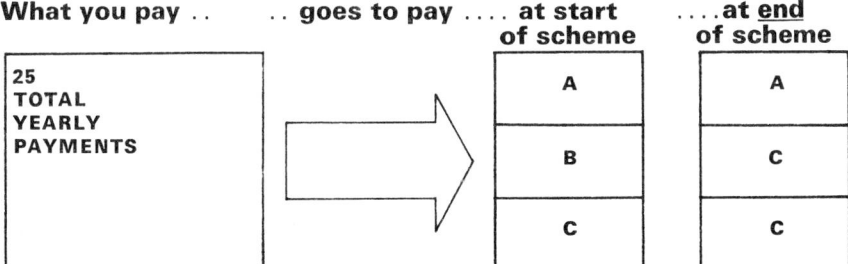

What you pay .. .. goes to pay .... at start of scheme ....at end of scheme

A = Interest on mortgage

B = Life insurance premium

C = With-profits scheme

than those on a low-cost policy. In example C the woman's payments after tax relief could be £71.69 a month.

It's silly to fall for this type of policy now that you can get low-cost endowment policies and option mortgages.

WHAT HAPPENS WHEN YOU BUY OR SELL A HOME

Buying a property is more complicated than buying a fur coat or a frying pan because the seller has first to prove to the buyer that the property is his to sell and the buyer has to undertake surveys and searches to check what he is buying. This is why the whole procedure is so laborious.

There's a government department called the Land Registry, where, slowly, the title of every bit of land and property throughout England and Wales will eventually have to be registered.

If the title to a property is already registered, the purchase rigmarole can be much shorter and simpler than if it isn't. Find out if it is by writing to the Land Registry, Lincoln's Inn Fields, London WC2A 3PH (☎ 01-405 3488). They will tell you whether or not the property is registered and if it is, the registration number. (*You* cannot get a copy of the entry on the register until the present owner of the property gives his permission for you to have it.)

When all properties are registered the transfer of ownership should be far simpler and cheaper because instead of wading through a wodge of deeds going back fifteen years or more a buyer will merely have to check the ownership with the Land Registry.

Having found a home to buy, you make an offer 'subject to contract' and pay a small deposit of, say, £250 (with a letter specifically saying that the *whole* of this sum is part of the house purchase price) to the seller's lawyer. (Usually the estate agent asks for it – ask him if he has a bond to protect you against his misuse of your money. At the time of writing there were government plans to force estate agents to have such bonds.)

You may be represented by a solicitor, the seller may be represented by a solicitor (not the same one) but a building society is *always* represented by a solicitor (often the same as yours).

The main job in conveyancing is to check that the seller really owns what he or she is selling and that he gets properly paid for it and that you really acquire what you are paying for.

All your letters up to exchange of contracts should be clearly marked 'subject to contract and survey' or you might find that you're contracted by accident, while you are still checking.

The main thing for a buyer to remember is *not to hand any money over* (including the deposit) without getting the *correct documents* in exchange and *correctly worded receipts* (watch out here).

If you are handling the transaction yourself without a solicitor, ask the estate agent:

1 Is the *whole* house occupied by the seller? (You should also ask the seller this question and be very suspicious of odd people in the house when you look over it.)

2 Is the title registered? (The seller

can find this out from the title deeds, which will be with his building society if he hasn't finished paying off his mortgage.)

Go straight to a solicitor or a reputable conveyancing company if the answers to both questions are not 'yes' or if any complication appears.

You will have to pay for more than the cost price of the new home, in order to move into it. You may have to allow as much as £1500 extra. Tot up the:

★ purchase price
★ building society solicitor's costs
★ building society survey costs
★ cost of conveyancing your former home (if any)
★ cost of conveyancing the new home
★ your survey costs
★ interest on bank bridging loan (if needed)
★ removal costs
★ estate agents' commission of $2\frac{1}{2}$ per cent of the price received on sale of former home (if any)

All this can be heartbreakingly expensive if a couple of deals fall through, when you have already incurred the costs of the items starred. A couple of gazumpings could cost you over £1000 for nothing. (It's legally impossible to gazump in Scotland, incidentally.)

Until recently, solicitors have had a legally protected monopoly of conveyancing, and it is a lucrative part of their work, so they don't want anyone else to do it.

Many people (including some solicitors and MPs) think that solicitors' charges are too high for conveyancing work. The government has also said that conveyancing charges are too high, in two reports in 1967 and 1971.

The work can be so routine and straightforward that it is often given to junior clerks when they first join a solicitors' office. Probably one conveyance in ten involves complicated legal matters that only an experienced conveyancer could handle. Solicitors cheerfully agree that routine conveyancing work is done by their clerks, but they point out that if the conveyancing suddenly turns out to be more than a routine job then the professionals in the office have the responsibility of protecting you, the client. It is expensive protection.

Some solicitors also cheerfully agree that on an expensive house they would charge perhaps *five times as much* as on a cheap flat for the same amount of work. Solicitors are *not* supposed to charge a percentage of the value of the property but you will probably find that they charge around $\frac{3}{4}$ per cent of the value *plus* £100 *plus* 'disbursements' *plus* VAT. That can be about £300 on buying a £25,000 house.

There may be *another* £300 to pay if you are also selling your present home. In that case it could cost £600 in solicitors' fees for you to move home.

If, instead of using a solicitor, you use an expert conveyancing firm you can cut the cost of conveyancing by about one-third and also get extra insurance protection thrown in for the price. Go to your local CAB for a list of local conveyancing firms.

You can handle the conveyancing yourself, if the situation is a straightforward one. It seems to take ordinary, intelligent, *in*experienced people about ten to fifteen hours' work spread over a three-month period.

Many people think that it's illegal to do conveyancing work if you don't use a solicitor. THIS IS NOT TRUE. It's illegal only to draw or prepare 'an instrument of transfer' for 'fee, gain or reward' unless you are a qualified solicitor, barrister or notary public. The actual transfer deed is traditionally drawn up by the purchaser's lawyer and can be the easiest part of conveyancing. So of course it's not illegal to do your own conveyancing (no fee, gain or reward, you see) and the specialist conveyancing firms subcontract the actual drawing up of the final deed to a qualified lawyer when they are acting for purchasers.

Reputable conveyancing firms do no other work: they are specialists. Some will quote you the all-in, package-deal cost of your job before they start. One firm includes title insurance in the package. The conveyancing and title insurance on a £25,000 house would cost about £125, all inclusive, and this may include *that extra insurance protection*, which solicitors do *not* provide. This pays court costs and compensation if there's a subsequent title problem – even if this happens long after the deal has gone through. But this sum does *not* cover stamp duty, search fees, or the fee to the Land Registry (neither does a solicitor's fee).

If you use an expert conveyancing firm the advantages are:

1 You know in advance what the price is going to be.
2 You can save up to half of the cost.
3 You can get peace of mind because of the insurance.

If you do your own conveyancing on a straightforward transaction, you must double-check *everything* and realize that you don't simply *swap* documents and forms with the other side and the local council, you have to read the things and check whether you need to ask any more questions. CTI Dominion Title Insurance, 22 Theobalds Road, London WC1X 8PF (01-405 4896), will insure your title to your new property if you decide to do your own conveyancing and would like this extra protection.

The work is clerical and consists mainly of filling in the agreed figures, dates, names and addresses. You can get all the forms from a local legal stationery shop or from the Solicitors' Law Stationery Society, PO Box 55, 237 Long Lane, London SE1 4PU (01-407 8066).

If you're selling your home, *write* and ask the solicitor who originally handled the purchase to give you back the file (it's yours, you've paid him heavily for it and you are entitled to it). Then you can use it, as a guide: (*a*) to repeat the process and answer the other side's questions and (*b*) to get an overall idea of the whole procedure, if you are buying again.

If you are thinking of doing your own conveyancing, read *The Conveyancing Fraud* by solicitor Michael Joseph, who describes conveyancing as 'the art of making the simple, complicated'. The book includes a step-by-step guide to doing your own conveyancing and costs £1.80 direct from the author at 27 Mole Park, Occupation Lane, Woolwich, London SE18 3JQ.

Another good book for do-it-yourselfers is *The Legal Side of Buying a House,* published by the Consumers' Association at £2.25. It's regularly up-dated and will be your Bible until completion day. Get it from bookshops or from Consumers' Association Subscription Department, Caxton Hill, Hertford SG13 7LZ (☏ Hertford [0992] 59031).

Another conveyancing guide is *How to Buy Your Property without a Solicitor* (£4.95, published by the Homes Organization, 4 Passey Place, London SE9 5DQ). A launching party in the House of Commons was given for this book by Christopher Price, MP, who said that he hoped this book could help to break 'the grip that the solicitors' monopoly has on the conveyancing market'.

The Homes Organization also published *How to Sell Your Property without a Solicitor* and provides a back-up service of advice and help for an extra £5. They say that the *total* cost of do-it-yourself conveyancing should be about £13!

If you are buying a freehold property with registered title, the conveyancing can be a straightforward matter. (If you run into any trouble, go straight to a solicitor.) If you are buying a leasehold flat or house, or part of a house, where the ownership is *not* straightforward, it is definitely risky to do it yourself. Go to a conveyancing firm or a solicitor.

Whether or not you do your own conveyancing, you should know *exactly* what's going on. Solicitors' offices are not always efficient, they don't always do things as fast as possible and they have been known to lose documents or send things to empty houses and make other mistakes that have lost deals for their clients.

Solicitor Michael Joseph says that a client may (wrongly) think that by going to a solicitor he is buying some sort of insurance to safeguard the house purchase. But he isn't. 'Even if you can prove that a solicitor has been negligent you'll have a very difficult job to find another solicitor to take your case and you'll have to have a *very* expensive lawsuit before you get compensation.'

HOW TO STAY PUT

If your happy fireside picture turns to one of sorrow, your first priority should be to hang on to your home, until the dust has settled and you can calmly decide what to do.

Sometimes a woman under stress may make a rash decision to leave (or be persuaded to do so). Perhaps she may feel (momentarily) that her home has too many unhappy memories. However, later she may remember only the happy memories of a shared home.

When there are a number of changes happening simultaneously in your life, you should try to reduce the possible number of stress situations – especially if one of the proposed changes is moving home (*see* The Stress League Table on *page 26*).

Sometimes families with children are forced out of their homes. But there is nearly always a good opportunity to stay put.

Whatever the reason, if a woman doesn't want to leave her home it can now be very, very difficult, if not impossible, to make her do so.

Never, never agree to leave if under pressure, even if the house or flat isn't in your name, even if you can't pay the mortgage, even if you haven't any money.

More and more families are buying their own homes and taking on high – perhaps too high – financial

TWENTY-ONE STEPS TO HAPPINESS

This is basically what happens when you buy a new home on a mortgage. In a straightforward sale of an existing house between an owner-occupier and a potential owner-occupier, there are approximately eleven main steps in this minuet to be taken by the buyer.

The documents involved may be as follows:

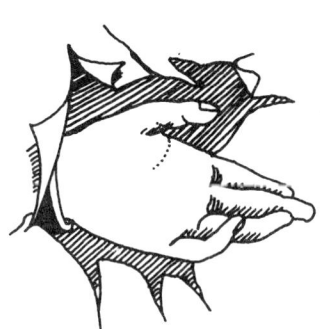

Buyer and Mortgagee
Survey reports
A mortgage application
Draft mortgage deed
Mortgage deed
Buyer and Local Authority
A local search certificate
A second local search certificate
Buyer and the Registry
(if applicable)
A copy of the old entry on the
    Land Register
The Land Register search
    certificate (form 94A)
Buyer and the Seller
Enquiries before contract
Answer to enquiries before contract
A draft contract
Requisition on title
Answers to requisitions
A financial statement on completion
The transfer

Here are the steps which may have to be taken to complete the deal:

STEP 1 BUYER sees surveyor. He instructs his own surveyor to report on the house (electrical wiring and drains will be extra and **must** be checked).

STEP 2 BUYER to building society, local authority or other money-lender, e.g. bank. He applies for a mortgage and finds out what other money he will have to raise.

STEP 3 Building society surveys property.

STEP 4 Seller to BUYER. **A draft contract** and a copy of the entry in the Land Register is sent by the seller or the seller's lawyer.

STEP 5 BUYER to seller. The buyer sends **enquiries before contract** to the seller's lawyer (concerning boundaries, etc.).

STEP 6 BUYER to local council. He sends local search and enquiry forms to the local council to ask whether there are *any plans that might affect the property* (such as running the motorway through the front garden).

STEP 7 Council to BUYER. The council responds to Step 6 with a local search certificate and answers to queries.

STEP 8 BUYER to seller. He checks that the seller satisfactorily answers Step 5 above.

STEP 9 Building society to BUYER. Assuming it gets a satisfactory report from its own surveyor, the building society then makes its mortgage offer to the buyer.

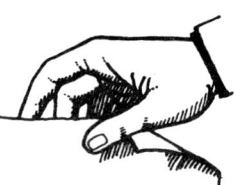

STEP 10 Surveyor to BUYER. By now the buyer should have his own surveyor's report. He should not be optimistic about the pessimistic parts. They should be used to beat down the selling price.

STEP 11 BUYER to seller. The buyer sends the seller a draft of **the transfer** and **requisitions on title** and arranges (with the seller) a date when completion will take place.

STEP 12 BUYER to seller. Having obtained satisfactory replies and (with luck) beaten the price down with the surveyor's report, the buyer signs and **exchanges contracts** with the seller or the seller's lawyer. (N.B. If the seller is trying to sell his present home, then contracts for both deals should be exchanged at the same time.) The buyer pays a deposit of 10 per cent less the original small deposit. This is paid to the other side's solicitor or estate agent (but preferably the solicitor) and the accompanying letter (and receipt) must clearly state what it is for. Otherwise it might be payment for a second-hand sofa, verbal advice from the other side's estate agent—anything!

STEP 13 Seller to BUYER. The seller sends a) approval of the draft transfer and b) **replies to requisition on title** and c) a **completion statement** showing how much money remains to be paid at completion.

STEP 14 BUYER to building society. The buyer sends copies of certain documents to the solicitors for the building society. These documents are copies of **the entries on the Register, the contract, the enquiries before contract, the draft transfer, the requisition on title, the local search,** and **any other information** the solicitor requires.

STEP 15 Building society to BUYER. The building society sends its own requisitions to the buyer.

STEP 16 BUYER to building society. The buyer replies to the requisitions and sends any documents, which may include forms for **the Inland Revenue and Land Registry.**

STEP 17 Money-lender to BUYER. The building society's solicitors send the buyer a **financial statement** and the **mortgage deed.**

STEP 18 BUYER to Land Registry. The buyer makes a final search of the Land Registry (to check that no *very recent* entries have been made). Before handing over the rest of the money he may want to get a **second search certificate.**

STEP 19 Land Registry to BUYER. The Land Registry sends a **search certificate** (form 94A) to the buyer.

STEP 20 BUYER meets seller. The money (bank drafts from the buyer and the building society) is then handed to the seller or the seller's lawyer, who gives the buyer the keys, the title deeds and all documents relating to the house and purchase. This is **completion** and the buyer can now move in, two minutes later.

STEP 21 BUYER to Inland Revenue. On properties that cost over £15,000 a tax (stamp duty) is payable to the Inland Revenue. If the sale price is £20,000 or under, the duty is $\frac{1}{2}$%; if it is £25,000 or under, the duty is 1%; if it is £30,000 or under, the duty is $1\frac{1}{2}$%. The top rate of 2% is payable on all properties costing over £30,000. In practice, the building society attends to the stamping and deducts the duty (along with its legal fees) from the loan.

commitments in order to do so. A small change for the worse can often tip the balance from 'can just manage it' to 'just can't'. If this happens, always pay *part* of the rent or mortgage regularly (no matter how small the amount) and write to explain that you can't pay more at the moment due to personal problems (no details necessary).

'All too often a small amount of mortgage arrears has been the start of a cycle which has led to a family being homeless,' says an excellent, simple guide, *Rights for Home Owners*, by Jo Tunnard and Clare Whately, who have worked in a Citizens' Rights Office and a Mortgage Advice Department, respectively. The book costs 60p from Child Poverty Action Group, 1 Macklin Street, London WC2B 5NH.

It explains how a woman with little or no money can get the maximum free money from the Welfare State to help her family stay in their home. It also gives step-by-step advice on how to negotiate with the mortagee, the Courts, local councils and unhelpful social security offices. Many women don't realize that social security can pay your mortgage interest and the council can pay part of the home maintenance costs (including rates, repairs, central heating and fuel bills).

HOW TO KEEP THE HOME IF YOU AND YOUR MATE SPLIT UP

Your partner cannot force you to leave your home without applying to a County Court for an eviction order (which will take weeks) and no matter who owns what, the Court may decide (especially if you have chil-dren) that he should leave, rather than you.

Don't leave because you are frightened of your mate. If he owns the home, *immediately* go to a solicitor and get an injunction to stop him selling the home over your head.

Don't leave because you are frightened of the cost of paying rent or mortgage when you haven't any money – check how to cut costs or increase your income (see later).

Don't agree to sell the home. If your husband leaves you may well be able to increase your income with supplementary benefit by as much as £2500 a year or reduce your housing costs through the local authority.

See a solicitor straight away. It is THE FIRST THING YOU SHOULD DO. But don't leave the matter entirely in the hands of a solicitor because he only knows the law and he probably doesn't know what can be done (unofficially, anyway).

Remember that possession really *is* nine-tenths of the law, so stay put, do your homework and immediately contact your local Housing Aid Centre, Law Centre or local Citizens' Advice Bureau. Also try CPAG, SHAC, Shelter and perhaps Gingerbread as well as the Housing Aid Centres that are run by local authorities or by voluntary groups (look for them in the telephone directory or apply to the town hall).

CPAG (Child Poverty Action Group) has branches throughout England and Wales, Scotland and Northern Ireland. Each branch has a Citizens' Rights Office attached, which can help you with legal problems. (Head office is at 1 Macklin Street, London WC2B 5NH; ☎ 01-242 9149.)

SHAC is the London Housing Aid

Centre and is invaluable to Londoners. SHAC has a list of all other Housing Aid Centres in London and many of the Housing Aid Centres in England, Wales, Scotland and Northern Ireland. (Their address is 189a Old Brompton Road, London SW5 0AR; ☎ 01-373 7841.)

Shelter (National Campaign for the Homeless Ltd) can help with all housing problems and has branches in England, Wales and Scotland (Scottish headquarters: 6 Castle Street, Edinburgh EH2 3AT; ☎ 031-226 6347; London head office: 157 Waterloo Road, London SE1 8XN; ☎ 01-683 9377). Shelter has no branches in Northern Ireland.

Gingerbread specializes in advising one-parent families, including advice on housing problems. It has over 400 branches throughout England, Wales, Scotland and Northern Ireland. (Headquarters: 35 Wellington Street, London WC2E 7BN; ☎ 01-240 0953.)

Your partner may try to borrow on the property (thus reducing its value) or sell it without your knowledge, but *if the home is in your joint names*, it cannot be sold without your agreement and your signature on the sale contract. You have an automatic right to occupy the place meanwhile.

If the mortgage payments are not kept up the building society has the right *eventually* to attempt to evict you and sell the property in order to get its money back. However, *as long as you remain in possession* a Court will not grant the building society a possession order if you can show that you can pay off the arrears in a reasonable time.

The executive in charge of evictions for a big building society has said (privately) that it can take *up to*

two years after a Court order to dislodge a wife with children, provided she isn't frightened of bailiffs, doesn't let strangers into the house, changes the locks, puts a peephole and chain on the front door and buys a bull-terrier or some similar, seemingly ferocious, dog.

If the home is in your husband's name only and he leaves, at once establish your rights of occupation by registering a 'caution' at the District Land Registry if the land is registered (*see page 218*) or a 'Class F' charge in the Central Land Charges Register if the land is unregistered. This action registers your interest in the home. It will deter any potential purchaser that your husband may be trying to interest in the home, and *should* prevent him borrowing any money on it.

If you take over the responsibility of making the payments on a joint mortgage your payments may entitle your husband to half the house (although he isn't paying a bean) so check that this situation is brought to the Court's attention when you divorce or legally separate.

Check, too, that you get permission from the Court *before* a divorce to re-register your right to occupy, after the divorce is absolute. Then check that your solicitor re-registers it.

Women who are not married to their mate can register a claim to a share of a house or flat in his name, provided that they have put some work into building, buying, working on or maintaining the home. This 'Mistresses' Charter' gives similar occupation rights to those of a married woman.

PAYING THE MORTGAGE

If your husband is no longer paying

the mortgage (or his share of it) *tackle this problem at once* both to prevent arrears building up and to establish your right to stay, your willingness and ability to pay and your general air of responsibility (as opposed to the defaulting man).

1 Visit the manager of the local branch of your building society. Your aim is to demonstrate your responsibility, your willingness to pay what little you can regularly, and your wish to keep up interest repayments.

Look sensible and tidy; wear good but not special Sunday Best or showy clothes – something you would wear if you were going to lunch at a good restaurant. Do not be flirtatious or pathetic; do not seek sympathy. You're supposed to be a sensible, reliable, practical business partner of the building society.

2 Briefly explain your inconvenient situation (give no details) and explain how you plan to resolve it. ('I have an appointment with the DHSS tomorrow, I am seeing my solicitor in the afternoon and I have already registered my right to occupation at the Land Registry.') Also mention your legal rights under matrimonial and property law, and make it clear that YOU ARE STAYING PUT, that you will firmly resist *any* attempt to dislodge you and will take advice from SHAC and CPAG on this.

You have the right to make the mortgage payments instead of your husband under section 1(5) of the Matrimonial Homes Act 1967, so don't let any petty bureaucratic local building society officer convince you otherwise because they don't like the idea of an unsupported mother with children taking on this financial burden. If they say that they've never heard of the Act, say that you will immediately contact your MP and SHAC and do so.

3 Suggest that the building society reduces your payments until you get on to your financial feet. (Make it clear that you are prepared to pay *something* regularly.) As already suggested, try to lower monthly payments, either by paying only the interest (or part of it) or by increasing the number of years over which the mortgage is spread – from twenty to twenty-five years, from twenty-five to thirty years. Or both.

If you want to rearrange the mortgage in this way and the house or flat is in your husband's name, then his written agreement must eventually accompany the formal request to the building society. Best get a solicitor to handle this.

4 Try to transfer your mortgage to the government option scheme, which means smaller repayments. The building society can fix this.

HOW TO GET SOMEONE ELSE TO PAY YOUR MORTGAGE INTEREST

The DHSS is empowered to pay the interest on the mortgage, if you can't. Remember that in the early years of a mortgage the greater part of the repayment is interest so if this is your case, much of your repayment could be paid by the DHSS either under the supplementary benefit scheme if you are not working (or only working part time) or under the family income supplement scheme if you are working full time but have a low income. Get the DHSS to write to the building society and confirm that they will do this. You may then be able to make other arrangements for paying off the capital (anyway, this is what you tell the building society office manager).

Don't feel guilty about this. It will cost far more for the state to care for you as a homeless family than to help you out until you can afford to take over the interest repayments (no need to think too far ahead on this point).

When you visit the local DHSS office, you will need to take a file full of documents. Allow plenty of time to assemble it beforehand. They may want to see details of:

1 The mortgage: the total amount repayable and the monthly payment.
2 What the ground rent and service charges are (if any).
3 The rateable value of the property, the rates and the water rates (find out from your last rate demand or from the treasurer's department at the town hall).
4 What child benefits you receive. They will want to see your child benefits book and you should also tell them of any other social security benefits you receive.
5 Details of any outstanding HP or other debts.
6 You will also be asked whether you have any income and what your husband earns (it doesn't much matter if you don't know this).

HOW TO PAY OFF THE MORTGAGE CAPITAL

If your husband is paying maintenance for you or your children, see if you can get him *legally* to earmark this 'specifically for paying off the capital on the home'. He loses nothing and you can avoid mainten-ance payment being counted as part of your weekly income, so your supplementary benefit or other State help will not be cut as a result of getting maintenance and your tax position may be improved.

In this relatively new way of getting round the question of keeping the family home, you can regularly pay off the capital and interest.

Snag: A judge may decide that if the wife has sufficient means she can take on the mortgage but that she must pay her husband a sum for *his* stake in the property. She will then have to raise this sum to prevent the property being sold.

Alternatively, the judge may decide that the husband should pay less maintenance in view of this. It may be well worth the wife accepting a reduced maintenance in return for the transfer of the home to her name. She will then have the main family asset in her name (and if she remarries she should see that it *stays* in her name: a remarriage is no good reason to alter this).

How property is split in a divorce depends on the incomes and proper-ties of the partners. When both have possessions the Court may split them fifty-fifty. If you are a non-earning wife with no assets of your own and the house is in your husband's name, you are likely to get one-third of the total value of the home plus mainten-ance (which depends on the Court order and husband's income).

OTHER IDEAS

Take a lodger. You can let part of the property in which you live and get repossession when you want it if you provide cleaning, meals or other ser-vices (for lettings which ensure repos-session *see page 234*).

You might sell your present home to the local authority for the full market value (especially if you have a registered right to occupy) or to a housing association, staying on as their tenant. You will have to pay rent but it will probably be a subsidized rent and it *does* mean that you can stay put.

IF YOUR HOME IS RENTED AND YOU CAN'T PAY THE RENT

See that you are claiming all your possible benefits. Single parents on low wages with dependent children can claim family income supplement, but they may do better to reduce their hours of work and claim supplementary benefit (check with Gingerbread).

All tenants in need can have part of their rent paid by their local council. Council tenants get rent *rebates*, private tenants get rent *allowances* (outright Giro payments). You will probably be entitled to this as well as a rate rebate. The council will work out (*a*) which part of your rateable value *entitles you to a rate rebate even if you don't pay the rates*; (*b*) which part of the rent entitles you to a rent rebate.

Councils in high rent areas can pay more than those in poor areas and the money simply arrives by Giro cheque every fortnight.

WHETHER YOU OWN OR RENT YOUR HOME

Apply to the council for *rate rebates* (sometimes these are more worthwhile than claiming supplementary benefit). Don't think that your income is too high to do this. *Try it.* People living in smart flats with ankle-deep carpeted entrances and uniformed commissionaires are claiming rate rebates – and getting them.

These rebates are confidential. Many people are entitled to them and the more children you have, the more rebate you get.

The old, the single, the married, the self-employed and the bankrupt can also claim rent and rate rebates, not only mothers with children. For instance, a single self-employed person who earns £35 a week might get one-third of her rent paid, so might a married couple with three children and an income of £3000 a year.

To claim a rent or rate rebate, call at the housing department at the local council offices. Declare your income, and prove it with a pay slip or tax return. Declare what rent you're paying and take a lease or rent book to prove it. Then leave it to them to work out how much they'll pay you. If a crisis hits you, get your application form in as fast as possible. It may take a while to process, as they say, but it's backdated from when you first claimed (so make a note of that).

If you think you have been too highly rated, you can appeal against assessment of the rateable value of the property.

When you get a rate assessment you should also get a form on which to object to it. If you do so, the valuation officer will try to come to an agreement with you.

If you don't agree and you want to go to Court, get advice from your local Law Centre or CAB or Shelter or a lawyer operating under the Green Form Scheme.

Incidentally, in Scotland the valuation officer is called the assessor and the Valuation Court is called the Local Valuation Appeals Committee. In Northern Ireland he's called the district valuer and if you want to argue against his decision you'll have to write to the Commissioner of Valuations in Belfast: Valuation Division, Department of Finance, 43 Downshire Road, Newry, Co. Down BT34 1EH (☎ Newry [0693] 4301).

IF YOU LOSE YOUR HOME . . .

. . . and want to raise a mortgage for a new home, then you must find a suitable property, get details of the exact amount you need for the interest repayments, then trot along to the DHSS (your local social security office). Ask them for a letter agreeing to meet interest payments on that amount *and ask the local authority* to act as your *guarantor* under section 45 of the Housing (Financial Provisions) Act 1958.

Yes, they really will . . . *anything* rather than have you on their doorstep with three kids for them to keep at over £135 a week *each. You are kindly saving them money by bravely trying to manage on your own – and never forget it.*

Alternatively, if you have children under sixteen and are homeless (or likely to be) the social services department can guarantee your mortgage payments under section 1 of the Children and Young Persons Act 1963.

Apart from that, your best financial bet will be to get the council to rehouse you, at a subsidized rent. You have a better chance than most if you are a single parent with children, but waiting-lists may be long, accommodation offered too far away, not good enough for you or not big enough.

If you qualify for a council flat *on no account move out of the district and don't move in with friends and relatives*. Go to your local Housing Aid Centre (it's probably run by the council) or the housing department as soon as you know that you'll be homeless. If you have a Court possession order, take it with you. Almost certainly you will have to stay in temporary accommodation until somewhere is found for you.

If you need support, contact your local Law Centre or CAB or CPAG and ask for the address of their local branch and their local citizens' rights office. Also try your local branch of Shelter.

Some housing associations are managed by trusts, set up to help particular groups of people, such as refugees, the old, professional workers on small incomes, and very possibly *you*.

They may receive financial help from a local authority. If your local authority helps a housing association in this way, it probably also nominates many of the tenants. So you could also try to become a tenant of an established local housing association in your area.

Ask your local housing department

for details of *all* the housing associations in the district. You may get yourself a very good home at a very modest rent. Most housing associations come under the fair rent requirements and some are required by the local authority to charge even less than that.

If your local authority isn't helpful, contact the *National Federation of Housing Associations* (86 Strand, London WC2R 0EG; ☎ 01-240 2771) and ask about housing associations in your area.

You could also contact the *Housing Corporation*, Maple House, 149 Tottenham Court Road, London W1P 9LL (☎ 01-387 1466) but not every housing association is registered with them.

Think about moving to a new town. They take families from large cities and the surrounding areas – and they have a special priority for single mothers. They may also help you to get a new job.

Write to the new town development corporation at the town you think you might want to live in. *Northampton* and *Milton Keynes* take overspill from London and the south-east; *Redditch* and *Telford* take overspill from Birmingham and the Black Country; *Runcorn* takes overspill from Liverpool and Merseyside; *Washington* takes overspill from Newcastle. Might be a good way to make a new start.

YOUR RENTING RIGHTS

Most tenants in England and Wales and Scotland now have some protection against unfair rents or unfair eviction.

If you have to rent privately try not to take a flat in the same house as that in which the landlord already lives; your tenancy will have only a limited protection from eviction.

Find a flat or a house through an estate agent, accommodation agency, or the small ads in the evening paper. Estate agents and accommodation agencies *by law* should not charge you a fee for supplying you with lists of addresses and introductions unless they provide other substantial services, such as ringing round to find you a flat or personally viewing the flat for you. Many agencies try to con you into paying them a week's rent if you take the flat – but they should be charging the landlord (and very probably are).

Your tenancy rights are affected by the sort of tenancy you hold. Basically, you are an unprotected, a protected, or a semi-protected tenant. If it is important for you to be certain–it is best to check your status for £5 with a legal aid lawyer (CAB are very competent in this area and will direct you to an expert lawyer).

Landlord and tenant law is a tangle but the most important statutory provisions were all gathered together into two Acts passed in 1977. The following pages give a brief outline of these Acts but if you are in trouble, then you must seek expert help: these pages will just give you some preparation.

PROTECTION FROM EVICTION ACT 1977

1 It is an offence to dispossess a tenant of his dwelling without a Court order.
2 It is an offence to harass a tenant in order to get him to leave or to refrain from exercising his rights under the Rent Act.

3 Landlord and tenant must give at least four weeks' notice to quit and it must be in writing.

DEFINITE TERM OR PERIODIC

There are basically two ways a landlord can agree to rent property to a tenant:

1 Landlord says, 'You can have this place for the next twenty-one years (or fifty years or until next Christmas or some definite time in the future) as long as you pay me rent.' In legal jargon this is called a lease (some lawyers prefer the word 'demise') *for a term of years certain*. It comes to an end when the twenty-one years, or whatever, is up and neither side has to give notice at the end. If the term is more than three years, an agreement of this kind must be in a deed.
2 Landlord says, 'You can have this place if you pay me rent every week (or month, or year) but either of us can end the agreement by giving notice.' The notice has to be at least four weeks. This kind of agreement does not have to be in writing but if rent is payable weekly then the landlord must give the tenant a rent book in the proper form.

RENT ACT 1977

This covers many residential tenancies. If your tenancy involves agricultural land or business premises then there are separate systems of protection which won't be dealt with here. The Rent Act gives tenants:

1 A limit on the rent that has to be paid.
2 Security of tenure – that is, the right to stay in the home when the agreed tenancy comes to an end (either because the term is up or because the landlord has given notice to quit). The tenant stays on as a 'statutory tenant' with the same terms and conditions as before. The landlord cannot get the tenant out without a Court order and the Court will only grant a possession order in specific circumstances (see below).

A tenant is not covered at all by the Rent Act:

1 If the landlord is the Crown, the Duchy of Cornwall, the Duchy of Lancaster or a government department.
2 If the property has a high rateable value – generally, above £1500 in Greater London and £750 elsewhere on 1 April 1973, but even such properties may still be protected if they once had a much lower rateable value.
3 If no rent is payable.
4 If the rent includes a substantial payment for food.
5 If the letting was only for a holiday.

Also there are special provisions in the Rent Act for tenants of housing associations and cooperatives which won't be dealt with here.

Under the Rent Act, you may also be:

1 Protected and controlled, or
2 Protected but not controlled (you're then called 'regulated'), or
3 Letting under a restricted contract.

Tenancies (furnished or unfurnished) that haven't been eliminated so far are all *protected* unless:

1 The landlord is a local authority,

the Commission for the New Towns, a new town development corporation, or the Development Board for Rural Wales.

2 The rent is a low rent (covering most leasehold houses and flats) – that is, the rent is less than two-thirds of the rateable value on 22 March 1973 (there is a lower limit for controlled tenancies, see later).

3 The tenancy was granted to a student on one of a number of courses which have been named in statutory instruments.

4 A substantial part of the rent is for services and fairly reflects the value of the services to the tenant.

5 It's a *section 12 tenancy*.

Section 12 of the Rent Act 1977 enables a householder to let off part of his house without fear that the tenant will claim a statutory right to stay for the rest of his life. It applies to any tenancy created on or after 14 August 1974 where the landlord (or his successors) always resides in the same building as the tenant and the building is not a purpose-built block of flats. A section 12 tenancy is not protected but it is a restricted contract (see later).

A protected tenancy is *controlled*:

1 If the dwelling has a very low rateable value: not more than £40 in London (which means the City of London and the Metropolitan Police District) or £30 elsewhere on 7 November 1956 *and* not more than £70 in Greater London or £35 elsewhere on 1 January 1974; *and*

2 The tenancy was created before 6 July 1957 and is *not* for a term of years certain of more than twenty-one years; *and*

3 The premises are let unfurnished.

The rent can be very low too: instead of two-thirds of the 1965 rateable value, the limit is two-thirds of the 1939 rateable value.

Controlled tenancies are the rats-and-hypothermia end of the market. Rents are rigidly tied to the 1956 rateable value though the landlord is entitled to charge a proportion of the costs of improvements. Landlords are given one not very effective incentive to improve the premises: if they provide the 'standard amenities' then the local authority grants a 'qualification certificate' and the premises cease to be controlled (though they are still protected).

If a protected tenancy is not controlled then it's called a *regulated tenancy* and a 'fair rent' for it is fixed by the local rent officer and entered in a register. The registered rent can't be altered for three years unless there is a substantial change in the quality of accommodation offered.

A protected (regulated or controlled) tenant can be succeeded in the tenancy (which then becomes a statutory one) on death by a surviving spouse or by a close relative who was living with the tenant in the six months preceding death. This first successor can again pass on the tenancy on death but the statutory right of occupation dies with the second successor.

A Court can give a landlord a possession order for a protected (regulated or controlled) tenancy only if it considers it is right to do so and the landlord can prove one of the following:

1 The tenant gave notice but did not leave and the landlord is now under

contract to sell with vacant possession.

2 The landlord bought the property before a certain date (which depends on the type of tenancy, e.g. 7 November 1956 for a controlled tenancy) and now needs it as a home for himself or a member of his immediate family. However, the Court will not grant possession in these circumstances if to do so would cause more hardship to the tenant than the landlord.

3 The tenant is in arrears with the rent or has broken an important condition of the tenancy agreement.

4 The landlord can provide suitable alternative accommodation.

5 The house goes with a job that the tenant no longer holds and the landlord needs the house for a new employee.

6 The tenant, or any person residing with the tenant, has seriously annoyed neighbours or damaged or neglected furniture or property or been convicted of using the premises for immoral or illegal purposes.

7 The tenant has assigned or sublet the whole of the premises without the landlord's permission.

8 The tenant has sublet part of the premises at an illegally high rent (the tenant has to obey the Rent Act as well).

In the case of regulated (not controlled) tenancies the Courts will always grant a landlord a possession order in certain circumstances, as long as the landlord gave the tenant notice of the possibility of repossession at the time the tenancy was created. The most important circumstances are:

★ Case 11, where the landlord occupied the dwelling as his residence before granting the tenancy and now reasonably requires it again to live in.

★ Case 12, where the landlord bought the dwelling as a retirement home and has now retired. In Case 12 the Court has discretion to grant possession even if notice was not given to the tenant.

Restricted contracts are lettings covered by section 12 (see above) and any contract by which accommodation is provided together with the use of furniture or services (which means anything except water and sanitation) unless the contract falls within the definition of a protected tenancy.

Rents for restricted contracts are settled by rent tribunals and entered in registers. Once registered they cannot be altered for three years without a significant change in the accommodation provided.

If a tenant under a restricted contract is given notice to quit he can appeal to the rent tribunal for a rent reduction. Rent Tribunals have a legally qualified chairman and the members will include a surveyor. The Tribunal will decide how much the tenant should pay, and meanwhile how long he can stay. The landlord may apply to the Courts for an order for the tenant to quit, but meanwhile he stays put.

Whether you are a protected or an unprotected tenant, go to your local Law Centre or to a lawyer working under the Legal Advice (Green Form) scheme to find out if you have a case. Or apply to Shelter, 157 Waterloo Road, London SE1 8UU (☎ 01-633 9377). You can then write to your local Tribunal or Rent Assessment Committee (address in telephone directory).

Rent Tribunals and Rent Assessment Committees operate in England, Wales and Scotland but not in Northern Ireland. Tenants who feel unfairly treated can apply to the Northern Ireland Commissioner for Complaints (River House, 48 High Street, Belfast BT1 2JT; ☎ Belfast [0232] 33821).

NOTE FOR LANDLORDS AND LANDLADIES

If you let your home (furnished or unfurnished) you should give the tenant written notice beforehand that you may recover possession of the place under Case 11 of the Rent Act 1977. Send it recorded delivery (to prove that it arrived) and stick the receipt to your copy of the letter. Ask for an acknowledgement of the letter (send two copies, ask the tenant to sign one, date the signature and return it by recorded delivery).

Do the same thing if you let your retirement home (furnished or unfurnished) under Case 12. If you let on a fixed-term contract, there is no need to serve a notice to quit.

Before a landlord applies to the Court for an eviction order (under Case 11 or 12) he must terminate any tenancy agreement that isn't for a fixed period. If you let the place on a periodic tenancy (by the week, fortnight or month) you must give your tenant at least four weeks' notice to quit in writing (recorded delivery). You must give a quarter's notice if you are paid quarterly or six months' notice for half-yearly or yearly payments.

Get any further information from CAB, a neighbourhood Law Centre, a Housing Aid Centre, Shelter, CPAG, SHAC, or the rent officer.

ADDRESSES

Building Societies Association, 14 Park Street, London W1Y 4AL (☎ 01-629 0515).

CPAG (Child Poverty Action Group), 1 Macklin Street, London WC2B 5NH (☎ 01-405 5942).

CPAG (Child Poverty Action Group) Northern Ireland, c/o Department of Social Administration, New University of Ulster, Cromore Road, Coleraine, Co. Londonderry BT52 1SA, Northern Ireland (☎ Coleraine [0265] 4141, extension 621).

CPAG (Child Poverty Action Group) Scotland, c/o Volunteer Bureau, 234 West Regent Street, Glasgow G2 4D2 (☎ 041-248 7671).

CTI Dominion Title Insurance, 22 Theobalds Road, London WC1X 8PF (☎ 01-405 4896).

Consumers' Association Subscription Department, Caxton Hill, Hertford SG13 7LZ (☎ Hertford [0992] 59031).

Gingerbread, Headquarters: 35 Wellington Street, London WC2E 7BN (☎ 01-240 0953).

The Homes Organization, 4 Passey Place, London SE9 5DQ (☎ 01-859 2001).

The Housing Corporation, Maple House, 149 Tottenham Court Road, London W1P 9LL (☎ 01-387 1466).

Michael Joseph, 27 Mole Park, Occupation Lane, Woolwich, London SE18 3JQ (☎ 01-855 2404).

The Land Registry, Lincoln's Inn Fields, London WC2A 3PH (☎ 01-405 3488).

National Federation of Housing Associations, 86 Strand, London WC2R 0EG (☎ 01-240 2771).

SHAC Ltd (London Housing Aid Centre), 189a Old Brompton Road, London SW5 0AR (☎ 01-373 7276).

Shelter, National Campaign for the Homeless Ltd, 157 Waterloo Road, London SE1 8UU (☎ 01-633 9377).

Shelter Scotland, 6 Castle Street, Edinburgh EH2 3AT (☎ 031-226 6347).

The Solicitors' Law Stationery Society, PO Box 55, 237 Long Lane, London SE1 4PU (☎ 01-407 8066).

Where to get money

It is a curious fact that, at a time when we are all supposed to be broke, there is an amazing amount of free money around. You can get a good deal of help from the Welfare State, some of it regardless of your contributions, if you are eligible and prepared to struggle through the form-filling and the interviews. All you need is the calm of a sphinx, the tenacity of a bull-terrier and a small amount of basic information.

HOW TO GET FREE MONEY

What is a Welfare State benefit? They aren't quite sure. There is unnecessary confusion about benefits because of the double meaning (in Civil Service literature) of the word 'allowances'.

You are allowed *tax reliefs* on various ways of spending your money and these are sometimes called 'allowances', although you don't get a penny. You are allowed certain *benefits* because of your National Insurance contributions (and some, whether you have paid contributions or not) but sometimes these benefits are also called 'allowances'.

Don't think of benefits as charity or something for nothing. If you have paid your National Insurance contributions, then you have paid for a fair share of help. Look upon the payouts as if they come from an ordinary insurance company, after you've been paying premiums for years. If you or your family have not paid National Insurance contributions, then the State may still be getting a bargain by giving you free money if it helps you to carry on independently, rather than putting your children into care or yourself into hospital or whatever would be the result of your not being helped.

The first thing to do if you are short of money, is to check that you are claiming all your allowances, benefits and straightforward CASH from (*a*) the State, (*b*) your local council. You can do this because you have contributed towards the State insurance scheme, because you have home responsibilities or because you have personal disabilities.

Check the list of benefits to which your National Insurance contributions entitle you and call at your local social security office (the address is on a poster in your local post office or look in the telephone directory under H for Health and Social Security, Department of) or CAB to discuss any particular problem. Leaflet FBI, *Family Benefits and Pensions*, from the Department of Health and Social Security gives full details of family income supplement and supplementary benefits and also of free medical benefits.

Once you have discovered what they are, claim *all* your benefits. The Department of Health and Social Security is concerned that millions of benefits that could be claimed are not being claimed.

Almost one in four of the families entitled to free school meals and family income supplement doesn't claim them. A million people are not claiming their rent and rate rebates. The DHSS is particularly worried about pensioners and families with children who do not claim supplementary benefits that might add between £2 and £5 a week to their incomes.

Some pensioners mistakenly believe that because they have some savings they can't claim supplementary pensions but this isn't true. In fact

you can have £1249 in savings in the bank as well as owning your home. And the average pensioner can certainly claim a rate rebate from the local council.

For families with very low incomes the benefits are:

1 *Family income supplement*, for those whose earned incomes are below a certain level.
2 *Supplementary benefit* for those who are not in full-time work, and who are *not* eligible for . . .
3 *Unemployment benefit*.

You can't claim family income supplement *and* supplementary benefit.

FAMILY INCOME SUPPLEMENT (FIS)

This is for families which have a very low income but do have a working breadwinner. The breadwinner has to work at least thirty hours a week and there must be at least one child under sixteen in the family.

From November 1978 a family breadwinner (with one child) earning less than £46 a week is eligible for FIS, but check the latest figure with your nearest CAB.

The qualifying income limit is increased by £4 a week for each extra child, so for three children it would be £54.

The DHSS looks at your actual income to see how far it falls short of the qualifying income limit. You get half of the shortfall but the most you can get in FIS is £10.50, plus £1 for each child after the first.

Example: Jim has a wife and three

children. He works thirty-one hours a week for £30.80 (agreed, it's unlikely, but if he works less or earns more he won't qualify for maximum family income supplement).

Maximum qualifying limit

£46 + £4 + £4 = £54.00
Deduct Jim's income = £30.80

= £23.20

Divide this in half $\frac{£23.20}{2}$ = £11.60

But Jim isn't entitled to the full £11.60, only the maximum £10.50 plus £2 (£1 for each child after the first) which is a *total weekly benefit of £12.50.*

If you're single or divorced then a parent of any sex can claim (half of the families that receive FIS are one-parent families).

If you're a couple (either married or living together) only the man can claim FIS, even if the breadwinner is the woman. If the man is not working, he is supposed to claim either supplementary benefit or unemployment benefit (see later). Unfairly, the State does not recognize couples in which the man takes the responsibility of running a home in order to take a degree or a technical course to go back to studying or whatever, while the woman takes on the responsibility for earning. The State doesn't recognize role swapping.

To claim family income supplement get form FIS.1 from your local post office or local social security office. To prove your earnings, enclose recent pay slips or tax assessments. Send it all off to DHSS Family Income Supplements, Poulton-le-Fylde, Blackpool, Lancs FY6 8NW

(the post office or social security office provides stamped envelopes). If you are eligible you'll receive a book of fifty-two weekly orders to be cashed at the post office. Your allowance is always for the year, whatever your change in circumstances, and at the end of the year you apply again.

Receipt of family income supplement entitles you automatically to various other *free* benefits. These include: *medical prescriptions, dentures, dental treatment, spectacles, wigs and elasticized stockings, school meals for children at school, refund of fares for members of the family attending hospital, legal advice (depending on capital, assets and savings).*

SUPPLEMENTARY BENEFIT

This can be awarded to any man aged sixteen or over, or any single woman over sixteen who isn't living 'in sin' (committing intercourse) with a man, and who earns not more than £6 a week.

It is called *supplementary allowance* if you are below retirement age and *supplementary pension* if you are retired. If you are married, your husband has to claim; if you are living with your lover, he has to claim.

If you don't have any dependants, are fit to work and are under forty-five, you will probably be told to register for employment and draw unemployment benefit instead. (This is why so many lone mothers who look after their young children claim supplementary benefit – because they can't do full-time work.)

Besides supplementary benefit you can probably get help with: *rent, rates, repairs, insurance, mortgage interest, special heating, dietary needs.*

You may also receive lump-sum

grants to help with *clothing, bedding, furniture, hire-purchase debts* and *fares*.

The amount you get depends on your income, the number and age of dependants in your family and how long you are likely to need help. The Supplementary Benefits Commission deducts any other social security benefits and maintenance payments in full from any supplement it allows you.

Deductions will also be made if your savings are £1250 or more, whether for a single person or for a married couple (which might encourage sock-under-the-mattress saving).

But the biggest, most iniquitous, most idiotic injustice about supplementary benefit is the cohabitation rule. If you have a man in the house, and the DHSS special investigators decide that you are living together as husband and wife (even if you are certainly *not*) then the Commission will refuse you supplementary benefit on the grounds that the man (even if he only met you last week) ought to be supporting you and your children. They would not feel this if you had another woman in the house, or a relative, who might reasonably contribute to expenses.

While this may stop a few fiddlers, it is a sort of sex tax on women. This system is deeply offensive because it assumes that every woman who sleeps with a man in her home is being paid to do so. It is also most unfair if the man is a lodger (highly likely, if a woman is short of money and she's letting off a room to help pay the rent) and their relationship is non-sexual. This rule, and the unpleasant behaviour of the special investigators (snoopers) who have to 'decide' when living under the same roof amounts to cohabitation, causes a lot of distress

and is very much resented by many people.

Women who have been unfair victims of this rule can appeal to a Tribunal and may be able to get help from their local claimants' union (see later; ask CAB for your local branch). Claimants' unions can be a valuable source of support and information and they will battle on your behalf and help with your claim in any case of injustice.

To claim supplementary benefit, collect form SB1 from your local post office or go to your local social security office, which is often easier. A social security official may call to interview you at home about your income, your needs, and those of your children.

Supplementary benefit is sent to you in a book of orders or by Giro order, which you cash at a post office. Once you have been awarded supplementary benefit, then you get the same free benefits that you get when you are awarded family income supplement (see above), including *free school meals, free prescriptions* and *fares to hospital*.

You can check whether you are eligible in the *Supplementary Benefits Handbook* published by HMSO. Get it from a Government Bookshop at:
★ 49 High Holborn, London WC1V 6HB (☎ 01-928 6977) (personal callers only).
★ PO Box 569, London SE1 9NH (☎ 01-928 6977) (mail order only).
★ 80 Chichester Street, Belfast BT1 4JY (☎ Belfast [0232] 34488).
★ 258 Broad Street, Birmingham B1 2HE (☎ 021-643 3757).
★ Southey House, Wine Street, Bristol BS1 2BQ (☎ Bristol [0272] 24306).

★ 41 The Hayes, Cardiff CF1 1JW   3AR (☎ 031-225 6333).
  (☎ Cardiff [0222] 23654).   ★ Brazennose Street, Manchester
★ 13a Castle Street, Edinburgh EH2   M60 8AS (☎ 061-834 7201).

Child Benefit Table

Apart from these main sources of benefit for people on low incomes, there may be other benefits that you can claim. If you have children, for instance, you might get:

Benefit	Weekly value	Who can claim
Child benefits	£3 for each child (£4 from 2 April 1979)	A person responsible for a child under sixteen, or sixteen to nineteen in full-time education.* (The mother must claim if she's there.)
Child benefit increase	£2	Single parents with children under sixteen, or sixteen to nineteen in full-time education*
Child's special allowance	£6.35 for each child (£5.35 from 2 April 1979)	A divorced woman with a dependent child (under sixteen or sixteen to nineteen in full-time education*) whose former husband has died. Entitlement depends on former husband's national insurance contributions
Guardian's allowance	£6.35 for each child (£5.35 from 2 April 1979)	Person taking orphaned child into family
Child increase with widowed mother's allowance	£6.35 for each child (£5.35 from 2 April 1979)	Widows with dependent children
Educational maintenance allowance (not available from all local authorities)	£1–£4	Parents with children over sixteen whom they wish to keep at school but can't afford to do so

* This means a course of a standard up to GCE A level or OND. For more advanced courses the child will get a grant.

Other benefits are available if you are *disabled* or *care for an invalid*. You may also be able to claim *extra unemployment* or *sickness benefit*.

If the whole idea of claiming sounds too slow and aggravatiing, consider the hypothetical case of Jane Ophelia Whittaker who gets paid £1955.20 a year, *tax free*, in benefits. Jane has three children, aged twelve, fourteen and fifteen and they live in a mortgaged house. Recently, her husband left her. Ladies who have just been left by their husbands are often too distraught to write the crisp, factual letter that is necessary to explain the situation before you can get the money. Here's the letter Jane wrote, which can be taken as a guide:

Her address

Address of local social security office
(in telephone directory under
Health and Social Security, Department of)

Date: 1 March 1979

Dear Sir

I wish to claim supplementary benefit because I have been deserted by my husband. I telephoned you after he left yesterday and you said that I should write to you, describing my circumstances. You arranged for me to come and see you tomorrow.

I have three children: Gary is nearly fifteen (born 14 April 1964), Joanna is fourteen (born 12 February 1965) and Petra is nearly twelve (born 9 July 1967).

I have a part-time job helping in Gosport Polytechnic Arts and Crafts Department two evenings a week, for which I am paid £10.

I get child benefits, which come to £11. So our weekly income is now £21.

My husband has not left me any money and I don't think he will send me any. I don't know where he has gone. I am very worried about the mortgage on the house as I don't want to have to leave, I don't see how I can keep up the payments, and I have nowhere else to go.

Our mortgage is with the XL Building Society (address) and is in my husband's name. The reference number is 12345678W. We still owe £5000 and the current interest rate is $12\frac{3}{4}$ per cent a year. The weekly interest repayment is £13.

The general rates are £250 per year and the water and sewerage rate is £12 a year.

We have central heating and our house has three bedrooms, bathroom, open-plan sitting/dining-room and kitchen.

Please let me know what benefit I can claim and how it is calculated. If you need to visit my home, I am in most afternoons. Please let me know by letter when someone will call.

Yours faithfully

Jane Ophelia Whittaker

Calculation: The first £6 of Jane's earnings are not included in the calculations. This leaves her with an income of £4 to offset against weekly outgoings of £18 for mortgage and rates, plus central heating and living expenses.

She is eligible for:

	£
Basic supplementary benefit	15.55
Two child supplementary benefits at £7.95 (for children aged thirteen to fifteen)	15.90
One child supplementary benefit at £6.55 (for child aged eleven or twelve)	6.55
Central heating allowance	1.60
Mortgage interest (this can be paid in full even though the mortgage is in Jane's husband's name)	13.00
	52.60
From which is deducted £11 ordinary child benefits and £4 of Jane's earnings	−15.00
	37.60

So Jane's weekly income is now £37.60 (supplementary benefits) plus £10 (earned) +£11 (child benefits) = £58.60 a week, which is £3047.20 a year. Her supplementary benefits are worth £1955.20 per year which is, of course, not taxed.

If Jane's husband decides (or is ordered) to contribute maintenance and stipulates in a recorded delivery letter that this is to be used primarily for repayment of the mortgage capital then none of Jane's benefits should be reduced until after the mortgage capital is repaid.

It might be more beneficial to Jane to arrange quietly for her husband to do this, rather than have him pay straightforward maintenance to her, which would then be subject to tax and which she would have to spend on the mortgage anyway.

For help with claims contact:

The National Council for One Parent Families, 255 Kentish Town Road, London NW5 2LX (☎ 01-267 1361).

The National Council for the Single Woman and Her Dependants, 29 Chilworth Mews, London W2 3RG (☎ 01-262 1451).

Child Poverty Action Group, 1 Macklin Street, London WC2 5NH (☎ 01-242 3225).

Claimants' Union, The Albany, Creek Road, London SE8 3PU (☎ 01-692 1047).

THE ROOF OVER YOUR HEAD

As a householder (even if you don't qualify for family income supplement or supplementary benefit) you may be able to claim a *rent rebate* or help with mortgage interest and/or a *rate rebate*.

Your rebate or allowance will be decided on the basis of your income and your needs. It is usually granted for six months at a time (twelve months for pensioners). You can re-apply at any time up to a month before, or a month after, your allowance runs out.

At time of writing the maximum rent rebate allowed in the Greater London Council area is £13 a week (£10 elsewhere) and the maximum rate rebate is £4.50 a week in London (£3.20 elsewhere), so some people might be able to claim £17.50 a week.

Rights Guide for Home Owners (published by Child Poverty Action Group) clearly and simply explains how to get free State cash and claim free money towards your *mortgage, rent, removals, central heating bills* (you can get £1.60 a week towards the heating if your home has five or more rooms), *house insurance and repairs* (£39.50 a year). They also advise how to get *free school meals, clothing, fares* and *study grants*.

UNEMPLOYMENT BENEFIT

To claim full unemployment benefit you must have paid, during the preceding tax year, National Insurance contributions equal to the minimum contribution you can make for fifty weeks. If you leave your job voluntarily without good cause, or you are dismissed with good cause, you have to wait six weeks before claiming.

Unemployment benefit ranges upwards from £15.75 according to your earnings in the preceding tax year and the number of your dependants. All unemployment benefits are tax free and you can draw them for up to a year.

To claim your benefit, go to your local unemployment benefit office, taking your income tax form P45 or a note of your National Insurance number with you. You should also register for employment at the same time at the local office of the Employment Service Agency.

Whilst you are drawing unemployment benefit, you must be prepared to apply for other jobs in the field of your experience and on a par with your qualifications. (The Employment Service Agency can't just order an out-of-work film director to take a job as a road-sweeper or cinema usher.)

You do not qualify for unemployment benefit if:

1 You are self-employed.
2 You take a part-time job which pays you more than 75p a day and/or prevents you from taking a full-time job.
3 You make unreasonable demands about where and when you will work, or the amount of pay you want.

HOW TO GET MORE MONEY

If you think that your SB officer is a bureaucratic, penny-pinching, unfeeling, unfair, all-round bastard (which is unlikely to be the case) and that your benefits should be higher, you can appeal to the local *supplementary benefit appeal tribunal*. You lodge the appeal at your local social security office: they will provide you with a form.

Get help in preparing your case from your local claimants' union or the Child Poverty Action Group.

The Tribunal is appointed by the Secretary of State for Health and Social Security. There is always a legally qualified chairman, one member to represent workers and another with special experience of the problems of claimants. After you have presented your case and the DHSS has presented its case, the Tribunal considers it and then sends you the decision by post.

You can get other benefits raised, including unemployment, pensions, invalid allowances, child benefits. If you think you have been unfairly assessed, appeal to your local *National Insurance appeal tribunal*. Get an application form from the DHSS or ask for the address of the relevant tribunal and just write to them direct.

If you don't agree with *their* decision and you are as tenacious as a limpet and as calm as a creek, you can appeal to the *National Insurance Commissioner*. The commissioners are all senior barristers and hearings are held in London, Edinburgh and Cardiff. Get expert advice from a solicitor or your trade union, and appeal within three months.

CHILDREN AND MONEY

Some women feel that they want to do something to help secure a good financial future for their children . . . or, at any rate, to help them financially in some way. To be blunt, what you can best do for them, that costs nothing at all, is to make sure that they know their way around the Welfare State claims system.

There is no need to do more for your children than see that they are educated as well as possible and bring them up to earn their own living at something they enjoy and are properly trained to do.

However, when they most need money seems to be when they're setting up their first home, not when they are in their late forties, when finances might be expected to be a bit easier.

So, if you can afford it, be generous by helping with the down-payment for a first home. Parent aid might be a money gift (you can give up to £2000 a year without running into capital transfer tax), an interest-free loan specifically for house purchase, a guarantee for a bank loan or mortgage or a combination of any or all of those four.

CHECK WHETHER ANYONE YOU DON'T KNOW WANTS TO GIVE YOU MONEY

Finally, if you are broke, don't qualify for benefits and have nothing to sell there are various benevolent organizations which may be able to help. Almost every profession has some sort of welfare organization and many of them are terrific support (not only with money but schooling, housing and general cheering up). Here are a few of them:

National Council for the Single Woman and Her Dependants, 29 Chilworth Mews, London W2 3RG (☏ 01-262 1451). Very good indeed, with a very good president; sympathetic, understanding and will *fight* for your rights.

Friends of the Elderly and Gentlefolk's Help, 42 Ebury Street, London SW1W 0LZ (☎ 01-730 8263). Can be a real help, especially if you need assistance with an elderly relative.

Distressed Gentlefolk's Aid Association, Vicarage Gate House, Vicarage Gate, London W8 4AQ (☎ 01-229 9341). For practical help with day-to-day problems. *Very* understanding.

Society for the Assistance of Ladies in Reduced Circumstances (once your silver salver has gone), Lancaster House, 25 Hornyold Road, Malvern, Worcestershire WR14 1QQ (☎ Malvern [068 45] 4645).

The National Benevolent Institution, 61 Bayswater Road, London W2 3PG (☎ 01-723 0021).

Royal United Kingdom Beneficient Association, 13 Bedford Street, London WC2E 9HH (☎ 01-836 2575).

Friends of the Clergy Corporation, 27 Medway Street, London SW1P 2BD (☎ 01-222 2288).

Clergy Orphan Corporation, 2 Verulam Buildings, London WC1R 5LS (☎ 01-242 7769).

Teachers Benevolent Fund, Hamilton House, Mabledon Place, London WC1H 7BB (☎ 01-387 2442).

Royal Medical Benevolent Fund, 24 King's Road, Wimbledon, London SW19 8QN (☎ 01-540 4656).

Professional Classes Aid Council, 10 St Christopher's Place, London W1M 6HY (☎ 01-935 0641).

Royal Air Force Benevolent Fund, 67 Portland Place, London W1N 3AJ (☎ 01-580 8343). Very good reports indeed of kindness and help.

Officers Families Fund, 21 Strutton Ground, London SW1P 2HW (☎ 01-222 4119). Kindly as well as helpful and very understanding.

Artists' General Benevolent Institution, Burlington House, Piccadilly, London W1V 0DJ (☎ 01-734 1193).

Musicians Benevolent Fund, St Cecilia's House, 16 Ogle Street, London W1P 7LG (☎ 01-636 4481). Have a very generous, warmhearted reputation.

National Advertising Benevolent Society, 3 Crawford Place, London W1H 1JB (☎ 01-723 8028).

GET YOURSELF A PRIVATE INCOME

This is not exactly light, bedside reading, but, believe it or not, it's easier to understand than anything else you're likely to read on the subject. As it will almost definitely affect your future personal income please try to plough through it.

National Insurance contributions are a compulsory tax on everyone who works and earns more than a minimum wage (£19.50 a week for the 1979/80 tax year). They entitle you to a range of welfare benefits.

There are four different classes of contributions and the rate of payment is different for each class. *Class 1* is for employers and employees. *Classes 2 and 4* are for the self-employed. All these are compulsory. *Class 3* is voluntary: it is for anyone who doesn't fall into the other groups.

Generally, in all classes you are eligible for benefit if you have paid in the past year the equivalent of fifty contributions at basic rate.

If you are drawing sickness or unemployment benefit your contributions are paid for by *the government* and your pension rights are unaffected.

CLASS 1

Class 1 is for employees and employers and is compulsory. If your employer does not provide you with an approved company pension then you pay $6\frac{1}{2}$ per cent of your earnings up to £135 a week, which is the ceiling. *You* pay nothing if you earn under £19.50 a week. Your employer pays the equivalent of $13\frac{1}{2}$ per cent of your earnings (up to £135 a week).

Because an employer has to pay between £2.63 and £18.22 a week National Insurance for each person on the payroll, he naturally wants to employ as few people as possible.

Just assuming you earn £135 a week, the total National Insurance contribution in your name would be £27 a week. A *lot* of money and you would get a better return for it if you invested it privately. But your contribution doesn't go towards protect-ing only you. Part of your National Insurance contributions funds the Welfare State benefits of other people: the able-bodied earners support the rest. Also the National Health Service has to provide you with a lot of treatment that private health insurance would not cover.

How you pay. Your employer keeps a card showing your PAYE and National Insurance deductions each week. He deducts your contribution from your pay before paying you. Provided you have made enough payments, this entitles you and your family to the following benefits: unemployment benefit; earnings-related unemployment benefit; sickness benefit; earnings-related sickness benefit; invalidity benefit; maternity benefits; widow's benefits (for widows of male employees but not for widowers); widowed mother's allowance; basic retirement pension; earnings-related retirement pension; child's special allowance; death grant.

All employees are entitled to compensation for injury or illness caused at work but this does not depend on the number of National Insurance contributions.

Your employer may decide to provide his own Occupational Pension Scheme for his staff and contract out of part of the National Insurance Scheme. This means that your National Insurance contribution will be reduced but you may have to pay a contribution to your employer's scheme.

Almost certainly an Occupational Pension Scheme will be more to your advantage than staying within the State scheme. All Occupational Pension Schemes have to meet very strict conditions laid down by the government.

There is one major disadvantage. If you change jobs several times, you will accumulate a lot of odd, tiny pensions when you finally retire. Private company pension schemes can't always be transferred to a new job, whereas the government earnings-related pension scheme will carry on regardless even if you switch jobs every month.

Class 1 contributors who are *not* in an employer's private Occupational Pension Scheme will get an earnings-related pension (*see page 254*).

CLASS 2

Class 2 is for self-employed people. They pay a flat rate of £2.10 a week. They can ask for exemption if they earn less than £1050 a year.

If you earn over £2250 a year (net after expenses) self-employed, you also pay an earnings-related supplement called Class 4 (see below) for which you get no extra benefits.

How you pay. You buy your own National Insurance stamp and fill up your own card. Or you can arrange to pay through your bank or National Girobank or your accountant can pay it for you annually. Provided you have made enough payments, this entitles you to some benefits but they are fewer than Class 1. You get: free medical and subsidized dental care; sickness benefit; invalidity benefit; maternity benefits; widow's benefits; basic retirement pension; child's special allowance; death grant.

You are *not* entitled to unemployment benefit, industrial injury or disablement benefit, industrial death benefit, or free medical treatment for you or your family when abroad.

Your retirement pension is a flat, basic pension, not earnings-related.

If you are self-employed you should invest in a private pension scheme because your contributions are *entirely exempt from tax*. This may well be worth several hundred pounds that you don't have to pay.

CLASS 3

See below.

CLASS 4

Class 4 is for the self-employed whose net income (after allowed expenses) is above £2250 a year. You pay the basic £2.10 a week on Class 2 plus 5 per cent of your net income between £2250 and £7000. So the maximum payment is an extra £4.57 a week, making a total of £6.67. Class 4 contributions bring no extra benefits to the payer; they are intended to distribute more fairly the contributions from the self-employed.

How you pay. Class 4 contributions are worked out by the Inland Revenue, along with schedule D tax.

CLASS 3

Class 3 is a voluntary payment for people who are not liable to pay Class 1 or Class 2 contributions, such as students, someone living on a private income, someone bringing up the family at home. Married women who have opted for reduced liability for Class 1 or Class 2 (see later) still have a liability so they can't pay Class 3 contributions.

Provided you have made enough payments you are entitled to the following benefits: basic retirement pension; child's special allowance; death grant; widow's benefits; maternity grant.

How you pay. Men and women pay £2 a week. As a voluntary contributor you buy your own stamps at the post office and fill up your own card, or arrange to pay through your bank or National Girobank.

NATIONAL INSURANCE FOR WOMEN LOOKING AFTER DEPENDANTS

If you are at home full time looking after your children or a dependant relative you obviously cannot be in paid employment nor (until recently) could you pay any class of National Insurance contribution. Now you can, if you choose, pay Class 3.

Is there any point in doing that? You can get a number of benefits anyway without making any contributions. In certain circumstances, you will even have your pension rights protected. So what extra benefits might Class 3 contributions bring?

Protection of your pension rights is not guaranteeing you the full national basic pension. You cannot get that unless you have paid or been credited with contributions for *at least twenty years apart from* the years spent at home looking after children under sixteen or a relative who is receiving an invalidity or retirement pension. If you don't meet those conditions, you get a reduced pension, worked out only on the contributions that you *did* pay. But you could make up the extra with Class 3 contributions and become entitled to a full national basic pension.

So if you aren't looking after the very young or the very old, if you have *never* worked, or if you are having a temporary period at home, whether it's simply to sun in the garden or write a novel, you should try to contribute to Class 3.

Paying Class 3 contributions is a *very, very* good deal. Let's say for argument that you pay £2 each week for twenty years. This is a total of £2084. You would get that back in just over two years, so after you are $62\frac{1}{2}$ it's profit all the way. And don't forget that pensions are virtually inflation-adjusted.

NATIONAL INSURANCE FOR MARRIED WOMEN

This section applies to married and separated women and to widows but not to divorced women.

1 Until 11 May 1977 a married woman with a job could *choose* whether to pay the full National Insurance contribution or pay a reduced contribution and obtain limited benefits from her husband's payments. If she opted out *before* this date and paid the reduced rate then she can continue to do so until she retires.

2 *If she opted out before 11 May 1977* she pays 2 per cent of all earnings up to £135 a week (maximum £2.70 a week). However, women earning less than £19.50 a week pay nothing. In this case her benefits depend on her husband's payments, not hers. If he has made twenty-six contributions in the previous year she can get the following benefits: maternity grant; basic retirement pension; death grant.

3 A woman who has chosen to opt out can stay out. But if she decides at any time to change from opting out to paying full contributions (opting in) she cannot later decide to opt out again.

4 She *cannot retain* the option if she divorces because she is then treated as a single person.

5 If she is divorced she can still benefit from her ex-husband's National Insurance contributions for a pension, so long as she doesn't remarry before she is sixty. After she is sixty, she can get the single person's pension on his contributions and, if she wants, get married as well.

6 A married working woman *cannot* now choose to opt out if she didn't do so before 11 May 1977 or (in a few cases) May 1978. After that she has no choice: she *must* pay the full contribution.

7 If she stops work for two consecutive years and therefore need not pay contributions she *cannot go back* to work and continue to opt out. She has to start paying full contributions.

If you opted out, when is it worth your while to opt in? It depends on your age and circumstances. However, there is one situation in which it is almost certainly worthwhile to opt in. That is when you are in full employment and know that you will shortly have to give up work in order to take on domestic responsibilities.

If you are giving up work to look after young children or a sick or elderly relative, you can be credited with insurance contributions for the period at home and so have your pension protected.

But, if you have opted out, you will receive no credits for the first two years at home. The solution is to opt in before you leave work (allow three months before leaving) and then you will get the credits for the first two years at home (this tip can be worth several hundred pounds paid into your insurance scheme).

THE WIDOW'S MITE

Do you know that no married woman is automatically entitled to a widow's pension?

Do you know that a widow can live in sin with a man and *still* get her pension, *provided she's over sixty*?

Do you know that your husband is being discriminated against, if you die, because (even if there are four children to look after) *he* won't get a State widower's pension? (In America, they do.)

Widows' pensions are unbelievably complicated, unfair and ungenerous, and won't get much better until 1998 (in May, to be exact), when the new rates will start to be paid.

It's not easy to follow the convoluted logic of widows' pensions and benefits. Only two things are clear: they were not drawn up by widows and they are not enough for anyone to live on. *They are below the poverty line*; widows should apply for supplementary benefit wherever possible. Women who are happily married should carefully work out what they spend now and what they would live on if widowed.

There is no one, simple, flat widow's pension, like the retirement pension. A widow is entitled to a range of benefits according to:

1 Her age at the time of her widowhood (there is no widow's pension for anyone who is under forty when her husband dies if her children have left home).

2 Whether or not she has young children.

3 Whether she was employed or retired.

4 Whether her husband was employed or retired.
5 Whether he has paid the required number of contributions.
6 Whether he died as a result of an industrial accident.

If a husband paid National Insurance contributions amounting to fifty contributions at basic rate during his last year at work his widow will receive benefits.

Whether or not you are working, if you are eligible for any sort of widow's pension *it is yours by right.* There is no means test.

Available benefits may include: the widow's allowance; the widowed mother's allowance; the widow's pension; the State retirement pension due to her husband; her husband's earnings-related pension; an industrial widow's pension.

Sounds good, doesn't it? But wait . . .

You may qualify for more than one benefit, but the general rule is that you are not entitled to more than one for the same set of circumstances. Either you receive the largest, or one benefit is reduced because you receive another. This rule, which is intended to prevent anyone living too well off State benefits, is very hard on some widows. For example, it means that after you have been widowed for six months you can't draw your widow's benefits *and* the grant you might get for going on a TOPS course (although married women can draw the grant while still having a family breadwinner).

Immediately after a husband's death a widow is paid the *widow's allowance* for twenty-six weeks, provided she is under sixty and her husband was employed when he died.

This imaginative and thoughtful allowance (currently £27.30 a week) is to tide the widow over while she readjusts to life on her own (and perhaps a frozen bank account). She continues to receive the child benefit for each child living with her who is aged under sixteen, or under nineteen and in full-time education (up to A-level standard).

She *may* be able to claim more in the form of an earnings-related addition based on her husband's National Insurance contributions and earnings in the tax year before his death. This is worked out by a complicated formula but from November 1978 the *maximum* could be £16.25 extra a week.

The widow's allowance, the widow's pension and the earnings-related addition are *classed as earned income and are liable for tax*! So they have to be added to any other income a widow receives, when her tax liability is being assessed.

After six months a widow with children may qualify for the *widowed mother's allowance* which will be paid until the children are nineteen, provided they live at home. This allowance is currently £19.50 a week *plus* a further £6.35 (£5.35 from 2 April 1979) for each child who is not receiving an educational grant for higher education.

After the last child has blown out the nineteen candles on his birthday cake, the widowed mother will be eligible for the *widow's pension.*

To claim the *full* State widow's pension (currently £19.50 a week) a wife must be over fifty when her husband dies, or when widowed mother's allowance ceases.

If she is between forty and fifty years old when her husband dies or when the widowed mother's allowance ceases she will *not* get the full widow's pension.

If she is under forty when her husband dies or when widowed mother's allowance ceases she will not get a widow's pension AT ALL.

The reduced benefit for a woman widowed between forty and fifty can be very unfair for a recently bereaved woman with no children or with children who have just left home. After twenty years of bringing up a family she is suddenly treated as if she has the earning capacity of a professional career woman who has never stopped work. But it may be difficult for her to get *any* job, let alone a well-paid one, particularly if she is unqualified; if she does get a job it's unlikely to pay as much as she would be earning had she not devoted her time to her home and her family.

You can continue to receive widow's pension until age sixty-five but after sixty you may be better off with a retirement pension based on your own contributions (you can't have both). After sixty-five the retirement pension is as least as much as the widow's pension.

If a woman is widowed when she is over sixty she will automatically get the *State retirement pension* due to her husband.

A widow who has worked and has her own pension rights is entitled to add her late husband's earnings-related record to her own, so she can be credited with *both* earnings-related contributions, up to the maximum that one person can be paid. This isn't worth much now but it will be in a few years.

In theory a future widow's pension will be related to earnings from April 1978 (when the National Insurance contributions changed) to the time of her husband's death. In fact, it will take twenty years before the benefits build up to what is intended. Until then widows will merely get a token amount above the basic widow's pension.

The structure of the new earnings-related widow's pensions means that pensions will always be inadequate for *young* widows, because it's unlikely that the husband will have made a long enough or big enough National Insurance contribution. And if a widow is too young (under fifty!) to receive the full flat-rate widow's pension, she will not receive the earnings-related widow's pension either!

You can claim an *industrial widow's pension* if your husband dies at work in an accident or as a result of an illness or injury contracted at work. You can claim this if he was supposed to be supporting you, *even if you were separated*, though not if you are divorced. You get it whether or not he had paid any national insurance contributions.

If you're an invalid and are receiving a *non-contributory invalid pension* at the time of your husband's death you are likely to have this reduced by the total amount of your widow's benefit.

If a widow remarries she loses her widow's pension *for ever* (even if there is a later divorce) but if she 'cohabits' the pension is merely suspended for women under sixty. Over sixty you can cohabit as much as you please, with as many as your please, and they can't stop your pension. Whoopee.

HOW THE SUN COMES OUT AT SIXTY

The unglamorous image of the

pension suddenly changes, Cinderella-like, when you start wondering if you're going to get one.

There are basically five sorts of retirement pensions:

1 *The Basic Retirement Pension* which is State paid and index-linked to prices.
2 *The Additional Pension* (officially called the Earnings-Related Pension) which is State paid and is also index-linked to prices.
3 *Civil Servants' Pensions* which are index-linked to prices.
4 *Employers' Pensions* (officially called Occupational Pensions). They are paid by an employer's pension fund and are *not* index-linked.
5 *Private Pension Schemes*, much used by the self-employed. They are run by insurance companies, big finance companies and private companies with their own investment department. They are not index-linked.

All pensions are taxed as earned income. This includes the basic State pension, the earnings-related State pension, your pension from an employers' Occupational Pension scheme or any pension you take out for yourself under a private pension scheme.

If you have two or three pensions and you are still working (which is nowadays quite possible) this can mean that you have quite a large income to declare and may find yourself in a tax bracket above the basic rate, just because of the pension schemes to which you have contributed.

We can all thank Barbara Castle for making sure that, for the first time in history, British women can now look forward to a decent pension – even if they *have* stopped work to have a family. Unfortunately, the full benefits won't be apparent until 1998, when it will have been operating for twenty years, but in that glorious year every sixty-year-old woman who has been making earnings-related contributions will get a basic, index-linked retirement pension *plus* her additional earnings-related pension, also index-linked.

If you have been in an Occupational Pension scheme for *all* those years, you will probably do even better, because your employer's scheme has to be as good as, or better than the government's scheme for it to have been allowed to operate. The new schemes will even out people's incomes over their total life spans. This will be a nice change from the minor economic miracle expected of today's old-age pensioner who, overnight, is suddenly expected to manage on about one-fifth of what she's been only just able to manage on to date.

Because the government pensions are going to be index-linked, even if inflation is reduced to a steady 10 per cent, today's basic old-age pension of around £1000 will be £6720 a year in twenty years' time.

We can also welcome pensions

which are protected against inflation although there remains one problem: who is going to pay for them? State pensions are financed out of *current* contributions (not from the pensioners' contributions) so that the *earners* in 1998 will be paying for pensioners in 1998.

WHAT WILL YOU GET?

Reading about pensions causes the eyes to glaze and cross, the attention to wander and all faculties to numb. But EVERYONE should know their pension rights, so try to plough through it as if it were a civil servant's game of snakes and ladders. Each type of contribution is a ladder and each qualifying clause a potential snake.

BASIC PENSION

Everyone who has made sufficient National Insurance contributions in Class 1, 2 or 3 for a sufficient number of years by the time they retire (women aged sixty, men aged sixty-five) is now entitled to the full basic pension – currently £19.50 a week for a single person. As it is index-linked you will get the same purchasing power whenever you retire; you don't have to wait twenty years for this.

Sufficient contributions means contributions at the minimum rate payable each year (this rate also goes up with inflation).

Sufficient years means thirty-nine years out of a national working life of forty-four years (from sixteen to sixty). If you aren't in paid employment all that time you may be credited with contributions (see later) or you can pay Class 3 contributions.

ADDITIONAL PENSIONS

Everyone who has paid Class 1 contributions equal to fifty times the lower earnings limit each year for twenty years (which need not be consecutive) will get this additional pension, which is related to what he or she has earned. The top earnings-related pension is currently about one and a half times the amount of the basic pension, so it's about £30 a week, and index-linked.

If you have a modest earned income, your pension can amount to over 60 per cent of your final earnings.

Married couples get one, joint, larger pension, even when the wife has not contributed to the scheme.

An example of a possible earnings-related pension based on 1978 figures is given opposite.

People who retire between now and 1998 will get the full basic pension plus *some* earnings-related pension, depending on the number of years they have contributed.

If you contribute for more than twenty years before reaching retirement, your additional earnings-related pension will be calculated on your best twenty earning years. Earnings in excess of the ceiling (£135 a week in the 1979/80 tax year) do not count and you won't have to pay any extra contribution on them.

If you're in the government scheme and you don't think your pension arrangements will provide enough retirement income, you can take out another private scheme with all the tax savings that are available for the self-employed.

WHAT DO WOMEN GET OUT OF STATE PENSIONS?

Seventy-two per cent of all British

Maximum Earnings-Related Pension

Contributor's weekly earnings	Personal pension	Percentage of weekly earnings	Married couple's pension	Percentage of man's earnings
£30	Basic £19.50 Plus £2.63* TOTAL = £22.13	74 per cent	Basic £31.20 Plus £2.63 TOTAL = £33.83	Over 100 per cent
£50	Basic £19.50 Plus £7.63* TOTAL = £27.13	54 per cent	Basic £31.20 Plus £7.63 TOTAL = £38.83	78 per cent
£95	Basic £19.50 Plus £18.88* TOTAL = £38.38	40 per cent	Basic £31.20 Plus £18.88 TOTAL = £50.08	53 per cent

* Earnings-related pension.

old-age pensioners who receive supplementary benefit are women, which means they either have no pensions or that their pension is so small that it's still below the breadline. Now:

1 *Single women* are included in the State pension scheme on exactly the same terms as men. They can earn both basic and earnings-related pensions according to their contributions. Of course, as long as women's average earnings continue to lag far behind those of men, so will their pensions. But they are included in the scheme on equal terms.

2 *Married women* can receive a pension either on a husband's contributions (provided he has made enough) or on their own contributions.

If you are a married woman and you have paid a sufficient number of Class 1, 2 or 3 contributions you can claim, at the age of sixty, *the pension which would be paid to a single person earning the same amount.* This is a major advance in married women's pension rights. However, if you claim a pension in your own right your husband only gets the pension of a single person (reasonable).

If you have not made sufficient contributions to qualify for the full single person's pension, you can get a proportionate amount. If that, together with your husband's single pension, works out at less than the amount which you would jointly get on the married man's pension, you can switch to the latter.

3 *If you are a married woman but have not contributed to the State scheme* you get your share of the married couple's pension paid to you separately. You will have your own pension book, and, if your husband qualifies for the full basic State pension, you will receive £11.70 a week (the rate from November 1978) as your share of the joint pension. You can claim this pension once your husband has qualified for a retirement pension, provided you are over sixty.

You can get the pension whether or not you are living with your husband, provided he is supporting you and your own earnings are very low.

If your husband has retired but you are under sixty, he gets *all* the married couple's pension until you are sixty. But if you reach sixty before he retires (say you're ten years older than him) you will *have to wait* for your share of the married couple's pension until he reaches sixty-five! (Another good strike against marriage.)

4 *If you are a married woman*, you cannot claim BOTH your earnings related pension on your own earnings and your share of the married couple's basic pension. But, instead, both you and your spouse can choose to receive your earnings-related pensions *as single people*. (This idiocy will continue until both men and women are all, logically, classed as people.)

5 However, if your earnings-related pension is less than your share of the joint basic pension, you can choose to be counted as a married woman and be paid the basic.

You will not be paid your full share of the joint pension if you are still working and are earning more than £45 a week.

6 *The married couple's pension* can only be earned on a man's contributions, not on those of his wife. But, from 1978, a widower has to have his wife's National Insurance contributions taken into account when calculating his own invalidity or retirement pension, provided he is over sixty-five or incapable of work when his wife dies.

7 Another major advance in the new pension scheme is that women now have an opportunity to qualify for a *personal* pension, even if they are running a home for a large part of their working lives.

You can qualify in two ways:
(*a*) If you have been working, and contributing under Class 1 or 2 and then give up work to bring up your family or to look after a sick or elderly relative, then your existing pension rights can be protected for that period.
(*b*) If you have never been paid to work, or alternatively if you want to make sure that you qualify for the basic pension, you can pay Class 3 contributions. The much resented and very unfair half-test whereby married women get no pension unless they have paid contributions on earnings for at least half the years between their marriage and their sixtieth birthday, is eventually being abolished. It was idiotically unfair on women who married late in life.

8 *If you get divorced* you are treated as a single person and contribute accordingly. But you can benefit from your ex's record, because you are allowed to count *his* National Insurance record up to the date of the divorce as contributing towards *your* personal pension. This scheme makes some recognition of the unfairness of depriving previous wives of joint pension rights.

9 More women than men reach the age of eighty. Many people now aged eighty or more do not receive any basic pension because they never paid any National Insur-

ance contributions. They can claim a non-contributory retirement pension if they live in Britain and have lived in Britain or the Isle of Man or Northern Ireland for at least ten out of the twenty years up to their eightieth birthday. This benefit might interest you if you have an elderly relative to care for.

10 If you don't want to retire at sixty, you can carry on working for another five years, which will slightly increase your pension. For every three extra National Insurance contributions in Class 1 or 2, you earn yourself another 2p a week on your pension (*who* sits around on their fat, index-linked Superpension working these things out?)

Of course, you can carry on with your job and still collect your pension after sixty. If you earn more than £45 a week, they'll reduce your pension, until you're sixty-five. After that they've got to pay you in full, however much you earn.

HOW TO PICK A PRIVATE PENSION

Today, the calculation of a person's real wealth should include his or her pension rights. While personal wealth is being stamped out in this country as a matter of policy, the government actively encourages you with generous gifts (via tax relief) to support yourself as lavishly as possible in your old age. They also put the screws on employers to ensure that they contribute even more than you do.

It's vital that a woman should know full details of her husband's pension scheme and/or make sure that her own future is similarly secured.

An enormous number of employers now have very good Occupational Pension schemes. They can be a good alternative to raising salaries in a time of wage restraint (especially for senior staff).

So, apart from the State pension scheme, you may also get a private pension because your employer runs an Occupational Pension scheme, or because you contribute to a private pension scheme as a self-employed person. Or you may have all three types of pension.

Even if your employer contracts out of the State earnings-related scheme, both you and he, by law, must still contribute to the State basic pension. You will still receive the State basic pension if you have made sufficient contributions.

Nobody has yet come up with a private pension scheme which has a guaranteed protection against inflation in the way that your basic State pension will have. This is because investment firms have to deal with the financial facts of life. The State is pledging that your pension will be paid in the future by other people who (they hope) will honour the State promise (some of these people haven't yet been born).

If you are in an *employer's Occupational Pension scheme* the advantages are likely to be:

1 The terms will be better than the State earnings-related scheme (legally, employers are obliged to match or improve on it).
2 A lot of tax relief (ask them for details).
3 A final pension that is *truly* related

Twenty Questions About Occupational Pension Schemes

1 What contributions will you pay?

2 What contributions will your employer pay?

3 How much is the tax relief?

4 How is the pension calculated?

5 Is a fixed sum allocated for each year of employment? . . .

6 Or is the pension based on your average earnings? . . .

7 Or your best years? . . .

8 Or your final salary?

9 What benefits does the pension provide for dependants?*

10 Can you choose which dependants you would like to benefit?

11 Can you alter your nomination (after death, split or a divorce)?

12 Can part-time workers join?

13 Could you stay in the scheme if you changed to part-time work?

14 Can you choose to be paid a lump sum on retirement and a reduced pension? (You won't be able to get all your pension in a lump sum but you might be able to choose the proportions between lump sum and pension.)

15 Does the scheme allow for early retirement? Could you retire early on a reduced pension if you wanted to? By how much would your pension be reduced if you did retire early? How early could you retire?

16 What would happen to your contributions if you left before the retirement age?

17 What will happen if you fall ill and have to stop work before pensionable age? Will you get the pension?

18 Do you have any claim on your husband's pension if you divorce? In Britain, the argument about the rights of previous wives to a share of a pension scheme is still going on, but it won't do any harm to ask the views of your company's pension board. In West Germany, pensions are apportioned amongst previous wives, primarily according to the duration of the marriage. This is a *very* important negotiating point if you are divorcing: this is where older wives get done in the eye.

19 Your contributions to a company pension scheme are allowable against the highest rate of tax you pay. So if you pay a high rate, you may want to increase your pension contribution rather than receive a salary increase. Can you do this?

20 Can you make voluntary extra payments into your Occupational scheme to ensure you get a larger pension? If not, you could consider taking out an extra private pension. You can invest up to 15 per cent of your salary (less some allowed reductions) in a pension and still claim relief.

* Widows are usually well provided for, and nowadays widowers may be. Until recently it was *illegal* to provide for widowers, a ruling that was changed after a small, determined campaign led by top women executives in J. Walter Thompson, the advertising agency. But many people have other dependants.

to your earnings, unlike the State scheme, which has a strict upper limit (so an Occupational scheme is better for high earners).

4 Better conditions for repayment and benefits if you retire early (but check that this is written into the contract).

5 A lump sum of possibly four times annual salary at death, which is a great, great advantage that you can't get on the State scheme.

6 A better pension for a widow.

Legal requirements for occupational pension schemes include:

1 If you leave your job and you're over twenty-six and have worked there for over five years your employer must protect your pension rights in one of various ways:
  (a) By transferring your contributions into the Occupational Pension scheme at your new job.
  (b) By keeping the pension you have earned so far and paying you the equivalent inflation-adjusted amount when you retire (they hate doing this).
  (c) By 'buying' you back into the State scheme (the employer pays into the State scheme the contributions that he would have made had you been in the State scheme all the time that he employed you).

2 Widows of men in Occupational schemes must get at least half the guaranteed minimum State widow's pension; the State makes up the other half.

3 Women must be allowed to join *on the same terms as men doing the same type of work*.

The Legal and General Assur-ance Society Ltd estimates that since this became law in 1978 about 2½ million more working women now have the opportunity of equal pension rights. That is nearly ONE WORKING WOMAN IN THREE – so check whether you are one of them.

Unfortunately, it's much harder to provide good benefits for women employees than it is for men because:

1 Women don't earn as much as men (on average) so their earnings-related Occupational Pensions are correspondingly lower.

2 Women work five years *less* than men before qualifying for a pension (retiring at sixty, not sixty-five) so they pay five years' *fewer* contributions to an earnings-related scheme. This leaves them with a smaller pension – although not in the State scheme.

If you're going back to work, try to pick a firm with an Occupational Pension scheme and, ideally, choose a company that mainly employs men, because the scheme is more likely to be a good one.

One of the reasons that you should know full details of your Occupational Pension scheme (and your husband's) is because it will affect all your other plans for spending on insurance, savings and investments. On page 257 there are twenty questions you should ask.

Once you have the answers to these questions you can compare what would happen to you if you joined your employer's scheme with what would happen if you chose to remain entirely in the State scheme (to find out *that* position simply telephone your local social security office or

CAB and ask them the same twenty questions).

Don't assume that your existing Occupational Pension scheme can't be improved. You can get your office or your union to campaign for extra benefits.

Remember that if you join an Occupational Pension scheme you still have to contribute to the State basic scheme (£0.44 plus 4 per cent of your weekly salary). If you stay entirely in the State scheme, you pay a total of 6½ per cent of your weekly earnings up to £135 (a maximum of £8.78 a week). This is a modest sum. But then, for high earners, so is the State earnings-related pension.

Once you see a pension as a three-in-one security pack of insurance, investment and savings (a large part of which is paid for by somebody else), you will realize that you own a large, valuable piece of property that may even be worth more than your home (although you can't raise a loan on a pension). A man earning £4000 a year (the national average) is worth £17,000 in pension benefits by the time he retires.

The best possible scheme is:

A TOP HAT SCHEME

This is a way of protecting highly paid executives who join a company too late to get maximum benefits from their contributions to the company's Occupational Pension scheme. The executive's own contribution is limited to a maximum of 15 per cent of salary but the employer's contributions to such a scheme are unlimited.

He or she can receive a pension (taxed as earned income) of up to 66 per cent of final salary, a widow's pension that is 36 per cent of final salary, a tax-free lump sum up to 150 per cent of final salary and life insurance up to four times final salary after ten years' service.

If you are married to a Top Hat Scheme, well, congratulations.

If you are in one in your own right, well done, Superstar!

PENSIONS FOR THE SELF-EMPLOYED

The self-employeds' State contributions only bring them the basic pension, not the earnings-related pension. But the State allows some very good tax concessions to the self-employed if they make their own arrangements to contribute to a private pension plan. You should consider putting as much money as you can afford into one of these.

Self-Employed Pensions is a good handbook with details of ninety policies and helps relate them to your circumstances. (It costs £6.50, published by Money Management and Unitholder, Greystoke Place, Fetter Lane, London EC4A 1ND.)

Don't be put off by the thought that your earnings are too up and down, or your future too uncertain for you to commit yourself. Today, most insurance companies understand these situations, which can affect all the self-employed. There's a flexible date of retirement (the date when they start paying you your pension) and usually you can suspend or reduce payments if you have a bad patch. (You may be able to catch up with your payments later. Otherwise your benefits may be reduced.)

If you invest in a private pension scheme, you get the following advantages:

1 Your premiums are offset against your highest rate of tax – so if you pay 75 per cent tax, the pension would cost you only £25 net for every £100 of money invested.
2 You can get a lump sum on retirement, as well as a reduced pension. The lump sum is tax free, up to three times the amount of your pension. You might use this to buy a home or a high-income annuity.
3 Your pension is taxed as earned income not unearned income.

You can invest in a private pension scheme up to 15 per cent of your net income, or £2250 a year (whichever is the less). You can pay monthly or in a yearly lump sum or both, and it can be an irregular arrangement for irregular incomes.

If you work for an employer who is contracted into the State earnings-related scheme you can *still* contribute to a private pension scheme with the amazing, relevant tax advantages. Very few people realize this.

Self-employed pension plans come in three basic forms:

1 *Non-profit*. These offer a high guaranteed return, short-term. But they won't bring in so much money as a with-profits plan after five years or so. Useful if you are shortly due to retire and want a guaranteed income.
2 *With-profits*. These don't offer such a high guaranteed return but a bonus is added every few years, so it should eventually bring you more money; the best bet if you have rather a longer wait for retirement.
3 *Unit-linked*. These offer dividends linked to the fortunes of a managed fund. You could do badly; but you could also make more money than you could on a with-profits plan. It's a gamble.

Pick your life insurance company with care when looking for your self-employed pension plan. The returns they yield vary enormously. Go to an insurance broker who will recommend several companies. Compare past performance and the benefits offered in the contract.

WHERE DO YOU PICK A PRIVATE PENSION?

The National Provident Institution, Equitable Life Assurance, the Prudential, University Life and Scottish Provident are companies which have performed well and steadily. So look at them, as well as what your broker suggests.

Money Management and Unitholder, Greystoke Place, Fetter Lane, London EC4A 1ND (☎ 01-405 6969).

The National Provident Institution for Mutual Life Assurance, The NPI Group, PO Box 227, 48 Gracechurch Street, London EC3P 3HH (☎ 01-623 4200).

Equitable Life Assurance Society, 4 Coleman Street, London EC2R 5AP (☎ 01-606 6611).

Prudential Assurance Company Ltd, Holborn Bar, London EC1N 2NH (☎ 01-405 9222).

University Life Assurance Society, 4 Coleman Street, London EC2R 5AT (☎ 01-606 6225).

Scottish Provident Institution, 3 Lombard Street, London EC3V 9AE (☎ 01-626 4661).

In confidence

One of the most cheering things to happen in the last ten years is that so many family skeletons have been brought out of the cupboard and into the open (where of course they aren't nearly so frightening).

There is now almost nothing that is too shaming to talk about and people will openly discuss such previously antisocial and pariah-like situations as being short of money, being bankrupt, being sacked, or having a drunken father. Nobody seems immune to trouble, even royalty is affected by mental illness, divorce and VD in racehorses.

Suicide is now sad, but not shaming, rape is a political issue, homosexuality, lesbianism and transvestism are no longer considered problems in some circles and divorce is almost normal. Yet only twenty years ago you were not allowed into the Royal Enclosure at Ascot if you were divorced.

CREAK!!

The only areas that are still taboo, to a certain extent, are incest and mental illness – in spite of the fact that one in six British women and one in nine men will at some time be hospitalized for mental illness and many, many more will be out-patients.

However, the more serious problems of family life are still sometimes too painful to face, let alone discuss. And people often try to blot out the pain with destructive behaviour. Sorrows are not only drowned in drink, but coated in chocolate, smothered in cigarette ash and numbed with tranquillizers. In this way one difficulty can lead to an addiction – and a second problem.

There are two sorts of problem: (a) the personal problem that directly affects you; (b) somebody else's problem that has a disastrous, spin-off effect on your life.

A PERSONAL BEHAVIOUR PROBLEM

(such as drink and/or adultery) that makes you feel guilty and ashamed can be very difficult to control. Whether it is compulsive of a habit, you often can't actually admit to its existence – and you can't cure something that doesn't exist.

A PERSONAL PRACTICAL PROBLEM is generally far easier to deal with. For instance, if you are deeply in debt then your bank manager, accountant or local CAB can help you extricate yourself by re-juggling your assets or you can actually go bankrupt and start again with a clean slate. There are usually practical solutions to a practical problem: all you have to do is face it, decide on the solution and then get on with it, painful though this may be.

A SPIN-OFF PROBLEM that is the consequence of someone *else's* drink or adultery can nevertheless make you feel deeply ashamed, guilty, frustrated and unhappy. Consider three examples:

★ The tyrannical Victorian Head of the Family is less in evidence today, but still, in many homes, a sadistic father can make life a misery for his family, wreck the self-confidence of his children, and possibly be the cause of worse family trouble, such as incest.

★ Realization of a mate's homosexuality can be chillingly gradual, unbelievable and disorienting. He starts spending more time with his men friends, he's 'too tired' or 'got a headache'. Then perhaps you see him touching a man friend in a seemingly innocent but unnecessary way, and from then on it inexorably develops. There is a frightening change in the person you married. You aren't on the alert, you don't notice, then you

don't *want* to notice, you shut your eyes to the clear signs, then suddenly, this is not the person you married, it is somebody else.

★ Mental illness, whether it involves regularly seeing a psychiatrist or indulging in a full-dress, nervous breakdown, is still frightening to many people. Anything severe, such as the onset of schizophrenia, is often called 'eccentricity' or 'Dad's funny ways' until some insensitive or dangerously violent bit of behaviour goes beyond the boundary line of normality, and he insists that the people in the flat upstairs are pumping poison gas down the chimney and that you must stop them, immediately.

Sometimes such problems are never discussed in the family although they are half-recognized and elliptically referred to by the children ('I'm not going to bring Jim home to meet you if Dad's in one of his moods') or the in-laws ('I know Peter is a problem, dear, but there must be *some reason* for it'). Reaction from the neighbours might range from unspoken, embarrassed sympathy to quivering disapproval.

Few women want, or know how, to face such situations; many wives dread the loss of face that acknowledgement will bring. Although the strain is great they push the problem to the back of the mind, bluff out or blank out the true situation and either bottle up their feelings or reach for other bottles.

Family skeletons may be openly discussed today, but there are still situations that you generally think of as happening to *other* people. But the five most serious problems of family life today are divorce, drug and drink addiction (increasingly among middle-aged housewives and teen-agers), mental illness and wife and child battering (17 per cent of *Woman's Own* readers admitted, in a survey, that they *regularly* got beaten up by their husbands).

It's no good saying, 'But that doesn't happen to people like *us*' or '*Our* family certainly doesn't go in for that sort of thing'. Statistically, the chances are that one of these dramas may well affect you, your family or your friends.

VIOLENCE IN THE FAMILY

'She must have been asking for it.' 'Every woman likes a bit of rough stuff.' 'If she doesn't like it, why doesn't she leave?' These are the fre-quent, cynical and not all male reac-tions to the problem of the family batterer. But there is nothing sexy about two broken ribs and a smashed nose or a ruptured liver and a blinded eye. Women and children are also battered inside the head, where they have no self-esteem and cannot imagine any other life; they lack the money and nerve to break away.

The consequences of violence within the family are traditionally considered by the Establishment to be less serious than violence outside it (although most murders are within the family). But the results of family violence are becoming more obvious and alarming: diminishing respect for the police, teachers and public property; a huge increase in motive-less crimes by tough schoolchildren under twelve (girls as well as boys) and dangerous *young* teenagers.

The primary socializing influence on the next generation is family life.

For some children the only pattern of family life has often been the imprint-ing of violence from birth – scream-ing, abuse, assault and rape. The boys grow up to be bullies and the girls grow up to be bullied. They may, in turn, batter their own children. Some may have been victims, some only witnesses to the battering of mother or brothers or sisters, but the majority of batterers spent their childhood with a violent domestic background.

They are conditioned to feel that this is how a father and a mother should behave. So when they grow up they seek out partners who behave similarly. A girl may even despise a non-batterer as being 'unmanly' while the boys grow up to say that every woman likes rough treatment or (if better educated) to mutter about walnut trees.

The outward signs of a father who beats his family are sadly obvious in doormat docility and nervous ten-sion, if not black eyes and bruises, broken arms and noses. But often a beater deliberately hits where the bleeding and bruises can be hidden by clothes. The mother knows that the children will leave home as soon as they can; she also knows that she will then be left with *him*.

Batterers tend to drink heavily. One medical study showed that 74 per cent of battering cases involved alcohol (although drink is often also a problem for the woman victim), 26 per cent involved gambling by the husband and, although it is thought of as a lower-income, slum-property problem, 6 per cent of batterers were professional men or senior business executives.

What help does the community offer the battered wife? Officially, very little, though aid is increasing rapidly, as the size of the problem and HM the Queen's concern is revealed.

The Housing (Homeless Persons) Act 1977 obliges local authorities to provide advice and assistance to battered women and to provide accommodation for battered women who are pregnant or have children, but this won't solve the emergency, midnight-escape problem. So refuges will still be needed.

Chiswick Women's Aid (the first Women's Aid Centre) was founded in 1972 by the redoubtable Erin Pizzey. CWA is the *only* battered wives' refuge in Britain with an 'open door' policy. It will not turn away women and children in need. Many of them turn up without warning, often in the middle of the night, which is when battering tends to happen (often after drinking).

Because CWA handles violent families, rather than a series of victims, professional visitors come from all over the world to study the methods used and the German government has recently set up a system of refuges based on the CWA methods.

There are now around 100 other refuges in Britain to which battered women can be referred by CAB and the social services, but they are mostly small and full and they will not accept refugees without warning. Some of them get small, local council grants but they get no government funds whatsoever, so the shelter is minimal.

The National Woman's Aid Federation also acts as a clearing house and will try to find a place for women who telephone because they can't find local refuge. They also advise women how to get legal help (51 Chalcot Road, London NW1 8LY; ☎ 01-586 0104).

WHAT SHOULD A WOMAN DO IF SHE IS BADLY BEATEN?

Make as big and as public a fuss as possible, *especially if it's the first time*. She shouldn't be ashamed of doing this; she shouldn't forgive and forget. She should tell her doctor, her parents, her family, his family, the neighbours. Remember (*a*) that the beatings will get worse, not better, (*b*) that beatings will not stop because he is remorseful afterwards.

Never try to hit back (try to dodge) and get to hospital if possible if the beating is at all serious. The police will not (cannot) help a woman in her own home but are very efficient if they see her bandaged up to the eyeballs in a casualty ward.

Whether or not she goes to hospital, a battered wife should *always* see a doctor about any injuries, as this builds up evidence that she is being damaged. This may not seem important, but it is, should she ever want legal help.

Battered wives can telephone the NWAF for help or the CWA. All general practitioners in the UK have been sent lists of refuges, says the NWAF, so a battered wife can ask her general practitioner. If he says that he does not know of a refuge, she can try her local police station or the local social security office. Or she can try the social services department of her local authority. A battered wife need not go to her local refuge; she can get the address of one further away.

HOW CAN A WOMAN LEGALLY STOP A BEATER?

She should see a solicitor. CAB will tell her where to go. He (or preferably she) will advise her on her legal position.

The Domestic Violence and Matrimonial Proceedings Act was passed in 1976 and came into force on 1 June 1977. Before this a woman couldn't get an injunction without first starting divorce or separation proceedings. It is now possible for a woman to apply to a County Court for an injunction ordering her husband (*a*) not to assault her or her children, (*b*) to leave her home and keep away from it, or (*c*) to let her back into her home. The injunction may be backed by powers of arrest.

HOW TO GET AN INJUNCTION

This procedure applies to a woman living with a man, whether or not they are married. If her case is very serious or she is very damaged or frightened, she can go to the Court *before* preparing the papers and promise to prepare them as soon as possible. If the judge is sympathetic he may grant her an injunction immediately.

1 To prepare her case herself she can simply write out what has happened (CAB will help). Three copies are needed. This is called an *originating application*.
2 Next, she prepares an *affidavit*, which is a statement that she formally swears to be true. Two copies are needed.
3 If possible, she gets affidavits from any witnesses – two copies are needed.
4 She takes the papers to the local County Court (look it up in the telephone directory) and pays £5 if she isn't eligible for legal aid.
5 She asks one of the Clerks of the Court for her application to be heard urgently.

6 Reasonably, the Court will not fix a date for the hearing before it has attempted to deliver to her husband a copy of her original application. So she may have to wait at least two or three days. However, if her case is extremely urgent or dangerous she can apply for the injunction to be granted without his having had prior warning.

7 Even if the injunction is granted straight away it doesn't normally become effective until the injunction is delivered personally to the husband by the Court.

8 If she is married and wants a divorce, she can apply for one before or after getting an injunction. She will probably need a solicitor (*see page 142*).

9 Since the passing of the Guardianship of Minors Act 1971 she and her husband have equal rights and responsibilities towards her children (*see page 152*). If she wants sole custody she must make another application and should get legal advice on it.

The law still has a long way to go. The Law Commission has recommended that magistrates should be empowered to grant injunctions (rather than the case going to a County Court) and the National Council for Civil Liberties is urging that each case should be heard from the beginning to the end by one judge.

Not only wives get beaten and it's not only men who do the beating. There is no typical child batterer, they come from all walks of life, but there is more beating in the lower-income groups, according to a recent medical study. There is more abuse from new parents who aren't used to children or who didn't want the baby and there is more beating of children who are handicapped, who have behavioural problems or whose mother is (or feels) isolated.

'There is a myth that all child batterers are sadistic ogres, whereas in fact a lot are parents struggling in difficult situations, who have difficult children and are living in difficult circumstances,' said Dr Neil Frude. 'Education in schools and in antenatal classes should do more to prepare mothers for the fact that there will be times when their children are difficult or impossible.'

Dr Frude suggests that potential batterers *literally* count to ten aloud; leave a screaming baby on its own or scream back at it; splash their face with cold water, smoke a cigarette, play a soothing record; telephone a friend or contact the local NSPCC. All branches of the NSPCC throughout the UK run a twenty-four-hour service to help with all problems of child abuse. Additionally, the NSPCC runs seven centres to help battering parents at Manchester, Leeds, Nottingham, Newcastle, Northampton, Goldthorpe (South Yorkshire) and London.

One voluntary group to help potential batterers is PAL (Parents Anonymous Lifelines) which was started by two battering mothers who were determined to control their violence towards their children. (Between 6 p.m. and 6 a.m. telephone 01-643 8878.)

INCEST

It is only since 1972 that wife and baby battering has been publicly rec-ognized as a problem. Now it looks as if incest may be far more common than people think and reported figures suggest that in some areas it is so frequent that it is 'more or less taken for granted'.

Incest is by no means confined to slum families but it *is* associated with unemployment, subnormality, overcrowding (where, perhaps, children have to sleep in the same bed as their parents), and drunkenness.

In 1978 Noreen Winchester, seventeen, was sent to prison for seven years for stabbing her father as he slept in a drunken stupor. The Court was told that he had sexually abused her *in all ways* since she was eleven. At first this aspect of the case was *not brought up by the defence because it was so common* in area of the town in which she lived (Belfast).

An appeal against the sentence was turned down but she was finally released by a Royal Pardon after groups of the Women's Movement had organized an international protest.

When this case was brought into the open, it unleashed the subject. Many women who had been similarly abused as children felt free (and unashamed) to talk about it for the first time.

Father-and-daughter incest is the most common of sexual assaults by adults on children but they are also assaulted by stepfathers, elder brothers, uncles and old family friends. The degree of assault varies from fingering the child's genitals to outright rape, and not only of little girls.

The children are often too bewildered and terrified to tell their mother because they fear that they won't be believed and will get walloped for telling wicked stories about Uncle Charlie or Mummy's new husband or some other family authority figure.

Sometimes the children are threatened, sometimes they are beaten and sometimes they are bribed to preserve secrecy.

Most researchers think that the mother generally knows what's going on, when it's a father-and-daughter relationship, but the wife may keep silent because she is terrified of her husband's violence, of losing the family breadwinner, or of losing her man altogether to some strange woman.

Incest with young children is sometimes discovered because a child gets VD or gets pregnant, or by the school doctor, but with an older girl it is more often a despairing wife who finally tells the doctor or Welfare Officer.

The wife wants the incest to stop, but she doesn't want anyone to know about it and still less to testify against her husband, which is why the cases rarely get to Court.

Unfortunately, the consequences of exposure can be very damaging indeed to the whole family, especially if the father is sent to prison.

Most researchers think that police intervention should be avoided. It is best to ask for help from a doctor or the NSPCC.

GAMBLING

It may be bridge or bingo, it may be the dogs, horses, poker or backgammon. It may be *any* probability, if he is a compulsive gambler. Gambling, in extreme cases, can cause almost as much unhappiness as alcohol. You also have to accept the lies and the cliff-hanging dramas, as well as the misery of having no money or sometimes no food, seeing your possessions sold and learning to moonlight flit.

Anyone who enjoys a flutter but who starts to lose regularly more than he or she can afford might try the following suggestions (straight from the horse's mouth):

★ Don't gamble with strangers (just like Gary Cooper said).
★ Only gamble with friends or colleagues.
★ Never pin your hopes on a win.
★ Never gamble more than you can afford TODAY.
★ Fix a target sum before starting and when you reach it, walk out.
★ If you win a pile, walk out immediately.
★ When you've lost as much as you can afford to lose today, stop playing.
★ Never try to recoup your losses.
★ Never follow the crowd on a bet, you don't get good returns.

★ (With cards) set yourself a time to stop, tell everyone else who's playing and *always stop then*.

★ (With cards) learn one or two games and stick to them (few successful poker players will play more than one or two versions of it).

★ (With cards) learn the odds on your speciality game.

Compulsive gambling which goes far beyond a flutter, which fritters away all earnings and renders your family miserable, isn't even fun for the gambler say *Gamblers Anonymous*. They claim that gambling isn't only a financial problem, it's an emotional one. They claim that the compulsion is a psychological illness which the gambler is powerless to control and that it is as serious a problem as alcoholism.

Gamblers Anonymous helps gamblers to get back to a normal life. Their equally desperate families can get help from Gam-Anon. Both associations are at 17–23 Blantyre Street, Cheyne Walk, London SW10 0EB (☎ 01-352 3060).

SMOKING

Older people smoke because it was a sign of adulthood when they were young, and they got into the habit. The young smoke to stay slim by cutting their appetite, to have something to hold on to when they feel nervous at parties, and because death has simply got nothing to do with their lives.

The young will even tell you that it hasn't actually been *definitely proved* that cigarettes can kill you. But the first report to suggest that smoking shortens your life came out in 1938

and the evidence has been piling up ever since.

People smoke for many reasons. They sometimes start smoking when under great strain and they also smoke more under strain. Whatever good reasons for smoking there are many better reasons for giving it up. Here they are.

★ Each cigarette shortens your life by five minutes (this is from a report by the Royal College of Surgeons, *Smoking or Health*).

★ A smoker is thirteen times more likely to die of lung cancer than a non-smoker.

★ Each year 30,000 people in the UK die from diseases related to smoking.

★ Smokers run a higher risk of getting heart disease, strokes, a peptic ulcer, cancer of the voice box and mouth, cancer of the bladder, emphysema and respiratory diseases like bronchitis.

★ If you smoke, are over thirty-five and on the Pill, you run an *exceptionally high* risk of heart diseases. Giving up smoking (not giving up the Pill) brings your risk down.

★ If you are pregnant and smoke, your baby will certainly suffer. Babies of smoking mothers weigh less at birth than babies of non-smokers. At seven years old they are *still*, on average, shorter, educationally less advanced and emotionally less adjusted than children of mothers who did not smoke in pregnancy.

★ If you smoke you also damage your children's health, because they inhale the smoke in the atmosphere.

★ It's very expensive. Twenty cigarettes a day costs about £165 a year. (How long does it take to earn that money? It would pay for a trip to Paris if you didn't smoke.)

★ Some smokers point out that the government cigarette tax pays for a big chunk of the Health Service. A big chunk of the Health Service wouldn't be needed if people stopped smoking. Take just *one* smoking-related illness – chronic bronchitis. It costs the country £116 million a *year* (£2 a year from every man, woman and child in the country) for people in hospital with chronic bronchitis.

★ It makes you much less attractive. Your breath smells like old ash-trays, your hair/hands/clothes/rooms smell unpleasant. Your teeth and fingers get stained. You can't breathe correctly and you'll get a horrible cough, especially in the morning.

★ You can't taste properly.

★ Smoking doesn't *make* you thinner: it cuts your appetite. People get fatter when they stop smoking only if they want something else to put in their mouth and choose food.

WAYS TO CUT DOWN

Stopping is better, but cutting down is worthwhile: every cigarette counts against you.

★ Check how many you *really* smoke by using a cigarette case, doling a certain number into it in the morning and never smoking anyone else's cigarettes or offering yours around.

★ Try to cut down by two a day.

★ Take puffs but don't inhale.

★ Smoke filter cigarettes; leave large stubs.

★ Change from cigarettes to small, slim cigars or an eccentric pipe.

★ Specify the times of day when you will smoke and smoke only then.

★ Don't cut out the cigarette you most look forward to – perhaps that first morning drag . . .

★ But try to postpone the first cigarette of the day. Light up later and later.

★ Specify where you will smoke and smoke only there. Choose one room and one chair (not a comfortable one).

★ Count to ten aloud before lighting up.

★ When you smoke, don't do anything else. Don't drink or read or talk or watch television or work. Just stare at the wall and puff.

GIVING IT UP

★ Be positive. Remember, you aren't just stopping smoking, you are getting healthier, richer and more attractive, day by day.

★ Be serious.

★ Contact ASH (Action on Smoking and Health) for information, advice and support (27 Mortimer Street, London W1N 7RJ; ☎ 01-637 9843).

★ Nicrobrevin and Respaton can cut down the craving (on doctor's prescription).

★ Go to a smokers' clinic (ask your doctor or public library or ASH where it is). You don't need an appointment, treatment is free, you will get personal counselling, medical and social therapy.

★ Read the compleat non-smoker *How to Stop Smoking or At least Smoke Less* by Oliver Gillie (Pan paperback, 70p).

★ Don't keep it a secret, in case you give up giving up. Tell your friends and family. Enlist their help. Ignore people who joke about it or tempt you. You are trying to do something very commendable.

★ Avoid situations where you will smoke heavily, along with other people. Situations such as the pub or drinks parties: drink seems to make smokers want to smoke more.

★ Go where you can't smoke. Choose non-smoking compartments, see non-smoking friends.

★ Chew gum and pencils, suck sweets, peppermints, straws, a baby's dummy if you like (that's where it all started after all) but don't kid yourself with special filters, etc.

★ Break old routines. Take a walk instead of a cup of coffee and a you-know-what.

★ Learn to relax (*see page 31*).

★ Try standing up, at ease, and do deep, slow breathing for a minute every morning (yoga breathing routines, if you know them).

★ Save your cigarette money. Every week put it in a glass jar on the mantelpiece, so you can see it mount.

★ Reward yourself by spending it *only* on a luxury.

★ Don't be put off by failure. Failure reinforces a smoking habit. You can't expect your body to give up a physical and mental craving without putting up a bit of a fight.

DRINK

Unlike smoking, there's quite a bit to be said in favour of drink. Taken with food it helps the digestion, a glass or two makes you less anxious and relaxes you at parties and initially it peps you up.

But subsequently, it acts as a depressant, and, for many people, drink is a serious, dangerous problem. Admissions to hospital for treatment of alcoholism have risen by over 500 per cent since 1960. Offences of drunkenness in boys and girls in the fourteen-to-seventeen age group increased by 30 per cent in 1974 alone, according to the Health Education Council. It is estimated that two to three million Britishers are now heavy drinkers. *They will almost certainly hide it, especially from themselves.*

The many influential factors that lead to alcoholism include:

★ *Social ones* (our social etiquette is built round offering and accepting a drink).

★ *Physical ones* (a person may have a body chemistry problem).

★ *Psychological ones.* Alcoholics Anonymous (AA) has come to the conclusion that a certain type of character is more likely than others to be an alcoholic. These people are often frustrated, impatient perfectionists who have set themselves impossible goals. Anger, resentment and repressed hostility also seem to have a close tie-up with alcoholism. Dutch courage enables a timid person to answer back (or imagine that he will), it removes inhibitions and unleashes pent-up aggression.

AA also think that certain people are 'addictive-prone' and that if you are likely to get hooked on drink then you're likely to get hooked on cigarettes, sleeping pills and drugs. So these people should go to great lengths to avoid all chemical mood-changers.

A parent who drinks heavily is the worst thing that can be inflicted on a child. It is a dreadful burden to have a parent who is unpredictable, maudlin, belligerent, ridiculous, stupid, incapable, disgusting, remorseful, tearful, violent and perhaps in debt (to name but a few drawbacks). Another grave result is that the children of alcoholics are more likely than other children to become alcoholics themselves. They are imprinted with this pattern of behaviour for dealing with problems.

More fathers than mothers are heavy drinkers. There are three main patterns of family response.

★ *Response 1* is perpetual bewilderment, fright and attempts only to avoid physical pain, but not to seek outside help.
★ *Response 2* is accusative and resentful. Every drunken action is later described to him when he's sober in an effort to shame the alcoholic. 'The wife sees herself as the director of the ungovernable,' says the Health Education Council, 'and she loses sight of much that is positive and good in her alcoholic husband.' (This attitude, of course, assumes that he is sometimes completely sober.)
★ *Response 3* is the most realistic. This is when the wife doesn't harp on drunken behaviour, is prepared to help her husband keep sober, and is prepared to leave him if he won't.

But the problem is not only drunken fathers. The National Council of Women reports that in ten years the number of *women* applying to Alcoholics Anonymous grew from one in eight to one in three. AA guesstimates that a quarter of a million women in Britain have a serious drink problem.

Studies also show that a woman who drinks heavily in pregnancy is more likely to give birth to a deformed child (the risk is higher than one in three). Serious deficiency is also likely and affected almost all newborn babies of chronic alcoholic mothers in a 1976 survey.

WHAT EXPLAINS THE GROWING NUMBER OF FEMALE ALCOHOLICS?

Possibly because women are now more willing to admit that they drink and to ask for help. Possibly greater freedom, increased stress and tension, or boredom in middle age.

Some women begin drinking seriously when they are unhappy or when trouble strikes (especially if they haven't been brought up to accept responsibility). Perhaps they may suddenly feel unable to cope with a problem about children, husband or money. Some start drinking for quick energy when they are tired, overworked or harassed or under stress (or all four).

Career women often start heavy drinking when they try to keep up with their male colleagues.

Housewives are now tempted to buy drink from cut-price supermarkets and to drink by themselves at home (these lonely women are called 'lace curtain' drinkers).

Some women begin drinking because their husbands are heavy drinkers (it is a high risk to have an alcoholic husband).

Middle age is a heavy-risk time, particularly if there are menstrual difficulties, pre-menstrual tension or menopause problems. Some women just like the stuff and suddenly find that they can't do without it.

Alcoholism leads to worse medical complications with women than with men. Almost all women alcoholics have liver damage (compared with only 65 per cent of the men); they also suffer more nerve damage and mental disturbance than do male drinkers.

Apart from wrecking your bank balance, your innards, your mind, and your looks (it gives you a florid, puffy face), excessive drink can also make you fat at the same time as you suffer from malnutrition: you get the calories but not the nourishment and not the essential vitamins. Drink destroys vitamins – especially the B group.

Alcoholism can also wreck families and friendships, it can lose you your home, your job, your savings, and your sanity, not to mention your driving licence. It can also kill you, and make you kill other people. Assault, child battering, homicide and suicide are frequently preceded by excessive drink.

SO WHAT *IS* EXCESSIVE DRINK?

When the drinker's behaviour, during and after drinking, regularly causes distress or damage to himself and others. It can take five to twenty-five years to develop into an alcoholic and true alcoholism tends to develop in the forties, says Dr Robert Kemp, author of the booklet, *Drinking and Alcoholism*, (published by Family Doctor Publications, BMA House, Tavistock Square, London WC1H 9JP, price 35p plus 8p for postage and packing).

Some people at risk don't necessarily drink a lot – just too much for them. And *the safe amount varies according to a person's degree of fatigue and general health*. (If you are lying on a sofa all afternoon you would probably be able to drink more in safety than after some exhausting crisis at work, when a couple of dry martinis might lay you out cold.) Anxiety also seems to weaken the head, which is why you may go on your best behaviour to an important function, or to meet your future mother-in-law and behave like a perfect fool after one glass of wine.

It is certainly possible for someone at risk to be drunk on the same small amount of wine that everybody else around the dinner table has consumed with no ill effect. Such drinkers may even appear all right and behave normally, so far as the onlookers can see, but later they may remember nothing of what happened.

You are probably drinking more than you should if you regularly sleep badly after drinking, if hangovers affect your efficiency at work or if you can't remember what you did the night before.

If you think you might be drinking more than you should:

★ Avoid getting overtired, very hungry or lonely.
★ Don't drink alone.
★ Try not to drink before a meal, never drink after a meal. Never drink a liqueur or brandy.
★ If necessary, avoid situations where you'll be offered a drink. Don't go to pubs or parties or business luncheons.
★ If you drink at lunchtime, don't drink in the evening.
★ If you drink in the evening, don't drink at lunchtime.
★ If you have a drink before going home, don't have one when you get home.

★ If you drink during the week (perhaps for business reasons), don't drink at weekends.

★ Drink small measures, never doubles. Drink half pints of beer from a large wine glass (not a hefty mug). Never refill your glass before it's empty and don't let anyone else.

WHAT IS AN ALCOHOLIC?

Alcoholics Anonymous defines an alcoholic simply as someone who can't control his or her drinking. The classic AA test is to decide that for the next two months you will have not less than one drink and not more than three drinks a day (standard pub measures). Make no exceptions. If you can do this you have your drinking under control.

The Health Education Council and AA see alcoholism as a perfectly respectable illness with biochemical reasons for it, definable causes and symptoms. It is not just wilful self-indulgence. Nobody could *wish* to be an alcoholic, they say.

HOW DOES AN ALCOHOLIC RECOVER?

Willpower, says AA grimly, is about as effective a cure for alcohol addiction as it is for cancer.

Cures differ in detail but, as the American Medical Association so aptly puts it, 'Treatment of the condition primarily involves not taking a drink.' There are several approaches to this.

One of the difficulties of treating alcoholism is the secrecy with which the problem is surrounded. The drinker is ashamed (and so is his or her family) to admit what is really the matter and seek professional advice. But a GP can help a great deal and he won't be shocked whatever he's told. He's heard it all before, and far worse. He can also refer a patient to a hospital or clinic for special treatment, and prescribe vitamins (especially the Bs) or tranquillizers to help cope with withdrawal symptoms.

The doctor can also prescribe drugs to encourage abstinence. The effect of combining many drugs with alcohol is to increase the effect of both. So a normal drug dosage *can become an overdose if you swallow it with a stiff drink*.

One particular drug, disulfiram (proprietary name, Antabuse) produces such a violent reaction to alcohol that it has been used to treat chronic alcoholics.

These treatments are used for in-patient and occasionally out-patient treatment. If after taking the daily tablet a patient drinks so much as a sip or two of alcohol, he quickly feels awful. He might turn red, get a throbbing headache, have difficulty breathing, feel sick, faint or dizzy.

The patient is supposed to find the consequences of drinking so unpleasant that he is put off. But the abstinence effect isn't lasting without the drug (only a permanent change in the patient's way of life will achieve that) and the drug can be dangerous. There are recorded instances of heart failure and death.

Many doctors suggest going to an AA meeting. No one will ask your name or any questions. You can sit as an observer. AA is not a teetotal organization; the meetings are informal, friendly, and deadly serious. AA is founded on sympathy, understanding and that fatal common interest. They are all experts.

Many people worry that they may meet someone they know, a friend or bank manager. If so, it is because he or she has the same difficulty; they are relying on your silence as much as you are relying on theirs. No one will lecture you; there is no pressure to join a group or go to meetings. You will be politely ignored unless you want to speak.

AA believes:

1 In avoiding temptation for only twenty-four hours at a time.
2 In not drinking, rather than stopping drinking temporarily.
3 In putting off the first drink. It's the first drink that does the damage, that triggers off the compulsion for a potential alcoholic.
4 In telephone therapy, so that you can telephone one of the group at any time of day or night, when the craving or the panic hits.
5 That once cured, an alcoholic is *still* an alcoholic, just as a diabetic is *still* a diabetic although he's on insulin. An alcoholic is always, afterwards, at risk and should try never to drink again.

Recommended reading: *Living Sober* (sent in plain wrapper, £1.10 including postage and packing from AA Sterling Area Services, PO Box 514, 11 Redcliffe Gardens, London SW10 9BG).

ADDRESSES
There are 700 AA groups in Britain. Look in the telephone directory for your nearest, or phone head office at *Alcoholics Anonymous*, 11 Redcliffe Gardens, London SW10 9BG (☏ 01-352 9779; 01-351 3344 for London area only).

Al-Anon Family Groups can help the families of alcoholics; get in touch with them at 61 Great Dover Street,

London SE4 4YF (☏ 01-403 0888). Al-Anon has established a fellowship for teenage sons and daughters of alcoholics called Alateen. Write to Al-Anon to be put in touch with your nearest Alateen group.

There are local *Councils on Alcoholism* in most large towns. For the address of your nearest information centre contact the head office: National Council on Alcoholism, 43 Great Peter Street, Westminster, London SW1P 3LT (☏ 01-222 1056).

The London Council on Alcoholism is not only interested in abstinence but can also help a heavy drinker to cut down. No fees are charged for individual counselling, group counselling, group discussions and training courses. London Council on Alcoholism, 68 Chalton Street, London NW1 1JR (side entrance) (☏ 01-387 2191/2214).

The Health Education Council is at 78 New Oxford Street, London WC1A 1AH (☏ 01-637 1881).

DRUGS

Not all drug addicts are grubby young men with hollow cheeks, drooping moustaches and dirty hair, who have had dreadful childhood experiences. Certainly your own children, exasperating though they may be at times, are unlikely to get hooked on drugs and you can't see *yourself* as a potential drug addict. Don't be too certain.

Drug *addiction* is the hopelessly hooked state, the desperate stealing-to-pay-for-a-fix, shooting-up-in-public-lavatory, ending-up-in-padded-hospital state.

Drug *dependency* is when you're

hooked but not hopeless. It includes dependence on alcohol and nicotine and the British Medical Association suggests that if the term 'hard drugs' is used to describe those such as heroin or opium, which are addictive to the point of physical dependence, then other, more common drugs should also be included in this category 'particularly drugs like the barbiturate sleeping tablets or capsules'. And like American President Ford's brave wife, Betty, it's possible to become addicted to a drug after receiving medical treatment of which the drug forms a necessary part.

By 1975, 12 per cent of British women were taking tranquillizers daily for a period of a month of more every year. (Valium, Librium and Mogadon were the most commonly prescribed.)

Most tranquillizers were taken by women aged sixteen to twenty-four (the time when they cope with young families) and forty-five to fifty-four (menopause). Over 15 per cent of women in the older group were regularly taking tranquillizers (at least one daily dose).

Drugs are an age-old way of dealing with unhappiness and anxiety. Tranquillizers and anti-depressants can be very useful for helping you through a short period of difficulty, but these figures suggest they were being prescribed to blanket out unhappy family situations or difficult personal problems.

'Often these drugs do no more than convert an anxious, but clear-headed, person into an anxious but woozy-headed person,' said Dr Samuel Cohen, psychiatrist at the London Hospital. Drugs provide no long-term solutions to your problems and they can damage you if you become dependent on them.

Tranquillizers and sedatives relax your muscles, can make you sleepy and slow down your reactions. So it might be dangerous for you to use machinery or drive. Sedatives are particularly dangerous when combined with alcohol because the sedative effect is greatly increased.

The effect of a drug varies greatly from person to person (not all doctors allow for this). A few people react unexpectedly. For instance, instead of becoming calmer they become less inhibited, excessively agitated and aggressive. They probably won't notice that their reactions are abnormal, but their families notice personality changes for the worse.

Changes of mood can be volatile. There may be sudden switches from sunny smiles to irritable depression, or from sleeplessness to lethargy. Patients may become absent-minded, forgetful and inefficient. Appetite either disappears or becomes insatiable.

Many a modern mother has sampled an upper or two in her time or politely puffed at the joint passed round at a party and been more worried about catching something as a result of passing the thing from mouth to mouth than the fear of addiction. Such experiences can lead people to underestimate the effects of extensive drug use. So, many a perplexed parent, complaining that she can't think what's come over Jim these days, has blamed on pubescence a change that is due to secret drug-taking.

Why might your teenager take drugs? Pep pills (*speed*) stimulate the brain and are often first taken to help study for exams or else to stay awake and full of beans until the party's over.

Taken over a period, speed destroys concentration, makes it difficult to work, makes it impossible to judge your own work (it may seem terrific but it's really inane), causes palpitations and agitation, produces personality changes and eventually psychosis.

Pep pills can lead to serious illness. *They are addictive* and many people come to depend on them to cope with their emotions. But every time they take a pill to ward off depression or exhaustion, they face a bigger load of exhaustion afterwards. The irritability, tension, fatigue, depression and paranoia which may follow taking a series of amphetamine pills can be so terrible that there may be a suicide attempt.

Marijuana has hundreds of nicknames, including hash, pot, grass and shit (it comes from a plant called cannabis which is a sort of official name for the drug). Marijuana is soothing, calming, lazily relaxing. It makes you giggle and feel at peace with mankind. It provides an escape from the system or your lack of success. *It hasn't been proved to be addictive.* No wonder it attracts the young!

Many students first try marijuana because it is forbidden, and therefore a challenge. Many do so from curiosity, many because they find hash preferable to alcohol with no resultant hangover.

It is estimated that some 20 million Americans and between 2 and 5 million Britons use marijuana regularly. They find it a much more attractive, less harmful form of achieving relaxation than either alcohol or tobacco. Many people would like to see alcohol and tobacco made illegal and marijuana legalized.

However, too much dope can become a substitute for living, for taking decisions, for solving problems; soothing calm can develop into inertia, the will to work or make any effort may disappear. Taking marijuana may be the introduction to taking hard drugs, which certainly can be addictive and which are extremely harmful.

Cocaine is the most fashionable drug of the moment. It's a fine white powder (ruinously expensive, as are most drugs except home-grown hash) and you sniff it up your nose. You can do this with a rolled-up pound note, a customized cocaine tooter, a special gold spoon, or a roll of cigarette paper without any tobacco inside.

Cocaine makes you feel young, pretty, brilliant, witty, happy, agile, sparkling, healthy and generally as if you were walking six inches above ground on top of Mont Blanc.

If you *sniff* coke, you have this agreeable sensation of self-confidence and power but *you don't risk physical addiction* although dependency is dangerous. Cocaine *injected* into the veins can produce even stronger feelings of well-being, but *it is highly addictive*, and an overdose produces terrible effects.

An overdose of cocaine is extremely expensive and nasty. You may have hallucinations or convulsions, go rigid or into a coma. You may have breathing difficulty and eventually stop breathing altogether or have a heart attack and die immediately.

LSD (acid) was the favourite hippy drug of the sixties. It provides extraordinary hallucinatory experiences. You may 'hear' colours, for instance. *LSD is not addictive but it is very dangerous.* Your mood can yo-yo violently from joy to depression and a bad trip can be a nightmare. Delusions of great power have led LSD takers to walk out of skyscraper windows, thinking that they could fly.

Hallucinations can recur long after the trip. Some people have become mentally deranged from LSD abuse and some develop acute leukaemia.

Morphine and heroin are based on natural opium and are addictive. You develop a tolerance to them and need increasingly stronger doses to get the same effect. One difficulty of treating addicts is the terrible pain they suffer when their supply of the drug is stopped. Withdrawal is called the 'cold turkey' treatment because the sufferer gets clammy gooseflesh and 'kicking the habit' refers to the agonizing jerking of limbs and painful muscle cramps.

Hard drugs – heroin and opium – blot out the pain of unhappiness (which is often why people try them in the first place). Adolescence is when you are yanked out of a predictable school and home routine and suddenly thrust into the outside world, where you have to start making your own uncertain decisions and then accept responsibility for them. The pressures of college, factory, office or first unhappy love affair, a dose of unemployment or VD can seem hopelessly depressing.

It can be bewildering to find that the Boy Scout code taught at school just doesn't apply in real life. It can be cqually unsettling to find that having loudly and publicly disagreed with parents, teachers, church and politicians, there remain no guidelines to life in a world that seems hypocritical, inefficient, and unjust but that forces you to live to its rules.

Adolescents, like adults, are clever at inventing new forms of drug abuse.

Release, the organization which helps both drug addicts and their relatives, says that main-lining barbiturates is still a common form of abuse with young people. You dissolve the tablets and inject the solution into your veins.

Glue sniffing is a growing problem among younger children – *Release* says sniffers are usually between eleven and seventeen. Lots of glues produce hallucinatory effects if sniffed. So do many household cleansers, weed killers and nail varnish. Glue sniffing may not lead to crime (because it's cheap and easy to find products to sniff), but it can be dangerous. Lungs, kidneys, and the heart can eventually be damaged. A glue sniffer may also accidentally suffocate: he puts his head in a polythene bag (to concentrate the strength of the vapour) and passes out before he has time to take off the bag.

According to *Release*, the next age group up – seventeen to early twenties – tend to take Mandrax or *mandies*, a combination of sedative and anti-histamine. They are addictive and can produce bad side-effects, but are much in demand on the teenage black market.

Drug dependants are not basically abnormal. No one sort of person is more liable than another to become dependent. Some people obviously become dependent very quickly, while with others the change is gradual. Even when dependent, some people show very little change in behaviour for a long time. But physical changes will have taken place, which means that withdrawal may cause great suffering and physical damage.

A person can shake off dependency, but it may take a long time if he or she is dependent on a physically addictive drug. The withdrawal may have to take place under medical supervision at a withdrawal centre or a hospital. Although drug dependants are not often mentally ill, just withdrawing the drug probably won't be the end of the cure. The dependant's entire personality and lifestyle may have to be reassessed; he will probably need professional help to do this and to lead him away from his habit towards new interests in life. Specialists will check the underlying reasons for his drug dependency. It may be a feeling of personal inadequacy, wanting acceptance from a group, fear of rejection, insecurity, or the reasons might simply be overwhelming practical difficulties, for which he really needs more help than he's been getting.

HOW TO CHECK WHETHER YOUR CHILD IS ON DRUGS

1 Sudden loss of interest and drop in performance at sport or school work.
2 Prevarication, evasiveness, truancy (if *any* story seems, somehow, a little odd, then *check on it*: phone the school or other parents or the people concerned; turn up unexpectedly *in person* if you are really worried).
3 Problems over discipline at school.
4 Bad timekeeping at work, rows with an employer, a sudden change of job.
5 Inexplicable changes in his or her mood or what he or she does.
6 Sudden, clandestine friendships, especially with older boys and girls.
7 Loss of appetite and weight.

Don't worry unduly. Practically all these symptoms might be the result of falling in love. But take no chances – check on them.

WHAT TO DO IF HE OR SHE IS

1 Phone *Release* (1 Elgin Avenue, London W9 3PR; ☎ 01-289 1123). They are terrific. They give advice and counselling on legal, social and medical problems related to drug taking.
2 Try to persuade him or her to go to the doctor.
3 Phone the social service department of your local council, who will know of local specialists and clinics (but so will the doctor).
4 Don't criticize. Accept it in a matter of fact manner (*very* difficult). Do what you can to help him or her, to keep him or her enjoyably occupied and find new friends (many adolescents start on drugs because they are bored and lonely).

HOW TO AVOID DRUG DEPENDENCY YOURSELF

1 Always ask the doctor or nurse to explain why you are being given a pill and what it is supposed to do for you. Patiently insist on a sensible answer ('because it will make you feel better' ain't good enough) and *write it down in front of him or her* (you'll find this often makes them think twice and they amend what they first said).
2 Ask how long you may need to take the drug. Write down *that* answer, as well.
3 Always ask your doctor what you can't eat or drink with your pill, to avoid tiresome or dangerous side-effects. Doctors don't always warn you how very bad the side-effects can be, because (reasonably) they don't want to suggest symptoms to you.

4 Check your reactions to the drug and report them to your doctor. Watch for the reactions of anyone else in your family who is on pills.

5 Immediately report to your doctor any severe side-effects that you *or your family* notice.

6 Don't beg your doctor for a prescription for large quantities. He can be prosecuted for doing this.

7 Make sure that clear instructions are written on the bottle (not 'take as directed', but 'two after breakfast').

8 Never take a bigger dose than it says on the prescription. Only *real* idiots think that twice as much will get you better twice as fast (of course we've all done it).

9 Flush any left-over pills or medicine down the lavatory.

10 Carefully check the 'What's what' list, especially for aspirin, tranquillizers and barbiturates. It has been estimated that Britain has about 80,000 barbiturate addicts, many of them middle-aged women who have become addicted after being prescribed barbiturates for their nerves.

RECOMMENDED READING

Your Everyday Drugs by William Breckon. This is a simply written, riveting and highly detailed account of coffee, tea, alcohol, cigarettes, aspirins and other drugs. It tells you what's in them, how they affect you and what medical conditions they can cause.

It is a straightforward and intelligent book about the drugs of modern civilization that have become a part of everyday life for everyone. (Costs £2.95, published by BBC Publications, 35 Marylebone High Street, London W1M 4AA.)

WHAT'S WHAT

In the following list, trade names used by pharmaceutical manufacturers are given in capital letters followed, where applicable, by the official approved names which are often used on doctors' prescriptions, or by slang names (in italics).

Amphetamines (*speed*)

Formerly prescribed to ward off middle-age depression. Also used by commandos in battle to ward off fatigue.

BENZEDRINE (amphetamine sulphate) (*bennies*)
DRINAMYL (amylobarbitone; amphetamine sulphate) (*purple hearts; blues; French blues*)

Anti-depressants (*uppers*)

Not physically addictive. The effect of these drugs in particular is strengthened if taken with alcohol. They come in two groups: the tricyclics; and the MAO-inhibitors. Doctors tend to prescribe tricyclic anti-depressants for patients who are depressed without any obvious outward cause. The drugs take two or three weeks to have an effect:

TOFRANIL (imipramine)
LAROXYL (amitriptyline)
SAROTEN (amitriptyline)
TRYPTIZOL (amitriptyline)

MAO-inhibitors are more likely to be given to patients who have good cause to be depressed, who have suffered some experience that would make *anyone* feel depressed, but who seem to be over-reacting to it. The drugs take one or two weeks to have an effect:

NARDIL (phenelzine)
MARSILID (iproniazid)
MARPLAN (isocarboxazid)

There are certain foods that you *must not take* when on these pills: cheeses; beer; wine; pickled herrings; chicken livers; yeast; broad beans; Marmite; Bovril; and Oxo. These foods contain tyramine and together with the pills will give you acute high blood pressure and can make you dangerously ill, sometimes very suddenly (too suddenly to get help, if you live alone). Because of this, the first group of anti-depressants is usually considered safer. But as you can see, they are used for slightly different conditions and one or the other may suit a particular patient.

Aspirin
Aspirin is a non-addictive pain-killer, but you can get into the habit of taking too much and that could lead to kidney trouble. A mild overdose (or a *normal* dose plus alcohol) can cause ringing in the ears; dizziness; sweating; nausea; confusion. It can cause ulceration and stomach bleeding (one cause of unsuspected anaemia). A large overdose can cause coma, breathing failure and death, if not treated promptly.

ASPIRIN (acetylsalicyclic acid)
ANADIN (acetylsalicyclic acid; salicyclamide; caffeine; quinine sul-·phate)
VEGANIN (acetylsalicyclic acid; paracetamol)
CODIS (acetylsalicyclic acid; calcium carbonate; anhydrous citric acid; saccharin sodium)

Paracetamol
Paracetamol is a mild pain-killer and useful if you're allergic to aspirin, but it can cause liver damage.

VEGANIN (see above)

Phenacetin
In the same chemical group as paracetamol. It has now been withdrawn from sale because it can cause kidney damage, but it may still be medically prescribed.

Barbiturates (*downers*)
Barbiturates are powerful drugs, you can become dependent on them and physically addicted to them. All barbiturates calm you down; some are used as anaesthetics.

PENTOTHAL (thiopentone) reduces pain quickly in childbirth; also given before a full anaesthetic.
SONERYL (butobarbitone)
AMYTAL (amylobarbitone) takes about half an hour to work, lasts for five or six hours.
SECONAL (pentobarbitone)
NEMBUTAL (pentobarbitone) works fast, lasts for up to three hours.
LUMINAL (phenobarbitone)
VERONAL (phenobarbitone) strong barbiturate. May take one hour to work, lasts for six to ten hours.
MANDRAX (methaqualone; diphenhydramine) (*mandies*) a combination of barbiturate and antihistamine. Doctors now try to avoid prescribing Mandrax because of its high risk of addiction and bad side-effects.

Anti-psychotics
Based on the phenothiazine group of chemicals. One of these chemicals is chlorpromazine. This is a wonder drug for severe mental conditions in

people who might otherwise spend their lives in hospitals or need ECT or brain surgery.

LARGACTIL (chlorpromazine)
AMARGYL (chlorpromazine)
THORAZINE (chlorpromazine)
MODECATE (fluphenazine) is a related drug which is given by injection to those patients who cannot be relied on to keep on taking their Largactil and Amargyl tablets (not unusual).

Opiates

Derived from opium (*see page 277*).

Morphine is the main derivative of natural opium; it is a powerful pain-killer that makes you sleepy. It is addictive.
Heroin derives from diamorphine (synthetic opium) and is even more addictive than morphine.
Codeine is derived from morphine but is much weaker in its effects.

Tranquillizers

Tranquillizers are based on the benzodiazepine group of chemicals. They keep you calm during the day and help you sleep at night. Although you don't become physically addicted to them you can become dependent. Barbiturates have the same sort of effect on you but they are much more powerful and you may become physically addicted to them as well as dependent.

LIBRIUM (chlordiazepoxide)
VALIUM (diazepam)
TROPIUM (chlordiazepoxide)
SERENID-D (oxazepam)
SERAX (oxazepam)
DALMANE (flurazepam)
MOGADON (nitrazepam)

WHERE THERE'S HELP THERE'S HOPE

All families have problems; there's nothing unusual about that. But in order to solve them or lessen the destructive effect it is necessary to admit that the problem exists, be prepared to discuss it and be prepared to do something active about it.

Until you admit it you may well, without realizing it, also be in a state of anxiety that can make you edgy, tense, quarrelsome and difficult to deal with. You may harbour unrealistic hope, procrastinate and postpone the confrontation (hoping that the lump will go away) until the situation is deadly serious. Or you grimly mutter, 'Well, if Francis Chichester sailed round the world with it, then I needn't go to the doctor until next month.'

Or there is the reverse situation. Women have been known to take poison because, *mistakenly*, they thought they had cancer or to hang themselves because they think they've got syphilis when it's only thrush but they dare not go to the gyno clinic to check.

Historically, if you were at the end of your tether and sought help, it was from the doctor who had no remedy, only sympathy and sal volatile. Or perhaps you confided in your mother, or the vicar, who told you (sympathetically) to go back and bear your cross and do your duty. What can't be cured must be endured they said, but they were wrong. The problem may not always be curable but today the situation can generally be improved.

Although we live busy, isolated lives and although man's indifference to man seems to rise at the same rate as the standard of living, although nobody seems to have time to dish out long-term assistance, the Age Of Self-Help is here!

It has to be. On the whole nobody else can help you *enough*. Medicine and the Welfare State are limited by time, money, lack of experience and bureaucracy, with its strain and inefficiency.

It's vital to realize that the solutions to personal problems cannot be *given* to you or passively purchased from experts with magic wands. You have to do the work yourself, but there are lots of people who can help you – if you look in the right place.

There's a self-help group for almost any personal problem, from psoriasis to depression. Fellow suffers have formed groups, clubs, discreet telephone services and books written from their own experience and UNDERSTANDING WHAT IT FEELS LIKE, rather than clinical observation.

Where advisable, the self-help groups preserve strict anonymity; they offer no criticism and you feel no shame. They understand the paralysing side-effects of bewilderment, self-disgust and hopelessness. They make you realize that you're *not* alone and *not* a freak – and that there are many, many others in the same boat, including the rich, famous and successful.

The self-support groups can offer legal advice, medical advice, facts and information, together with empirical support, comfort, encouragement and practical help. Best of all, they offer to share the undeniable strength of a group, whether it is the grim, tough strength of AA or the cheerful, party atmosphere of Weightwatchers.

When you analyze the systems that they have evolved for dealing with drunkenness, anorexia or cancer after-care, the basic methods may seem ridiculously simple.

But it is the simplicity of experience and genuine interest, rather than the simplistic, logical and often unrealistic advice that is frequently dished out in irresponsible agony columns. It is NO USE some television personality advising you to send your husband to Alcoholics Anonymous. As far as your husband is concerned, he's *not* an alcoholic and he won't go to AA until he's so frightened that he can't do anything *but* face his condition. (What's more, AA can't do anything for him until this point.) But *you* can go to Al-Anon, which is a support group for the relatives of alcoholics.

Some self-help societies operate on a rather simple, friendly level. Going to one of the amazingly successful Weightwatchers meetings can be like watching a lot of healthy puppy-dogs gambolling in a basket. The intellectual level is not noticeably high; that is not what they are meeting about. It's important to meet people only on the level of everybody's problem.

It's also important not to expect free magic. One very intelligent woman writer complained that when she telephoned Samaritans (the voluntary association that helps would-be suicides) they were 'rather banal'. Did she expect a sort of computerized R. D. Laing, waiting at the ring of a telephone to sort out her life in ten minutes and free at that?

Unfortunately, people who are desperate enough to need help are seldom gracious, often disagreeable, critical, over-demanding and obsessed with themselves to the exclusion of the helper's feelings.

They may be paranoid and feel that everyone's against them, everybody hates them, everybody is plotting against them. They may suddenly become ridiculously over-sensitive in certain areas: you might offer a job to someone who's out of work or a gift cheque to a long-standing friend in money trouble and they immediately react as if you had prodded a raw burn. Luckily, most self-help organizations understand this as well – which is another reason why they are so successful.

Two outstanding guides to self-help organizations (ask for both at your library) are *The Sunday Times Self-Help Directory*, edited by Judith Chisholm and Oliver Gillie (published by Times Newspapers Ltd) and *Do Something!* by Betty Jerman, which has a foreword by the Duke of Edinburgh (published by Garnstone Press).

The Sunday Times Self-Help Directory consists of three main sections:

1 Help that may be available from the State.
2 A large alphabetical directory of helpful organizations.
3 A classified book list, most of them obtainable from your library.

Do Something! lists and describes organizations that deal with children and parents (such as the Pre-school Playgroups Association and Gingerbread), medical self-help groups (such as the Disablement Income Group and the Spastics Society), groups that provide individual help (such as the National Housewife's Register and Neurotics Anonymous), and campaigning groups (such as the Women's Peace Groups and the National Federation of Consumer Groups).

HOW TO PULL YOURSELF TOGETHER WHEN YOU CAN'T: A BLUEPRINT FOR SURVIVAL

We all have problems that we would like to eliminate, but, alas, the All-Purpose Pocket-Size Problem-Solver doesn't exist. Trying to cope with grave problems such as alcoholism or drug dependency is obviously a far, far more serious matter than a bad habit such as scratching spots or biting nails.

With a serious problem, such as drink, a fatal spiral may start: your friends and family cannot treat you honestly, the unmentionable overshadows your relationships. Some friends may fade away, some frankly tell you to do what to them seems obvious and are exasperated when you don't. It's like living with a corpse in the middle of your sitting-room that people are supposed to step over and not mention. Life is scripted by Harold Pinter.

But there are steps that can be taken to face a problem (always the most difficult part): analyze it, meet other people who are successfully tackling a similar problem, and plan to wobble slowly towards controlling the difficulty.

Obviously every part of the following plan won't apply to your problem. But by jotting down your comments on the parts that *do* apply, you can: *draw up your own problem-survival blueprint.*

STEP 1

TALK TO YOURSELF ABOUT IT
Does your problem provide you with anything that's enjoyable, good

or useful? (Distraction, relaxation, oblivion, poise, sensuous pleasure, compensation, avoidance of responsibility, avoidance of mental or physical pain?)

If so, can it be replaced by anything else?

What's bad about it?

What effects don't matter much?

What are the worst effects on you?

What's the most frightening thing about it?

When was the worst moment?

Does it affect your family? Who? How?

Why are you doing something harmful and self-destructive that you don't really want to do?

How did you come to start in the first place?

Does any particular situation increase the problem?

What part of the situation is unlikely to change?

What could you not give up? Why?

What's the worst that can happen if you don't stop it? (Death, loss of job, loss of income, loss of family?)

Why do you want to do something about it?

What might be altered or improved?

What might be changed?

What's unlikely to change?

What *must* be changed to avoid possible disaster?

What must you NEVER do?

What must you NEVER say?

What's the best improvement you can hope for?

What is the least that you will settle for?

STEP 2

WHO ELSE KNOWS ABOUT IT?

Who else knows? (Put all 'possibles' on this list; make it as long as possible.)

Which person on this list is most fond of you?

Which person on the list is the most sensible?

Is there anyone in your family on the list?

Do you know anyone else who OPENLY is struggling with a similar problem? Two bingo addicts, two slimmers, two eighty-a-day smokers stand more chance together than alone.

STEP 3

CONTACT THE EXPERTS

Is there a self-help group specializing in this problem? (Telephone the local librarian anonymously – NOW and ask.)

Why not telephone the group NOW and ask if they can recommend any book on the subject? Use a false name if you like: they all understand shyness or anonymity. They are unlikely to *ask* your name.

STEP 4

KNOW YOUR ENEMY

Find out all you can about the problem from the reference library, newspapers, magazines, lectures, radio or television.

STEP 5

GET HELP

Telephone the self-help group (still anonymously) but tell them about your problem and ask what they suggest you do.

STEP 6

MEET THE EXPERTS

If the self-help group suggests that you contact one specific member, do so (still anonymously, if you like).

OR contact a trained professional (doctor, vicar, teacher, librarian, welfare officer).

OR talk to one of the people you named in Step 3. Possibly show them this plan.

It may help if you eventually tell several people what you are trying to do. If they can help you, ask them to do so – and don't yell at them when they do.

STEP 7

WINNING SIGNS

What is the smallest step forward you can take?

What will you see as a sign of improvement? (When you do – or don't do – what?)

What would be a setback?

How will you cheer yourself when things don't go according to plan? When you take one step forward, then totter two steps back?

Who can encourage you and comfort you?

Be on your guard against relapse.

Relapse, then carry on.

Don't let a relapse be an excuse for giving up.

STEP 8

COUNT YOUR OLD EXCUSES

Count your old excuses and write them *all* down. You're cunning enough about the excuses; you've got to be even more cunning to trap yourself inventing new ones, to catch yourself out.

STEP 9

IGNORE THE FUTURE

Never plan in detail how you will cope with your problem. Never think more than one day ahead (today). Try not to do it – just for today.

Don't ever think you have conquered your problem or you will be lulled into false security. View the demon with respect; keep him at a distance, but assume that he will *always* be a potential threat and will *never* disappear.

STEP 10
KEEP BUSY

Give yourself something to do that will take your mind off the habit. Start going to pottery classes, start gardening, repaint a room. Check what's offered at your local evening classes. Aim for something with a low failure potential and fairly quick, easy-to-see results.

You might consider choosing a campaign group to work for. This often helps to channel frustrated, aggressive or hurt feelings into productive channels, such as income-tax reform.

Instead of feeling that things are done *to* you, which you impotently cannot prevent, you feel that *you* have group power and that *you* can diminish a problem for other people or perhaps (as with cancer research or wife battering) help to alleviate or solve it.

Or you might start a support group in your problem area if there isn't one (this is how the cystitis and anorexia groups started). Write a SHORT letter to your local newspapers, television and radio stations, asking people with a similar interest to come to a meeting on a specific date. (Don't hold your meeting alone and be prepared for one or two nuts to turn up: every good cause has its lunatic fringe.)

STEP 11

BE SELF-INDULGENT IN OTHER WAYS
Get enough sleep.
Get enough food.
Try to exercise.
Get in the fresh air.
Think of one tiresome task you can dump NOW.
Plan at least one selfish treat a week that doesn't involve temptation.
Where can you be quiet and alone? (If that's what you want.)
Where can you go to be in a friendly atmosphere? (If that's what you want.)

STEP 12

BE BRAVE AND RUTHLESS
If you have a really grave problem, put avoiding it before anything or anyone else.
Avoid friends that may depress you (richer, smarter, cleverer, thinner, etc.).
Ruthlessly avoid distressing situations and people if they precipitate your problem. You may even have to abandon that part of your life that includes the habit (and with a drastic habit you sometimes have to make a drastic break).
If you only bite your nails when you read – don't read. If you drink too much at parties – cut out *all* parties, including weddings and business lunches, and never take a job as a barmaid or in public relations. Nobody can resist constant temptation.

The end . . .

. . . ought to be the beginning. The maddening thing about life is that it's only at the end of it that you're qualified to start it. By then, of course, it's too late.

It's only after you've *really* experienced adult life – after the nappies and before the arthritis – that you can start to *really* enjoy yourself; because by then you probably know what you want and – even more important – what you *don't* want.

With any luck, you'll have the time to go out and get what you want and the experience to avoid what you *don't* want, instead of being tossed around by circumstances, like a rag doll in a washing-machine.

On the whole, everybody gets an equal share of good luck and bad luck. Sometimes Life is a downhill path sprinkled with daisies, sometimes tin-tacks on an uphill stretch.

Some people rarely let a good opportunity pass, some people are too busy moaning about their bad luck to notice an opportunity, let alone go out and look for one.

Some people never want to make an effort. But if you don't shake the tree a bit, the golden apples of good luck might not fall into your lap.

Some people simply give up too soon, but tenacity is one of the secrets of success.

As Sir Francis Drake said: 'Teach me, O Lord, that it is not in the beginning but in the carrying out of an enterprise that lies the true glory.'

Life is everybody's major enterprise. You may not be planning piracy on the high seas, or a way of singeing the beard of the King of Spain, or the defeat of the Armada. Your aims may be altogether more modest. But, hopefully, not too modest. Because you never know what you can do until you try. So don't let anyone stop you. Especially not yourself.

Index

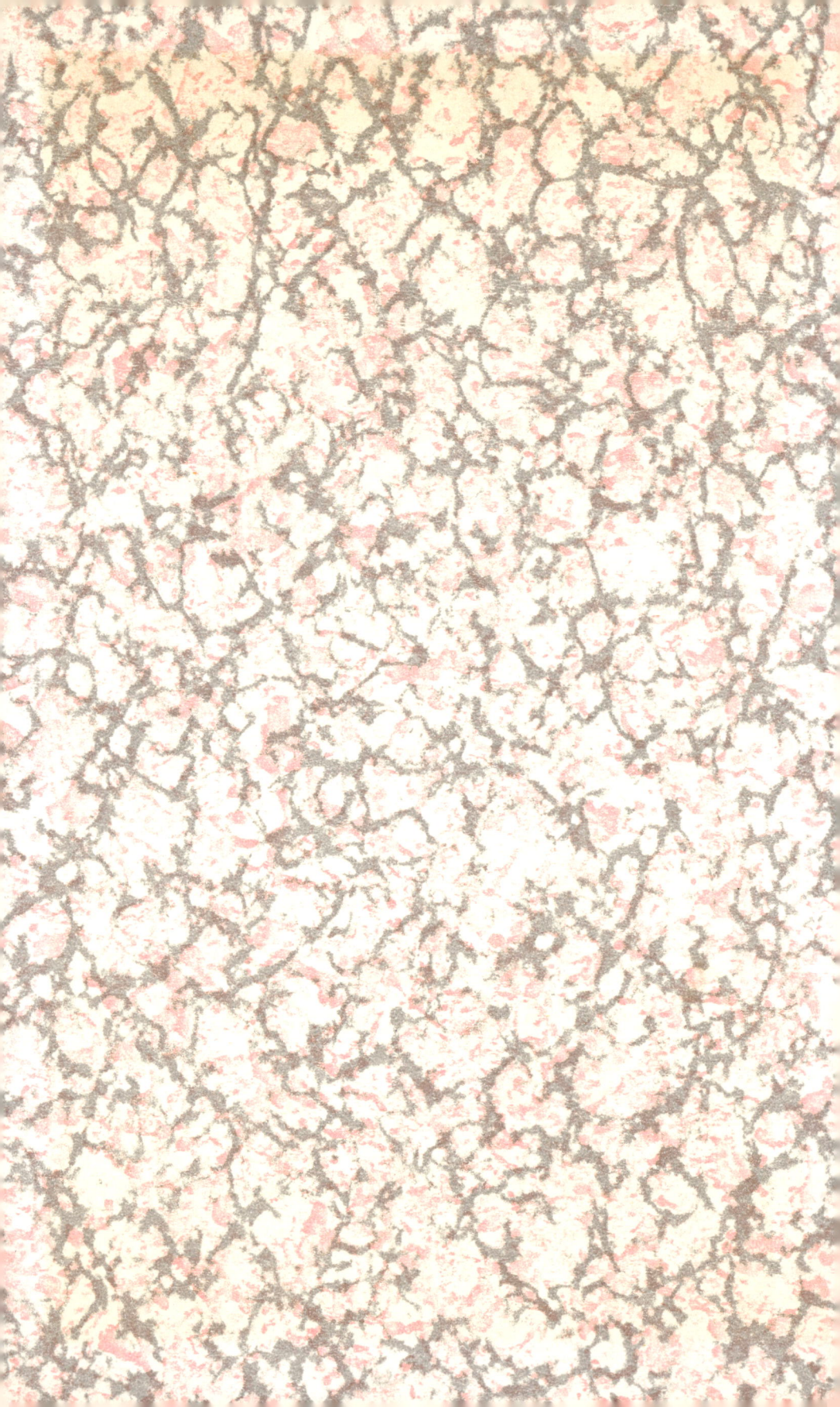